HISTORICAL ESSAYS

harper 🜂 torchbooks

A reference-list of Harper Torchbooks, classified by subjects, is printed at the end of this volume.

HISTORICAL ESSAYS

BY

H. R. TREVOR-ROPER

HARPER TORCHBOOKS
THE ACADEMY LIBRARY
HARPER & ROW, PUBLISHERS, NEW YORK

HISTORICAL ESSAYS

Printed in the United States of America.

This book was originally published in 1957 by Macmillan & Co., Ltd., London; and, in the United States, by Harper & Brothers, New York, in 1958, under the title *Men and Events*, with an additional chapter, "Arnold Toynbee's Millennium."

First HARPER TORCHBOOK edition published 1966 by
Harper & Row, Publishers, Incorporated,
New York, N.Y. 10016.

Library of Congress Catalog Card No.: 58-6157.

CONTENTS

FOREWORD

Ought one to reprint historical essays which have already been published once? This is a question which faces any historian who happens to have written such occasional essays. They may look well enough in their place, in the weekly or monthly press, but when they reappear, strung together, they often wear a miscellaneous look, as if they formed not a book but a scrap-heap. Since I am aware of this fact, and since these essays, ranging unevenly over so many centuries, may seem to invite such criticism, perhaps I should introduce them with an apologia. I should state why I have been so bold as to republish essays which have already appeared in well-known periodicals, and particularly in that distressingly radical organ, for whose space however I am most grateful, *The New Statesman and Nation*.[1]

My answer to this question is simple, perhaps presumptuous. Essays like these, various in time, depth and subject, can only bear republication if they receive an underlying unity from the philosophy of the writer: a philosophy, I would add, which is best illustrated by their very variety. Such a philosophy may be criticised as a bad or questionable philosophy, but if it is discernible through all these essays and gives them consistency, that is enough for my purpose. It will ensure that this volume is not a scrap-heap but a book.

It is perhaps anachronistic to write of a historian's philosophy. Today most professional historians 'specialise'. They choose a period, sometimes a very brief period, and within that period they strive, in desperate competition with ever-expanding evidence, to know all the facts. Thus armed, they can comfortably shoot down any amateurs who blunder or rivals who stray into their heavily fortified field; and, of course, knowing the strength of modern defensive weapons, they them-

[1] Of the essays reprinted in this book No. 7 first appeared in *Encounter*, Nos. 20, 27, 29 and 31 in *History Today*, No. 23 in *Commentary*, No. 30 in *The Spectator*, No. 39 in the *Times Literary Supplement*, No. 42 in *Problems of Communism*. All the rest appeared in *The New Statesman*.

selves keep prudently within their own frontiers. Theirs is a static world. They have a self-contained economy, a Maginot Line, and large reserves which they seldom use; but they have no philosophy. For a historical philosophy is incompatible with such narrow frontiers. It must apply to humanity in any period. To test it, a historian must dare to travel abroad, even in hostile country; to express it he must be ready to write essays even on subjects on which he may be ill-qualified to write books. This was a truism to the great historians of the past: who would ever ask what was Gibbon's period? Today it is a heresy: with few exceptions, we do not even enquire after the philosophy of our masters.

If these essays are united by any such philosophy, the reader will discover it. He will also discover any special interests or eccentricities of which I may be guilty. Here I will only say that to me the interest of history lies not in its periods but in its problems, and, primarily, in one general problem which is its substance in all times and all places: the interplay between heavy social forces or intractable geographical facts and the creative or disruptive forces which wrestle with them: the nimble mind, the burning conscience, the blind passions of man. For history, I believe, is not static, a mere field to be mapped out. It is not predictable, nor yet aimless. It is an endless play of forces, all determinable, except one: and that one is the dynamic element, the human mind which sometimes triumphs, sometimes destroys, sometimes founders. If these essays, random samples from a great ocean, nevertheless illuminate different aspects of that central problem, I can collect and republish them with a clear conscience.

HUGH TREVOR-ROPER

Christ Church
Oxford

CHAPTER I

THE HOLY LAND

From one narrow area — the borderlands of Arabia and Palestine — three great religions have been carried abroad. What peculiar character gave to one corner of the earth such spiritual concentration? For answer we must look not to history, but to geography, or rather to historical geography. In particular we may look to that great work, George Adam Smith's *Historical Geography of the Holy Land.* No other book so vividly re-creates the character of that eventful country or so skilfully calls in the rocks and valleys to explain its three thousand years of history. For the Scots professor was no academic observer: he had not only read but ridden his way through every corner of his subject. And in the end it was not only past history that he explained. Twenty years later Palestine became once more a battleground of great armies, and the book which was written for scholars became the manual of statesmen. The Prime Minister, Lloyd George, was 'absorbed' by it; the victorious General Allenby carried it with him on his campaign; it was used at the Peace Conference; and the first High Commissioner, before taking up the government of the new Mandate, sought out, as his adviser, the Hebrew scholar from Aberdeen.

What is the essential, the permanent character of Palestine? From the first it has been double: Palestine is both 'the bridge between Asia and Africa' and 'the refuge of the drifting populations of Arabia'. Great armies have passed through it to battle: the armies of Sennacherib and the Pharaohs, of Cambyses and Alexander, of Ptolemies and Seleucids, of Pompey and Caesar, the Caliphs and the Crusaders, Sultan Selim and Mehemet Ali, Napoleon and Allenby. Monotonously they have followed the same great highways, picked up in the Serbonian Bog the same fearful plague, and fought their crucial battles in the same natural theatre, the passage and gateway of Jezreel. There Sisera and Saul were destroyed; there, at Megiddo, Josiah was destroyed by Pharaoh Necho; and the greatest battle of all, where the Kings of the Earth are to be destroyed, was naturally placed, by the heated Zealots who imagined it, at Megiddo, or Armageddon.

But what were these Kings of the Earth and their great transient armies to the mountain tribes of Israel? Like the beduin of the desert in our wars, they looked down upon the passing chariots from above and only descended afterwards, for the leavings. For the Hebrews were a highland people: their very language shows it. Their word for valley is 'depth', their visitors 'come up', even their hilltops are viewed from above. To them horses and chariots were exotic beasts and unfamiliar machines. All the great chariot-rides in the Bible take place in the north, in Samaria. The horse, until Solomon, was not used; if captured, it was hamstrung; and the Prophets, those die-hard conservatives, continued to frown upon it as an irreligious novelty. It was in 'the high places of Israel' that the Hebrews settled; it was there that their own unique history took place; they left the valleys to foreign armies and caravans, the sea coast to the sea-faring Phoenicians and the sea-borne Philistines.

Furthermore, these drifting tribes of Arabia who had settled in Palestine were both wedged in and split up by the shape of the land. On the east the Jordan, sunk in its tropical valley, is not, like other rivers, a trade-route: it is a barrier. On the west the inhospitable sea coast was not, like the tempting archipelago of the Greeks, a highway to other continents: it was 'a stiff, stormy line', a border, a horizon. There is no word in Hebrew for a bridge — no bridge over their only river; nor for harbour either — no harbour in their only sea. And between these two barriers the country is further broken up into 'shelves and coigns' into which the swarming clans of Arabia fitted themselves by tribes and, thus fitted, preserved, as in Alpine cantons, their different cultures.

Thus when history first lights up within Palestine, what we see is a confused medley of clans — all that crowd of Canaanites, Amorites, Perizzites, Hivites, Girgashites, Hittites, sons of Anak and Zamzummim which is so perplexing to the student and yet in such thorough harmony with the natural conditions of the country and with the rest of the history. . . . Palestine, formed as it is, and surrounded as it is, is emphatically a land of tribes.

At first it was the land of these Canaanite tribes, scattered and sedentary, an agricultural and commercial people dwelling in strong places and practising like all primitive agricultural peoples, orgiastic rites. Each tribe had its tutelary deity, like local madonnas in Italy: they 'practised abominations' and worshipped Baal 'on every high hill and under every green tree'. Later, when the Hebrews conquered and absorbed them and became, like them, an agricultural people, they fitted as naturally, tribe by tribe, into the same local niches and adopted as naturally the same local cults. They 'went a-whoring after strange gods'.

And yet, in the end, they were not seduced. They did not persevere along the path of their predecessors. Why not? Once again geography offers an answer. For over and above the local subdivisions of Palestine stands a greater, more fundamental division: the division between Arabia and Syria, between the desert and the sown. The Hebrews were not, like their predecessors, a sedentary, agricultural people: they were beduin from the desert and their religion was the religion of the desert, 'the sour Wahaby fanaticism' and yet also 'the great antique humanity of the Semitic desert' which Doughty afterwards found in his solitary Arabian wanderings. From the nomadic Kenites, the outcast tinkers of the desert, they had learned their grim religion, the worship of Yahveh, the god of the volcano in Sinai; and now they carried it from 'the waste, the howling wilderness' into 'the land of corn and wine' which they had conquered. Then the miracle happened. Absorbed, Canaanised, civilised, they yet contrived to retain their desert religion with its violence and its humanity. The Old Testament, in so far as it is history, is the history of a great ideological struggle: a struggle between the invading gods of the desert and the native gods of the sown.

How splendid are the stories of its human agents! Politic kings, setting up their new regality with its officers and tax-gatherers and incorporated court-chaplains, might seek to tame the old aristocratic anarchy of the desert; but always the beduin with their *marabouts*, the prophets, intervened. Sometimes their intervention was disastrous. The greatest of all the kings of Israel, Ahab, by his foreign alliances and religious toleration, might have saved his country, had not the terrible Elijah, the mad mullah from the mountains of Gilead, swept up from the wilderness of Jeshimon to mobilise the fanatics against him. Sometimes it was heroic. In the last century of Hebrew independence, while bulwark after bulwark crumbled before the revived empires of the East, the great prophets preached again their gospel of primitive equality. The liberties of Israel were gone, they repeated with grim relish, irretrievably gone; and why? Because the old equality of the desert had been sacrificed. The luxurious royal court, the court of Solomon, that ancient Ismail or Farouk, had replaced the patriarchal tent, and the *latifundia* of the new pashas had swallowed up the land of the peasant. The shepherd democrat Amos and the metropolitan aristocrat Isaiah speak the same language: the new landlords 'join house to house and lay field to field'; they 'oppress the poor and crush the needy'; and the only hope is in the repudiation of urban civilisation, a return to the desert, so that 'the cities be wasted without inhabitant and the houses without man and the land be utterly desolate'. It was among the Kenites, the original founders of Yahvism, that the austere Rechabites pledged themselves to retain for ever, even in civilised Palestine, the old nomad simplicity which was alone agreeable to their desert god.

Israel foundered, and with it Judaism which returned from the Babylonian Exile a fossil of itself. Ezekiel, the pedagogue of the Exile, had hardened it into a dreary ritualism; the prophet had yielded to the scribe and the high priest; the simple religion of the old Prophets was now encrusted with a luxuriant Persian apparatus. If the voice of the desert was raised, in this new age, it was no longer the confident voice of orthodoxy: it was the voice of the Zealot, the rebel, the heretic. John the Baptist, that *fakir* of the wilderness, protested against the Hellenised court of the Herods and was beheaded. Jesus, the prophet of cosmopolitan Galilee, whom the spirit however had driven into the wilderness for his inspiration, protested against the ritualism of the high priests and was crucified. Israel had repudiated the desert. Thereafter Palestine might remain the highway of great armies, but it was no longer the westward receptacle of the

Arabian tribes: it had become an eastern province of the Mediterranean empire of Rome.

Nevertheless, the rejected inheritance ultimately found another heir. In due time the voices of Moses and Elijah, of Amos and Isaiah and John the Baptist were raised again. The Mosaic monotheism, the Rechabite austerity, the prophetic intransigence (and the patriarchal polygamy) of the Old Testament were resumed not by the now Westernised Jews, the commercial travellers of a cosmopolitan empire, but once again in desert Arabia, to inspire a new Exodus and a new conquest. In the seventh century of our era, Palestine was reconquered for the East; and the true heir of Moses, of Joshua and of the Prophets was not among the rabbis of Safad or of the ghettoes in the West; it was the Arabian conqueror, the fanatic of the desert, the new 'prophet', Mohammed.

In our day the desert has once again been driven back by the West. Ironically it is the exiled Jews who have done it. Having first entered Palestine as the tribesmen of the Eastern desert, they now return to it as the spearhead of the avenging West. Ironically too they find facing them the truer heirs of their own lost tradition. For history is only accidentally the continuity of peoples: fundamentally it is the continuity of countries — and ideas. The modern Jews who have re-created Israel may please themselves with the fancy that they are resuming a lost inheritance. In fact they can hardly be surprised if the Arabs of Palestine, still poised upon the historic hills of Judaea, look down upon these sea-borne invaders of the coastal plain as the ancient Hebrews looked down, in their day, upon the encroaching settlers from the West, the Philistines.

CHAPTER II

THE WORLD OF HOMER

Our own Dark Ages are dark enough: those of ancient Greece are darker still. What happened in those four centuries between the crumbling of Mycenæan civilisation and the sudden rebirth of Greek culture? Not so much as a monkish chronicle glimmers through that night. Mycenæ we know. We know it, imaginatively, from its heroic myths: that great tapestry from whose shreds half the great tragedies of the world have been composed. We know it in a more real sense as its great palaces are explored and its new records deciphered. But when it had fallen — and its fall is itself mysterious — we are suddenly in the dark. Four centuries later, when we hear the first contemporary voice, we find ourselves in an altogether new world. All the old magnificence is gone. The heroic age is a distant myth. We are in the fifth age of men, the 'iron age' of stagnant, rural poverty. 'Would that it were not my lot to live among this fifth generation of men, but had either died first or might be born later; for this is the Iron Age, when day and night we are wasted by toil and suffering. . . .' It is the voice of Hesiod, the cantankerous, taboo-ridden peasant, nagging his idle brother on a squalid Bœotian farm.

Homer is the poet of Mycenæan splendour; Hesiod the first, last, only poet of the Greek Dark Age. So we easily generalise. But when, in fact, did Homer write — or, rather (to escape the snort of the scholar), when were the Homeric poems composed and recited in the form in which they were afterwards written down? Their subject, their heroes, their geography, their apparatus are Mycenæan. But what about those breastplates, that iron, those numerous un-Mycenæan details which earlier scholars, to preserve the Mycenæan virtue of the poet, had to write off as later 'interpolations'? Unfortunately, we cannot stop there. Homer, says Mr. Finley, 'knew where the Mycenæan civilisation flourished, and his heroes live in great Bronze Age palaces unknown in his own day. And that is virtually all he knew about Mycenæan times, for the catalogue of his errors is very long.' So he lists them. Homer's arms, though 'persistently cast in antiquated bronze', are post-Mycenæan in form. 'His gods had temples and the Mycenæans built none, whereas the latter constructed great vaulted tombs in which to bury their chieftains and the poet cremates his.' And then there are the battle-chariots. 'Homer had heard of them, but he did not really visualise what one did with chariots in a war. So his heroes normally drove from their tents a mile or less away, carefully dismounted, and then proceeded to battle on foot.'

In fact, it now seems agreed, the Homeric poems were composed in the Dark Age. Recited over many generations, their pedigree may stretch back to Mycenæ; it may be that it was in the courts of diminished Mycenæan dynasties that they were handed on — for such dynasties survived here and there in Ægæan islands, like Roman villas in barbarian Europe, preserving fragments of past culture. But the society around them had changed and changed radically. Homer may tell Mycenæan stories; his *dramatis personæ* and his stage properties may be Mycenæan; but his basic assumptions are far more modern. The social conditions which he reflects are those not of Mycenæ, nor indeed of his own time (for in traditional poetry there is always a certain time-lag), but of the tenth or ninth century B.C. — deep in the Dark Age.

Once this is admitted, what a field for deduction is open! The superficial anachronisms can be pared away and the society of the Dark Age laid open. Of course there is room for argument. The Iliad and the Odyssey are sundered in time and space, and there are varying degrees of anachronism. But Mr. Finley faces these risks boldly, and the result is a most exciting, most readable book.[1] He has filled a gap in history, reconstructed an era, a society, a culture that seemed lost, and done it — what adds a relish to his achievement — not in a remote Polynesian island or from the mute evidence of stones, but in a crucial stage of our European history, and from the two greatest, best-known epic poems in the world.

And what kind of a society was it? First, he makes clear, it was

[1] M. I. Finley, *The World of Odysseus* (London 1956).

a very shrunken society. The Lords of Pylos and Mycenæ, whose economy is newly being revealed to us, had a 'centralised bureaucratic social organisation'; they had writing and records; and these records reveal an economic development which makes the later, illiterate, world of Homer, though equally Greek, seem primitive by comparison.

> The poet exaggerates whenever numbers come in — of slaves and heroes and gold tripods and cattle — yet his overblown figures are tiny compared with the quantities inscribed on the (Mycenæan) tablets. The lords of Mycenæ . . . controlled far more extensive holdings in land and cattle and slaves (male as well as female) than the heroes who fought at Homer's Troy, and they organised their work on their properties through an elaborate bureaucratic hierarchy of men and operations, requiring inventories and memoranda and managerial controls; but Eumæus could carry the inventory of Odysseus' livestock in his head. Something like one hundred different agricultural and industrial occupations have apparently been identified on the tablets, each with its own word, and Homer only knew of a dozen or so. It was not merely a matter of the poet's having no occasion to mention other occupations; that society had no place for them, as it had no place for tenants or foremen or scribes. The difference between the two societies was in structure, not merely in scale or dimension.

Within this shrunken society what was the social and economic unit? It was, says Mr. Finley, the *οἶκος*, the household of a chief. Everyone had his status determined by his relationship to the household, whose basis was the family, but which incorporated also a hierarchy of attendants and slaves. Only within the system of the household and the family were there bonds of loyalty or obligation; and so the most wretched of all men was not the slave, who had his status in the system, but the *θής*, the casual day labourer who had not: the wandering, rootless man who hired himself where he could and belonged nowhere. When Achilles, among the Shades, deplored the state of the dead, it was not the slave but the day-labourer whose plight, at its worst, he preferred to kingship over all the tribes of the dead.

This household, family system, with its limited obligations, is reflected in politics and war. When a city or country was attacked by foreign raiders, then, indeed, its inhabitants united to strike back, as all Troy, not merely Priam and his house, struck back at the Achæan invaders. But 'it was Menelaus who was aggrieved by the flight of Helen, not Sparta; it was his brother Agamemnon who assumed leadership of the war of reprisal, not Mycenæ; it was Amphimedon and Odysseus to whom Agamemnon appealed for assistance, not Ithaca'. And when Odysseus finally came home and fought his great battle with the usurping suitors of Penelope, he could count on no support from his subjects. He had no 'subjects', only a household. 'The king could count on no one but his wife, his son and his faithful slaves.'

What kind of royalty was this, in which every great household was an independent centre and there was no political obligation? Clearly it was an aristocracy, and the power of the kings was a personal ascendancy, precariously maintained — as they discovered when they returned from Troy. Nestor and Menelaus might smoothly resume their rule in Pylos and Sparta; but in Mycenæ Agamemnon was murdered by an usurper, and in Ithaca Odysseus, who had secured power at the expense of his father, found himself faced by a conspiracy not merely of subject nobles, but of other 'kings'. As his son remarked, 'here in sea-girt Ithaca there are many other kings among the Achæans, young and old, one of whom may take the place of Odysseus, since he is dead'. Kingship in fact was merely personal: the accidental primacy of one family in the aristocracy which was permanent. It was so in heaven as on earth. Zeus was recognised as king on Olympus, but he had had to fight for his position; and like a somewhat undignified Hanoverian king, he was reduced to persuasion and patronage to get his way with the fractious whig oligarchy of gods over whom he impatiently presided.

Of course, if the aristocracy was permanent, that was because the economic structure made it permanent. Every important *οἶκος*, like a monastery in our Dark Ages, was self-sufficient, based on land; and once the system had been established, it was frozen in caste-like rigidity. There was no social mobility, no trade (that was left to Phœnicians), no possibility of new fortunes, or therefore of new nobles. Only in one substance did this society feel the need of imports, and that was in metal. Metal could justify even trade. 'Even a king could honourably voyage in its search. When Athena appeared to Telemachus as Mentes, the Taphian chieftain, her story was that she was carrying iron to Temesa in quest of copper. That gave no difficulties.' But when one of the Phæacians suggested that Odysseus was a merchant, what a rumpus followed! Nor was it only for tools that metal was needed; in that static society, in which morality too was static, reduced to a set of conventional responses, metal was needed also for a great social convention which criss-crossed the Homeric world, binding household to household in an ever-widening system: the interchange of gifts.

Everyone who reads Homer is aware of the regular, almost ritual exchange of gifts. In the most fascinating part of his book, Mr. Finley has shown the essential character of this operation. The giving of 'gifts' or 'treasure' was, in Homeric Greece as in the Trobriand Islands, the only regular economic activity; it was also the badge of status, the nexus of obligation among equals. Gifts have economic value, of course, and this economic value is carefully estimated: but it is estimated as the concrete and therefore only intelligible expression of their real value, which is symbolic — symbolic of status. For of course if a man has accumulated a great store of gifts, it is unquestionable that he has given as much — exactly as much, neither more nor less. So, architecturally, the heart of the οἶκος, the symptom of its greatness, is the store-room, piled with gold and copper, not for use but for giving away, as it had been received, as gifts. 'No single detail in the life of the heroes', says Mr. Finley, 'receives so much attention in the Iliad and the Odyssey as gift-giving, and always there is a frank reference to the adequacy, appropriateness, recompense.' It was a kind of trade, but one that was motivated by imports only, never by exports. 'There was never a need to export as such, only the necessity of having the proper goods for the counter-gift when an import was unavoidable.' Nor was it aimed at economic profit, but entirely at status, which, in spite of all that Marx has said, perhaps still remains the *primum mobile* of social man, at least of those who are above the starvation line.

But what of those who live on that line? Homer hardly refers to them. But who pays for these gifts? It is Alcinous, King of Phæacia, Homer's ideal of kingship, who lets the cat out of the bag. 'Come now,' he tells his nobles at dinner as they speed the parting guest, 'let us give him a great tripod and a cauldron; and we in turn shall gather among the people and be recompensed, for it is burdensome for one person to give without recompense.' Homer makes no comment. He takes it all for granted. Besides, he is a royalist: it was at the court of kings that he and his fellow poets were retained. But we happen also to have another view. Hesiod, the peasant poet, saw the same system from the underside. To him, with his radical *New Statesman* querulity, kings were predatory hawks, oppressors of the people, and his regular word for them is *δωροφάγοι*, 'consumers of gifts'.

They did not consume them much longer. Already, in Homer's and Hesiod's day, royalty, that precarious primacy, was foundering, and the more permanent aristocracy at its base, no less oppressive, was asserting itself throughout the Hellenic world. And yet even that, it soon seemed, was not so permanent after all. Suddenly, with the enriching contact of the East, with the discovery of coinage and the renewal of trade, the Greek Dark Ages, like ours, came to an end. On the ruins of royalty and aristocracy alike, mercantile and military tyrants inaugurated a new age, an age in which there was no longer any room for old-fashioned epic poetry. But let us not be ungrateful. The great mercantile tyrant of Athens put all Europe in his debt. Having driven Homer out of business, he preserved him for posterity; he caused the Iliad and the Odyssey, which might otherwise have been lost for ever, to be written down.

CHAPTER III

THE DARK AGES

All history is contemporary history: even the Dark Ages are not now as remote as once they seemed. An imperial civilisation, as mature as our own, by a seemingly organic mortality declined and crumbled; a vast commerce dwindled and the world it had united dissolved; wealth and culture evaporated from Europe, and instead there arose, based on barbarous tribes, a new ideological power, unimaginable hitherto. How did it happen? In the serenity of the last two centuries such a problem seemed remote and inconceivable, and philosophers easily dismissed it by effortless generalities. They referred it to the inevitable effects of climate, happily beyond the control of man; or to some inherent principle of superannuation in bodies politic; or to barbarian invasions, formerly repelled, then mysteriously successful. To us, who face more closely the reality, such explanations are unsatisfactory. Faced by a similar prospect, we ask for practical answers to the questions: What were the Dark Ages? How did they occur? How were they surmounted?

Our civilisation is an urban civilisation and we can most easily understand other urban civilisations. The city states of Greece, the urban kingdoms of the Hellenistic world, the imperial city of Rome, all seem nearer to us than the centuries between us and them — which, in Europe, were rural centuries. Only Byzantium, 'the City' *par excellence*, had no Dark or Middle Ages; but that vast metropolis, custodian and continuator of ancient culture, could no more effectively control the destinies of Europe than the great coastal cities of China can to-day govern the vast rural areas behind them. From the infinite steppes of Asia, from the forests of the North, successive invaders swept past that powerless capital whose statesmen could only play one against the other with despairing diplomacy. Germans and Slavs, Northmen, Magyars and Avars — the impact of their coming was met not there but in the rural west: the Magyars settled deep in Hungary and were converted from Rome; the Avars were ultimately destroyed not at the gates of Byzantium but far in the rear, in Central Europe, by Charlemagne — that great organiser whose stature dominates the impoverished backwoods of abandoned Europe.

The Dark Ages are still very dark, but there are shafts of evidence to illuminate them, and some of the greatest historians of our time — Henri Pirenne, Marc Bloch — have answered the challenge of their interpretation. The ruralisation of Europe was not caused by the barbarian invasions: already, under the Roman Empire, it had begun. Rome itself, by the fifth century, had long been a provincial town; the economy of the empire had already become decentralised in great rural estates; and even after the official dissolution of the Western Empire, the German princes, revealing themselves through the shreds of a dissolving suzerainty, continued to rule over their portions as Romanised kings — only to face, in their turn, the same mysterious problem of decay: a decay which their ancestors had not caused, but merely exploited; a decay which now fretted in turn their own feeble images of Roman civilisation.

For in fact European culture was not being overborne in the fifth century, nor disintegrating; it was slowly drying up; the stream of world commerce which, under the Empire, had temporarily fertilised that barren peninsula, was perishing. Pirenne, in the course of a famous thesis, has marked the stages of evaporation: the disappearance from Europe of Eastern products — of gold and papyrus, spices and Oriental cloths — and of the 'Syrian' merchants who had carried them. What was the cause of this change? Was it, as Pirenne suggested, the Moslem conquests in Asia and Africa which 'bottled up' the economy of Europe, cutting it away from the old sources of its vitality? That theory is now hard to defend. Rather, it seems, it was a drainage of gold that reduced Europe to its natural dimensions in the world, as a drainage of dollars may now reduce it again. The Romans, a poor but warlike tribe, had conquered the gold and thereby the trade of the world, and drawn it westwards; now, by a 'perpetual hæmorrhage' it had run back to the East, there to be immobilised in the palaces and temples of the Persian

Empire. There was no more purchasing power in Europe, nor the military power to recover it. When another poor and warlike tribe issued from Arabia to conquer the cities and liberate the gold and trade of the world, the great age of Islam began; but the great age of Europe, that derelict continent, seemed to have passed for ever.

In fact, it had not. Gradually, after centuries of depression and exploitation, the poor and warlike tribes of Europe again asserted themselves. Towns began to revive, nourished by a new Eastern commerce: first Venice and Amalfi, Bari and Salerno, linked to the great Eastern commerce of Byzantium; then, as the rich Moslem world drew more and more upon European slaves and furs, arms and timber, and purchasing power returned, city life spread northwards. Finally the tables were completely turned. Europe was able once again to enslave the currency and commerce of the world; to stay, as Rome had stayed, that fatal hæmorrhage: by different means indeed — by wider conquests, new techniques, new industries; and yet perhaps no more permanently.

How was it possible for Europe, once so decayed and dissolved, to rise again? What were the institutions, the secret power, which enabled it to bridge the dark centuries? Mr. Christopher Dawson, in his Gifford Lectures,[1] offers an explanation. It was the Church that did it, he says, the medieval Catholic Church, whose rise he traces from the fall of Rome till the recovery of Europe. How well, how clearly he describes it! How rich and various is his scholarship, how happily presented! It is a stimulating experience to read these dozen chapters, covering almost as many centuries, full of learning, and yet clarifying, not compressing, that crowded history of vast migrations, obscure events, and fragmentary evidence. Faced by the mysterious problem of decay, how narrow was the basis of the newly-established Church! 'There were only eighteen years,' he reminds us, 'between Theodosius' closing the temples and the first sack of the Eternal City by the barbarians. The great age of the Western Fathers from Ambrose to Augustine was crammed into a single generation, and St. Augustine died with the Vandals at the gate.' Nevertheless, in that brief period, the Western founda-

[1] Christopher Dawson, *Religion and the Rise of Western Culture* (London 1950).

tions were firmly laid; doctrine, discipline and propaganda were developed and extended; Rome, sacked and deserted, revived as a centre of priestly power-politics; missionaries brought the furious tribes of the North and East into dependence upon it; and monasteries, not towns, like islands of culture in the ocean of barbarism, became 'the spiritual and economic centres of a purely rural society.' Nobody can like the Church in those days. It was intolerant and obscurantist, and did not improve with time. St. Augustine read the classics — like Marx, the Founding Father was himself a humanist: the old bigot could weep over Dido, and puritanism struggled in his soul with light. His contemporary St. Jerome with difficulty overcame his taste for Cicero. But he overcame it in the end, and once the insidious spirit of humanity had been beaten down, no quarter was shown: it was crushed. St. Augustine organised the rabble in Africa, reducing doctrine to rhythmical slogans wherewith to drown the voice of opposition. St. Cyril organised a blackshirt claque to applaud his oratory in Alexandria. St. Gregory, the Stalin of the early Church, banned all profane learning as offensive and abominable. Truly they were no saints, those terrible old ideologues, past whose history Mr. Dawson so discreetly slides; and what was the solemn liturgy which he so extols but a narcotic formulary? And yet these men did their work as perhaps no others could have done in those barbarian centuries, and left it so firm and solid that when commerce returned to Europe and urban civilisation revived, it did not perish. As a great power in its own right, the Church could make terms with the new age, reform and adjust itself to cope with new needs or profit from new opportunities. New politics, new machinery, new orders preserved its vitality; it fostered the crusades which re-directed the commerce of the East; it colonised the towns and made them its allies against a less versatile institution; it colonised the new universities, sending out in each generation new missionaries of up-to-date learning; it participated in new economic ventures and became one of the great financial institutions of the world. Only when its own capacity for self-reform was spent, in the thirteenth century, did it enter into that long decline which led, at the Reformation, to its permanent division.

What are we to deduce from this? That Christianity alone is

a formative religion, alone can change the world: that other religions are static and conservative, it alone dynamic? This is Mr. Dawson's conclusion. It seems inconceivable that he should draw it, that so learned a scholar should appear, in this one respect, so parochial. To point the contrast he reminds us of the 'immobile' religions of China and India; but what of Islam? In the very centuries in which he dwells upon the barbarians of Europe, the followers of Mahomet were sweeping over three continents, pressing upon Paris in the West, and, in the East, twenty-six years later, storming the city of Canton. Is it then not Christianity only, but religion in general, that moves these mountains, that is, as Mr. Dawson says, 'the dynamic element in civilisation'? What of the Roman Empire, that colossal achievement of cynical greed and political skill? Religion may have been the dynamic of European civilisation in the Dark Ages, but what of the eighteenth century? Even when he reaches the twelfth century Mr. Dawson begins to find himself in difficulties, and his argument that even humanism, even the paganism of the Renaissance, was fundamentally Christian requires, to be significant, a special use of words. And yet, within the centuries of which he writes, it is hard to dispute his conclusion. It is difficult to conceive — indeed to me impossible to conceive — of the re-creation of Europe in the Dark Ages without the Church: without that doctrine whose unheroic content could yet subdue barbarian kings; without that institution whose versatile power-politics could use and exploit in turn Franks, Slavs and Normans; without those wandering missionaries who lit their temporary candles in Bulgaria, on the coast of Northumberland, and by the Arctic Sea. The history of the Church gives both unity and quality to the centuries when commerce and city life seemed to have left Europe for ever; without it, they seem meaningless.

So too, no doubt, our new idealogues view our present state, and their liberal fellow-travellers console themselves with an ultimate respectability. Doctrine — unintelligible, reversible, but indubitable; inexorable discipline; insistent propaganda; missionaries and local cells; the cult of saints; a mind-drowning liturgy — all the old machinery has become familiar again. Culture can always wait a few centuries, Hitler wrote in *Mein*

Kampf. . . . The parallel could no doubt be extended infinitely. It is more profitable to remember the differences. Christianity, even in its most barbarous period, at least never forgot the dignity of the human soul. Besides, it is worth remembering that Christianity did not save the civilisation of the ancient world: it was not a solution but a substitute: the Dark Ages came first. If Western civilisation is to be saved from darkness now, it can only be by Western methods: ideologies are only applicable when night has already fallen. That, no doubt, is why Hitler and Goebbels preached a gospel of destruction, and Stalin hungrily scans the future for unemployment, misery and slumps.

CHAPTER IV

THE MEDIEVAL ITALIAN CAPITALISTS

We Europeans are parochial in our historical outlook. We recognise antiquity and our modern civilisation — for both are European ages: but the intervening period of Asiatic domination we dismiss as the Dark Ages. Now that the Dark Age of Asia is receding, the greatness of Europe, so long taken for granted, begins again to require explanation. How was it that that ruined and forgotten peninsula, whose civilisation once seemed to have passed away for ever, recovered power and wealth and culture to dominate the world again?

Partly, no doubt, thanks to the Church. Christianity, that Asiatic religion, profoundly modified by its adoption among the barbarians of Europe, provided, from the eleventh century, such slogans of war and conquest as Marxism, a European religion, similarly modified, now supplies to the natives of Asia. The crusades were Europe's protest against the dominance of Asia, Pope Gregory VII our Mao Tse-tung. And yet crusades alone are not enough. Fanaticism we have always with us: it only succeeds when it can also finance itself at a profit, and thereby tame and rationalise its own spirit. The revival of Europe was not achieved by Peter the Hermit, that Frankish *marabout*, but by the merchants of those Italian cities, last links with antiquity and the East, who, by financing and exploiting the crusades, led trade and civilisation back to the West.

What a debt we owe to those few survivors of antique capitalism! Europe around them was almost entirely rural; trade had shrunk to the peddling of pilgrims; the techniques of large-scale commerce, denounced by the furious Fathers of the Church, had been largely forgotten; and in the Rome of Gregory the Great, capital of the Christian world, there had been, it seems, but a single banker. But in Venice, Bari and Amalfi — outposts of Byzantium and the East — the old techniques were preserved or rediscovered: the Venetians, financing and insuring their voyages by a system of partnership, settled at Constantinople and Alexandria and monopolised the trade of the Empire; and when the brief splendour of Amalfi and Bari was snuffed out, the fishermen of Genoa and Pisa inherited their commerce. By the time the Papacy was ready to proclaim the crusades, these three capitalist cities were equipped to finance, transport, and supply them. They earned their reward: their quarters and capitulations in captured towns throughout the Mediterranean — even in Constantinople itself — gave them the trade of the whole sea; they became bankers to the Popes who directed the campaigns, to the impoverished noblemen who fought in them. The Syrian seafarers retreated before them; the Jews declined into local usurers; and by tapping African gold in the Barbary ports they refreshed, indirectly, the economy of the whole continent. Behind them, in Piedmont and Tuscany, capital was accumulated, the wool industry organised, and banking begun: and industry and banking in turn raised up two inland cities — Milan and Florence — to rival the sea ports of Venice and Genoa as capitals of the mercantile world.

Throughout the Middle Ages these four cities held their position. In the great trade-boom which followed the crusades, when the Mongolian peace opened all Asia to their agents, they eclipsed all their rivals and solemnised their ascendancy by minting their own coins in the gold which they had reintroduced to Europe. In each of them, in the thirteenth century, the mercantile classes rose to political power; in each of them the form of that power was different; in three of them the nature and history of that power has been analysed by M. Yves Renouard, one of that brilliant group of historians inspired by Marc Bloch.[1] The relationship between economics and ideology, between the bourgeoisie and culture, has been so bedevilled by the new dogmatists that it may be well to examine, in these scholarly pages, three such historical laboratories as the medieval communes of Venice, Genoa, and Florence.

Venice, the earliest of all, retained throughout its original character. It was the city not of industry, nor of international

[1] Yves Renouard, *Les Hommes d'Affaires Italiens du Moyen Age* (Paris 1949).

finance (its only industry was the state-owned naval arsenal, its only borrower the city government), but of commercial capitalism and Eastern trade. Further, Venice was not merely (like Genoa) an oligarchy of great merchants: it was a mercantile state, whose machinery of government served not the interests of the merchants, but the commerce of the state. The 200 great merchant families might organise themselves around their political members; they might build, as families, commercial empires in the Levant; but policy, appointments, war, the rules of commerce itself, were strictly determined by the state. There were no private fleets, no private monopolies, but a state fleet, state monopolies, a whole economy directed by the state. In no Italian republic was the power and intervention of the state as firm as in the classic whig republic, in which alone, in a long history, the aristocracy was not split by faction nor attenuated by exile — which alone gave to Europe not only wealth and culture, but a new political ideal: the 'Venetian aristocracy'.

What a contrast with Genoa! Genoa too was a purely commercial state, without industry. There too the government was controlled by great capitalist families. But there was no state. Government was the prey of faction: families with great private monopolies, great private fleets, struggled to control it. Having cornered the alum of Phocaea, Benedetto Zaccaria, in the thirteenth century, became admiral of Genoa and used his own fleet, headed by his flagship *Divizia* — 'Wealth' — not only to crush the rival commerce of Pisa, but also, by capturing a personal empire, to monopolise every process in his cornered goods; and when the impecunious city wished to send a naval expedition against Monaco, it could only finance it by converting the sailors into a company to capture Chios on a profit-making basis. This cut-throat individualism, this religion of private wealth, enabled the Genoese to perfect many commercial techniques — portulan maps, book-keeping by double entry, professional insurance; it denied them civic prosperity. Even when the creditors of state amalgamated themselves into a state bank, the Casa di S. Giorgio, the bank did not serve, it exploited the state: it became the means whereby a few rich families managed the treasury, the colonies, and trade in the interest of their private monopolies. And meanwhile the defeated families fled abroad or sold their skill to foreign powers — like that Genoese bank-agent who, having learnt his employers' philosophy that gold is the key of earth and heaven, transferred his service to Spain and discovered America for the new masters of his city.

Those who suppose that the spirit of capitalism is hostile to art, should clutch at the solitary instance of Genoa to support their fantasies: alone among Italian communes it was exempt from the Renaissance. But what of Venice, what of Siena, what of the Flemish towns, what of the greatest capitalist city of Italy — Florence? Tuscany came late to world commerce: Florence was a banking and industrial city long before it possessed a sea-port, and the vast financial power of its great family companies was based first on a highly organised cloth industry, then on a fortunate alliance with Rome. In the thirteenth century a group of exiled Florentine citizens financed the papal conquest of Sicily and thereby their own return to power in Florence; and thereafter 'the Guelf alliance' of Pope, King of Sicily, and Florentine bankers remained a constant in politics. At the end of the century, when the crash of the Bonsignori, 'the Rothschilds of the thirteenth century' ruined the great banking houses of Siena, the Florentine companies were supreme. In Italy they organised a multiplicity of business, in food and clothing, metals and spices, relics, *objets d'art* and slaves; they had branches in Italy and abroad; they accepted deposits and advanced loans; they handled the revenues of Popes and kings; they established mints and insurance companies, postal and intelligence services; until in the end their vast fortunes depended on credit and their credit on the politics of their royal clients. A political scare in 1342 caused a rush on the banks that ruined the lesser companies; and even the three great survivors — the Bardi, the Peruzzi, the Acciaiuoli — 'the columns of Christendom' — crashed four years later with the failure of their greatest client, Edward III of England. Nevertheless, the system was reorganised and continued: its leaders controlled government and policy and finance in their own interest; they seemed immune — except from proletarian risings or *coups d'état* by ambitious individuals among themselves. In the end it was the latter that prevailed: the greatest financial dynasty of Florence — the Medici — became the Grand Dukes of Tuscany.

Meanwhile what of the Church, whose alliance, whose war-slogans, whose financial needs had so favoured the communes? Christianity was a pacifist religion, and its original anti-capitalist doctrines had been reformulated with an added emphasis for a society of rural barbarians. The pacifism indeed had been rejected in the eleventh century; what of the anti-capitalism, now that the Church and its allies were alike great capitalist organisations? Little by little the orthodox faced their dilemma. Sometimes there were spectacular *crises de conscience*. So a Sienese financier in 1360 abandoned his office and, magnifying the name of Jesus through the villages of Tuscany, founded the mendicant order of the Gesuati. Others compromised less painfully by vicarious sacrifice: the Florentine millionaires gave largely to the poor, commissioned Giotto and Orcagna to glorify holy Poverty in paint, and arranged for their own burial by the mendicant orders which they had enriched. But this delicate equilibrium could not last for ever. Already at the end of the fourteenth century a mendicant friar was preaching that wealth was an estate pleasing to God (he soon became a rich cardinal); a few years later a Sienese saint would affirm the legitimacy of usury, the utility of high finance; and a Florentine bishop would argue that wealth, however acquired, was intrinsically good. A century later, when the Genoese plutocracy hovered on the edge of heresy, a Jesuit reclaimed them by his famous sermons on the rate of interest.

M. Renouard does not reach this last point. To him the sixteenth century, the beginning of our world, was the end of the Italian cities, eclipsed by new discoveries and new conquests. But great histories do not end so abruptly. Venice long dominated the trade of the East, a model of government to other merchant states; Tuscany, with its new port of Leghorn, became a great commercial power; and the century of Spanish predominance has been called, in the history of finance, 'the century of the Genoese'. And if Genoa and Florence had lost their civic independence, their exiled citizens, like Europeans to-day, carried their talents abroad. The Genoese bankers became grandees of Spain, the Florentines peers of France. Even in

England the family of an exiled Genoese financier propped up, by a quadruple marriage, the Protectoral house of Cromwell, and a member of the expatriate Florentine family of Dante's Beatrice designed, for Queen Elizabeth, the fortifications of Berwick-on-Tweed.

CHAPTER V

IBN KHALDOUN AND THE DECLINE OF BARBARY

In the two thousand years between Thucydides and the Renaissance there are two, perhaps only two, great philosophers of history. Both were Berbers, born a hundred miles from each other in North Africa. Devout believers in different religions, they were impelled by the political disasters around them to seek the meaning of history and give it a new philosophical dimension. St. Augustine was moved by Alaric's sack of Rome to write his *City of God*, and he revised his last works in Algeria with the Vandals at his gate. Nearly a thousand years later, from a castle in the Little Atlas, another great African looked out over a similar desolation. The nomads and the Black Death had ruined the Maghreb. 'Once the whole of this country was populated from the Roman Sea to the land of the Blacks, from outer Sous to Barca. Now almost everywhere there is nothing but abandoned plains, empty wastes, and desert. . . . *God inherits the Earth, and He is the best of inheritors.*' Such was the mood in which Ibn Khaldoun sat down to write his great work, *The History of the Berbers.*

Like many great historians, Ibn Khaldoun was a pessimist. He had tried politics and failed; but the attempt had enlarged his observation and the failure had sharpened his thought. He had sought, like Socrates and Plato, to be the educator of tyrants, but like them he had found his pupils incorrigible. So from the courts of Tunis, of Fez and of Granada, he had retired to this castle of Taour'zourt and there, for three years, had studied and digested the history of the Islamic world. How trivial its previous historians seemed to him, with their anecdotes and exaggerations, their lack of philosophy or purpose or comparative method, their failure to see the essential continuity of history! When Ibn Khaldoun looked around him, he felt the need for a new and deeper interpretation. 'When the universe is being turned upside-down, we must ask ourselves whether it is changing its nature, whether there is to be a new creation and a new order in the world. Therefore to-day we need a historian who can declare the state of the world, of its countries and peoples, and show the changes that have taken place in customs and beliefs.' Ibn Khaldoun determined to be that historian. He had discovered, he thought, 'the secret which had eluded everyone else'. He had 'devised a new method of writing history, and chosen a path which will surprise the reader, a course and system entirely my own'. History, as seen by him, was 'a new science, as remarkable for originality of interpretation as for the extent of its usefulness: a science which I have discovered after long research and profound meditation'. It transcended even the science of the Greeks, even Plato, even Aristotle. 'It was divine inspiration', says Ibn Khaldoun complacently, 'that led me to this undertaking, introducing me to a new science and making me the custodian and faithful interpreter of its secrets'.

Of Ibn Khaldoun's originality there can be no doubt: it is shown by what seems to us his 'modernity'. This fourteenth-century Berber stands out from his contemporaries and seems one of ours. He is a modern social scientist who found the 'essence' of history in that social organisation and social dynamism which underlies the 'accidents' of political change, and who sought to penetrate and analyse that essence. But he was also, as Dr. Muhsin Mahdi emphasises,[1] inseparable from his own contemporaries. He was an intellectual conservative in the classical Arabic tradition, a devout believer who sought a *via media* between the strict and the liberal interpretation of the Law. Though he applied rational criteria, he was not a rationalist. He might end with applied science, but he began with Revelation. Life, to him, was bounded by miracles. Even in human history there were divine interventions not to be explained by science. The first Arab conquests, for instance, were 'completely outside ordinary events . . . one of the miracles of our Prophet; and between a miracle and an ordinary event there is no analogy'. The purpose of man also is not political or even social: it is 'to practise religion, which will lead him to bliss in the future life, by way of God, Lord of everything in Heaven

[1] Muhsin Mahdi, *Ibn Khaldoun's Philosophy of History* (Allen and Unwin 1957).

and Earth'. Therefore, even in intellectual matters, dogma must always come first. Wisely the Prophet forbade the rational examination of his truths: such an exercise, says Ibn Khaldoun, is but 'a gorge in which the mind wanders without avail'.

Nevertheless, though he started from these premises, Ibn Khaldoun saw a large field for rational investigation. His religion, if it limited his steps, also guided and strengthened them: for it elevated history, making it, instead of mere secular diversion, an essential part of the divine work, to be approached, like Nature, with circumspection and a sense of 'grave moral responsibility'. Mishandled, it might lead men to disaster; correctly understood, it might teach wisdom to governors. It might also explain why it was that Ibn Khaldoun, setting out with the best of intentions, had failed in his politics. Could it be that the impersonal laws of history were set against him?

It could indeed. For having deduced those laws, Ibn Khaldoun saw that the civilisation around him was sick unto death. A cultivated aristocrat, he knew well that civilisation is essentially a product of settled cities. Only in great capital cities, where a resident court, a large population and a rational division of labour create wealth and opportunity, can such luxuries as art and science thrive, softening manners and adorning life. But when he looked at the cities of North Africa and Moslem Spain, what did he see? Only petty tyrants levying punitive taxes on a people rotted by past luxury. How different from the great civilisations of Damascus or Baghdad under the Caliphs or of Fatimid or Mameluke Cairo, 'the Mother of the World, the Palace of Islam, the spring of crafts and sciences'! Something had gone out of this urban life: something that could still be found among the nomads of the desert, barbarians though they were. Ibn Khaldoun hated the nomads, whom he knew so well and among whom he composed his *History*. When he writes of them, he writes sometimes with a burning detestation. The 'Arabs' to him are the destroyers of all civilisation, the enemies of all arts and crafts, 'of all people the least fit to rule'. Nevertheless, reluctantly he allows their virtues. They are aristocratic, self-reliant, frugal; and above all they have, in embryo, that elixir without which civilisation is impossible: '*aṣabiyya* — that 'public spirit' or 'social solidarity' which transcends the ordinary bonds of kinship and clientage and which can create the civilisation which then, alas, dissolves it.

'*Aṣabiyya* is the key-word in Ibn Khaldoun's philosophy. '*Aṣabiyya* is generated in the desert, never in cities; but it takes a Prophet to generate it. The Israelites in Egypt were a slavish people: the Prophet Moses had to keep them forty years in the desert to breed up a generation which possessed it and, possessing it, could build a state. It was in the desert that the Prophet Mohammed conjured up the '*aṣabiyya* which inspired his incredible conquests, that the Mahdi of the Almohads found the force to overthrow the rulers of Barbary and Spain. But what happens once the conquest is over? Prophetic power may perhaps preserve that spirit; but even prophetic power tends to turn into secular power, caliphs and imams into sultans and kings. At first the new rulers are civilised by the great cities they have conquered: while the '*aṣabiyya* lasts, the two forces are in harmony. These are the golden ages of civilisation — which however hold in perfection but a little moment. For soon the spirit is dissolved, rotted away by luxury and court-life, bureaucracy, taxes and the irreversible process of change. For the process is quite irreversible. 'Several rulers, men of great prudence in government, seeing the accidents which have led to the decay of their empires, have sought to cure the state and restore it to normal health. They think that this decay is the result of incapacity or negligence in their predecessors. They are wrong. These accidents are inherent in empires and cannot be cured.' 'Sometimes, when an empire is in its last period, it suddenly shows such strength that we think its decay is halted; but this is merely the last flicker of a candle that is going out.' So the rotten state languishes until a new barbarian conqueror pounces on the unresisting prey.

Is there then no hope? No, says Ibn Khaldoun, there is none. The stages of decline are invariable, infallible, predictable. And yet sometimes he seems to offer an escape. For why, he asks, has civilisation proved so much stronger in the East than in the West, in Persia and Iraq, Syria and Egypt than in the Maghreb? And he answers that the East had a settled urban civilisation which had thrown such deep roots that it could continue under successive conquerors. In Spain, too, sedentary civilisation had had time to take root and flourish, immune from nomadic invasions. How then, we ask, did such civilisations acquire such strength? But Ibn Khaldoun does not answer. 'My intention', he had written, 'is to confine myself to the Maghreb, its tribes, peoples, kingdoms and dynasties. I will not deal with other countries for I lack the necessary knowledge of the East and its peoples'. So he answers only for the Maghreb, which had no such settled civilisation under the successive thin crusts of Roman and Arab domination. The two urban poles of the Maghreb had always been Córdoba and Tunis, but neither really belonged to it. Córdoba was Roman and now Christian again; Tunis, as Ibn Khaldoun remarked, was a colony of Cairo.

It was to Cairo that he retired after writing his great work. He had had enough of the desert, the 'Arabs', and he spent his last twenty-five years in that magnificent metropolis, a teacher, a judge, a courtier under its Mameluke sovereign. He sent for his wife and family and worldly goods, but all were lost by shipwreck on the way. He travelled at last to Eastern Islam, to Mecca, to Jerusalem, to Damascus. At Damascus, while the city went up in flames, he was lowered from its walls and conveyed to the tent of the invading war-lord; and so the great doctor of Islam, who had begun his diplomatic career as ambassador to Peter the Cruel of Castile, ended it by a *tête-à-tête* with the Terror of the World, Tamerlane.

What of Ibn Khaldoun's *History*? It is a wonderful experience to read those great volumes, as rich and various, as subtle, deep and formless as the Ocean, and to fish up from them ideas old and new. Sometimes he seems marvellously precocious, as when he deals with the division of labour, the social origins of wealth, the distinction between the form and substance of history. Often we are struck by his maturity, his capacity to see good and evil in the same thing: his disdain for the corruption of city life, which alone he recognises as civilised, his admiration for the primitive simplicity of the nomads whom he detests as the destroyers of culture. Always he brings us back to the nomads with whom he had lived, among whom he had written, from whom he was to flee. Suddenly, in a few brief sentences, he can recreate their whole life: their camels, their vigilance, their self-reliance, their long, incessant journeys, their bare pastures, and themselves, 'the fiercest of men, whom the townsmen regard as wild beasts, ungovernable beasts of prey'.

How truly he understood the Arab world! There indeed, as he wrote, 'the past and the future are as like as two drops of water,' and the history of Morocco or Arabia, even in the twentieth century, still illustrates his theme: the puritanism of the desert, triumphant, converting itself into urban royalty and then rotting with luxury, bureaucracy and taxes. But it is well to remember his limitations. He was a philosopher of history, not a universal historian; and though his great genius, addressed to his narrow field, drew therefrom profound reflexions, they were not and could not be of general application. He missed — because it was outside his field — what was to be the most significant factor even for Arab history.

For although Ibn Khaldoun wrote of the civilisation of cities, he had never, at that time, seen a European or even an Eastern city. He had been to Castile, but Castile neither was nor is Europe. To him a city was a sultan's capital, which lived by the court and died with it: a city with a large and varied artisanate, but without independent economic life and, above all, without civic spirit — for his *'aṣabiyya* was a spirit of the desert aristocracy, or of the Prophet and his *élite*: in cities it must inevitably perish. Ibn Khaldoun might admit the possibility of 'settled urban life' in happier lands, but he did not pursue this fertile path. He had seen the merchants of Europe who came to the Barbary ports and had marvelled at their wealth and splendid way of life 'beyond all description'; but he never conceived the character of the cities which had sent them forth: indeed, he remarked casually, 'God knows best what goes on in those parts'. And yet it was these cities which were ultimately to invalidate his rules. For they were cities whose life was quite independent of courts and sultans, which did not consist of a mere artisanate, and which had an urban patriciate with an *'aṣabiyya*, a civic solidarity of its own. In the end it was not a new rural dynasty that was to pounce on the rotten civilisation of Islam. After many revolutions, the cycle of history was suddenly broken. It was broken by the mercantilist states of Europe, the heirs of those mercantile cities of Italy whose character has never even been envisaged by the Philosopher of the Maghreb.

CHAPTER VI

UP AND DOWN IN THE COUNTRY: THE PASTON LETTERS

To some readers *The Paston Letters* are a cosy work. They show the unchanging face of Norfolk society. That social competition, those provincial interests, those irreconcilable manor houses, those rural viragos, those farming, hunting, poaching clergymen — there they all are, with High Church exhortations from the laity at Bayfield, midnight assaults in the churchyard of Plumstead, Wyndham darkly threatening from Felbrigg, cousin Gurney in the courts, the parson of Snoring in the stocks, and unedifying scenes at Paston, when 'we fell out before my mother with "thou proud priest!" and "thou proud squire!" ' Might it not all be to-day, instead of the mid-fifteenth century?

Possibly it might. But below this unchanging face there is another very different world. It is a pre-capitalist world, a world in which the great majority of men had not yet discovered our innocent but absorbing methods of getting and spending. Consequently their whole society was different. It was different in structure, different in aims, different in social values. It is unrecognisable to-day, even to that small minority of Englishmen who still have to find ways of reducing the tedium of rural life.

Consider the aims of the fifteenth-century Englishman. He lived — according to all the outward evidence — not for himself, or for God, but for the family. Not to make the family rich or comfortable, but to raise its status — a status that might be illustrated by wealth (as long as it was conspicuous), but to which comfort must certainly be sacrificed. The Marxist heresy that man lives for profit would have seemed disgusting to him; the capitalist heresy that he lives to cosset his children would have been incredible. Children were imperfect, stunted creatures whose sole purpose was, when grown up, to help forward the family. To this end life, marriage, everything was openly subordinated, as young Elizabeth Paston discovered when she drew the line at an elderly, deformed widower. For three months she was, by her loving mother, 'beaten once in a week or twice, sometimes twice in one day, and her head broken in two or three places'. The same truth was experienced by Margery Paston who, having stubbornly married the bailiff, was summarily informed by the family chaplain that neither her mother nor her mother's friends would ever receive her again. Margery was 'lost'; 'but remember you, and so do I,' her mother wrote consolingly to her son, 'that we have lost of her but a worthless person.' She was 'worthless' and 'lost' because she was now useless to the family. These loving mothers are the Paston women whom Mr. Warrington, in his introduction to this new selection,[1] finds so admirable.

Of course, we must not think of the family only in the strict sense. It extended to include, in their proper stations, cousins, allies, clients, 'servants'. All these were held together in a great system of mutual dependence and patronage; and it was within and through this system that a family, in the strict sense, 'rose' — that is, acquired land and influence, was feared and, therefore, obeyed, deserved the patronage of the great, the alliance of other 'rising' families, the service of clients whom to defend and reward was also a sign of success. The successful man was he who, thanks to such a combination, had won all his lawsuits, married an estate clear of debt, built a large house, and would die sure of burial by an impressive number of priests, in a monumental tomb already built, and with masses prepaid in *sæcula sæculorum*.

Nevertheless, in saying this, we have already stumbled on an apparent contradiction. Why must the tomb be prefabricated, the masses prepaid? It is because, in spite of all this lip-service to the family, no one really trusted anyone else, not even his sons, once his power over them was gone. In reality the family was not cultivated as such: it was a necessary alliance from which every man hoped individually to profit: 'every gentleman that hath discretion waiteth that his kin and servants that liveth by him and at his cost should help him forward'. Such an

[1] *The Paston Letters*, edited by John Warrington (London, Everyman's Library, 1956)

alliance was cultivated only so long as it served its purpose. Hence that ruthlessness to the black sheep, those 'lost' and 'worthless' members who, by their weakness, failed to help the others forward. A struggling society has no room for passengers: every member must pull his weight, for once the boat ceases to go forward it will surely go back, and once it is seen to go back, the rats will leave, the enemy will attack, and it will sink. As Mrs. Paston wrote: 'if we lose our friends, it shall be hard in this troublous world to get them again'.

The operation of these social laws is clearly seen in the history of the Paston family. In one generation they were made, by an energetic lawyer. Always it is the lawyers who are the self-made men: the Pastons' Norfolk has no great tradesman, except Sir Geoffrey Boleyn, and he had made his fortune in London. Judge Paston was the son of a husbandman, but in his heyday none durst oppose him and he left to his heir both good manors and good advice. 'I advise you,' his widow told his son, 'to think once a day of your father's counsel to learn the law, for he said many times that whosoever should dwell at Paston should have need to know how to defend himself.' The whole Paston correspondence is a commentary on this judicious remark, for as soon as the formidable judge was dead the plunderers descended. An ex-friar, patronised by the Duke of Suffolk, attacked the manor of Oxnead. Lord Moleyns sent a thousand men, 'a company of brothel that reck not what they do,' to rifle and sack the manor house of Gresham. At once it was clear that the Pastons were fair game. 'Here dare no man say a good word for you in this country,' Mrs. Paston wrote to her husband. 'God amend it.'

To stop the rot it was essential to show that one could hit back. One must win a lawsuit. Unfortunately, this also depended on power. John Paston duly sued Lord Moleyns; but to what end? The sheriff assured him that whereas he would gladly pocket a bribe and fix the verdict accordingly in any other case, in this one case it was impossible: the King had written commanding him to make 'such a panel to acquit Lord Moleyns'. The answer was for the Pastons to find a patron as powerful as Lord Moleyns. Once again we are brought back to the central fact of feudal society: patronage.

High above the Pastons' Norfolk, like the gods above Homer's

Troy, live the great patrons, the arbitrary, cynical and yet epicurean managers of these desperate human struggles. There is the Duke of Norfolk at Framlingham; there is the Duke of Suffolk at Costessey, maintainer of 'all the traitors and extortioners of this country', without whose 'good-lordship, while the world is as it is, ye can never live in peace'; and at Caister Castle, his newly-built seat, there is Sir John Fastolf, once major-domo of the Regent of France, now old and heirless among his books and tapestries, his artists and chroniclers. Upstart gangsters, fattened with the spoils of war and injustice, these men yet appeal to us more than the dreary, pushing, grasping county society beneath them: for it was they or their peers — a Tiptoft, a Duke Humfrey — who brought to England the Italian or Burgundian Renaissance, who built great colleges and libraries, churches and tombs, to house their pride or expiate their sins. Unfortunately, these great patrons of art and learning proved less useful as patrons of the Pastons.

It is true the Pastons — by hook or crook — netted most of the Fastolf property; but it proved, as the Bishop of Norwich observed, an inheritance full of 'sorrow and trouble'. It did not make them stronger, only a richer, more tempting prey. The Duke of Suffolk grabbed the manor of Drayton and wrecked the manor house and profaned the church of Hellesdon. 'If my Lord of Norfolk would come,' wailed the Pastons' bailiff, 'he should make all well.' But, alas, the Duke of Norfolk had been wooed in vain, for he, too, had designs on the Fastolf property. So he now deserted his former clients and suddenly besieged and captured Caister. Exultant, the two dowager duchesses declared that what they had they would hold, and lesser families — Heydons, Yelvertons, Boleyns — pounced upon the leavings of the feast. The Pastons seemed finished — was it not getting about that they were selling their woods? — but no: fortunately, those fatal accidents which had brought them temporarily so low could happen to other families too — even to their oppressors. Within four years the last Mowbray Duke of Norfolk was suddenly dead and Sir John Paston, in an access of energy, was able to seize Caister again — and this time to keep it.

Such was the social round of fifteenth-century England. It will be said that that was an exceptional age, the age of 'bastard feudalism'. But in fact what were the special circumstances? Only the weakness of the Crown which gave wider scope to these social struggles and the *Paston Letters* which open a window into them. A century later, when the Tudors have reimposed the royal power, we can still see the same social pattern, even if it is now more limited in scope and must be sought in obscurer records. Landlords may not sack each other's houses, but they break down each other's enclosures. Private war continues, formalised in ceaseless litigation. Wards are still 'bought and sold as beasts'. The rules are the same, too. Two hundred years after the death of Judge Paston, a successful Crown servant urged his son, as the prime condition of survival, to be sure to win his first lawsuit: otherwise the whole county would turn and rend him. And the result was the same: long after Judge Paston, the great houses of Norfolk continued to be raised by an oligarchy of lawyers: Heydons, Yelvertons, Hobarts, Cokes. And at the summit of national society still we find upstart olympian magnates, Howards and Seymours, Dudleys and Sidneys, great patrons of art, letters and injustice, advertising by their magnificence their brief triumph in the social war. Only one social group still plays no public part: the 'capitalists'. If the Boleyns are still there, in Tudor times, it is no longer as merchants. They, too, have 'risen' and joined, triumphantly but briefly, in the great game.

But as for a modern parallel, it is not to be found in England, even in Norfolk. In spite of cousin Gurney and the parson of Snoring — those fleeting forms — the substance is unrecognisable. For a modern parallel we must look elsewhere, to Persia or the High Atlas. The modern Sir John Fastolf or Duke of Suffolk is not among the English aristocracy: he is a great caïd or pasha, who has cornered water-rights, distributed uneven justice, prospered in war, subjected other tribes, and built up a private empire of patronage which suddenly dissolves with his death: a man like the late El Glaoui, Pasha of Marrakesh.

CHAPTER VII

DESIDERIUS ERASMUS

Desiderius Erasmus was a scholar who, in the early days of printing, sought to give his contemporaries clear and accurate texts of certain neglected works. He re-translated the Bible, and edited the Christian Fathers. He also wrote, in his clear, elegant Latin, colloquies, satires and works of evangelical piety; and he carried on, mainly with scholars, a gigantic correspondence. Offered opportunities of practical responsibility, he consistently evaded them, and in the crisis of his time he appeared to many a timorous neuter. He was neither a courtier in the age of courts, nor a revolutionary in an age of revolution. Though a friend of kings, his ideal society was the republican city-state. In religion, Luther and Rome alike accused him of tepidity. He was not even an admirer of fashionable classical culture: ancient Rome displeased him both by its paganism and by its empire. His personal character was not heroic. He was a valetudinarian, comfort-loving, timid and querulous. He lived in his study and died in his bed.

And yet Erasmus is a giant figure in the history of ideas. He is the intellectual hero of the sixteenth century, and his failure was Europe's tragedy. For his failure seemed, at the time, immense and final: as immense as his previous success.

Consider his success. Born the illegimate son of an obscure priest, he rose, merely by his pen, to a position of undisputed supremacy in Europe. Cosmopolitan in an age of awakening nationalism, he was born in Holland, studied in Paris, found his intellectual home in Oxford, took his doctorate in Savoy, travelled to Germany and Italy, published his works impartially in Louvain, Paris, Venice and Basel, and had disciples throughout Europe. When he travelled, customs-officers treated him as a prince, princes as a friend. The royal bastard of Scotland was his pupil, the King of Poland his correspondent; the King of Portugal tried to lure him to Coimbra; the King of

France wrote twice, and in his own hand, to tempt him to Paris. He was offered professorial chairs in Bavaria and Saxony, bishoprics in Spain and Sicily. The Emperor made him his Privy Councillor, the Pope offered him a cardinal's hat. His disciples formed a European *élite*: they included, he once proudly wrote, 'the Emperor, the Kings of England, France and Denmark, Prince Ferdinand of Germany, the Cardinal of England, the Archbishop of Canterbury, and more princes, more bishops, more learned and honourable men than I can name, not only in England, Flanders, France and Germany, but even in Poland and Hungary. . . .' Such was the fame of Erasmus in 1524, when it was almost at its peak.

Eleven years later, his failure seemed complete. The great crisis of the Reformation had split his followers and Popes and Princes could not help him. To save his independence, Erasmus had declined their gifts, avoided their courts, and fled to die in a republican city in Switzerland. He died defeated, foreseeing the future. Soon his name and works would be condemned, his disciples persecuted, his patrons unavailing. 'If that is a crime', protested a Spanish thinker whom the Inquisition accused of having corresponded with Erasmus, 'it is a crime committed also by many great princes, many men of all conditions in all countries . . . among whom I see the Pope, our Lord the Emperor, and most Christian princes, as well spiritual as secular. . . .[1] It was in vain. By mid-century Erasmus had become a heretic. In Catholic countries it was dangerous even to have known the last great thinker of united Catholic Europe.

How did this great tragedy come about? For it was a real tragedy, not only of one man but of a whole generation. The disciples of Erasmus, in the early sixteenth century, were the spiritual and intellectual *élite* of Europe. There is scarcely a great name in those years which is not among them. They were the saints, the humanists and the reformers who, by their universal diffusion, might have created a new Europe but were in fact swallowed up in the great and widening gulf which they had sought to bridge. To understand this tragedy of a generation it is not enough to study their leader only. We must consider the century which produced both him and them.

[1] Juan de Vergara, quoted in M. Bataillon, *Erasme et l'Espagne* (Paris 1937), p. 493.

In the fourteenth century the decline of Medieval Europe began. The great age of medieval industry, medieval art, the medieval Church was then over. Particularly of the Church, whose vitality then began, as it seemed, a long, uninterrupted ebb. This spiritual ebb was accompanied by other developments. First, the wealth of the Church was increased. New religious orders were not founded, but the old became increasingly rich, and none more arrogant, more ostentatious of their wealth, than the former 'Mendicant' orders, the Franciscans and Dominicans. This increasing wealth of the Church led, as a natural consequence to greater aristocratic control. The system of 'commendation' — 'the leprosy of the Church' as Montalembert called it — made the Church, in the fifteenth as in the eighteenth century, into 'a system of outdoor relief for the upper classes'. Hence those aristocratic teen-age bishops, those highly promoted papal bastards who so enliven the history of the pre-Reformation Church. Meanwhile, as spiritual life ebbed away from religion, new forms of piety were developed upon its arid crust. In the schools, Thomism triumphed: a mechanical dissection of dead doctrine; among the people 'works' replaced 'faith': mechanical devotions — pilgrimages, veneration of images and relics, ostentatious ceremonies, and finally, the sale of indulgences. Genuinely religious spirits turned away from this oppressive incrustation of religion to an inner mysticism. It was not for nothing that the fifteenth century was the great age of mysticism. Mysticism, as so often, was the refuge of the defeated.

But Christianity was not everywhere defeated. Sporadically, throughout Europe, the evangelical protest was raised. In England the Lollards appealed to — and translated — the Bible. In Medicean Florence, the new Platonists, Ficino and Pico della Mirandola, challenged the formalism of the schools and Savonarola, the puritan friar, preached his crusade against the mechanical 'works' of religion. In the other great centre of European wealth, the Netherlands, Gerard Groote founded the evangelical order of the Brethren of the Common Life, whose new primitive Christianity spread through the monasteries of Northern Europe and produced the greatest mystical work of the century, *The Imitation of Christ.* But all these remained local movements, doomed (it seemed) to local extinction. By the end of the fifteenth century the Lollards had been crushed in England, Savonarola had been burnt in Florence, and the Brethren of the Common Life remained rude and parochial in their Northern simplicity. None of these was able, by themselves, to mobilise the scattered forces which demanded the reform of the Church.

For all over Europe there were practical men eager to reform both the Church and society. Princes, noblemen, officials, clergy, lawyers, scholars only asked to be inspired and used. Already serious efforts had been made within the Church itself, but the machinery was clogged by its own vested interests, against which even a reforming Pope was to prove helpless: the prisoner of his own patronage and the powerful monastic orders around his throne. Other reformers obtained local successes by invoking the lay power: which, however, had dangerous appetites. So Cardinal Ximenes in Spain, thanks to royal support, was able to purge monasteries, to reduce papal patronage, to advance biblical study, and to found the new humanist university of Alcalá. But Ximenes was exceptionally fortunate: generally these early reformers were broken by the impossibility of their task or achieved success only among a few disciples. They remained a scattered minority of enlightened men in an apathetic or hostile world. Then Erasmus appeared and gave them not a constitutional programme but a message, not new machinery but a new spirit. He turned the disconnected reformers into an army which seemed — for a time — invincible.

How did he do it? One technical advantage which he possessed must not be overlooked. Erasmus had the good fortune to coincide with the spread throughout Europe of the printing-press, first used ten years before his birth. The great printers of his time were his natural allies. They were scholars and humanists, members of that educated urban patriciate from which the reformers naturally sprang. Thierry Martens of Louvain was a pupil of the Brethren of the Common Life; so was Josse Badius of Paris, who had also studied in Italy; and Aldus Manutius of Venice was a humanist and a Greek scholar. These men, his publishers and friends, lent their services to Erasmus and his contemporaries as they could not have done to his predecessors.

The printing-press, coinciding as it did with a European Church, a European movement of reform, and an international language, gave to the educated classes a weapon of sudden, miraculous potency: a new way to learning, to the Scriptures, even to heresy, by-passing the control of the Church. The age of Erasmus was that golden age which lay between the European discovery of printing and the discovery of its antidote, the *Index Librorum Prohibitorum*.

But of course this was not the only reason for Erasmus's success. Erasmus did not go to the printing-press: the printing-press came to him. He was the first modern best-seller, the first great writer whose works publishers competed to commission, to print and to distribute. They did so because he had discovered, as none other had done, a universal idiom. Behind his lucid, nimble, pungent style he had united the intellectual appeals of all the reformers: Lollard biblicism, Dutch piety, Italian scholarship and Florentine Platonism. Fusing all these he had made them into one message. And finally, there was his irony, which carried that message everywhere. Like Pascal after him, he discovered that in moral questions it is not earnestness but irony that kills.

This great achievement, the uniting in one cosmopolitan message of the various local protests of the fifteenth century, occupied Erasmus for the first forty years of his life as a wandering scholar. The process began in his native Holland, where he studied under the Brethren of the Common Life at Deventer and there discovered the deep evangelical piety which marked him for life. In Holland also he made his first contact with the exact classical scholarship of Renaissance Italy, and particularly of Lorenzo Valla, the papal secretary who had exposed the false Decretals of the Church. As a scholar, Valla remained Erasmus's master all his life; it was by Valla's strict and disconcerting textual methods that Erasmus would afterwards delete, as spurious, the only reference to the Trinity in the New Testament. But Erasmus's most fruitful contact with Italy was not with the Italy of the philologists: it was with the Platonist Florence of Ficino, of Pico and of Savonarola; and he made that contact not in Italy, where it was already extinct, but in England. There, in Oxford, English scholars — Grocyn,

Linacre, Colet — returning from Italy, had grafted Florentine Platonism on to the stump of Lollard Biblicism and produced a new movement, Platonist and Pauline, by which Erasmus, coming to England in 1499, was at once inspired. From that moment, Oxford became his spiritual home. He became a disciple of Colet, the fellow-pupil of Thomas More, and for the rest of their lives remained intimately attached to both of them. After that discovery, Erasmus's intellectual experience was complete. He visited Italy, only to be disappointed by the cold, proud cult of pagan antiquity which had now replaced the Florentine renaissance. He went to Cambridge, but, as his biographer observes, '*l'esprit de Cambridge n'est pas l'esprit d'Oxford*',[1] and he was disappointed there too. Thus, from four sources, from Wyclif and Gerard Groote, from Lorenzo Valla and Savonarola, Erasmus drew together his philosophy of reform. Out of these separate elements he had created a single cosmopolitan force, a combination of Latin and Northern piety capable of inspiring the army of reformers throughout Europe and conquering, from its northern base, even orthodox France, even Jewish Spain, even pagan Rome.

And what was this philosophy? Erasmus himself called it *Philosophia Christi*, the philosophy of Christ. Rebelling against the dead intellectual apparatus of the Schoolmen and the mechanical devotions which monks and friars had multiplied among the ignorant people — the 'works' which seemed no longer to express or illustrate but to have replaced that 'faith' which St. Paul had preached — he urged men to turn to the Bible and, in particular, to the New Testament, and there to discover the primitive spirit of Christianity, as it had been before a jealous priesthood had desiccated it in formal dogma and overlaid it with 'judaic' observances. After all, thanks to the new art of printing, the Bible need not any longer be withheld from the Christian world; thanks to the new scholarship of Italy, the text could be cleaned of all excrescences and incrustations and presented widespread in its original form. The message of Christ, he wrote, was not either complex in itself or a mystery of state which princes, out of prudence, must conceal: it was simple, and it should be spread. 'I would have women read the Gospels

[1] A. Renaudet, *Erasme et l'Italie* (Geneva 1954), p. 110.

and the Epistles of St. Paul; I would have the ploughman and the craftsman sing them at their work; I would have the traveller recite them to forget the weariness of his journey. Baptism and the sacraments belong to all Christians; why should knowledge of doctrine be reserved to a few men only, theologians and monks, who form but the smallest part of Christendom and often think only of their lands and goods? True theology is possessed by every man who is inspired and guided by the spirit of Christ, be he a digger or a weaver.' The theologian, said Erasmus, by his expert knowledge, has a duty to divulge the simplicity of the Scriptures; but it is the layman who, if he understands it, is the measure of Christianity.

This teaching was soon to become 'Protestant' teaching; but when Erasmus first advanced it 'Protestantism' had not yet been heard of. Luther had not yet spoken, nor the Church panicked. Therefore clergy and laity alike listened to it without alarm. It seemed a new and fruitful message, capable of renewing the Church from within. In all Erasmus's works this 'Philosophy of Christ' is expressed. It is in his *Adages*, in his *Paraphrases*, in his *Colloquies*, in his *Praise of Folly*, in the introductions and dedications of his great scholarly editions, in the vast correspondence by which he held together, throughout Europe, the ever-growing Erasmian *élite*. But most simply it appears in one of his earliest works, *Enchiridion Militis Christiani*, 'the Manual of a Christian Soldier'. When the *Enchiridion* was first published, in 1504, it attracted little notice, for Erasmus was not yet famous. But in 1508, with the publication in Venice of the great Aldine edition of his *Adages*, his fame was established, and in 1516, his wonderful year (for it saw the publication of his New Testament, his edition of St. Jerome and his *Institutio Principis Christiani*), it swept over Europe. In that year the *Enchiridion* was rediscovered and began its conquest of Germany. Two years later a new edition, prefaced by a new manifesto of the Philosophy of Christ, was printed at Basel. Translations soon appeared in German, Dutch and French. The great French reformers — Lefèvre d'Etaples and his friends — accepted Erasmus as their leader. And meanwhile (for in 1517 the Archduke Charles, ruler of the Netherlands, had gone with his Flemish court to be

King of Spain) the works of Erasmus had crossed the Pyrenees. In 1522 began that extraordinary phenomenon, the Erasmian conquest of the Peninsula. 'It is astonishing,' wrote one of his disciples, 'this devotion to Erasmus among all classes of Spaniards, learned and ignorant, clergy and laity alike.' 'They say', another reported to him, 'that in reading your works they feel illuminated by the spirit of God. They say that you alone know how to publish the teaching of God for the peace and consolation of men's souls.' In 1524, the *Enchiridion* was translated into Spanish. The translator himself was astonished by his success. 'At the court of the Emperor,' he wrote, 'in the towns, in the churches, in the monasteries, even in the inns and on the roads, everyone now has the *Enchiridion* of Erasmus. Hitherto it was read only in Latin by a few scholars, who did not always understand it; now it is read in Spanish by men of all conditions, and those who had previously never heard of Erasmus now know him through this little book.' From Spain the *Enchiridion* soon conquered bilingual Portugal. In 1531 an Italian translation was published at Brescia. The rest of his works soon followed. The piety of the North had triumphed throughout Europe.[1]

Thus Erasmus conquered the *élite* everywhere. He conquered them because they were ready to be conquered. Particularly they were ready for him in Spain, where the reformation of Cardinal Ximenes had prepared the ground and the upper classes were deeply penetrated by a leaven of converted Jews. This connexion between Erasmianism and the Jews in Spain is interesting. The fact is indubitable; it is also somewhat paradoxical, for Erasmus himself was anti-semitic and hated Spain and Portugal, which he declined ever to visit, precisely because of their indelible Semitic tincture: 'Italy', he once wrote, 'contains many Jews, but Spain scarcely contains any Christians'; and he dismissed Portugal (whose 'Grocer-King' had been offended by Erasmus's strictures on the royal spice-monopoly) as 'that Jew-

[1] The Erasmian conquest of Spain has been the subject of one of the greatest historical studies of Erasmus and his work, M. Marcel Bataillon's *Erasme et l'Espagne* (Paris 1937). For the cult of Erasmus in Portugal, see M. Bataillon's volume of essays, *Etudes sur le Portugal au temps de l'Humanisme* (Coimbra 1952). For his influence in France, see Margaret Mann, *Erasme et les Débuts de la Réforme Française* (Paris 1934); for his influence in Italy, see A. Renaudet, *Erasme et l'Italie* (Geneva 1954).

ish race'.[1] But in fact the paradox is explicable, and explicable partly by Erasmus's own confusion of terms. To him Judaism was a religious term: it meant Talmudic formalism, pharisaical observances — in fact, precisely those 'mechanical devotions' which, in his eyes, had stifled, in official Christianity, the Philosophy of Christ. But the Spanish Jews of his time were of course converts to Christianity — the believing Jews had been expelled from the Peninsula before he had begun to publish; and being converts, newly arrived at Christianity, they had not acquired, and were not prepared to acquire, that heavy apparatus of dogma which the born Christian has more gradually learnt to wear. Ironically, it was the born Christians, the *cristianos viejos*, who, in Spain, represented the 'judaism' hated by Erasmus, and who, mobilised by the Orders and the Inquisition, ultimately destroyed Erasmianism in Spain: it was the 'new Christians', the *conversos*, who were the natural Erasmians. Thus the Spanish Jews, by that same emancipation from dogma which afterwards made them prominent among the Spanish mystics, provided Erasmus with some of his greatest disciples and helped to make Spain, for a time, the bulwark of Erasmianism in Europe.

Such then was the position in the early 1520's. At that time the ultimate triumph of Erasmianism in the Church must have seemed almost certain. For what power had the corrupt Court of Rome against so unanimous a Europe? And this Erasmian Europe was, moreover, politically mobilised under an Erasmian sovereign. Since 1516 Erasmus had been a privy councillor of his own native sovereign the Archduke Charles, ruler of the Netherlands, to whom he afterwards dedicated his *Education of a Christian Prince*. By 1520 the Archduke was not only King of Spain, the most powerful military monarchy of the day, but also, as Emperor in Germany, the greatest lay sovereign in Europe; and both Spain and Germany were now deeply penetrated by movements of reform. Further, the Emperor was surrounded and advised by what has been called an 'Erasmian

[1] The connexion between Erasmianism and the Peninsular Jews is amply documented by M. Bataillon. For Erasmus's antisemitism see the accumulation of references given by P. S. Allen, *Opus Epistolarum Des. Erasmi Roterodamensis* (1906–47), IV, 46.

general staff'. Mercurino Gattinara, his Piedmontese chancellor, was a devoted disciple of Erasmus. So also was Alonso de Valdés, his indispensable secretary. Finally, in 1521 the Pope himself was a Netherlander. He was the Emperor's old tutor, Adrian of Utrecht, a compatriot, almost a friend of Erasmus, and he had taken to Rome, just as the Emperor had taken to Spain, an entourage of Netherlanders, familiar with the Christian revival of the north. To complete his triumph, all that Erasmus required was a period of peace: for it is peace, not war, he always insisted, that forwards spiritual movements among men. Unfortunately, Europe did not obtain peace. Moreover, two other forces threatened from either side the victory which Erasmus sought: two rival fanaticisms to which his whole spirit was hateful: Luther and the Monks.

From first to last monks were the bane of Erasmus's life. Between them there was no peace. He hated and despised them as the irreconcilable enemies of learning and true piety, and they in turn pursued him with the vindictiveness of a depressed class whose very livelihood is threatened by reform. For if the spirit of monasticism was now dead — save among the Carthusians whom Erasmus himself, like More and Colet, excepted from his condemnations[1] — its vested interests were still living, and these vested interests were threatened at their very base by Erasmus's Philosophy of Christ. Were there monks in the New Testament or in the primitive centuries of the Church? What did monks do, asked the Reformers, except perpetuate among the ignorant people those mechanical devotions, those 'works', those pilgrimages, those relics, those indulgences which the Philosophy of Christ had never admitted? In the last two centuries, all agreed, monks had contributed nothing to religion, nothing to society, nothing to learning. They had become a mere religious vested interest, a pressure-group which, by its wealth and its influence with the illiterate people, could intimidate even the sometimes liberal court of Rome. In the early sixteenth century all liberal men believed that monasticism must be abolished: it

[1] Both More and Colet at one time contemplated becoming Carthusian monks, More at Sheen, Colet at Richmond. Erasmus's respect for the Carthusians is shown by his colloquy *Militis et Carthusiani*, as also by a letter of 1527, written to a monk, evidently a Carthusian, who was contemplating a return to the world (Allen, *Opus Epistolarum*, vol. VII, No. 1887).

was a disease in the Church. In the same year in which that practical reformer, Thomas Cromwell, was legislating against it in England, a committee of cardinals, appointed by the Pope, and including Cardinal Pole and the future Pope Paul IV, advocated its gradual abolition throughout Christendom. The battle-cry against the monks had been uttered thirty years before, by Erasmus, in his *Enchiridion: Monachatus non est pietas*, Monkery is not piety. It was a phrase which the monks would remember and revenge.

The monks, of course, had their answer. The Philosophy of Christ, they could say, was all very well for educated men: for bishops and cathedral clergy, princes and officials, cultivated merchants, lawyers, scholars — that educated bourgeoisie in which Erasmus found his disciples. But what of the poor and unlearned who could not understand such an intellectual message? For them visual images, 'mechanical devotions', pilgrimages, relics, ceremonies, were the necessary evidence of the Church. The images which the Reformers attacked were the Bible of the illiterate. Erasmus might credit the ploughman and the craftsman with a capacity for apprehending the truth apart from such visual aids, but he was wrong: he romanticised the gross faculties of the fallen plebs. And as for the monks and friars, the religious tribunes of that plebs, the recruiting-sergeants of that Christian army, who purveyed to their crude senses this necessary trash and *bric-à-brac* of religion — was it not their living also? Pigs'-bones and indulgences, spiritual necessities to the ignorant people, were bread-and-butter to their tub-chaplains. . . . Unfortunately, this argument, though strong as a cement to rally the monks in defence of their interests, did not seem very cogent to the Princes of the Church — at least as long as those Princes were not frightened. Unfrightened, the educated classes turned naturally to Erasmus: it was only if they were frightened and needed an army that they would turn to the recruiting-sergeants, and lower their intellectual standards in deference towards them. Fortunately for the monks, a benefactor arose who did so frighten the upper classes in the Church and drove them into dependence on these hitherto despised allies. This benefactor was, appropriately enough, a renegade monk: Martin Luther.

When Luther made his frontal attack on the Roman Church, he incorporated in it, of course, many of the criticisms already made from within the Church by Erasmus. Consequently he naturally looked to Erasmus for support against Rome. But Erasmus, though a critic, was still a Churchman. He would support the Church of Rome, he replied, until he saw a better: and although he sympathised with Luther's criticism, he did not think that Luther offered a better alternative. Consequently the Roman Church also looked to Erasmus for support against Luther. From 1519 onwards both sides began to court Erasmus: each hoped that the greatest uncommitted spiritual writer in Europe would declare roundly against its adversary.

What was Erasmus to do? He could not support Luther, whose philosophy he rejected and who was seeking to disrupt the Church. On the other hand he could not denounce him completely, without repudiating his own criticism of the Church — in other words, without ceasing to be Erasmus. The more he was pressed, the more he refused to commit himself, or use his unique position to endorse the rage of either party. He urged the Elector of Saxony to protect Luther against the Catholic fanatics; he urged Luther to persevere 'against the tyranny of the See of Rome and its satellites, the mendicant monks'; on the other hand he disavowed the heretical views of Luther. But the proper answer to Luther, he insisted, was not condemnation, for 'the accusations of Luther against the tyranny, the rapacity, the corruption of the Court of Rome' were only too true — 'would to God', he wrote to the Pope's chaplain, 'that they were not'. The true remedy for Lutheranism was not denunciation, it was 'to cut the roots from which the evil continually springs: of which one is the hatred of the Court of Rome, with its intolerable avarice and tyranny, and other certain human ordinances which weigh heavily upon Christian liberty'. These 'human ordinances' were, of course, monasticism and mechanical devotions.

To this philosophy of reform Erasmus remained constant. He sacrificed to it his comfort, his influence, his friends, his peace of mind. He has often been accused of timidity, but in fact his refusal to take sides is a sign rather of consistency: consistency to his ideal of a still united Church peacefully reformed from within. Pressed by Luther, he refused to support him or separate himself from Rome. Pressed by Rome, he refused to deny the truth or justice of Luther's criticism. 'All the Princes urge me to write against Luther,' he said; 'I will not, or if I do, I shall so write that the Pharisees will wish I had kept silent'; and rather than be converted into an inquisitor in the Netherlands, he fled to the free city of Basel to preserve his intellectual integrity. The monks were delighted. From now on Erasmus, though he had opposed Luther and been spurned by Luther, could be blackened as a Lutheran. The monasteries set to work: packs of monks dived into Erasmus's writings; and soon a series of clerical tally-hos denoted the flushing, in many a deep theological thicket, of suspected heresy. In reply to the Erasmian phrase 'Monkery is not piety', a monk of Cologne invented a rival battle-cry which was to become just as famous: '*Erasmus posuit ova, Lutherus eduxit pullos*. . . . Erasmus laid the eggs, Luther hatched them. God grant that we may smash the eggs and stifle the chicks.'

But Erasmus's patrons were not yet prepared to abandon him to such enemies. In 1527 the Spanish monks prevailed on the Inquisitor-General to permit a general inquest on the works of Erasmus by an assembly of theologians in Valladolid. Erasmus was attacked for his doubting spirit, his inconvenient scholarship, his insinuating style. Had he not advocated toleration in religion, basing it on uncertainties which the monks in no way felt? Had he not maintained that questions of *hypostasis* and *homoousia* did not justify setting fire to the world? But it was no good. The great of the world stood by Erasmus. The Inquisitor-General himself championed him. The Emperor wrote personally to promise his support. Even the Pope would not favour the monks. From the Conference of Valladolid Erasmus, thanks to his great patrons, emerged triumphant. Alas, it was his last triumph. In the very same year an event occurred which led to the loss of those patrons and precipated the ultimate defeat of Erasmus, the ultimate victory of Luther and the monks.

For in 1527 the Spanish Erasmists appealed to the sword. Erasmus hated war. Only in peace, he thought, could the spirit reform the world. It was his great grievance against the kings who patronised him that they treated war so lightly, as a royal sport. Never did Erasmus's basic republicanism express itself more eloquently than when he attacked the whole tribe of kings for their crimes against peace, their cynical profusion in dissipating the prosperity built up by the ceaseless labour of 'that despised and humble crowd', the people. Rightly, he once declared, was the eagle chosen as the symbol of royalty, since it is 'neither beautiful, nor musical, nor fit for food, but carnivorous, greedy, hateful to all, a curse to all, able and eager to do more harm than all.' Even Popes, instead of controlling the warlike rage of kings, now joined and encouraged them in their crimes in order to establish their families in Italian duchies. Even theologians and clergy committed *la trahison des clercs*, prostituting their learning in support of secular wars. Even the Erasmians, he was now to discover, were not exempt from this disastrous fever. In 1527 the government of Charles V, fired by Erasmian visions of reform, launched the invincible Spanish *tercios* against the corrupt Court of Rome, and the Spanish Erasmists applauded both the war and the violent sack of Rome which it accidentally entailed. Meanwhile the Erasmian chancellor Gattinara applied to Erasmus to re-edit, as an imperial manifesto against the Papacy, Dante's *De Monarchia*. Once again Erasmus refused: he declined to be the agent of the messianic Erasmianism of Spain.

He was wise in his refusal. The sack of Rome was, for him, a fatal turning-point. Shocked by his own action, the Emperor himself lost his nerve: he moved gradually over to the papal side. And the Pope, shocked by his own failure, decided — if only the Emperor would secure his family in the duchy of Florence — to become an imperialist. On these terms the bargain was sealed. The Medici returned to Florence, the Pope decided to live and die an imperialist, and the Emperor decided not, after all, to clean up the Papacy. Thus the Emperor abandoned the Erasmians, and soon afterwards they suffered still further blows. In 1530 Gattinara died, in 1532 Valdés. Five years after the sack of Rome the 'Erasmian general staff' was dissolved. Against Luther and the monks the Erasmians were left to rely on themselves. At once they began to feel the increasing pressure of persecution. Already his books had been censured in Paris, his French translator burnt at the stake. In Spain, too, some of his disciples were burnt and even the Inquisitor-General could not save them. From now on the pace quickened. Rome, said its nuncio with satisfaction, was only waiting for Erasmus to die in order then to declare him formally a heretic.

Erasmus died in 1536 in Basel, already by then a Protestant city. He died uncondemned — indeed it was in his last year that he was offered, by a new 'Erasmist' pope, the cardinal's hat: but this honour he refused, as he had always refused other than purely intellectual authority. Nevertheless, he died defeated and defeatist. His hope, which had once seemed so near to fulfilment, of seeing the Philosophy of Christ accepted throughout Europe, was broken. Already, on the first emergence of Luther, he had foreseen the future: the recrudescence of monkery, the defeat of the Philosophy of Christ, the victory, within the Roman Church, of the Council of Trent. 'A fine defender of evangelic liberty is Luther!' he had then written. 'By his fault the yoke which we bear shall become twice as heavy. Mere permissible opinions shall become articles of faith. It will become dangerous to teach the Gospel. . . . Luther behaves like a wild man; his adversaries goad him on. But if they prevail, we shall be left to write only the epitaph of Christ, dead without hope of resurrection.' Erasmus was a true prophet. After his death all this came about. Nevertheless, a whole generation passed before his ideals were formally defeated; and the fate of this generation is interesting, for it bears some resemblance to our own. It was the generation of the liberals who were obliged to choose between rival orthodoxies.

The period from about 1530, when Erasmus lost his protectors, until 1559, when his teaching was most emphatically condemned by Rome, was the generation of the Erasmian *epigoni*, the men who had grown up under his influence and who were now feeling the ever-increasing pressure, on either side, of Lutheranism and the Monks. What were they to do in such a crisis? Liberal men, believers in the Philosophy of Christ, they wished to remain true to that ideal, but they could no longer hope to realise it within an undivided Church: they must make the difficult choice between opposing bigotries. Some, in hope, chose Catholicism: but it was a 'Protestant' Catholicism, the

Catholicism of Erasmus himself and, after his death, of the 'reforming' cardinals, Contarini, Sadoleto, Morone, Pole. They believed in such 'Protestant' doctrines as Justification by Faith, the renovation of the soul by Grace, and in the cult of mental prayer. They looked back, through Erasmus, to Savonarola and *The Imitation of Christ*, and their favourite contemporary book was a little work which a Benedictine disciple of the Spanish Erasmian, Juan de Valdés, had composed in a monastery on Mount Etna, *The Benefit of Christ*.[1] Others, in despair, chose Protestantism, but it was a 'Catholic' Protestantism, the Protestantism of the German Melanchthon, the Swiss Bucer, the Spaniard Encinas, still hoping for reunion across the narrowing Erasmian bridge. But ultimately such attempts proved futile: the gulf widened, the bridge crumbled, and the Erasmians who sought to meet upon it had to scramble to opposite sides or perish in the intervening abyss. The middle position became impossible.

Thus, little by little, in the generation after Erasmus's death, the Erasmian *élite* was dissolved. Death, desertion or martyrdom carried away its members and they were not replaced. But before each desertion, or each martyrdom, what a crisis of conscience occurred! Wherever we look, it is the same: groups of friends broken up by the agony of divergent choice and retrospective recrimination. Of the liberal cardinals who in 1538 had proposed the abolition of monasticism, one — Caraffa — became a reactionary, persecuting Pope and threw another of them, Morone, into prison as a heretic; a third, Pole, died in disgrace, accused of heresy. The little book of devotion which they had read together, *The Benefit of Christ*, was so thoroughly dealt with by the Inquisition that 300 years afterwards no copy of it could be found.[2] It had become a Protestant work, like its

[1] For Juan de Valdés and his connexion with Erasmus see Bataillon, *Erasme et l'Espagne*, pp. 373–92. He was the twin brother of Alonso de Valdés, Charles V's Erasmian secretary, and founded an Erasmian circle in Naples.

[2] Before its total condemnation in 1570, *The Benefit of Christ* was often reprinted and widely circulated in Italian, and translated into French, Spanish, Croat and perhaps other languages. After 1570 it was translated into English (from the French version) and reprinted three times before 1640. By Macaulay's time the original was thought to be 'as hopelessly lost as the second decade of Livy'; but by 1855 two copies had been discovered in Cambridge and Vienna, and the Cambridge text has been twice reprinted. See Churchill Babington, *The Benefit of Christ's Death* (Cambridge 1855) and G. Paladino, *Opuscoli e Lettere di Riformatori Italiani del Cinquecento* (Bari 1927).

precursors, *The Imitation of Christ* and the devotional writings of Savonarola.

Everywhere it was the same story. But perhaps the most famous of these Erasmian separations was that which divided not the living but the dead, the separation of Erasmus himself from his closest friend, Sir Thomas More. In all their lives, More and Erasmus had never diverged. Florentine Oxford had been the inspiration of both. Both had admired Pico della Mirandola and translated Lucian (afterwards a suspect author). Both had rejected monasticism, but exempted the Carthusians from that rejection. They had influenced each other's work, shared each other's irony, believed alike in toleration and republican city-government. And yet these inseparable allies were separated after death by rigid divisions of belief which they had never admitted. In the foundering of the Erasmian 'Third Church', More was converted into a saint of post-Tridentine Rome; Erasmus was utterly disowned by the same Rome, discarded, and accepted, as a Protestant. Already in the Protestant England of Edward VI his *Paraphrases* were printed for use in churches; by 1559 all his books were on the Roman Index; thereafter, while the Inquisition was obliterating even his name from Catholic Europe, his works, which had once been universal, were printed only in Protestant cities. The imprints of Paris, Augsburg, Mainz, Alcalà, Seville, Zaragoza, Venice, Modena gradually disappear from their title-pages, to be replaced by Basel, Geneva, Amsterdam, Leyden, Hanover, Heidelberg, Leipzig, Oxford, Stockholm, Aberdeen.[1]

Thus by 1560 the division seemed complete. The Reformers were outside the Church; and within the Church the Counter-Reformation, as it was formulated by the last session of the Council of Trent, was a victory for the monks. Every specifically Erasmian position was emphatically rejected by Rome and declared a mark of Protestant heresy. Thereafter the remaining Erasmists in the Church, however distinguished, were summarily dealt with. Even an Archbishop of Toledo, Primate of all Spain, was persecuted by the Inquisition and thrown into prison to die because of his Erasmian views. To avoid such a

[1] This protestantisation of the works of Erasmus appears clearly in A. van der Haeghen, *Bibliotheca Erasmiana* (Ghent 1893).

fate, the European Erasmists went over to the Protestantism of which they were accused, the Spanish Erasmists took refuge in mysticism — only to find that mysticism was persecuted also as an 'Erasmian' deviation. And on the other side, all that Erasmus had attacked in the Roman Church was now strengthened, reasserted, multiplied. Instead of appeasing the Reformers, Rome had decided to defy them. New monastic orders, new relics, new images, new devotions — this was now the order of the day, and art was called in to advertise ever more ostentatiously this reinvigorated apparatus of belief.[1] Of the old concessions to reason nothing was left. Even the achievements of Erasmian biblical criticism were rejected, by both sides: the Book of Revelation crept back into the canon of the New Testament, the Epistle to the Hebrews was restored to St. Paul, the spurious *comma iohanneum* returned, for two centuries, into the New Testament. Erasmianism, it seemed, was killed stone-dead.

It would be easy to end here, as has often been done; but it would, I think, be unfair. Political programmes may be defeated entirely, but not ideas: at least, not great ideas. Political circumstances may alter around them, ideological frontiers may be formed against or across them, but such convulsions merely alter the terrain: they may divert or divide, but they do not permanently dam the stream. The idea of ideological blocs systematically opposed to one another in intellectual matters is a naïve idea such as can only occur to doctrinaires and bigots. The Age of the Reformation had of course its bigots: monks who, in sixteenth-century Spain, denounced Liberal Catholics as 'Lutheran' heretics, puritans who, in seventeenth-century England, denounced Liberal Protestants as 'popish' conspirators. But the historian of ideas is not interested in these stunted McCarthyites. The victims of persecution are always more interesting than their persecutors; and if we wish to discover the heirs of Erasmus, rather than to assume too easily that they were crushed by the Counter-Reformation, we should not accept as final and mutually exclusive the barren categories of 'Pro-

[1] The use of art as official propaganda in favour of challenged Roman doctrines and practices has been brilliantly illustrated by E. Mâle, *L'Art Religeux après le Concile de Trente* (Paris, 2nd edition, 1951).

testant' and 'Catholic' into which Christendom was officially and superficially divided. There was an Erasmianism after Erasmus, a secret stream which meandered to and fro across those loudly proclaimed but ill-guarded frontiers, creating oases of rational thought impartially on either side.

In Protestantism this stream is, of course, more easily identified, for the Protestant Churches openly adopted Erasmus and used his name. In some ways his direct heir was Calvin. Calvinism, at least in its early days, had a double appeal: it appealed to the laity in general, the simple gentry revolting against the privileges and usurpations of the priesthood, and it 'exercised its most profound attraction not on this or that economic class but on the intellectual *élite* of all classes'.[1] Now these were precisely the two social groups to whom Erasmus also had appealed. The ideal of Erasmus had been the ideal of lay piety, simple, sincere, animated by faith, nourished by prayer, free from the ostentatious trappings of priestly 'works'; and his scholarly rationalism had drawn to him too 'the intellectual *élite* of all classes'. When Rome had yielded to the monks, the intellectual *élite* moved over to Protestantism: from Italy, Spain and Marian England there was an exodus of Erasmists to Geneva and Basel;[2] and Calvin, for those harder times, cast the ideas of Erasmus into his harder mould. It is easy, if we are blinded by the later, less intellectual form of Calvinism, to overlook its earlier character; but if we look more closely, it is clear. Calvin was brought up under the influence of Erasmus and himself professed the 'Philosophy of Christ'; the inspiration of Erasmus is clear in his works; and it was in Basel, the capital of Erasmianism, that

[1] I take this phrase from a most interesting passage in J. H. Hexter's book, *More's Utopia, the Biography of an Idea* (Princeton 1952), p. 93. The intellectual ascendancy of Calvinism *in the early period* of the Counter-Reformation deserves further study. In my opinion a great deal of historical error has been caused by failure to distinguish the successive phases of religion, e.g. between the intellectual Calvinism of Calvin's own time (contrasting with the intellectual poverty of Rome), and the backward Calvinism of the early seventeenth century, which appealed to different classes and contrasted with the intellectual revival of Rome. For the influence of Erasmus on Calvin see Margaret Mann, *Erasme et les Debuts de la Réforme Française* (Paris 1934), pp. 161 foll.

[2] For the flight of the humanists to Switzerland in the 1550's see (for Spain) Bataillon, *Erasme et l'Espagne*, p. 749; (for Italy) Delio Cantimori, *Gli Eretici Italiani del Cinquecento* (Florence 1939), pp. 88–92, and A. Pascal, 'Da Lucca a Ginevra', a series of eight articles in *Rivista Storica Italiana* 1932–5; (for England) G. H. Garrett, *The Marian Exiles* (1938).

Calvin, in the last years of Erasmus's life, wrote and published his *Institutes*. Admittedly Calvinism had also many features which Erasmus would have condemned, and in theocratic Geneva was dogmatic and intolerant; but as practised under more tolerant lay rulers in England and the Netherlands, it could become, in many ways, the continuation of Erasmianism. Unfortunately, Calvinism, becoming intolerant, was unable to retain for long the intellectual Erasmian *élite*. Falling back therefore on its other basis, the poorer gentry, it degenerated into a religion of backwoods squires: the Huguenot *hobereaux* of Southern France, the Covenanting lairds of Scotland, the Orangist *petite noblesse* of Gelderland. With this change, the spirit of Erasmus left Calvinism and sought, within Protestantism, another body.

It found it in the 'rational theology' of the seventeenth century, a theology which was 'unitarian' in origin and began with Erasmus. Erasmus, on purely scholarly grounds, had correctly rejected from his New Testament the Trinitarian interpolation in the Epistle of John. Under pressure from the orthodox, he had in the end wearily restored it, but he had made it clear — to the fury of the monks — that he only did so for the sake of peace. Erasmus was therefore regarded as a unitarian, the founder of a rationalist unitarian school. The other founders were the French and Italian rationalists, Castellio, Acontius and the two Sozzini who, fleeing from the Inquisition to the Erasmian city of Basel, there formulated their views and published the first systematic defence of toleration, *De Haereticis an sint Persequendi*.[1] Afterwards the younger Sozzini went on and preached these views, under the name of Socinianism, in the italianised kingdom of Poland. Thus fathered, Socinianism incorporated not only anti-trinitarian conclusions but also Erasmian tolerance, Erasmian rationalism, and Erasmian respect for the Bible as the purest source of Christianity. In the late sixteenth century England and Poland were the two most tolerant countries in Europe, and it was no accident that they proved the most accommodating homes for the unorthodox spirit of Erasmus. But by the next

[1] The book is anonymous, but according to Cantimori (*op. cit.*, p. 160) Castellio and Fausto Sozzini were certainly the principal contributors to it. Toleration was afterwards regarded, and attacked, as an exclusively 'Socinian' doctrine. See quotations given by H. J. McLachlan, *Socinianism in Seventeenth-Century England* (1951), p. 9, note.

century the Jesuit reconquest of Poland was complete; the Socinian university of Rakow, 'the Sarmatian Athens', was snuffed out, and the Erasmian professors fled to a new area of tolerance which had been reconquered from the Counter-Reformation: the United Provinces of Erasmus's own home, the Netherlands. There already Calvinism had begun to harden into a rigid, illiberal system. The fresh breath from Erasmian Poland suddenly regenerated it, creating in its midst the liberal, tolerant 'Arminianism' of Amsterdam;[1] and from Amsterdam the same refreshing air was carried back to increasingly puritan England and there recreated the religious liberalism which Erasmus himself had found there 130 years before.

What an extraordinary revenge it was! In 1500 Erasmus had helped to create in Oxford that Florentine, Platonist piety which challenged the rigid Catholicism of the Middle Ages. Now, in 1630, his spirit, having fled first to Poland, then to Holland, had returned to Oxford to challenge the rigid Calvinism which had at one time seemed his more direct inheritor. Throughout the 1630's 'Socinian' books poured into England from Amsterdam. Their ideas penetrated both parties in the Church alike, showing themselves both in Independency to the Left and in Laudianism to the right of strict Calvinism. It was in high-church Arminianism that they first made themselves noticed. Lucius Cary, Viscount Falkland, and 'the incomparable John Hales of Eton' were each described as 'the first Socinian in England'; John Chillingworth and Jeremy Taylor were also, for their tolerance, called Socinians; and Archbishop Laud himself, for all his illiberal politics, was regarded as too liberal towards such ideas. The great patron of this 'Socinian' reception, Lord Falkland, who built up a fine Socinian library and made his house at Great Tew into the centre of such studies, was a particular admirer of Erasmus; and it is from the famous *convivium theologicum* of Great Tew, the headquarters of the new Oxford Movement, and from the Cambridge Platonism of the next generation, that rationalist Christianity ultimately spread over England.[2]

[1] Arminius himself explicitly based his teaching on that of Erasmus. See A. W. Harrison, *Arminiamism* (1937), p. 17. He was also regularly accused of Socinianism (*ibid.*, 25, 37).

[2] For this reception of Socinianism in England, and its consequences, see H. J. McLachlan's important work, *Socinianism in Seventeenth-Century England* (1951), and

Meanwhile, what by the Catholic Church? Ostensibly, of course, Erasmus had no place in it. His name and works were carefully blotted out of its official records. But if Sir Thomas More could ultimately find a place in Rome of the Counter-Reformation, could Erasmus really be excluded? Silently, secretly, anonymously, he returned. He returned by two roads: first with the Jesuits; afterwards, when they had degenerated from his exact spirit, with the great mystical revival of seventeenth-century France.

For although the Counter-Reformation was, ostensibly at least, a victory for the monks, it was not *only* a victory for the monks. That indeed would have been impossible. The Holy Office might condemn all Erasmian doctrines; it might repudiate the Erasmian cult of prayer, the Erasmian teaching of grace and faith; it might burn the books of Erasmus in Rome; it might forbid the translation of the Bible in whole or in part; it might reject rational criticism; and instead of all these it might offer again, redoubled, the old apparatus of religion on whose dead weight Erasmus had poured his irony, the other reformers their scorn. But if it had done no more than this, how could Rome have reconquered, as it did, a third of the provinces lost to Reform? In fact the Counter-Reformation was more positive than this. It rejected Erasmus indeed, but in name only. It stole his spirit and used it not to purge away but to reanimate the lifeless cumber of monastic religion. The first to do this, the real architects of the Counter-Reformation, were the newest order, the Jesuits. It was they who showed that both the new learning and the new piety of Erasmus could be used to reinvigorate the old forms of religion. The *Philosophia Christi* of Erasmus could become the Spiritual Exercises of Loyola; his fluent Latinity could be continued in their polished schools; his Biblical criticism could become ultimately the astringent scholarship of the Bollandists. Thus refreshed, the spirit of Christianity could carry still that deposit of previous centuries whose dead weight Erasmus had sought to lessen: perhaps it could even be enriched by it.

J. Tulloch, *Rational Theology and Christian Philosophy in England in the Seventeenth Century* (1872); and cf. C. J. Stranks, *The Life and Writings of Jeremy Taylor* (1952), pp. 23–4, 229.

The Jesuits, of course, had to walk warily, especially in Spain and at Rome where the power of the orders was greatest. They had to denounce one half of Erasmianism before they could safely appropriate and exploit the other. Thus Loyola himself had read Erasmus's *Enchiridion*, and he based his *Spiritual Exercises* fundamentally upon it; but he was careful to ensure that his pupils read it only in an expurgated and anonymous version, and he added to the *Spiritual Exercises* the rigorous and corrective *Rules for Thinking with the Church*.[1] And of course the Jesuits, like the Calvinists, rejected altogether the Erasmian belief in toleration. Even so they often found themselves in trouble on account of their 'Erasmian' innovations. They were distrusted by Pope Paul IV, whose total condemnation of Erasmus they deplored. Their 'Erasmian' cult of 'mental prayer' was attacked as heretical by Dominicans and Pope alike. They supported, against the Pope, Cardinal Morone, who was accused of heresy for disseminating the Erasmian book *The Benefit of Christ*; their support, against the Inquisition, of the Erasmian Archbishop Carranza nearly compromised their order and they had to wriggle out of their commitments; and they were constantly suspected of 'illuminism' — that heresy of direct contact with God, without the expensive and oppressive help of the Church, for which the Spanish Erasmists were persecuted by the Inquisition. Nevertheless, by opportune denials, tactical tergiversations and firm discipline over their indiscreet members, the Jesuits survived these difficulties: they made room for some at least of the ideas of Erasmus in the monk-ridden Church of Rome; and thereby, in half Europe, they saved it. It is not surprising that the writers of Counter-Reformation Europe in whom the spirit of Erasmus has been most observed were often the pupils, sometimes the admiring pupils, of the Jesuits.[2]

[1] For the Erasmian inspiration of Loyola's *Spiritual Exercises* see Henri Brémond, *Histoire Littéraire du Sentiment Réligieux en France*, XI, 60; M. Bataillon, *Etudes sur le Portugal au Temps de l'Humanisme*, p. 255 and note. For Loyola's expurgation of the *Enchiridion* see François de Dainville, S.J., *La Naissance de l'Humanisme Moderne* (Paris 1940), p. 230.

[2] The differences between the Jesuits and the official Church — always on an 'Erasmian' issue — can be followed in L. Pastor, *History of the Popes* (English translation), vol. XIV, pp. 246–58, 278, 302, and in Bataillon, *Erasme et l'Espagne*, pp. 747, 757, 760, 795, 814–15. Melchor Cano, the Dominican high-priest of ortho-

The intellectual supremacy of Jesuits in the Catholic Church, like that of the Calvinists among the Protestants, was brief. In the seventeenth century it soon declined into mere intellectual smartness. But just as the desiccated Calvinist orthodoxy of the seventeenth century was refreshed by the 'Socinian' spirit from Poland, so the courtly vapidity and moral 'laxism' of the seventeenth century Jesuits was challenged — at least in Northern Europe — by a new liberalism: the great mystical revival which triumphed in France. Once again, since it was a Catholic movement, the name of Erasmus was suppressed: Erasmus was still, in the eyes of orthodox French Catholics, 'malheureusement catholique, s'il est encore digne de ce nom,'[1] and only a bold writer, like Claude Joly, could openly name him as the source of his inspiration.[2] But the ideas of the new mysticism were his: they were, in the words of one of its historians, 'idées érasmiennes débaptisées';[3] and they came into France not from Italy, dominated by the now disreputable Jesuits, nor from Spain, reconquered by brute monkish reaction, but from the Catholic Rhineland and, above all, from the Catholic South of Erasmus's home, the Netherlands.[4] Just as the Protestant Netherlands received back the 'Socinian' spirit of Erasmus and therewith refreshed the wooden Calvinism of Holland and England, so the Catholic Netherlands, recreating the mystical spirit of Erasmus, discharged it upon France to refresh the wooden orthodoxy of the Sorbonne. The result was what the Abbé Brémond called 'the mystical invasion' of France: an invasion which, like the 'Socinian' invasion of England, flowed alike in all parties in the Church, bearing fruit in the 'dévots' and the Jansenists, in Bérulle and Pascal, in St. Francis of Sales and St.

doxy, denounced the whole Jesuit order as illuminists and Gnostics such as the Devil had constantly thrust into the Church. He urged their ruin, as did another Dominican, Fray Alonso de la Fuente de Llerena. See H. C. Lea, *Chapters from the Religious History of Spain* (Philadelphia 1890), p. 291, Fermin Caballero, *Conquenses Ilustres, II, Melchor Cano* (Madrid 1871), pp. 347–67. For the Erasmianism of Cervantes, a pupil of the Jesuits, see Bataillon, *op. cit.*, pp. 819 foll.

[1] André du Val, quoted by J. Dagens, *Bérulle et les Origines de la Restauration Catholique* (Bruges 1952), p. 42.

[2] Brémond, *op. cit.*, IX, 328, note.

[3] Dagens, *op. cit.*, pp. 78–9. For an instance of the widespread, if unavowed, influence of Erasmus on French devotional literature of the seventeenth century, see Brémond, *op. cit.*, IX, 358–9.

[4] See the statistics of Dom Huyben quoted in Dagens, *op. cit.*, p. 105, note.

Vincent de Paul — the great figures who gave to Catholicism in seventeenth-century France a warmth, a richness and a humanity which it could claim nowhere else. At the beginning of the new century the fact could be admitted. In his 'Apology or Justification for Erasmus', a French Catholic, in 1713, paid a last open tribute to 'that great man' whose work, so long resisted, had at last been achieved. The age of rational, tolerant piety had begun.[1]

That age now seems to be closing. Therefore it may be useful to consider Erasmus, who was, in a sense, both its prophet and its martyr. What does a humanist do when bigotries swell, black and red, on either side? There are some to-day who say that intellectuals should line up on either side as a species of army chaplains to encourage the troops. I well remember the spectacle, five years ago, in Berlin, when a so-called 'Congress for Cultural Freedom' mobilised the intellectuals of the West and invited them to howl in unison against the rival intellectuals similarly mobilised in an opposite 'Intellectual Congress' in Breslau. But I do not think that Erasmus, if he had yielded to political pressure and joined the Gadarene stampede of Lutherans or monks, would have had so lasting and beneficent an effect in the history of thought as he did by continuing to advocate peace for the diffusion of unarmed sense. Intellectuals may be citizens; they may even, as such, have to become soldiers; but it is not their business to be recruiting-sergeants. If their rational message is not heard in their time, let them still utter it rather than turn it into a battle-cry: it may still be heard to-morrow. For history, closely considered, suggests that opposite sides in an ideological struggle, for all their high-sounding abstract slogans, are not so opposite as they think that they are. The humanist message in fact can be understood by both. It may take a long time and a devious route; it may have to sur-

[1] Marsollier, *Apologie ou Justification d'Erasme*, quoted in Dagens, *op. cit.*, p. 79. This revival of Erasmus within the Catholic Church even penetrated — timidly and for a brief period — to Spain. See Jean Sarrailh, *La Crise Religieuse en Espagne á la Fin du XVIIIe Siècle* (Oxford, Taylorian Lecture, 1951), *L'Espagne Éclairée* (Paris 1954), pp. 193, 637, 681. Even when Erasmus is not cited by name, the programme of religious reform described by M. Sarrailh, with its cult of 'interior religion', its biblicism, its lay piety, its opposition to 'pratiques machinales, purement extérieures', is in fact the *Philosophia Christi of Erasmus*. See below, pp. 269–70.

vive by stealth; but there is no proper alternative to it. Whether we think of secular or religious ideologies, the words of a sensible eighteenth-century Whig bishop remain true: 'the Church, like the Ark of Noah, is worth saving: not for the sake of the unclean beasts that almost filled it, and probably made most noise and clamour in it, but for the little corner of rationality that was as much distressed by the stink within as by the tempest without.' In the ideological struggles before the Age of Reason, that 'little corner of rationality' was occupied by Erasmus; and it is he, not Luther or Calvin, the Pope or the Jesuits, who still speaks to us with a human voice.

CHAPTER VIII

NICCOLÒ MACHIAVELLI

In 1530 two Italianate Englishmen discussed politics together. Reginald Pole, who tells us about the conversation, was a somewhat priggish character: his ideal, he said, was Plato's *Republic*. Thomas Cromwell was sceptical. Such views, he said, were now out of date: the duty of a statesman was to see through such verbiage to the reality of politics; and since Pole's studies in Padua had evidently been inadequately supervised, he obligingly offered to lend him, in manuscript (for it had not yet been printed) a more up-to-date manual of politics. He afterwards forgot to send the book (he was rather busy in the next decade), but Pole read it and remembered it with a good deal of virtuous pain. It was, he said, 'written by the finger of Satan'. It was *The Prince* of Machiavelli.

No man, perhaps, until Marx, has had so various, so revolutionary an effect on political thought as Machiavelli. A scholarly official and observant ambassador of the Florentine Republic, a friend (in spite of his views) of Popes and Cardinals, he seemed, in his lifetime, a distinguished academic figure. After his death, his most famous work, *The Prince*, was at last published, with papal blessing, and in twenty years ran into twenty-five editions. Then, at mid-century, opinion began to harden. The Council of Trent ordered the destruction of his works. At Rome he was denounced as a detestable atheist. In Germany the Jesuits burnt him in effigy. In France the hatred felt for Catherine des Medicis and her Italian court was concentrated on his head. He penetrated to Scotland as 'Mitchell Wylie', the spirit embodied in that sceptical politician Maitland of Lethington. In England the dramatists made him a universal bogey-man, 'the murderous Machiavel', the type and patron of poisoners and assassins. His works were banned in England as in Rome. Poets, peoples, governments, Protestants, Pope — all seemed united in detestation of that name.

And yet, behind that solidarity of ignorance and prejudice which so often unites governments and people, the greatness of Machiavelli was never forgotten. Long before his works had been printed, the Italian booksellers had employed professional copyists to reproduce them. Long after they had been banned, manuscript translations passed from hand to hand in England, and the Italian text was piratically printed in London for learned readers. Already by 1540 Pole declared that Machiavelli 'had poisoned England and would poison all Christendom'. Thomas Cromwell's disciple, Richard Morison, read him privately in Germany with his secretary Roger Ascham, the tutor of Queen Elizabeth; Sir John Cheke read him, the tutor of King Edward VI; Cheke's brother-in-law William Cecil, Lord Burghley, read him, and Queen Elizabeth's other servants, Sir Christopher Hatton and Sir Thomas Smith; Sir Walter Raleigh read him, and Sir Francis Bacon, and Raleigh's friend 'the Wizard Earl' of Northumberland.[1] And as they read, little by little the cloak of respectability wore gradually thinner, the pretence of secrecy was dropped, the name of their master was discreetly avowed and quietly praised. Even so, it was not till the eve of the Puritan Revolution that his greatest works, *The Discourse on the First Ten Books of Titus Livy* and *The Prince* were at last published in English. Even then the editor took care to apologise for so bold a gesture. *The Prince*, he allowed, was a poisonous work; and yet, he added, even poisons, if carefully used, can be medicinal: 'the Lamprey, they say, hath a venomous sting runs along the back of it; take that out, and it is served in a choice dish for dainty palates.' Within a few months the twenty years' crisis had begun. In that revolution the last shreds of humbug were torn away, and the greatest of its political thinkers, examining their revolution with a new technique, were no longer afraid to glorify their teacher. John Lilburne, and the twin authors of *Oceana*, James Harrington and Henry Neville, all praised 'the divine Machiavel' — 'the best and most honest of all the modern politicians', 'one of the wisest,

[1] That Hatton read Machiavelli is shown by Thomas Bedingfield's dedication to him of his translation of the *Florentine History* (1595), 'which . . . your Lordship hath heretofore read in the Italian tongue '. The 9th Earl of Northumberland's copy is still at Alnwick Castle: it is the Italian text secretly published in London (with the imprint of 'Palermo') in 1584.

most judicious and true lovers of his country of Italy's liberties and freedom, and generally of the good of all mankind, that ever I read of in my days'; and when at last, in 1675, the first English translation of Machiavelli's whole works was published, its editor was the surviving republican philosopher, Henry Neville.[1]

What was the new science which Machiavelli had invented; which had so outraged the world that only revolutionaries, a hundred and fifty years later, could dare to praise him openly? To us it seemes innocent enough. Machiavelli humanised the study of politics. Rejecting old ideas that human institutions depended on divine prescription or *a priori* reasoning, he declared the simple proposition that the material of history does not change, that valid general laws of political behaviour can therefore be deduced from the past, and that modern politics should be regulated by these scientific laws. These laws are of course as many and various as human experience: there is one set of laws for tyrants wishing to seize and retain absolute power, another for democrats wishing to prevent such tyranny. Machiavelli is not directly concerned with such differences of purpose: he is a pure intellectual concerned to work out the general laws of political cause and effect, regardless of the practical use to which they may be put. To work them out, all that is needed is a deductive faculty and a stretch of history. Since history is recurrent, one stretch is theoretically as good as another; in fact, as an Italian humanist, Machiavelli chose to comment on contemporary Europe by reference to the history of Republican Rome. So a book with the dry title of *Discourses on the First Ten Books of Titus Livy* became the medium of the new theory which shocked the world.

Thus in theory the science of Machiavelli, like all science, is

[1] It is frequently stated that Neville himself was not only the editor but also the translator of Machiavelli's works. This statement derives ultimately from the Life of Neville prefaced to Thomas Hollis's edition of Neville's *Plato Redivivus* (1763). But in fact this preface is an unacknowledged plagiarism — with additions and omissions by Hollis — from Antony Wood's *Athenae Oxonienses*, and the statement that Neville 'translated Machiavelli's works' is one of Hollis's additions. I can find no evidence for it; and in fact one at least of the translations in Neville's edition was taken from an earlier publication which seems quite unconnected with Neville (*The Marriage of Belphegor*, printed in *The Novels of Dom Francisco de Quevedo*, London 1671).

entirely neutral as to political aims. Political forms and political methods are to be valued not in themselves but according as they achieve the purpose for which they are intended. Whatever the political form, the real rulers are seldom more than forty or fifty men, and certain institutions, certain rules of method are essential to any form of government. A republic can no more dispense with ultimate dictatorial authority (like the Venetian Council of Ten) than a prince; religion and certain other forms of fraud are essential instruments of all governors; no revolutionary power can tolerate its avowed enemies: 'he who establishes a tyranny and does not kill Brutus, and he who establishes a republic and does not kill the sons of Brutus, will not last long.'

And yet, however he try, can a political philosopher really be entirely neutral? It may be that the rules for establishing or overthrowing tyranny are, for their different purposes, equally valid; but what if the question is asked whether tyranny or freedom is more conducive to the peace, the prosperity, or the happiness of a people? This is an entirely neutral question soluble, in Machiavelli's theory, by entirely neutral methods; nevertheless, its answer implies a preference which can hardly be distinguished from a moral preference. So, obliquely, but by his very method, Machiavelli in his *Discourses* allows his own political preference to emerge. Fundamentally he is a citizen, and a republican. He does not believe in single rulers or unitary states. Political life is to him an essential of civilisation, and feudal gentry, who render such life impossible, he abominates. If vigorous city life leads to class-conflict, these are a sign of health, not corruption: 'to me those who condemn the quarrels between the nobles and the plebs seem to be cavilling at the very cause of Rome's continued freedom'. Further, as between aristocracy and democracy he is a democrat. Aristocracies, like Sparta and Venice, may preserve themselves longest, but only democracies, which refresh their ruling class, can expand. The methods of expansion for all governments are the same: war and conquest; and war and conquest also have their scientific rules.

Nevertheless, if Machiavelli is a republican, his very theory requires that such a preference can never be absolute. Times and necessities change and different circumstances have different rules. 'No state, be it republic or kingdom, is either first established or radically changed except by a single person.' Machiavelli lived in a time of European crisis: he saw French and Spaniards and Swiss invading Italy and a corrupted Papacy strong enough to foment the evil, too weak to cure it. For such a crisis he judged that a single person was necessary; and so in the end this Florentine republican, with absolute intellectual consistency, called for a tyrant to save Italy. Tyranny has its own rules, and Machiavelli never pretended to like them. But if there was one thing which he liked less it was intellectual muddle, half-measures, 'that middle course which is the most prejudicial that men can take,' the technical failure to relate means to ends. If the situation called for a tyrant, then it called for the methods appropriate to a tyrant. . . . So the writer of the *Discourses* became also, without any change of philosophy, the writer of the *Prince*.

So also he acquired that bad name which has never really forsaken him. It is an *idée fixe* among men that neutrality is impossible, and no protestations have really persuaded them that Machiavelli did not secretly approve his own propositions. Certainly he protested. He did not, like those modern ideologues who miscall themselves his disciples, pretend that cruelty and treachery were positive virtues. The methods of Philip of Macedon, he declared, 'are exceedingly cruel and repugnant to any human, let alone any Christian community. It were far better to avoid them and live in obscurity than to reign as king by such methods. Nevertheless, if a man wants to reign. . . .' He protested in vain. The doctrine that the end justifies the means has been firmly ascribed to him. Even the Jesuits, who hated him, could not altogether rob him of the discredit of that doctrine; and when John Donne staged his infernal competition for Satan's favour, he chose as his finalists Ignatius Loyola and Machiavelli.

The controversy continues. Machiavelli's latest editor[1] (himself a Jesuit) almost overheats himself in his eagerness to clear his order of the dreadful imputation. 'Let me begin by stating plainly', he writes, 'that I reject this doctrine root and branch,

[1] *The Discourses of Machiavelli*, translated and edited by Leslie J. Walker, S.J. (London 1950).

and regard it, together with its corollaries, as most pernicious'. But why all this moral indignation? Machiavelli's clarity is more instructive than Fr. Walker's heat, and if we examine the question coolly, we soon find the answer. Machiavelli and the Jesuits both in fact taught that the end justifies the means, but their meaning was different. The word 'end' is misleading: it can mean 'intention' or it can mean 'result'. Machiavelli's word was *effetto* — 'result': he had no patience with good intentions and expressed his contempt of the Gracchi 'whose intention was more creditable than their prudence'. A neutral political analyst, observing cause and effect, he only justified one in relation to the other. The doctrine of the Jesuits was different. They were not neutral observers. Indeed, they set themselves up as the official leaders of anti-machiavellianism, and it was against Machiavelli that their prize pupil, Giovanni Botero, advanced his theory that it is not the result but the intention which justifies the means, and thereby launched his new phrase *Ragion di Stato*, Reason of State.

It is interesting to look back at the last four centuries of history and observe the consequences of these two different doctrines that the end justifies the means: the doctrine of Machiavelli and the doctrine of the Jesuits. Machiavelli was a layman, and empirical philosopher who, believing no form of government to be absolute, sought only to recommend, for whatever purpose seemed desirable, the most practical, the most scientific, the least costly means. His great disciple is Bismarck, to whom politics were 'the cult of the possible'. The Jesuits, having ideals, believed that all means were justified which were intended (even if they failed and whatever the cost) to serve those ideals. From Plato's priest-king to Lenin and Hitler that tradition is clear. On the whole, like Thomas Cromwell, I prefer Machiavelli.

CHAPTER IX

THE TWILIGHT OF THE MONKS

According to Cardinal Gasquet, the monks had no ill-reputation until the days of that wicked Whig historian, Bishop Burnet. On the contrary (he insisted), monasticism was a noble institution which, until its overthrow by Protestants and plutocrats, had protected the poor from the rapacity of the rich. Unfortunately, to reach this conclusion the Cardinal found it necessary to cheat. In the writing of history it seldom pays to cheat — least of all where one can be found out by Dr. Coulton — that formidable scholar whose evangelical zeal and gigantic erudition could be not only fatal to bogus scholarship but also (as we now know) very exasperating in the home. His exposure of Gasquet is well-known. We have heard enough about his home. Let us now look at his positive achievement; his great work on medieval monasticism, a miracle of documented erudition, whose last volume has now issued, posthumously, from the Press.[1]

What was the state of monasticism in the century before its overthrow in England? Dr. Coulton is not content with a parochial view. To illuminate the last days of a cosmopolitan institution, he takes all Europe for his field. For two centuries before the Reformation the Church was in decay: no new orders had been founded, no new impulse given, no general statutes of reform devised. Learning had been abandoned to the laity. Even the newest of orders — the two orders of friars — had followed their predecessors into an opulent apathy which only their mutual hostility sometimes stirred. The three vows of monasticism — chastity, poverty, obedience — were almost everywhere neglected. Only the Carthusians preserved to the end their ancient virtues. The Mendicant Orders boasted openly of their wealth: 'True we are Mendicants', declared the Domi-

[1] C. G. Coulton, *Five Centuries of Religion*, vol. IV, *The Last Days of Medieval Monachism* (Cambridge 1950).

nicans as they launched their counter-attack against the Franciscan doctrine of the Immaculate Conception, 'but we have more than 40,000 crowns of gold in reserve for this purpose'. Opulence has its uses: the late Middle Ages were a great age of church building; but the former spirit of religion had fled from those graceful cloisters, those soaring towers, with which great ecclesiastical pluralists signalised their economic magnificence. Ignoring all the elaborate institutions that sought to capture and contain it, that fugitive spirit expressed itself in private devotion and direct — sometimes heretical — communication with God. The fourteenth and fifteenth centuries were the age of mysticism: of Thomas à Kempis and Ruysbroek, of Hilton and Rolle, of Margery Kempe and the Lollards; and mysticism is the religion not of hope but of despair.

And yet not everyone despaired — or Dr. Coulton's history had been a dreary chronicle. In fact it is the story of heroic attempts to reform the irreformable. For the facts, which Gasquet distorted, which 'the purblind laborious Janssen' tries to ignore, and the prim, judicious Pastor skilfully minimises, were clear enough to contemporaries. At the great Ecumenical Councils of Constance and Basel the need had been recognised, the plan proclaimed: all that seemed necessary was a supply of apostles. The apostles were there. Already in the Netherlands Florence Radewin and Gerard Groot had founded the Brethren of Common Life at Deventer and the reformed Augustinian convent of Windesheim stood at the head of twenty Dutch and German monasteries. Mount St. Agnes, where Thomas à Kempis wrote the *Imitatio Christi*, was one of them. Bödekken was another, which could later boast of having brought another twenty houses into the reformed congregation. Thither serious-minded aristocrats, answering, even in its decline, the original call of monasticism, secretly and inexorably converged; there the new monks built their own houses, with granges and herds, beehives and fishponds and the earliest sawmills in Europe; thence, as it seemed to the despairing churchmen gathered at Basel in 1435, the spirit of Reform might be breathed again into the decaying body of monasticism. Two years later Johann Busch, a monk of Windesheim, set out on his missionary journeys, eager to reform the world.

To reform is a frustrating task: to be reformed is maddening. The old monks and nuns regarded their long-neglected rule (if they had ever read it) as an obsolete formula, like the Creed, to which no sensible person can be expected to give more than a vague and general assent. Cloisters, to their inhabitants, were country clubs; to the outer world they were useful receptacles for unemployable or half-witted sons and unportionable daughters. To such men, the suggestion that the rule should be executed — that roast beef disappear from the menu, that private property be abolished and (worst of all) that chastity be enforced — naturally seemed an outrageous revolution. Fortunately, they reflected, they had ample funds for resistance. They could bribe the great, prevaricate at law, appeal to their relatives and clients in the world, mobilise their tenants, arm their serfs; and ultimately, at the summit of the system, they could rely on their greatest asset of all: the patronage, or the apathy, of the Court of Rome.

But if the old monks always had allies, so sometimes had the reformers. Laymen, fortunately, demand from their clergy higher standards than they set to themselves; and many lay princes — the Emperor Sigismund, his successor Duke Albert of Austria, Duke William of Brunswick, Count John of Egmond — put authority on the side of the Reformers. In some cities — as Cologne and Geneva — the municipal authorities did the same. Thus, when the missionaries set to work, a series of local struggles began which set in motion innumerable interests, and were decided now this way, now that, as the balance of wealth and power and skill and chance incalculably inclined.

Johann Busch was a man of infinite tenacity, and in the Duke of Brunswick he had a powerful ally: but the struggle was nevertheless exhausting. The nuns were particularly recalcitrant: when the reformers entered the nunnery of Wennigsen, near Hanover, 'the nuns all lay down on their bellies in the choir with arms and legs stretched out in the form of a cross' and chanted an anthem parodied into a Black Mass. At Mariensee, where the nuns had bought the protection of the Bishop of Minden, 'at the first visitation, the Abbess and her nuns climbed to the roof of the choir and ran about there like cats', ready to pelt the reformers with tiles and stones. After a sharp physical struggle they were reformed, and the reformers were able to report that the ringleader of the nuns (who had been crushed under the prostrate Duke in the mêlée) 'after regaining her breath, consented also with us in all things'. Cardinal Cusanus, the greatest of the orthodox reformers, struggled for five years before he could reduce the great nunnery of Sonnenburg in his own diocese 'where the young daughters of the Tyrolese nobility led the freest and most luxurious life under the cover of the veil'. At Klingenthal, the richest abbey in Basel, the recalcitrant nuns tried to burn down their convent, assailed the reformers with spits, cudgels and swords and demanded that the reformers 'be delivered up to them for strangling'. New nuns were stuffed into the convent, but the old rakish nuns clung to the cash, retained their organisation, bribed Duke Sigismund with 800 florins to put robber-knights at their disposal, and in the end, returning triumphant to Klingenthal, obliged the reformers to pay them the huge sum of 11,500 florins as damages and interest. 'The pious virgins had demanded even 36,000, for disturbance in their possessions *and for the harm done to their reputation!* After all, they had to reward the devotion of their protectors; and neither the Lord of Klingenberg nor the Count of Thierstein nor the needy Sigismund were men to content themselves with the not very devout prayers of their clients.'

In every country the same struggle was fought, with varying results. Windesheim and its congregation stood firm, but the next greatest reformed congregation, Bursfelde on the Weser, soon declined again: the old party enlisted the support of the great financier and industrialist Jakob Fugger, and beef and mutton introduced a disastrous schism among the monks. The great abbey of Melk, the richest in Europe, on a rock above the Danube, was reformed; Santa Giustina at Padua and Monte Cassino became islands of reform in Italy. In France, if the Cordeliers of Paris filibustered against the reformers by perpetual psalmody, the abbey of Chezal-Benoît became a centre of Benedictine reform. But, in general, the movement failed; and the reason for its failure was fundamentally the same. The Court of Rome was too heavily committed to the old system. The most authoritative of the reformers, Cardinal Cusanus, found himself sabotaged at Rome; the most influential of them,

Ambrose of Camaldoli, found the personal favour and genuine support of the Pope powerless against the interests of a whole system. It was the system of *commendam*, 'the leprosy of monasticism,' as Montalembert called it: a system which had converted the great offices of the Church into the private patronage of secular Popes and orthodox kings: a system which even a reforming Pope could not omit to exploit, and which converted the Church of the fifteenth, as of the eighteenth century into organised outdoor relief for the privileged classes. The cast-off royal mistresses who reigned as great abbesses in Castile were unlikely to welcome monastic reform.

And yet, ironically, it was this very abuse of *commendam*, which, in the end, under energetic princes, offered the only hope of effective orthodox reform. *Commendam* hardly existed in England until Wolsey, that gigantic pluralist, awarded himself bishopric upon bishopric and sought to use these powers for a general reform. In France the Cardinal of Amboise, a French Wolsey, prime minister and papal legate, sought the same end. In Spain Queen Isabella gave a similar monopoly to Cardinal Ximenez. Ximenez was successful. The monasteries were disciplined, their privileges burnt, their revenues usefully redistributed; the old monks, outraged at the new demands of Christianity, migrated to Africa and embraced the more agreeable religion of Mohammedanism; and in Spain, alone in Europe, there was never even a threat of religious revolution.

The English Cardinal failed. Perhaps he did not try very hard: he had other, more magnificent, more grandiose personal ambitions, which interested him more. At all events, none of his plans came ever to full realisation, and Reform in England was ultimately achieved by other hands — the hands of powerful, serious-minded laymen. But the methods were the same. Henry VIII followed the most orthodox precedents. Popes and cardinals and orthodox kings had been praised for their earlier suppressions; the distinction between great and small monasteries was as old as St. Benedict and as modern as the Cardinal of Amboise; and Cromwell's visitors repeated the methods and questions of episcopal visitors. The difference between Cromwell and Wolsey was not in their methods, or even in their orthodoxy, but in their serious purpose and its result: one failed, the other succeeded.

It was a drastic success: in England the whole, irreformable fabric of monasticism sank painlessly and unlamented to the ground. But perhaps no other remedy was possible. A century later a far greater man than Wolsey sought to repeat his less revolutionary methods. Cardinal Richelieu, by exploiting the abuse of *commendam*, had himself appointed abbot-general of the three great exempt orders of Cluny, Cîteaux and Prémontré, and held in *commendam* other of the great abbeys in France or Europe — Marmoutier, La Chaise-Dieu, Chezal-Benoît. Then he set out to reorganise and reform. In this alone the greatest of clerical statesmen achieved nothing. Indeed, some of the incidents are worthy of the fifteenth century. To Marmoutier, where disorder had increased under the abbacy of two royal bastards, the cardinal sent twenty-four reformed monks under royal escort. 'But lo! at 9.0 at night a strange concert broke out under the cloisters and in the dormitory. The young monks had hidden there, and until 1.0 a.m. they did nothing but howl, imitate the cries of animals, blow hunting-horns, discharge fire-arms, and belch out a thousand insults against the newcomers.' Even when they were expelled, the former monks returned: they came into the choir in riding-boots, disconcerted the services with strange noises; and from their headquarters in the third prior's lodging, where they danced and feasted, 'nothing was heard but oaths, blasphemies and obscenities, the echo of hunting-horns and musket-shots'. So much for the work of the Counter-Reformation.

But if Henry VIII and Thomas Cromwell succeeded, history takes its revenge on such absolute success. In England when the monks had been pensioned off and their monasteries destroyed or converted, a strange myth gradually attached itself to those deserted ruins which the accident of inaccessibility had here and there preserved: in the haunted Yorkshire dales, in the wild fells of Westmoreland, in the remote solitudes of the Border lands. Already in the seventeenth century Aubrey, the first romantic, sighed for their revival: a hundred years later 'in the full light and freedom of the eighteenth century', Dr. Johnson wished to kiss the site of a dissolved monastery; and in the next century Cardinal Gasquet, exploiting nostalgia in the interest of faith, paraded portentously documented mythology as research. Myths are all very well, but facts are better. The Cardinal and his pretentious historiography are now dead. The Russian Savine, the evangelical Coulton, the high Anglican Baskerville have killed them. Four great volumes and a few lapidary sentences make for both their final tombstone.

CHAPTER X

ENGLAND'S MODERNISER: THOMAS CROMWELL

Thomas Cromwell has not had a good press in history. Catholics and Protestants have ganged up against him. The support of Froude has hardly recommended him. His own biographer has been his most open enemy. He has been accused of establishing a police-state based on a network of spies; of destroying ancient institutions merely for the sake of the spoil; of ruling the King by subservience and Parliament by 'packed elections, fraud and violence'. The evidence? The misquoted spite of a bewildered foreigner; a long-exploded academic tirade by an embittered *émigré*; and a snowball of repetition.

Politicians should be judged by their work, not by the caricatures of their enemies, and if we examine Thomas Cromwell's work, what an astonishing, and, above all, what a durable achievement we find! No man has examined his administration more closely than Mr. G. R. Elton, but even his detailed study, a fine piece of pioneering history,[1] only shows one side — the bureaucratic centre — of that massive revolution which, incredibly, was achieved in only seven years. For Thomas Cromwell was a freak in English history, and that, perhaps, is why he has been so disliked: an iron-fisted bureaucrat who crammed into his brief reign the kind of process which in England, we like to maintain, is carried out insensibly, over centuries. He overhauled the machinery of government as it had never been overhauled since the reign of Henry II; and he overhauled it so drastically that much of it was not radically altered till the reign of Victoria. In six hundred years of history he stands out as the most radical of modernisers. Modern history, if it begins anywhere, begins, in England, with him.

[1] G. R. Elton, *The Tudor Revolution in Government* (Cambridge 1954).

Not, of course, only with him. The sixteenth century was an age of modernisation and every Renaissance prince surrounded himself with up-to-date administrators, canonists and civilians, bishops and lawyers, to help him. It was the age of the *letrados*, the *gens de la robe*, the 'officers' who had not yet grown, as they would grow in the top-heavy courts of the next century, into privileged sinecurists. They were working officers; and everywhere their work was similar. Whether clergy or laity, Catholic or Reformers, they were working in the same direction: national churches, centralised states, more closely controlled patronage, and, to man and sustain this new machinery, better education and higher revenue. But among all those who thus served their sovereigns, Thomas Cromwell stands, in one respect, alone. Others might lubricate and modify the machine; they might even change it — for their lifetime; but he not only changed it, he so institutionalised his changes that they outlasted his brief reign, outlasted his fall, outlasted it, in politics, for a hundred years, in administration for three centuries.

From his master Cardinal Wolsey whom, according to the Black Legend, he betrayed, but whom in fact he served and helped until death, Cromwell inherited a medieval administrative system, first nursed, then galvanised into life by the careful husbandry of Henry VII, the immense human energy of the Cardinal. Wolsey might send out commissions, might cram the Court of Chancery with business, might 'teach the law of the Star Chamber'; but behind the temporary power and *panache* of his career, the institution had remained the same. Cromwell changed them. His methods were simple, of a classic, universal simplicity: first statistics, as the basis of change; then statutes, as the sanction of change; finally, to make change permanent, new institutions, new courts. How did he dissolve the monasteries — not, as his biographer says, 'undoubtedly to fill the royal Treasury with the spoils of the Church' but, like so many other statesmen of the time, in order to strengthen the working part of the Church, to found new bishoprics, new schools? First, he carried out his great statistical survey, the *Valor Ecclesiasticus*: the first systematic valuation of the Church since 1200, and still, in 1836, when it was published for the Ecclesiastical Commissioners, the most up-to-date. Then he proceeded to legislate; finally a new

Court, the Court of Augmentations, was set up to handle the endowments thus nationalised. Every power taken from Rome was thus institutionalised in England, and everywhere the traces of the change, even when it was left imperfect by Cromwell's fall, linger on until the next great decade of overhaul: the Whig decade of the 1830's. It was not till 1832 that Cromwell's Court of Delegates was superseded as supreme ecclesiastical court by the Judicial Committee of the Privy Council. It was only in 1836 that Cromwell's legislation reducing the palatine powers of the Bishop of Durham was completed. Of the eighteen new bishoprics planned by Cromwell only six were in fact founded: but they were the first new bishoprics to be founded since Henry II, the last before Victoria.

We look back upon the work of Cromwell through religious spectacles — for the event obscures the aim. But Cromwell and the Catholic bishops who helped him saw it quite otherwise. To them the reform of the Church was only a part of the Reform of the State. The power of the Pope was merely another exempt jurisdiction to be rationalised along with other such private empires: were not the Bishop of Durham, the Marcher Lords of Wales, the magnates of the West, similarly finding part of their powers transferred, by statute, to new or re-modelled 'conciliar' courts, limbs of the Privy Council, in York, Ludlow and Exeter? If the new ecclesiastical revenue reached the King through the new Courts of Augmentation and — afterwards — of First Fruits, so would the old feudal revenues reach him, more fully, through the new Court of Wards. And always, at the back of these changes, we can see at work the mind not only of the Reformer who had read the works of Erasmus, and the politician who had read the works of Machiavelli, but also of the statistician and merchant who had learnt accountancy in Italy and traded spermaceti to Flanders, the economist who reorganised the extravagant royal household, the lawyer who had handled the debts and petitions of private clients, and who was now, in the intervals of managing the first Long Parliament and carrying through the first Reformation, centralising and registering the private money-lending of the country (the register lasted till 1775), setting up overseers of the poor (the nucleus of his Poor Law, embedded in the Elizabethan Act, lasted till 1834), and founding, as a statistical preliminary to the reconstitution of local government, those parish registers which are still kept up to-day.

Political careers under Henry VIII were sometimes brief. In seven years Cromwell did all this and more; then suddenly, as an incident of foreign policy, Henry VIII sacrificed, as he afterwards ruefully complained, 'the best servant he ever had'. In the years of conservative reaction after his fall, when the royal lethargy was interrupted only by spasms of personal government (years of relief, says his biographer, from 'the temporary madness and terror inspired by his personality'), Cromwell's work appeared to founder, or at least to stand still. A few disciples might here and there place a coping stone upon the unfinished building, but meanwhile the ground itself on which Cromwell had built was being undermined: the nationalised endowments were being squandered, the finances of the Crown had been built up only to run away, and amid faction in Court and Church, and mutiny in the country, all firm government seemed for a time to have dissolved. Nevertheless, Thomas Cromwell's work was solid enough to survive even those years of crisis, and in the reign of Elizabeth, when political careers were long, it was resumed. In 1572 Cromwell's most constant ally, Sir William Paulet, at last died. He had survived all the changes of the century and died in office, a marquis, and ninety years old; for he was sprung, as he genially observed, not from the oak but the willow; and dying, he handed over the white staff of the Lord Treasurer to his own greatest disciple, the third in the apostolic succession of Tudor bureaucrats, William Cecil. Thus the great work of Tudor government had survived its greatest crisis and could be continued, on the same foundation still, in the hands of the two Cecils, father and son, for another forty years.

For what was the essence of Tudor government? It was government by the Privy Council, that close, compact body of well-chosen officials who, without force but by perpetual vigilance and through a new machinery of legal centralisation, supervised the whole country and the working of it and gave to England internal peace while her neighbours were rent by civil war. And who was the architect of this Privy Council? Not Henry VII, that cautious steward with his medieval 'household' rule; not

Wolsey, that princely personal despot. It was Thomas Cromwell who in 1534, made a note 'to remember the King for the establishment of the Council', and who, by 1536, had in effect created it. Moreover, like all great bureaucrats, it was not through great office that Cromwell directed this institution which he had created: it was by 'unique administrative ability'; and — although he held other and more glorious offices — it was as Secretary that he wielded his greatest power. When Cromwell took over his office the Secretary was 'still merely a cog in the machine, an upper civil servant, not a minister of state'. When he left it, it had become 'the linchpin of the administration'. By the end of the century, when the post had been held by the two Cecils and Walsingham, it could be described in even more rhetorical language. 'You shall address yourself', King James of Scotland instructed his ambassador, 'especially to Mr. Secretary, who is king there in effect'. Tudor England, like Vasa Sweden, had its 'rule of the secretaries'; and this, too, was founded by Thomas Cromwell.

Twelve years later 'Mr. Secretary', now first Earl of Salisbury was dead; and in that year Cromwell's political system, already rotted from within, crumbled at the heart. How could it be otherwise when a system requiring constant vigilance by efficient, conscientious officials, had been handed over to the gilded spivs of our Scottish kings? The citadel had been converted into a playhouse, and when the attack came, within a generation, the archaic ecclesiastical battlements, desperately built on by Archbishop Laud, were powerless to save it. The Council and its Prerogative Courts, the State Church and the feudal taxes — all that was left of Cromwell's political work foundered in that great rebellion. So did his credit. He was the founder of 'Tudor despotism', and the Whigs, unwilling to defend him, jettisoned his body to the papists, hungry for posthumous revenge upon the Hammer of the Monks. In the 1830's they probably did not even know that it was his more durable administrative work whose now obsolete relics they were at last sweeping away. But now that the Whig era is over and bureaucrats, with their virtues and their faults, have become more obvious, we may perhaps allow a little belated praise to the first and greatest, if the most formidable, of our modern bureaucrats: Thomas Cromwell.

CHAPTER XI

THE CRISIS OF ENGLISH HUMANISM: REGINALD POLE AND HIS CIRCLE

In 1529 Cardinal Wolsey fell from power in England and in the next ten years the whole structure of known society seemed to crumble. In 1535 Sir Thomas More went to the block; in 1536 Reginald Pole burnt his boats in Italy. The two most distinguished living Englishmen had repudiated the new order. Emperors and Popes were gladdened on their thrones: they pronounced More a martyr and made Pole an ambassador; and they declared, with gloomy satisfaction, as their co-religionists have since declared, that humanism was dead in England.

Of course it was not. All his life Henry VIII remained an enthusiast for learning, and Thomas Cromwell, who had himself travelled in Italy and read Machiavelli, was the patron of another generation of scholars — men who would face the problems from which More and Pole had recoiled. It is with this second generation of humanists, the link between the Oxford humanists and the Elizabethans, that Mr. Zeeveld's excellent and scholarly book[1] is concerned — in particular with two of them, Thomas Starkey and Richard Morison.

The story begins with Wolsey, in the new college which he had founded at Oxford to commemorate his magnificence. Thither he gathered picked young men from every source, even from Cambridge. Being bright, some of them were radical, and the Cambridge group infected Oxford with some undesirable doctrines which seriously disconcerted the Warden of New College; but Wolsey, with a founder's partiality, turned upon them a blind, indulgent eye. Next year he fell and falling, appealed for his tottering handiwork. 'In the way of charity and for the

[1] W. Gordon Zeeveld, *Foundations of Tudor Policy* (Harvard 1949).

love that ye bear to virtue and *ad bona studia*', he wrote to one of his servants, now the King's secretary, 'be means to the King's Highness for my poor colleges, and especially for the college of Oxford. Suffer not the things which by your great learning, study, counsel and travail hath been erected . . . to be dissolved or dismembered'; and to another servant, now the King's chief minister, he made the same appeal for his twin foundations of Oxford and Ipswich 'for they are in a manner *opera manuum tuarum*'.

Henry VIII refounded Cardinal's College as Christ Church, but it took time, and in the meantime what were those hand-picked scholars to do? Some attached themselves to Wolsey's son, that exquisitely pampered young man Thomas Winter, in his successive households in France and Italy. But Winter, in spite of the care bestowed upon his education and finances (at fifteen he was Dean of Wells, archdeacon of Richmond and Provost of Beverley), seemed equally incapable of remaining solvent or becoming learned, and most of the scholars converged, directly or indirectly, on that great centre of English humanism, the household in Padua of the King's cousin, Reginald Pole.

In all Europe at that time there was scarcely a university to compare with Padua. There, in the tolerant Venetian Republic, Pomponazzi taught philosophy and Leonico Greek, and Vesalius, by his experimental surgery, was causing a renaissance in medicine. Thither the Venetian aristocracy, by the law of the Republic, sent their sons to study; thither enthusiastic scholars made the long journey from Oxford and Cambridge, sent by their own teachers who had also studied, in their generation, at 'the Athens of Europe'.

At nineteen Pole had gone to Padua with a splendid allowance from his royal cousin and letters of introduction from his Oxford tutors, Thomas Linacre and William Latimer. There he lived, in appropriate comfort, and in his house English and Italian humanists met. Bembo and Sadoleto, Priuli and Contarini and Caraffa were among his Italian friends — liberal Catholics who would have reformed the Church if they could; but a formidable decision was to divide them, as it was to divide his English friends, into persecutors and victims: for the intellectual crisis of the century struck indifferently throughout Europe. And in the same house lived a growing cluster of English scholars, mostly from Oxford, many from Cardinal's College, and several of them from those bright young men who had infected the new foundation with sudden reforming doctrines. Many of these young men were poor and of humble birth, but in that almost royal house they lived together, studying Galen and Aristophanes, Euripides and Plutarch — and of course that most fashionable, most useful subject, the Roman Law — in complete intellectual equality. In Padua, in Pole's time, 'was preserved the same democracy among scholars that had characterised the generation of Erasmus, Colet and More'.

For what were they studying? Not for the sake of study. That monastic concept no longer appealed to the new, uncontemplative world of the Renaissance. They sought not to glorify God but to perfect man. And once perfected, for what purpose did they mean to use that laboriously achieved and finely polished instrument? Of course, to govern the affairs of the world. Humane scholarship was the secret of success: it had broken down the old barriers of birth and wealth; it had liberated politics from taboo; to some it had even revealed a new method, a method which shocked the old and excited the young, the analytical method of Machiavelli. Through humane study Wolsey and Wolsey's numerous servants had risen to power and fame. Pole and his friends studied to the same end. It was an agreed convention: agreed by themselves — Pole said he was studying 'to lay his attainments at the King's feet'; agreed by the King who was paying their expenses, and by his new minister who had himself risen through his education. If Henry VIII looked to Padua, it was to find another generation of judges and bishops, councillors of state and ambassadors abroad.

In 1534 the fruit was ripe and Thomas Starkey, 'judging all other secret knowledge not applied to some use and profit of others to be but a vanity', wrote from Padua to Thomas Cromwell offering his services. He duly returned to England to become chaplain to Pole's mother, and within two months he was chaplain to the King, an important architect of the new world. Within two years he had persuaded Cromwell to fetch Richard Morison also from Padua and Pole. Never was there such a market for talent. The monasteries were being dissolved — they could plan schemes of social reform and education with the proceeds. The Church was being reformed — they could devise an Anglican *via media* for its reformation. Ultimately they might bring back to England the most distinguished of possible apologists, their friend and master Reginald Pole.

Starkey assured Cromwell it could be done: 'upon the earth liveth not a more sincere and pure heart, and less spotted with dissimulation, than Master Pole.' For two years, at the King's instance, he pressed Pole to declare himself on the important issues of the day. He wrote to Padua describing, with enthusiasm, the new England. There were crabs of course: the Carthusians (and Pole's earliest teachers had been Carthusians) had been executed. Starkey explained the matter. It was a pity, he allowed, but they had behaved most irrationally; he himself had remonstrated with the superior, an intimate friend of Pole, but he had found him incurably superstitious, so of course he had to be hanged. Meanwhile would not Pole, who had so usefully championed Henry's divorce in the Sorbonne, continue his services? The King would be lavish of rewards, 'for sorry he is that there among strangers, without profit to your country, your virtues should be so utterly drowned, and like as in a dream vanish away'. But Pole was strangely silent. Ever since his visit to England in 1530, when Cromwell had shocked him by preferring Machiavelli to Plato and he had immured himself perversely in a Carthusian monastery, he had remained wrapped in enigmatic doubt. He was turning away from humanism, back to contemplation, asceticism and the unfashionable heresy of 'perpetual philosophy'. He was in the clouds, said his friends in Padua, 'undergoing a great change, exchanging man for God'. Then, in the sixth year of doubt, he complied with Starkey's request. He gave the King his opinion. It filled a whole book of uncompromising denunciation and bitter personal invective. Having thus rewarded the patron of seventeen years, Pole gathered up his robes and left Venice for Rome, to be a cardinal.

Pole's bombshell shattered the humanist group around him. Some, like George Lily, followed him in his retreat. The prudent trimmed. Starkey was dismayed. Shocked at Pole's behaviour, he remonstrated with him against 'your detestable unkindness towards your prince'; discredited at Court, he begged Cromwell not to impute to him any part of Pole's folly, 'which hath already more grieved me than ever yet hath done the deed of any man living upon earth'; and yet he could not altogether renounce his former master: first among his misfortunes, he told the King, was 'the perpetual loss of the conversation of so faithful a friend'; the hero of his last book, the *Dialogue* which he dedicated to Henry VIII, and which is his greatest claim to memory, is still Pole; and when he died, two years after the blow, a broken and divided spirit, in his will he remembered, as a humanist, his Oxford college, the poor scholars, and Lord Montague, the brother of Reginald Pole.

No such doubts tormented Richard Morison. If Pole could bite the hand of his host and patron, so could Morison. 'The kindness of Signor Pole', he had written in 1534, 'has rescued me from hunger, cold and poverty.' Two years later he was to become the King's propagandist-in-chief against 'Mr. Traitor Pole' and his associates, a successful literary champion of the new order, dashing off his pamphlets against the rebellious Pilgrims of Grace 'in my boots . . . in an afternoon and a night'. When the King, grown inveterate in tyranny, liquidated Pole's two brothers and aged mother (she had been indiscreet in her embroidery), Morison was there with a prompt and learned justification. He was rich and successful, Sir Richard Morison, M.P., the King's ambassador in Germany, a political thinker of real weight and learning, builder of a great house, founder of a noble dynasty. Well might he preach equality of opportunity, the virtues of a new, freely-formed aristocracy, an aristocracy of talent, an aristocracy of Morisons, to replace the old aristocracy of privilege, the aristocracy of the Poles.

Who betrayed whom in this strain of politics, ideas and loyalties? The question is irrelevant. An intellectual crisis faced a group of men and dissolved it. History is indulgent to the defeated, and in liberal minds there is always, and rightly, a suspicion against those who, with ready theories of consistency on their lips, leap nimbly and profitably on to the rising stair of a new despotism. Pole is a tragic figure. More and more he sank into mysticism; his friend Caraffa, as the most bigoted of Popes, became his most relentless tormentor; and he died, the last Roman Catholic Archbishop of Canterbury, a suspected heretic and a universal failure. The humanist tradition was to be continued not by him but by the brassy Morison and the young men whom he had collected around him: Roger Ascham, his secretary, the teacher of the Elizabethans, who read Machiavelli with him in Germany; William Cecil, their statesman, who also, perhaps through Morison's influence, studied Machiavelli's *Discorsi*; and those great Cambridge humanists who shared the exile of them all in the days when Popery and Pole had returned to England — Bishop Ponet, John Cheke, Sir Thomas Smith.

CHAPTER XII

HUGH LATIMER AND THE ENGLISH COMMONWEALTH

In 1555 the first two of the 'Oxford Martyrs' — that is, of the three distinguished Cambridge men, Cranmer, Ridley and Latimer — were burnt at the stake outside Balliol College. If Cranmer's position and temporary recantation earned him a brief delay, he emphatically expiated it by thrusting first into the fire the right hand that had testified to his timidity. The epitaph of all three was the last words of Latimer: 'Be of good cheer, Master Ridley, and play the man. We shall this day light such a candle, by God's grace, in England, as I trust shall never be put out.'

What was the common quality of these three men? All were Protestant humanists. They believed, like the Catholic humanists of the previous generation — of whom they, not Rome, were the heirs — in a purified religion: a diminution of external forms and superstitions, a return to the Gospel and that inner devotion, that *Philosophia Christi*, which Erasmus, Colet and More had learnt from the unavailing Catholic reformers of Windesheim. But to this common basis of belief each added also his own personal gift. Cranmer was a scholar who sought the truth even among the violent politics in which he was compromised and misunderstood. Ridley was a controversialist, a learned disputant, the champion of Protestantism in the schools. Latimer was none of these. He was no great scholar: he knew no Greek: he took his doctrinal position from Cranmer and left disputation to Ridley. He was a preacher, and a court preacher, too. Not a fashionable court preacher, like John Donne or the great Jesuit preachers of the next century, exploring and illuminating the intimate spiritual recesses of rich patrons and great ladies, but a tribune of the people who preached his message menacingly, like Hosea or Amos, to the face of Kings. 'Let the preacher never fear to declare the message of God unto all men,' he once said, '. . . if he preach before a King, let his matter be concerning the office of a king; if before a bishop, then let him treat of bishoply duties. . . .' Such preaching was, of course, dangerous. Small wonder he 'ever affirmed that the preaching of the Gospel would cost him his life'. Small wonder that in fact, in the revolutionary politics of the sixteenth century, it did.

And what was Latimer's message? It was, of course, a religious message — all messages of that time were, at least in form, religious, and the late Dr. Darby, in his useful new biography,[1] shows clearly the development of his religious views. But it was also a social message. Like so many of the Reformers, Catholic and Protestant, Latimer saw the old forms of society being broken up by new economic opportunities, and he appealed to that fashionable new Leviathan, the Christian Prince, not only, in religion, to amend doctrine but also, in society, to arrest change. It was the appeal of secular humanism: not the new, radical humanism of the schools only, but the old, conservative humanism of the villages and fields from which, in Leicestershire, the historic centre of both religious dissent and agrarian trouble, he himself had sprung. In 1547, when that erratic Christian Prince, Henry VIII, who had alternately promoted and imprisoned the reformers, was dead, and a new, docile, young prince sat more attentively on his throne, Latimer, who had renounced a bishopric in order to preach the Gospel, found at last his great opportunity. Was not Protestantism now at last officially recognised as the religion of England? Was not the Regent himself, the Protector Somerset, an indulgent patron of humanism in all its forms? And did not the rural society of England, under that too tolerant ruler, cry louder than ever for the conservative protection of the State? Never was the pace of rural change brisker, or its human cost heavier, than in those years when a rapacious oligarchy, by its scramble for the spoils of power, seemed to justify Sir Thomas More's sour definition of government as 'nothing but a certain conspiracy of rich men procuring their own commodities under the name and title of a Commonwealth'.

Thus began the last great ministry of Hugh Latimer. Again

[1] Harold S. Darby, *Hugh Latimer* (London 1953).

and again, in that brief period of fatal liberalism in politics and cut-throat economic scramble, he preached before the Court, the King and the Protector; and his message was always the same — it was the definition of a true Commonwealth, based upon the essential equality and dignity of man. 'Peers of the realm', he told the King and his court, 'must needs be'; but 'the poorest ploughman is in Christ equal with the greatest prince that is.' In King Henry's day he had welcomed the fall of the monasteries; but when Jervaulx Abbey had been destined for a royal stud-farm, he had protested: 'abbeys were ordained for the comfort of the poor' — it was their crime that they had failed to provide it — and, therefore, though they were justly dissolved, 'it was not decent that the king's horses should be kept in them' and 'the living of poor men thereby minished and taken away'. For the same reason he had welcomed the attack upon images, not blindly and fanatically like his unpleasing doctrinaire colleagues Knox and Hooper, but in the name of humanity: for was it not monstrous that 'dead images' should be richly clad in silk garments and laden with jewels and beset by wax candles burning wastefully through the noonday,

> as who should say, here no cost can be too great; whereas in the meantime we see Christ's faithful and lively images, bought with no less price than his most precious blood (alas, alas), to be an-hungered, a-thirst, a-cold, and to lie in darkness, wrapped in all wretchedness?

It was a commonplace of the Reformers: the contrast which Cranmer also made between 'the lively images of Christ' and the 'dead images . . . which be things not necessary, and without which the Church of Christ continued most godly for many years'; the real social meaning of that fierce iconoclasm which modern writers are content to dismiss as mere rowdy philistinism: a supercilious, superficial view which finds its ultimate expression in Mr. A. L. Rowse's brutal reversal of the humanist formula, deploring 'burnings of people and (what was more valuable) works of art'.[1]

Such was Latimer's basic philosophy, even in the reign of King Henry. Now, when the more sympathetic government of King Edward faced a more urgent problem, he pressed his

[1] A. L. Rowse, *The England of Elizabeth*, p. 510.

views ever more insistently. Let the clergy preach, he declared, and preach constantly,

> for the preaching of the word of God unto the people is called meat: Scripture calleth it meat; not strawberries that come but once a year and are soon gone, but it is meat, it is no dainties —

and let them preach particularly against 'covetousness', that covetousness of landlords which, he assured the King, had caused the peasant revolts of his reign.

> Speak against covetousness, and cry out upon it. Stand not ticking and toying at the branches nor at the boughs, for then there will be new boughs and branches spring again of them; but strike at the root, and fear not these giants of England, these great men and men of power, these men that are oppressors of the poor; fear them not, but strike at the root of the evil, which is mischievous covetousness....

Latimer, of course, was not alone; he was but one — the most outspoken indeed and the most inflammatory — of a group, that group whom their enemies hated as 'the Commonwealth Men'. They included his fellow-preacher Lever, who also declared that 'covetous officers' of the Crown had 'offended God, beguiled the King, robbed the rich, spoiled the poor, and brought a commonwealth into a common misery', and his fellow-bishop John Scory who attacked the same 'covetousness' of 'the great sheepmasters' which had brought 'the ancient and godly yeomanry of England' into the same state as 'the slavery and peasantry of France'; they included officials like John Hales, Clerk of the Hanaper, and Sir Thomas Smith, scholar, ambassador and secretary of state, the author of their greatest document, the *Discourse of the Common Weal*;[1] and if they did not include, at least they influenced other conscientious officials and clergy, men like Sir Walter Mildmay, the Protector's commissioner for education, and Sir William Cecil, and Cecil's brother-in-law, King Edward's humanist tutor, Sir John Cheke, and Latimer's friend, Matthew Parker, vice-chancellor of Cambridge, who had preached to the rebellious peasants of Norfolk — almost all, like Latimer and Cranmer and Ridley, Cam-

[1] The *Discourse of the Common Weal* is anonymous. Elizabeth Lamond, in her edition of 1893, ascribed it to John Hales, and this ascription is generally taken for granted. But I am convinced by the arguments of Professor Edward Hughes who in the *Bulletin of the John Rylands Library* (1937) ascribes it to Sir Thomas Smith.

bridge men, those 'Cambridge humanists' who, more than any others, fertilised the Tudor age in England.

It was in the brief reign of the Protector Somerset that 'these men called Common Wealths and their adherents' seemed most influential. Was it not at the direct prompting of Latimer that the Protector summoned the suits of the poor to his own house — that vast house which he too had built out of the spoils of three bishoprics — and earned from his despairing colleagues the reputation of an infatuated demagogue? Was it not at the instigation of Hales and 'that Commonwealth called Latimer' that he sent out those Midland enclosure commissions which, by uniting the landlords against him, precipitated his overthrow? The Protector, declared the indignant gentry, was bent on the decay of the gentlemen, for 'there was never none that even spake as vilely as these called Commonwealth does'. Naturally, when he was overthrown, his friends shared his fall. They disappear from the history-books as if they had been but a bright flash in a dark pan. Nevertheless, they did not disappear from history; for they had a sequel after, as they had had a beginning before, that brief, virtuous, unsuccessful government of All the Talents in Edwardine England.

For the Commonwealth Men, in their beginning, had been the disciples of that great, maligned, tyrannical, constructive minister, Thomas Cromwell. To build, out of the fabric of an old and corrupted Church, a new ministry and a new administration, new schools, new colleges, a new system of poor relief — that had been his, and their, ambition. Cromwell, Latimer thought, had been providentially raised up 'to hear and help the little ones of God in their distress'. When Cromwell had fallen, his constructive schemes had fallen too, or been suspended, and his disciples had either made their peace with the new ministers, 'the giants of England', or — like Latimer — gone to prison. Under Edward VI they had reassembled and viewed again the half-built, half-ruined structure of the great minister, from which already an army of privileged robbers was carrying away, for their private houses, the crumbling stones. Encouraged by the Protector, they had set to work once again; but once again the changing pattern of politics had soon frustrated their endeavours. In the scramble of court factions they were submerged and then, in the Marian reaction, they disappeared — this time, as it seemed, for good. What hope was there of the Reformers' Commonwealth when the old Church and the new landlords had united against them, when King Edward was dead, his two Protectors executed, and his preachers burnt? To Sir John Cheke in Basel, to Sir Thomas Smith in Padua, to Bishop Scory in Emden, to Matthew Parker, living like a hunted hedge-priest in England, it must indeed have seemed that their failure was, this time, final.

Fortunately, while there is death there is hope. Within five years Queen Mary, too, was dead, and a new generation of politicians, preachers and officials had accepted the martyrs' ideas. In the reign of Queen Elizabeth the Commonwealth Men at last achieved a more durable power. Cecil, Mildmay, Parker, Smith all returned, with the exiled Protestant clergy and the next generation of Seymours and Dudleys. And now at last the era of spoliation was over, the work of reconstruction seriously resumed: statutes of artificers and husbandry were devised, colleges and schools and almshouses founded, economy regulated, a poor law instituted — not hastily and by force, as under Cromwell, nor ineffectively, by good intentions, as under Somerset, but gradually, carefully and, within human limits, effectively, under the long rule of William Cecil, the practical heir of the Commonwealth Men. Well might Sir Thomas Smith, once again ambassador and secretary of state, supplement his tentative early dialogue, the *Discourse of the Common Weal*, by an authoritative, analytical textbook, *The Commonwealth of England*. The Commonwealth was no longer a subject of debate but of exposition: it had arrived. It was not to religion only that Latimer's last words had been applicable. The candle had been lit for society also.

CHAPTER XIII

SIR THOMAS MORE AND THE ENGLISH LAY RECUSANTS

On July 6, 1535, Sir Thomas More went to the block. He was the first English lay recusant, for he had refused, to a Catholic sovereign, that supremacy over the Church which the Pope had already allowed to the Catholic — but now outraged — Crown of Spain. Afterwards, when England had become Protestant, the recusant laity acknowledged in More their prototype and protomartyr; at every crisis in their fortunes, his works were rehandled, his biography (or hagiography) rewritten; and they confidently assumed, as even Protestants also assumed, that he would soon, 'after a hundred years expired,' be canonised. Curiously they were wrong: More and his fellow-martyr Fisher were not canonised for four centuries; and some explanation is required of this surprising delay.

Partly, no doubt, it was due to the view held of More in Rome. Like Newman long afterwards, More was suspect as a Liberal Catholic, a Catholic who appealed (as he still appeals) to Protestants, who was indeed himself half-Protestant. Belonging to the age and sharing the views of his friend Erasmus, he had doubted the value of monasticism, wished to reduce the externals of worship, to admit lay reason into dogmatic studies, to meet Reform half-way and salvage thereby a purified religion. But in fact, when Rome was saved it was not by such measures: the Counter-Reformation was not a compliance with Reform but a defiance of it: monastic orders, images, miracles and mumbo-jumbo were not attenuated but multiplied; and Erasmus, whom in his lifetime orthodox Kings and Popes had honoured, who had been offered bishoprics and cardinalates, and whom the Inquisitor-General himself had defended against superstitious friars, was after his death denounced and condemned. His books were placed on the Index, his name no longer uttered, his disciples bullied into recantation or burnt.

But for the accident of his great refusal and his martyrdom, the posthumous history of More might well have been similar to that of his greatest friend.

But another and far stronger reason for the long neglect, at Rome, of Sir Thomas More lies no doubt in the obstinacy of his devoted successors, the English lay recusants. For over three centuries, they too, like him, clung to the image of an English, unpolitical, pre-Counter-Reformation Catholic Church, and laboured in consequence under the imputation of 'liberal Catholicism', of anti-Romanism, even of crypto-Protestantism. It is this, I think, that makes them still, in history, attractive to Protestant readers: so attractive that, in spite of their negligible contribution to English life (how feebly they compare with other persecuted minorities — with Huguenots, Jansenists, Quakers, Jews!), they are still paraded before Protestants as appropriate decoy-ducks by those new Irish and Italianate clergy who, in the course of the last century, have finally crushed them.

The great age of the recusants was, of course, the age of Elizabeth: for that was the age of their greatest dilemma. They were Englishmen; they accepted — all but a few extremists — the fact of a rightful though Protestant Queen; and they hoped, by separating religion from politics, to practise their old religion, accommodated to a Protestant country, in peace. Mostly they were gentry; particularly they were backward gentry in remote counties, living on their estates, excluded — or excluding themselves — from other opportunities of enrichment; and gradually, as society hardened in its Protestant mould, they formed a rural freemasonry, inter-marrying only within the group. Scattered everywhere, most numerous in Lancashire and the North, their most active centre was in the Midlands, the rural heart of England, where social strains were always most harshly felt and expressed. There the leaders of the recusant laity — Vauxes of Harrowden, Treshams of Rushton, Catesbys of Ashby St. Leger, Throckmortons of Coughton, Fermors of Easton Neston, Brudenells of Deene — formed a compact nucleus, whose carefully orthodox marriage-alliances extended the system outwards, through Brownes in Sussex, Ropers in Kent, Tyrwhitts in Lincolnshire, Rookwoods in Suffolk, into the larger world. Thus self-contained, thus self-protecting, why should they not, loyal and tolerated, preserve their private religion in their native land?

Alas, there was every reason why they should not. Their ambitions of peace and toleration were regarded, in Counter-Reformation Rome, as signs of contemptible sluggishness. Toleration! exclaimed Pope Clement VIII, in reply to one of the documents in which they expressed their aims: 'Do you wish to be among thorns and yet not be pricked?' As for the separation of religion from politics, how could they entertain so naïve a notion? For now the Roman Church was recovering lost ground; now the feeble days of Erasmus and More, the days of appeasement, were over; now religion *was* politics, and it was the duty of religious minorities everywhere not to seek toleration from their native governments but to act as the advanced fifth-columns of an international headquarters. In 1570 the Pope declared Queen Elizabeth to be no longer a rightful Queen. In 1580 the first Jesuit missionaries landed in England to organise the fifth column, and the great dilemma penetrated, through the priest-holes, into the remote unpolitical country houses of England.

What were the recusants to do? On the one hand they welcomed the priests, devout, enterprising, persecuted men, who preserved for them the continuity of belief and ministration; on the other hand, they disclaimed the political designs of which these priests were the sometimes unconscious agents. It is true the priests told them not to subvert the Queen's government; but they told them so because they had been instructed to tell them so; and they could easily be instructed otherwise. At the moment it was not opportune to preach rebellion. At the moment it was more essential to build up and foster the Catholic body, so that a new Catholic monarch, when he could be inserted, might find an effective basis for his work. The failure of King Sigismund in Sweden — as afterwards of James II in England — was adequate proof of this necessity. So the Jesuits laboured to sustain and activate their innocent fifth column against the day when a Catholic Mary, or a Catholic James, or a Catholic Infanta should inherit the throne, and then suddenly — as in Poland, as in Bavaria, as in Belgium and the Rhineland, as afterwards in Bohemia — the apparatus of a Catholic despotism could rumble in and Protestantism be finally snuffed out. And if hope should fade or that day should be too long postponed? Then at any moment a change of tactics might bring it nearer. The same Jesuits who now preached acceptance, *pro tempore*, of Queen Elizabeth, were the inventors of the doctrine that rulers who displeased the Church ought to be destroyed by their subjects. Even the Catholic Philip III sent these offensive theories to the bonfire: small wonder that the Protestant ministers of Queen Elizabeth determined to strike not only at the immigrant priests, but also at the often innocent fellow-travellers who harboured them. It was all very well for Sir Thomas Tresham, the type of the loyal English recusant, to protest that he would defend Queen Elizabeth 'against all persons without exception, be it Prince, Pope or potentate whosoever'; it was all very well for the missionaries to coo like sucking-doves; but why, the English Protestants asked, did these missionaries come straight from the dominions of the Queen's declared enemy, the King of Spain? Why did some of them, like Fr. Walpole, receive their instructions from the King of Spain in person? Why did the most influential of all the English Jesuits, Fr. Parsons, who was safely outside England, openly declare that the rightful ruler of England was not Queen Elizabeth but the King of Spain? And why did some enthusiasts continually hatch, around the refugee Queen Mary, their assassination-plots? The modern priestly biographers of the recusants, who hide behind the loyalty of the laymen, are discreetly silent about the politics of the priests: the government, they scream, was 'totalitarian'; and having said so, they slide naturally into such terms as Gestapo methods, Reichstag fires, and concentration camps. It does not occur to them that a society at war has the right to protect itself not only against traitors, but against their dupes; nor that their own predecessors, the Roman clergy of the sixteenth century, regarded the loyalty of the recusants not as a virtue but as a fault.

The dilemma of the recusants, between the Protestants and the priests, was of short duration. It lasted for one generation; then, with the Gunpowder Plot, all was over. The government used, indeed exploited the Plot to crush the political priests, and thereafter the recusants, relieved of this incubus, achieved their aim: they were loyal and, within limits, tolerated. Even under the Republic, they were not seriously persecuted; and although the schemes of enthusiastic priests, excited once again by the prospect of a Popish heir-presumptive, could unleash terrible passions, the laity on the whole remained quiet; it was converts and timeservers, not the reluctant recusants, who forced the pace under James II. The recusants paid fines indeed, but did those fines impoverish them? All past taxation seems trivial to us, and evasion was as common then as now. Certainly recusants could spend as freely as Protestants if they wished. Heythrop and Wardour are the evidence, and the great houses in which Lord Petre and Mr. Weld of Lulworth magnificently entertained Hanoverian royalty. By the beginning of the nineteenth century the recusants, freed for two centuries from their Counter-Reformation priests, were as prosperous, as liberal, as 'half-Protestant' as in the days of Sir Thomas More. Some were even more liberal. The Pope they dismissed as 'a foreign prelate'; 'popery' — that is, the new superstitions of the Counter-Reformation — they explicitly disclaimed; and Sir John Throckmorton was even prepared to recommend that English Catholics should swear to a Protestant King that Oath of Supremacy which More had so fatefully refused to the Catholic, if schismatical, Henry VIII. Only one hurdle had still to be crossed: legal emancipation. If that could be granted the recusants would have nothing left to refuse: they would be as free as Protestants in the Protestant world. And why should they not be emancipated? Did not they too, they protested, like other Englishmen, believe fundamentally in 'freedom of thought and toleration'?

Alas, like so many dreams of the eighteenth century, this hope of the recusants — the 'Cisalpines', as they were now called — dissolved in the nineteenth. The nineteenth century was once again the age of the priests, and long and bitter was the battle which, through three generations, they fought to victory. The violent, unscrupulous Milner, with his Irish allies in the vendetta against 'the encroachments and aberrations of powerful laymen'; the ascetic, inflexible, *intrigant* Manning with his Italian politics and mystical exaltation of the priestly office; the hard, narrow zealot Vaughan with his unsympathetic organiser's efficiency — these were the architects of victory; and their enemies and victims were always the same: the laity, the old recusants who had escaped, in 1605, from an international political priesthood. 'Liberty of thought and toleration' indeed! Were not these the doctrines which the Popes of the sixteenth century had condemned as 'detestable', 'abominable' heresies? In 1864 Pius IX, in the same terms, condemned them again. Why should the laity demand emancipation? Once again, did they expect to live among thorns without being pricked? Emancipation from the prickly hedgerow, it was clear to Dr. Milner, meant emancipation also from the prickly hedge-priest; and so he waged against it, and against the 'lay juntos' which advocated it, his long delaying action. The universities at last opened their doors to Catholic laymen; for forty years Archbishop Manning forbade them to go in. The laity, he declared, must be kept away from English influences: they must be educated by priests alone. In despair the laity sought to express themselves in print. Then their ventures were stifled: Acton's reviews, the *Rambler* and *Home and Foreign Review*, were suppressed by Manning, the *Tablet* was bought up by Vaughan, and the Catholic Press thus fell entirely into priestly hands. It was for writing an article on consulting the laity in matters of dogma that Newman fell, at Rome, into his deepest disfavour. What is the province of the laity? asked Bishop Milner; and answered: to transact public business 'after it had been made known to them by the prelates'. What is the province of the laity? asked Cardinal Wiseman; and answered: to finance, assist and defend the Church, but on no account to be consulted. 'What is the province of the laity?' echoed Manning's agent in Rome, Mgr. Talbot; and answered even more firmly: 'to hunt, to shoot, to entertain', but on no account to interfere in religion. 'Dr. Newman is the most dangerous man in England,' he wrote to the Archbishop, 'and you will see that he will make use of the laity against Your Grace'; and he urged him to strike hard, lest the Holy Father 'begin to regret Cardinal Wiseman, who knew how to keep the laity in order'. 'Dr. Newman', he declared further, in language that might have been used by Fr. Parsons of Sir Thomas Tresham, 'is more English than the English. His spirit must be crushed'.

Thus, in the nineteenth century the old dilemma of the recusants, between England and Rome, between Protestants and priests, returned. But whereas in 1605 they had escaped from their priests, by 1905 — thanks to Irish reinforcements — the priests had recaptured them. The battle was over, and the gratified conquerors prepared magnanimously to throw a few sops to their now finally defeated victims. Having carefully emptied them of their intellectual contents, they decided to restore to them, as mascots, the great names of their former champions. First Newman, whose broken, aged body was robed in purple shortly before his doctrine of Development was implicitly condemned by Pius X. Then Acton, who had denounced the policy of the Counter-Reformation Papacy as organised murder, but who, when he was safely dead, and his letters had been safely expurgated by an abbot, was duly hailed (against a Jesuit protest) as a great Catholic historian. By 1935, the Church judged it safe at last to canonise the great hero of the lay recusants, Sir Thomas More. And now the recusants themselves — the Treshams and Vauxes — have become heroes, and clerical biographers praise them for that 'English national spirit' which, at the time, Fr. Parsons so desperately denounced and which, long afterwards, it was Cardinal Manning's greatest boast to have crushed. Dead as mutton, the recusants can still serve to bait a priestly trap. Come unto us, say the Roman clergy, come into the Church, says Mr. Evelyn Waugh (for in the intellectual emptiness of modern English Catholicism only the snob-appeal is left) . . . and join the old English recusants in their armigerous tombs.

CHAPTER XIV

ELIZABETH AND CECIL

Great partnerships are rare in politics, and the few that have lasted are justly famous. There was Ferdinand and Isabella, there was Gustavus and Oxenstjerna, and — most lasting of all — there was Elizabeth and Cecil. For forty consecutive years that alliance governed England, making the most splendid reign in our history; and the alliance was ten years older than the government. In 1548, when Elizabeth was a fourteen-year-old princess, she had singled out William Cecil as the one honest man whom she could trust and had written to him as 'your friend'. Fifty years later, when he lay dying, she brought him chicken-broth made with her own hands and afterwards, hardened actress though she was, wept in council when his name was mentioned. In a time of ideological convulsions, diplomatic somersaults, treacheries, conspiracies and *coups d'état*, they remained constant in their mutual dependence. Only once — in the time of the Queen's fury at the execution of Mary Queen of Scots — was there a coolness between them; but how brief, perhaps unreal, was that politic estrangement. Meanwhile, in the same forty years, the Catholic sovereigns of France, Spain and Scotland had all disembarrassed themselves of their counsellors by treachery and murder. Judged as an employer alone, the record of Queen Elizabeth was indeed extraordinary.

What was the secret of this long, unbroken partnership? At first sight the differences between Elizabeth and Cecil seem more obvious than the similarities. Cecil was a man of exact habits, firm convictions, puritan severity. How carefully he husbanded the royal revenues! How strictly he accounted for every detail of his many duties! How censoriously he frowned upon the lavish gaiety, the cynicism, the recklessness of that most magnificent of European courts! Conservative in everything, he believed in a jealously preserved hierarchy, its social distinctions guarded by sumptuary laws, entails and medieval regulation of labour. And how he worried over the future, and the Protestant succession, those great problems to which his mistress was, alas, so painfully indifferent!

For Elizabeth, it was only too clear, was very differently constructed. She was niggardly indeed, but that was not because she had an accountant's mind. There was no economy in her wardrobe, no sumptuary laws in her court. Not for her a rigid society. She would have order, 'degree', majesty — yes: but in her immediate entourage there must always be movement, animation, jostling crowds. She had little doctrinal interest, little political forethought. The Protestant succession, which obsessed her subjects, hardly troubled her. She uttered magnificent phrases about it: 'I hope I shall die in quiet with *Nunc Dimittis*, which cannot be without I see some glimpse of your following surety after my graved bones'; but the unspoken phrase was always the same: *après moi le déluge.*

The unconcerned can afford to be liberal, and seen from our safe distance, Elizabeth's regal tolerance is often more attractive than the prudent severity of her minister. To protect Protestanism at home, Cecil would make fires in his neighbours' houses: he would sustain Scottish, French and Dutch rebels against Catholic rulers — a policy which Elizabeth was reluctant to follow. And then there was that unfortunate adventuress, Mary Queen of Scots. To Cecil Mary was 'that dangerous traitress and pestilence of Christendom': Elizabeth, holding out alone, for fifteen years, against her subjects' clamour for Mary's blood, must always seem the nobler character. And how unusual, in her age, was her refusal to persecute for religion only! In vain Cecil protested that 'the papists' humours, by the Queen's Majesty's lenity, grow too rank'; it was no good: the Queen would not, in her own majestic phrase, 'make windows into men's souls'. But the fact remains that Cecil was always thinking, and thinking seriously, of the English people; Elizabeth was not. She looked no further than her own life. Rather than take out an insurance policy for her subjects (that, she said, was to contemplate her own winding-sheet), she speculated irresponsibly on her survival. Miraculously, she survived; but had she perished with Mary living, then indeed our history would have been different and Mr. A. L. Rowse and his followers would be singing to-day a very different tune.

How was it then that between these different characters so long an alliance was built up? How was it that Cecil was able to control his imperious but flighty mistress, and make of her, as he did, the conciliator of the classes, the head of European Protestantism, the idol of later generations? It was done in the first decade of their joint reign, the decade covered by Professor Conyers Read's new and scholarly book,[1] the period between their joint accession to power and the most formidable attempt to separate them: the rebellion of the Northern Earls and the palace conspiracy of 1569. It was in those years that Cecil achieved his authority with Elizabeth. But the origin and basis of the alliance lay, I think, further back, in the reign of Edward VI, that brief but portentous reign in which English Protestantism and the great Elizabethan statesmen who established it were formed.

For the Elizabethans — Elizabeth herself and all her first advisers — were (it is too often forgotten) a party: a political, an intellectual, even a revolutionary party; and all their personal differences were slight compared with the great bond which united them. All were intellectuals, all Protestants: for indeed how could any intellectual fail to be a Protestant in the 1550's, when Protestantism still wore the liberalism of the Reformers and Rome had surrendered to abject monkish reaction? Some of them were more sceptical, or more serious, or more doctrinally minded than others, but Protestantism was the essential cement which united that *avant-garde* of scholarly radicals. There was Catherine Parr, the last wife of Henry VIII, that erudite Hellenist queen who so zealously supervised the education of her precocious stepchildren and whose devotional writings were edited by Cecil. There were the Dudleys, that learned family, and Lady Jane Grey, whom a tragic royalty overtook when she was reading the *Phædo* in Greek. There was the bluestocking Cooke sisterhood, who made brothers-in-law of Cecil, Sir Nicholas Bacon and Sir Thomas Hoby. There were the professors John Cheke (Cecil's other brother-in-law), Roger Ascham and Sir Thomas Smith. Cecil himself was a scholar. He carried Tully's *Offices* 'either in his bosom or his pocket' to his dying day,

[1] Conyers Read, *Mr. Secretary Cecil and Queen Elizabeth* (London 1955).

and in the crisis of that reign, when faced by prison or flight, resolved his doubts by reading Plato's *Crito*. And in the midst of this severely cultivated *côterie* sat the young King, reading Aristotle and Thucydides and that famous work of liberal devotion, *The Benefit of Christ*, and the young Princess, reading Sophocles and Cyprian and her stepmother's edition of Erasmus; and around them their learned Protestant clergy — Cranmer, Parker, Coxe — chaplains, tutors and confessors to this incredibly sophisticated court.

Such was the little ruling world which the death of Edward VI and the disastrous accession of Mary suddenly broke up. At once all were scattered. Some fled to the Continent, some hid privately at home, others were dragged to the block and the stake; and in their stead there ruled, for five years, a starched and stuffy court of antiquated reactionaries. But the scattered remnant did not despair. For five years they waited, still a party, always in touch, sustaining their hopes, formulating their plans in secrecy and danger. Elizabeth at Hatfield, as heir to the throne, was the centre of their hopes, and it was then that she learnt the perils of a designated successor. 'I stood in danger of my life,' she afterwards said, 'my sister was so incensed against me. I did differ from her in religion, and I was sought for divers ways; and so shall never be my successor.' Cecil, still her adviser, prudently conformed; but he made himself, in Parliament, the champion of the Protestant refugees, and he kept in his private diary, a careful record of the Smithfield fires. Then, suddenly again, with the death of Mary, all was reversed. 'O Lord, Almighty and Everlasting God,' Elizabeth prayed in her exultation,

> I give Thee most hearty thanks that Thou hast been so merciful unto me to spare me to behold this joyful day. And I acknowledge that Thou hast dealt as wonderfully and as mercifully with me as Thou didst with Thy true and faithful servant Daniel, Thy prophet, whom Thou deliveredst out of the den of the greedy and raging lions.

At once the old Edwardian party reunited around her. The refugees poured back from abroad, the timid emerged from their obscurity. 'There is not a heretic or a traitor in the country', wrote the Spanish ambassador sourly, 'who has not started, as from the grave, to seek the new Queen with expressions of delight'. And the Queen sent for Cecil, that her secretary, from the secretary of her party, might be her secretary of state. 'This judgment I have of you,' she told him, 'that you will not be corrupted by any manner of gift, and that you will be faithful to the state, and that, without respect of my private will, you will give me that counsel which you think best.'

Thus the alliance of Elizabeth and Cecil had already been cemented long before it was tested in action. It was the alliance of a revolutionary party, tried by failure and eclipse, and now suddenly faced with a second prospect of power. Parrs and Dudleys, Cookes and Bacons, Smiths, Hobys and the rest all came back in 1558, a united front determined this time not to fail. There were differences, of course: power always reveals differences which opposition has concealed. Some of the returned *émigrés*, like the Duchess of Suffolk, that formidable patroness, found Cecil's Protestantism too tepid; others, like the Queen and her irresponsible favourite, Robert Dudley, found it sometimes too hot. And then what bewildering political problems must face any intellectual group of 'Souls' which suddenly finds itself a revolutionary government! No wonder, in those days of machiavellian diplomacy and vertiginous royal nuptial flights, if differences arose between the Queen and Cecil — if, in Professor Read's words, 'there were times when even Cecil must have felt a strong urge to wring the lady's neck'? But in the end the Queen, who after all, like her father, knew a good servant, was guided by him as by no one else. To her, as to her Protestant critics, he was indispensable; for who (wrote one of them) 'can as well stand fast against the Queen's arguments and doubtful devices? Who will speedily resolve the doubtful delays? Who shall make despatch of anything?' So, in the great crisis of 1569, she stood by him. The Edwardian reformers, in council and church and parliament, remained solid to the end; so solid that historians sometimes forget how revolutionary a group they had been. It should not be forgotten. The English Protestant revolution was still a revolution, even if, unlike later revolutions, it did not devour its own children.

CHAPTER XV

THE LAST ELIZABETHAN: SIR WALTER RALEIGH

In 1603 the greatest English royal dynasty came to an end. With surprising smoothness King James succeeded to Queen Elizabeth. Directly, that transition made the fortune of a great private dynasty, the Cecils of Hatfield; incidentally it ruined one of the greatest living Englishmen, Sir Walter Raleigh.

In November 1603 Sir Walter Raleigh was accused of treason — of seeking, with Spanish and popish aid, to overthrow the new king and substitute on his throne a puppet-queen. The evidence for this charge was simple: first, a group of desperate popish gentry in the Midlands, having hatched an absurd plot in the obscurity of Sherwood Forest, admitted that they had pleased themselves with the fancy of Raleigh's support; secondly, a single thrice-perjured witness alternately alleged and denied and re-alleged that it was so. At his trial at Winchester Raleigh contemptuously dismissed such evidence and demanded to face his accuser. Was it likely, he asked, that he would consent to be 'a Robin Hood, a Wat Tyler, a Jack Cade, a John Kett'? And did not the law anyway demand two witnesses? It was in vain. Over against him was the King's Attorney, Sir Edward Coke. No lack of evidence could disconcert that great Panjandrum of the Common Law. 'Damnable atheist,' he cried, 'thou hast a Spanish heart and art thyself a spider of Hell.' 'Many horse-stealers would escape,' declared another sententious lawyer, 'if they could not be hanged but by the mouth of two witnesses.' These arguments convinced the special judges of that tribunal — Sir Robert Cecil, the King's secretary, Raleigh's former friend, who would himself silently pocket, among other bribes, a pension from Spain; Lord Henry Howard, Raleigh's inveterate enemy, himself a secret papist; their friends, allies and kinsmen. By one of the most famous injustices in our history Raleigh was condemned to death and led out to execution.

Then, having submitted to all the formalities of approaching death, he was suddenly, at the last moment, reprieved; the British Solomon admired, in this solemn farce, the evidence of his own magnanimity; and Raleigh disappeared, for fifteen years, into the Tower.

Raleigh's condemnation in 1603 was a climacteric in his personal life and evoked from him his finest poems — his *Passionate Man's Pilgrimage*, his *Petition to the Queen*. He had always been a poet, of all the Elizabethan court-poets 'most lofty, insolent and passionate'; but beneath the polished surface of his occasional verse there lay, half-hidden, qualities which separate him from his rivals in that field: an insatiable intellectual ambition, a deep and proud melancholy. He was the patron not only of Spenser but of the disquieting 'School of Night': of the atheist Marlowe, 'still climbing after knowledge infinite,' and, indirectly, of that self-torturing laborious introvert, George Chapman, forerunners of the mystical poets of the new century. So now, on the eve of execution, Raleigh struck a new vein and expressed in poetry his latent metaphysical melancholy:

> Give me my scallop-shell of quiet,
> My staff of faith to walk upon,
> My scrip of Joy, immortal diet,
> My bottle of Salvation,
> My gown of Glory, hope's true gage,
> And thus I'll take my pilgrimage.
>
> Blood must be my body's balmer,
> No other balm will there be given,
> Whilst my soul, like a white palmer,
> Travels to the land of Heaven. . . .

Then, turning like all the poets of that litigious age to the processes of law for his images, he pronounced, indirectly, his sentence on the corrupt and unjust tribunal that had condemned him, and particularly on the King's Attorney, Sir Edward Coke:

> From thence to Heaven's bribeless hall,
> Where no corrupted voices brawl,
> No conscience molten into gold,
> Nor forg'd accusers bought and sold,
> No cause deferred nor vain-spent journey,
> For there Christ is the King's Attorney. . . .

Raleigh's trial, which recreated his poetry and gave him the leisure to write his most ambitious work, the *History of the World*, was also the cause of his remarkable posthumous reputation; but legally it was an outrage, which has to be explained. Of course it was a political trial; and the politics of the last years of Elizabeth bring us back always to the meteor of her declining court, Robert Devereux, Earl of Essex.

Raleigh and Essex, famous as rival courtiers, sustaining on the spoils of church-lands, court offices and war their ambitions, their retinues, their dependent poets, their elaborate gestures, were nevertheless not court figures only. Behind the court was the country, divided — like the court — by brisk party struggles between those who enjoyed and those who coveted the sweets and opportunities of office: between the Cecils and their ever-growing system of patronage on the one hand, and, on the other, Essex at the head of the excluded peers at court, the excluded gentry in the country. Against the day when the old Queen should die, the parties manœuvred and counter-manœuvred; then, in 1601, Essex was out-manœuvred and destroyed; the peers who had rashly followed him made their submission; and the court at least was united round Sir Robert Cecil, who could now negotiate from strength with the King of Scots and ensure, under a new king, the continuation of the old system, the vast monopoly of office which he had so nearly closed.

But if the court was united, what of the country? If the peers had forsaken them, the gentry would look to other champions. If Essex was dead, they would look to his old rival, himself by birth 'a bare gentleman'. Raleigh, by his individualism, his isolation, his survival, became the hope of all whom the Cecil system excluded; and Cecil and his allies the Howards were convinced that, to complete their monopoly, Raleigh must be destroyed. In secret letters to the King of Scots they denounced, with sanctimonious spite, the 'atheist' and his friends; and when the King's mind had been sufficiently poisoned, they struck. A few desperate plotters mumbled the name of Raleigh. It was enough. The all-powerful secretary, with unctuous magnanimity, presided over the trial, and could rely on his own kinsman, Attorney-General Coke, to demand the death-sentence. Raleigh was ruined; and the empire of Cecil was safe for ever.

Thereafter the excluded gentry, leaderless and resentful, looked from afar upon the gay, corrupt, extravagant court of James I, and the words which Raleigh, in his temporary eclipse by Essex, had once applied to the old court,

> Say to the court it glows
> And shines like rotten wood

now seemed to them doubly applicable to the new. The great Cecil racket was succeeded by the great Buckingham racket; court and country drifted ever further apart; and the distant protests of the gentry, as they beat inaudibly upon the frivolous world of privilege and pleasure, assumed by opposition a puritan earnestness. Naturally their minds turned to their most distinguished fellow-victim, whose name recalled the happier days of 'Queen Elizabeth of glorious memory': the solitary prisoner who now, still insatiable in his boundless intellectual quest, was practising chemistry in a shed under the Tower Wall, or writing for Prince Henry the *History of the World*. 'Only my father', exclaimed the indignant prince, 'would keep such a bird in a cage.' Then, in 1618, the bird was let out, and the second visit to Guiana was followed by the second and final ruin. Fifteen years after his freedom had been sacrificed to Cecil, Raleigh's life was sacrificed to the Spanish ambassador, Count Gondomar. So once again, still on the old charge, he was condemned to death; once again he penned — or rather, as we now know, remade — a valedictory poem, those famous lines inscribed in his Bible:

> Even such is time which takes in trust
> Our youth, our joys and all we have,
> And pays us but with age and dust;

once again he was led out to the block. Only this time there were differences. In 1603, thanks to his 'damnable pride', Raleigh had been the most hated man in England — at his trial at Winchester he had barely been brought alive through the crowd; in 1618 he was everywhere hailed as a martyr. In 1603, to the disappointment of the observers, the axe had not fallen; in 1618, to their dismay, it fell.

Thence also sprang the strange history of his later fame. Raleigh, the outrageous intellectual, the arrogant courtier, rich, elegant, flamboyant, with his satin clothes and huge pearl eardrops, the cosmopolitan, the machiavellian, the atheist, whose casual table-talk had sent a Dorset parson mumping to the Privy Council, was gradually transformed, by their common misfortunes, into the idol of earnest, conventional, parsimonious, provincial, puritan inland squires. In their country houses they transcribed his casual poems, or they had them carved upon their tombs;[1] they expressed their views in pamphlets with such titles as *Sir Walter Raleigh's Ghost*; they read, in half a century, twenty editions of his *History of the World*; and when, in the Great Rebellion, they rose at last and swept away the whole court, the court of Charles I, the last Renaissance court in Europe, they did it in the name of the greatest of all courtiers and virtuosi, Sir Walter Raleigh, whose minor works were first collected and published under the English Repulic; whose dreams of a Caribbean Empire became the policy of the Puritan Protectorate; whose *Prerogative of Parliaments* was copied out by Sir John Eliot; whose apocryphal works were edited by John Milton;[2] whose *History of the World* was, after the Bible, the favourite reading of Oliver Cromwell. Truly, until Disraeli, no man inspired, or was followed by a more incongruous party than he.

[1] Raleigh's lines 'Even such is time . . .' are inscribed on seventeenth century tombstones in Herefordshire, Cumberland and Surrey (see letters in *The Times Literary Supplement*, 12 and 26 October 1951).

[2] Mr. Ernest A. Strathmann has shown (in *The Times Literary Supplement*, 13 April 1956) that *The Cabinet-Council*, which Milton edited and ascribed to Raleigh in 1658, is not in fact by Raleigh but by one 'T.B.', possibly Thomas Bedingfield, the translator of Machiavelli's *Florentine History*.

CHAPTER XVI

THE JESUIT MISSION IN ENGLAND AND THE GUNPOWDER PLOT

On October 26, 1605, Lord Monteagle, a papist peer, suddenly ordered supper to be prepared in his long-unvisited house at Hoxton. At supper a servant as suddenly brought in a letter, handed to him (he said) by a stranger in the street. In spite of the mysterious circumstances, Lord Monteagle did not read the letter himself: he ordered a servant to read it aloud to the whole company. It was the famous letter revealing, in effect, the Gunpowder Plot. By this prearranged manœuvre Francis Tresham, a wavering conspirator, sought at the same time to prevent the Plot and to forewarn his friends.

In his first object Tresham succeeded. The gunpowder never exploded. But the consequences could hardly have been greater if it had. The horror of that discovery was universal. Lord Monteagle, as its revealer, became the hero of the nation, his dubious past forgotten, his praises sung by Ben Jonson, his rickety finances restored by a state pension. For 200 years the Christian name Guy was ostracised from England; for 250 years the conspiracy was annually denounced in the national churches; after 350 years we still symbolically celebrate that famous last-minute deliverance. Further, from that date, gentry opposition to the English court took a puritan, not a papist, form; and with that date the heroic age of the English Jesuits was over.

For several years gentry opposition had been breaking out in such desperate conspiracies: In 1601 the Earl of Essex, his lucrative monopoly withdrawn, his case hopeless, and his creditors pressing, had drawn around him other desperately impecunious men and attempted a *coup d'état*. He had perished, but his followers survived — Lord Monteagle, the Markham brothers, Robert Catesby, Francis Tresham. Next year Catesby's debts had forced him to sell his estate of Chastleton: almost automatically he and his friends, Monteagle and Tresham, 'by reason of my Lord of Essex's death and the want of his purse to maintain them,' had secretly offered themselves as a fifth-column to the King of Spain. A year later, when Sir Griffin Markham's debts had overtaken him and a warrant was out for his arrest, he also had planned a *coup*: to seize the person of the King as a hostage for change. He too had been condemned and exiled. By 1605 only Monteagle, Tresham and Catesby were left, and that group too was disintegrating. Monteagle had detached himself, 'he had done with all former plots,' he said, 'and wished to stand wholly for the King'. Tresham, having suddenly inherited an estate, wavered at the last minute. Only Catesby, 'exceedingly tangled in debts and scarce able to subsist', with some old and some new allies, persevered to the end. The Gunpowder Plot was the last fling of the old Essexians, the idiot-fringe of the indebted gentry.

It was also something more. Tudor society was an aristocratic society and political action required aristocratic leadership. But by 1605 the peerage had ceased to invest in conspiracy — it did not pay. Eight peers had followed Essex in 1601; the Markhams had congratulated themselves on having two; the Gunpowder Plotters had none. They were all gentry, 'gentlemen', as Guy Fawkes declared, 'of name and blood'; 'gentlemen', as Cecil retorted, 'spent in their fortunes and fit for all alterations' — but still gentry. As for the nobility, said Catesby, he made account of them 'as of atheists, fools and cowards'. And yet, if practical leadership was lacking, some substitute was needed. The substitute in fact used was religious intoxication, the fanaticism of the new popery. Though popery had been an element in the previous plots, it had never been exclusive — Essex and the Markhams had both relied on Protestant, even Puritan allies. Catesby, in his more desperate venture, relied on popish bigots alone, the pupils and converts of the Jesuit mission.

For the generation before the Plot had been the great age of the English Jesuits. Agents of a hostile power, propagandists of a foreign system, they were understandably regarded as traitors by the Elizabethan government, and cruelly treated if found. Individually they might be innocent unpolitical idealists; but their order was a political system, used by the enemies of England, and they, if not its agents, then its dupes. Had not the Pope declared Elizabeth a heretic and a usurper and sent papal troops to fight her in Ireland? Did not their own doctors pronounce that heretic sovereigns might lawfully be destroyed by Catholic subjects? From 1585 to 1604 England was at war with Spain; for nine of those years the chief English Jesuit sat at the Spanish court protesting that King Philip was rightfully King of England and advocating military invasion. In 1593 Fr. Walpole came to England direct from Madrid with the personal blessing of the King; in 1602 Fr. Garnett, the English superior personally presided over the treacherous session of Catesby and his friends, and Fr. Greenway personally carried their offer of a fifth column to the King of Spain. Even the instruction to the English missionaries not to speak against the Queen bore a significant rider which made it a matter of tactics, not principle: 'except in the presence of proved Catholics'. The function of the Jesuit missionaries was not to excite direct political opposition, it was to create and maintain a potential fifth-column. How that fifth column should be used would be determined not by them, but by the enemies of England. Understandably, they protested that they had no politics, they only preached a gospel. Understandably, the English government failed to make that distinction. When the Cominform preaches war, local communists vainly, even if genuinely, insist that they mean peace.

Nevertheless, idealism has an appeal independent of the uses it may serve, and against the superior resources, the corrupted interests, the vulgar instruments of even liberal power, the lonely, hunted, disinterested agents of even illiberal systems shine with the purity of the spirit contending with the world. One of these idealists was John Gerard, whose autiobiography[1] (written in Latin after the failure of the Plot) was first translated by John Morris eighty years ago. Now we have, from Fr. Caraman, a fellow-Jesuit, a new, excellent and most readable translation. Born of an old Romanist family in Lancashire, Gerard had become a Jesuit in Rome, and in the year of the Armada, with Fr. Oldcorne and two other Jesuits, secretly

John Gerard: An Elizabethan Autobiography. Translated and edited by Philip Caraman (London 1951).

landed on the Norfolk coast to begin a life of extraordinary adventure. Posing as a falconer who had lost his hawk, he wandered through Norfolk till he found, in a recusant family, a home and a base of operations. Then, going out hunting with the local gentry, or talking in a window with a lady in the evening, he drew them quietly into religion. Compared with the go-getting, competitive, successful world with which the State Church was associated, he offered to those remote gentry families, often casualties in that competition, a more dignified, more ancient, more spiritual consolation; and they, contrasting this gentle evangelist, whose cultivated tastes and elegant clothes concealed such secret courage and serious devotion, with their own local vicars of Bray, were 'blessed in hearing him' and felt their roof sanctified by his presence. So, from family to family, *via* the Counter and the Clink, the torture-house (he was barbarously tortured) and the Tower (from which he perilously escaped by rope), he carried his message and, so doing, built up, and in his narrative reconstructs before us, that freemasonry of recusant gentry families which was so soon to be split by politics and convulsed by the Plot. Here and there we see local cells — his own, first in East Anglia, then with the Vaux family at Kirby and Harrowden; Fr. Southwell's with the Countess of Arundel in the Strand; Fr. Oldcorne's at Hinlip House in Worcestershire with its eleven priest-holes disguised as chimneys. Now and then his tale is punctuated by martyrdoms — two of his original companions in 1590 and 1591, Walpole in 1595, Southwell in 1598, Page in 1602. And over the whole story hover two central figures: Fr. Garnett, the Superior, in London, who for eighteen years controlled all things from his secret headquarters; and Garnett's servant Nicholas Owen, called 'Little John', the architect of all those priest-holes which so often baffled the keenest poursuivant. Had he been unfaithful, 'Little John' might have ruined the movement, 'knowing the residences of most priests in England and all those of the Society, whom he might have taken as partridges in a net, knowing all their secret places, which himself had made'. Fortunately he was not.

Then, suddenly, came 'the catastrophe of the Powder Plot'. If others had lit the train, the priests had laid it: naturally there was a hue and cry after them. The Superior himself and Fr. Oldcorne were taken at last, forced out of their priest-hole at Hinlip by bad air, looking 'like two ghosts' after twelve days' concealment, and both were tortured, tried and unjustly executed. 'Little John' was taken and cruelly tortured to death. Fr. Greenway, who knew more than any priest about the Plot, escaped abroad in a cargo of dead pigs. Gerard also, after nine anxious days in the priest-hole at Harrowden, escaped abroad, never to return. Split by faction, discredited by the Plot, the English mission, for all its heroism, had failed altogether, and the next generation of English Jesuits, living more comfortably under the tolerance of a 'romanising' court, somehow made less appeal to earnest country gentry whose non-conformity, being opposition to court-religion, now took a puritan form. The order which, in those thirty years, had recovered Poland and Bavaria, had not recovered England. But then in England, unlike Poland and Bavaria, they did not control the ruler; and although, eighty years later, they might think that they had found their ideal King even in England, the English perversely chose that occasion to adopt the Jesuit doctrine that orthodox subjects may depose a heretic ruler.

Such political considerations did not occur to Fr. Gerard in his thirty years of exile after the failure of the Plot. He was an idealist, not a politician, and to him his mission did not seem a failure. Had he not, with feminine aid, after patient angling, skilfully caught Sir Everard Digby 'in Peter's net'? It is true Sir Everard, in consequence of this conversion, had joined the Gunpowder Plotters and so perished miserably at twenty-five instead of living happily with the hawks and hounds in which he had formerly delighted; but what of that if his soul was saved? And had not Gerard also ensured the safe keeping of certain important relics—a chip of St. Thomas Becket's skull, a complete spine from the Crown of Thorns, and 'a large piece' of the arm of St. Vita, a West Saxon royal virgin? Such were the positive results of the heroism, the devotion, the purity of the Jesuit missionaries.

CHAPTER XVII

TWICE MARTYRED: THE ENGLISH JESUITS AND THEIR HISTORIANS

These Elizabethan martyrs, these Jesuits who kept the faith alive, creeping from priest-hole to priest-hole in the days of persecution, until they were barbarously executed or escaped back to Rome or Seville to write their autobiographies, have become a great bore. It is not their fault. Many of them were admirable men, and the sympathy of Protestant Englishmen is naturally given to those who dedicate their lives to a dangerous cause. Such men are an *élite*, with the moral firmness, the self-discipline, the intellectual quality of an *élite*, and in our comfortable, uninspired age we listen readily to their voices: those clear, eloquent, sensitive voices which speak to us so freshly, without advertisement or self-pity, even from the catacombs, even from the scaffold. And yet after only five years — for it is only five years since Father Caraman's excellent translation of Gerard's autiobiography set the fashion — — they have become bores. Poor things, they have been martyred again : martyred not by Protestants but, once again, by those more comfortable co-religionists who push them forth, *perinde ac cadavera*, to maintain an unreal position in a real world.

Consider their first martyrdom. The Jesuit order had a policy: a perfectly clear and consistent policy. It was the reconquest of the Protestant world. It was also a scientific policy, taking account of practical politics. For instance, in monarchical Europe, it was absolutely essential to capture the sovereign. Without a Catholic sovereign there was really, as history showed, no hope. On the other hand even a Catholic sovereign — as was shown in Sweden — could not succeed against a firmly Protestant people unless he could rely, at the crucial moment, on a compact nucleus of educated supporters, ready and able to occupy all key positions. Therefore, in Protestant countries, the Jesuits had a double policy. First, they would look forward to a Catholic sovereign. They would fish for the right heir or groom a pretender. Secondly, and in the meanwhile, they would build up, by missionary work, that essential nucleus of administrators, councillors, inquisitors which such a sovereign would need. When the great day came, when the heretical sovereign was to be removed or the orthodox sovereign installed, these men would have their orders. But meanwhile, of course, they must not compromise themselves. The missionaries were to build up, nurture, extend the Fifth Column, but not to use it — at least not yet. As Pope Gregory XIII clearly instructed them, 'in all civil matters they must recognise the Queen of England as their rightful sovereign, respecting her in outward form and speech, *until the Holy See decides otherwise*' (my italics). The ban on disloyal expressions while in England was, as the Jesuit General made clear in his instructions, a matter not of 'piety and virtue' but of 'prudence'.

The policy of the English government, which faced this threat, was equally clear. Queen Elizabeth was a tolerant ruler. She refused 'to make windows into men's souls'. She did not reciprocate the policy which Pope Pius V, that saint of his Church, enjoined upon Catholic sovereigns: 'If your Majesty continues to fight openly and zealously against the enemies of the Church until they are all slaughtered, you may rest assured of divine support.' But she was not prepared to tolerate a reconquest. Therefore, if Catholic priests were to avail themselves of her toleration, they must be genuinely unpolitical. It was not enough to be merely discreet, out of 'prudence', 'until the Holy See decides otherwise'. It was not enough to be merely the naïve instrument of politicians abroad. They must accept the fact of the Reformation and enjoy — unlike the Protestants of Spain or Italy — 'a Mass in a corner'.

Between these two policies the Jesuit missionaries had a thin time of it. Some of them were no doubt genuinely unpolitical. But they were agents of a political programme. Their sending was a political act with a political purpose. It was all very well for Fr. Southwell or Fr. Walpole to talk of loyalty to their 'most beloved Princess'; but both came over during the war, secretly, from enemy country, Walpole personally bidden Godspeed by King Philip himself. Meanwhile their superiors, who sent them, were singing, at a safe distance, a very different tune. Cardinal Allen, the founder of the Mission, was declaring Elizabeth 'a most unjust usurper of all nations, an infamous, depraved, accursed, excommunicate heretic, the very shame of her sex and princely name, the chief spectacle of sin and abomination in this our age, the only poison, calamity and destruction of our noble Church and country', and was urging all Catholics to assist the Spanish troops when they landed. As for Fr. Parsons, the chief manager of the enterprise, whom the missionaries were ordered to obey in all things, he had been demure enough when he was himself a missionary in England, but now, in the years of war, he was sitting in Spain, laboriously proving King Philip to be rightful King of England and lamenting the inability of the Spaniards to make good the claim. And at the summit of the system, the oracle of Rome itself was declaring that anyone who, 'with the pious intention of doing God service,' would undertake 'so glorious a work' as to send that guilty woman, Queen Elizabeth, out of the world, 'not only does not sin but gains merit'. These were the men that sent Campion, Southwell, Gerard, Walpole to England with instructions not to meddle in politics but only to lay the spiritual foundations of conquest. In such circumstances the English government might well find the boundary between religion and politics obscure. Nevertheless, they sought to draw it. Some priests, who seemed politically innocent, they interned or exiled. Those who suffered were the victims not merely of the government but of those who sent them — and, it must be added, of their own almost indecent passion for martyrdom.

Now they are being sent forth again. The aim is a second conquest, the result a second martyrdom. This time it is not Douay but Farm Street which sends them forth, not Spanish politicians but convert-novelists who puff them from behind. The argument is the same: these innocent men, politically so loyal, were destroyed for religion only. The method is the same: the connection between their dove-like innocence and the serpentine subtlety of their managers is obscured. Unfortunately, the result is the same also. The modern reader, like the Elizabethan Council, remains unimpressed. He feels that his tolerance is being abused. The special pleading is too special. The arguments, references, texts, so plausibly exhibited have an unfortunately irreducible smell of fish. Consequently, like our ancestors, we cannot take it. Like them, we put 'the Bloody Question' — whose orders, in politics, do these men take? It is bloody because it is inconveniently clear; and when it only leads to equivocation we do as our ancestors did. They sent the priests to the scaffold, to cold storage, or back to Flanders; we send their biographies to oblivion, the shelf, or back to Boots.

For what is the technique of these new manipulators of devoted lives? The basic principles are simple. First, there is the distorting background. Nowadays, to carry conviction, a historian must document, or appear to document, his formal narrative, but his background, his generalisations, allusions, comparisons remain happily free from this inconvenience. This freedom is very useful: against an imaginary background even correctly stated facts can be wonderfully transformed. If Elizabethan government, for instance, is regularly described as 'totalitarian', if priests are sent to 'concentration-camps', if Catholic plots are darkly compared with the burning of the Reichstag, then an image is created which, though undocumented, dominates the mere detail for which alone the author takes responsibility. Moreover, such a background does not even need imagination. Pedestrian apologists who play for safety can construct it very effectively by mere omission. Just as Fr. Philip Hughes has contrived to write a portentous three-volume history of that 'immensely harmful' movement, the English Reformation, in which the great religious movement for reform of the Church is unobserved and such details as the burning of Cranmer, Latimer and Ridley are never explicitly mentioned, so Fr. Devlin, in his new biography of Robert Southwell,[1] contrives never to make clear the interesting and relevant fact that throughout Southwell's mission England and Spain were at war. This is a remarkable achievement. Needless to say, it greatly helps his argument. The argument, it may be added, can do with such help.

The second principle of this new technique is more positive.

[1] Christopher Devlin, S.J., *The Life of Robert Southwell: Poet and Martyr* (London 1956).

It is the principle of unequal scholarship: the scrupulous straining at small historical gnats which diverts attention from the silent digestion of large and inconvenient camels. How choosily these Jesuit historians nibble when the matter is of no great significance (thus winning tributes to their scholarship from lay reviewers), and yet what enormous gulps they take when no one — they think — is looking! How learnedly Fr. Caraman, for instance, annotates those minor recusant gentry, tracing their manors, their marriages and their movements; and yet, when it comes to a significant point — say, Sir Robert Cecil's attitude to the Spanish claims — he unhesitatingly gives us an answer which, though convenient to him, can be blown sky-high by mere reference to the sources. How learnedly Fr. Devlin refutes his own misquotation from Professor Conyers Read (whose name he regularly mis-spells); and yet, when a document is inconvenient, he summarily declares it first a probable, then, by an inconspicuous transition, a known forgery! Whenever the Jesuits are involved in controversy, their version of the facts, we are told, is 'the only accurate account', 'far closer to the truth' than any other, contemporary or modern. On the Babington Plot, for instance, through whose intricacies Fr. Devlin has led the grateful Fr. Caraman, modern scholars receive 'serious reproach' for accepting 'a whole edifice of lies . . . in violation of the known truth' — i.e. what a Jesuit said was the truth. And then there are those nasty priests who really did wish to separate religion from politics and refused to follow the Jesuit line. They, of course, get short shrift. They were, we are told, 'a small faction among the clergy which was to do incalculable damage to the recusant cause' and whose 'claim to represent the English clergy was fantastic'. A mere whisper is enough to prove them all 'Walsingham's spies'. The 'real recusant spirit' was, of course, that of the Jesuits only.

Was it really? If the Jesuits had succeeded — as they might very easily have done, had the Queen of Scots lived and Elizabeth died — that argument might be advanced, for then at least it could not be disproved. But in fact they failed. They played for high stakes — total reconquest or nothing — and lost, leaving behind them only heroic martyrdoms, bitter quarrels and a bad name for centuries. And yet Catholicism was preserved in England; emancipation, delayed by the recollection of Jesuit claims, was at last achieved; the faith, by then, had dwindled but not died. Who had preserved it? It was the lay-recusants, the despised secular clergy, 'Walsingham's spies'. No doubt they will continue to preserve it; but now, as then, their task is not made easier by these incorrigible manipulators of those poor missionaries.

CHAPTER XVIII

THE JESUITS IN JAPAN

In 1549, when St. Francis Xavier arrived from Goa as the first Christian missionary in Japan, the state of the country was hardly encouraging. There was war of all against all. Aristocratic chieftains fought each other in a bewildering series of combinations through all sixty-six provinces; bellicose Buddhist monks, after ravaging the countryside, retreated to hilarious potations in the heavily fortified 'monastery of the Original Vow'; and the Lord of the Heaven and his courtiers were reduced to supplementing their meagre incomes by selling autographed verses. And then there were the differences of language, customs and ideology between two highly developed, self-satisfied nations. Christianity, being (in theory at least) a religion of humility, seemed at first disgusting to the aristocratic Japanese, who also despised the Portuguese for their lack of self-control and a proper system of ceremonial etiquette; while Portuguese missionaries were inclined to dismiss the grave Buddhist philosophers of 'the Three Treasures' (Buddha, the Law and the Priesthood) as 'a bunch of pederastic hypocrites'. And yet, in spite of these difficulties, within thirty years the Jesuit missionaries had achieved an astonishing success. Patronised by the great war-lords, indispensable in trade and diplomacy, they had extended their influence throughout the country, and confidently promised to redeem, for the Papacy, the loss of England by the conquest of Japan. Within another thirty years those hopes were utterly dashed. Christianity was outlawed, the missionaries were expelled, their converts relapsed or were burnt; and Japan, for two centuries, alone among Oriental kingdoms, successfully resisted the otherwise universal expansion of Europe.

How can we account for this spectacular success, this sudden reversal? Professor Boxer's brilliant study[1] (a work of wonder-

[1] C. F. Boxer, *The Christian Century in Japan* (Berkeley, California 1951).

ful scholarship admirably presented) provides the answer. The Jesuit success was an incident in that other miracle of the sixteenth century, the Portuguese commercial empire in the East; its failure was a consequence of a separate development in the same century: the transformation of Japan from an aristocratic to a feudal state.

The Portuguese empire was indeed a miracle. How was it that the seamen of an underpopulated Atlantic kingdom suddenly, within a few years, appeared in hitherto unknown waters and controlled the commerce of two continents? Partly it was good luck. By a happy chance the Portuguese arrived in Asia to find a vacuum in sea-borne trade. The Chinese fleets, which had once penetrated to Arabia, had now, in the decline of the Ming dynasty, disappeared from the Indian Ocean; the Arab ships could not compete with the great Portuguese vessels — those giant carracks whose sudden arrival so amazed the East. The vast trade of Asia — of which the long-distance trade with Europe was but a fragment — lay open to the first comers. The Portuguese came and took it; and while the vacuum lasted— until Europe overtook them or Asia resisted them — it was their monopoly.

This vacuum, this temporary monopoly, extended also to Japan. In the period of aristocratic anarchy the *Wako*, or Japanese sea-pirates, had so enraged the Ming Emperors that all trade between China and Japan was, by imperial order, forbidden. But the Japanese nobility could not dispense with foreign wares. In their anarchy they still remained aristocrats, with aristocratic tastes: builders of majestic palaces, lavish patrons of the arts, connoisseurs of exquisite tea-kettles, consumers of Chinese silk. Further, for their politics, they needed two other essential imports: weapons for war and, increasingly as their politics became more complex, gold for finance. To them therefore the *Kurofune* or Portuguese 'Great Ship' which sailed annually from Macao, with a cargo worth a million ducats, making a fortune for its captain on every voyage, came, like the annual flooding of the Nile to Egyptian pashas, a blessing from Heaven; and eagerly, as it groped in the stormy China Sea for a safe harbour, they competed to receive it. Did it not bring the firearms of Europe, the gold of Africa, the silks of

China — for which, moreover, they could pay in native silver, marketable throughout the East?

It also brought the Jesuits. Soldiers of Christ, or at least of the Pope, the newest, most militant, most devoted, and yet most flexible of religious orders, founded indeed by a Spanish bigot, but quickly transferred to more skilful Italian management, the observant Jesuits, in every country, studied the rules of politics and deduced the terms of success. In Japan those terms were two: an aristocratic society and the Great Ship; and between these two forces the Jesuits quickly made themselves the essential intermediaries. From the start they recognised their dependence on the Great Ship. 'Your Reverence must understand', wrote the greatest of them, the Italian Alessandro Valignano, to his superior at home, 'that after the grace and favour of God the greatest help that we have hitherto had in securing Christians is that of the Great Ship'; and this truism was infinitely repeated. Able linguists, essential interpreters, obviously respected by the Portuguese captains, the Jesuits seemed to the Japanese an inseparable part and condition of the Great Ship, and many a *daimyo* or lord begged them to settle on his fief, confident that the Great Ship would not be far behind. In this competition it was Omura, Lord of Nagasaki, who triumphed over his rivals. In 1571, to lure the Great Ship annually to his fief he handed over the great natural harbour and fortress of Nagasaki, with all its revenues, in perpetuity to the Jesuits. There was indeed one inconvenient limitation of their sovereignty — Valignano complained that 'since we cannot order people to be killed when we wish, we do not derive so much benefit from it as did its former lord'; and there were some criticisms of such temporal ambition in spiritual men — even the Jesuit General, Aquaviva, had momentary doubts about its propriety. But in the end all was well: after a dose of prayerful meditation, the General swallowed his doubts; the cession was confirmed; and thenceforth the Great Ship came annually to the Jesuit port of Nagasaki.

The Jesuits never lost their connexion with the Great Ship. Indeed — thanks to a contract skilfully negotiated between Fr. Valignano and the Macao capitalists — they increased it: for to finance their activities they themselves invested directly in its profitable cargo. In the Jesuit warehouse in Macao an accomplished priest handled their official quota of silk; they also traded unofficially, on the black market; and they acted (though reluctantly) as bullion-brokers for ambitious Japanese lords. Nevertheless, they did not lose sight of the other condition of success: the condition imposed upon them by the aristocratic character of Japanese society. St. Francis Xavier had preached Christian humility; his successors dropped that inconvenient pose. Prudently disguised as Buddhist priests, attended by deferential negro slaves, they turned the poor from their doors and sought, by their elegant establishment and courtly manners, to please those great lords whom the lower classes (they said) would always obediently imitate. Successive tyrants, who personally conducted Jesuit missionaries over their newly-built palaces and pleasure-gardens, were charmed by the appreciative flattery of these visitors, who seemed not only to direct the treasures of the Great Ship but also to be, like their hosts, the aristocratic leaders of a military society, cultivated, self-controlled, polite. The Jesuits, on their side, returned the compliment, and admitted the Japanese *samurai*, alone among Asiatics, into their Order. They therefore found it very irritating when this carefully cultivated aristocratic monopoly was suddenly threatened by a rival 'Great Ship', bringing rival, and much less aristocratic missionaries. This was the Spanish Manila Galleon which, in the 1590's, began to appear in Japanese waters, bringing with it, from the newly-settled Philippine Islands, an incidental cargo of proletarian Spanish friars.

Loudly the Jesuits protested. Was not Japan within the sphere of Portuguese patronage which King Philip, now King of both Spain and Portugal, had promised to respect? Now these 'idiot friars', only fit to bash down the idols of American savages, were blundering into the formal civilisation of Japan, ruining the delicate diplomacy of the experts, and (what was worse) disgracing Christianity by their attention to the lower classes, by admitting to their hospices 'the poxy rabble', by openly wearing their monastic habits, and by preaching the unedifying doctrine of Christ crucified. Pope and King alike supported the Jesuits; but it was not enough. The friars continued to come; open war broke out between the orders; and from their mutual recriminations new deductions could be drawn by those successive Japanese magnates Nobunaga, Hideyoshi, Ieyasu, who were gradually triumphing over aristocratic anarchy. For why, they asked, were the Christian priests there at all? Was it not as a fifth-column of King Philip, who had already, with their help (as they boasted), conquered almost the whole world? Already a clumsy Portuguese Jesuit had hinted as much. If only Hideyoshi could have done without the Great Ship, he would gladly have dispensed with these dangerous missionaries as his random gestures showed: the expulsion (on paper) of the Jesuits in 1587, the crucifixion, ten years later, of a batch of friars. The Manila Galleon might be welcome as an alternative to the Macao carrack; but it also doubled the danger. Then, at the turn of the century, came other sailors, Dutch and English, denouncing King Philip's plans of world conquest, from which their own countries (they said) had only been saved by the timely expulsion of that sinister Fifth Column, the Jesuit missionaries.

Could the new rulers of Japan do the same? Only if they no longer needed the Great Ship. By the reign of the third great centralising tyrant, Ieyasu, who had totally subjected the aristocracy, that condition was fulfilled. Already the Portuguese monopoly had been broken — for the piracy of the *Wako* had been suppressed, and Japanese vessels, under government charter, were trading direct with China and the South; already in Japan great native capitalists were in control of foreign trade; soon native manufacture would render Japan independent of Chinese silk. Thus the terms of the Jesuit success no longer applied; and Ieyasu, who, like Bismarck, suffered from *le cauchemar des alliances*, decided finally to expel the unpredictable 'Southern Barbarians'. In 1614 he did it, by edict; and since an edict proved insufficient, his successor Iemitsu, a more capricious tyrant, turned to active persecution. So the agents of the new bureaucracy set to work; the misbelievers were hunted out; and the flames of the *auto-da-fe* burnt as merrily in Nagasaki as in Lisbon or Rome. For the aristocratic converts of the Jesuits this was enough. Already a court nobility, they returned with ease to the religion of the court. Only the humble converts of the 'idiot friars', the downtrodden peasantry, to whom Christianity still bore its original social meaning, proved the Jesuits wrong by refusing to follow their masters' apostasy. In 1637 at Shimabara the Christian peasantry broke out in rebellion against their lord and thereby hastened the last stage in the closure of Japan: the final and permanent banning of the Great Ship.

For how, argued Iemitsu, could the doltish peasantry of Kyushu have thus rebelled unless encouraged from Macao? The Great Ship, no longer indispensable to Japan, now seemed a positive menace to it. The Macao capitalists, to whom the Japanese trade remained indispensable, protested their innocence; but in vain. The Portuguese, they were now officially told, were banished for ever from Japan, on pain of death. In despair, the City Fathers decided on a last hopeless embassy. Four of their leading members, with attendant train, set out by sea to plead for their trade. Before embarking, passengers and crew took the sacrament, for they hardly hoped to return alive. In July 1640 they reached Nagasaki, and were at once arrested pending the answer of the Shogun. On August 1 it came: an executioner for every member of the party. In the end thirteen of the native seamen were reprieved, and having witnessed the execution of their sixty-one companions and the burning of their ship, were sent back to Macao, in a crazy vessel, to inform the Portuguese that even if 'King Philip himself, or even the very God of the Christians, or the great Buddha, should disobey this ban, they shall pay for it with their heads'. Thus ended the Macao Great Ship, the mainstay of Japanese Christianity, and with it, for two centuries, European contact with Japan. Only the Manila Galleon continued, during those two centuries, its astonishing annual journeys across the Pacific with its priceless cargoes of silver and silk: but even the Manila Galleon no longer touched Japan. There 'the Christian Century' was over: it was *Sakoku*, the Closed Country.

CHAPTER XIX

FULLER'S 'WORTHIES' AND THE AGE OF ENGLISH CHARITY

Every age has its worthies and by its choice of them shows its own character. Dark Ages have their Lives of the Saints; the nineteenth century had Samuel Smiles; seventeenth-century England had our first English Dictionary of National Biography, Fuller's *Worthies*. It is not an exhilarating work like Aubrey's exquisite *Lives*; it is not a majestic work, like the incomparable portrait-gallery in Clarendon's *History*; it is not even a scholarly work, like Antony Wood's gigantic *Athenæ Oxonienses*; nevertheless, as a record of a great age in our history, it is perhaps better, because it is more representative, than any of these. It represents not a class, nor a court, nor a literary coterie, but the solid substance of English life — the virtues admired, the standards imposed, the examples demanded by that great shapeless dictator to whom its author bowed: the Public.

For Thomas Fuller, unlike his rival biographers, wrote, as he was not ashamed to say, for money: 'to procure some honest profit to myself'. Aubrey who wrote for himself and his friends, might specialise in the elegant, the convivial, the 'ingeniose'; Clarendon, who wrote for posterity, might reveal the dangerous *arcana* of politics; Wood, the cantankerous hermit of Merton College, might laboriously catalogue the clergy, the pedants and the bores. None of these made a penny by his writing. Rather, they courted trouble. Fuller could not afford that: not for him the recriminations, the lawsuits, the public burning that greeted Wood's great work: he must be prolific, readable and conciliatory. In consequence, he prospered. 'No stationer', he boasted in the preface to this, his last work, 'hath ever lost by me'; and if he did not himself live to profit by his *Worthies*, it seems that the stationers, since they have reprinted it[1] are still confident that it will sell.

[1] Thomas Fuller, *The Worthies of England.* Edited by John Freeman (London 1952).

And what, to Fuller and his public, was a Worthy? What, in particular, was a Worthy of what Mr. Betjeman has compendiously and usefully called the Jacobethan Age? There are bishops of course, and statesmen, and Lord Mayors of London, and soldiers, and writers: but these are common to all ages. Two categories seemed to flourish peculiarly in that era: lawyers and 'benefactors of the public'. Of the lawyers little need be said; already they overfill the literature of that time. How could 'Tudor despotism' have been exercised without those indispensable 'civilians', or Stuart Parliaments have resisted them without those indispensable common-lawyers, or Cromwellian gentry and artisans have held together without that indispensable common bugbear, the 'Egyptian caterpillars' of Westminster Hall? But 'benefactors of the public' are less well-known representatives of that age; and since Fuller included them, and carefully classified them, for a particular purpose, and since Mr. Freeman, by his omissions from this new edition, has concealed that purpose, perhaps it is worth dwelling a little upon it.

How much we still hear of the unfortunate social effects of the Reformation — the 'Protestant individualism' which broke up the social solidarity of Merry England, plundered the poor, turned its back on charity, neglected education, and checked the advance of 'true' humanism! The rubbish of Chesterton and Belloc is happily disposed of; but something always sticks. From a worthless article in the *Dublin Review* it crept into R. W. Chambers's *Life of Sir Thomas More*. The article has since been exploded, but the biography still perpetuates its doctrine. It was accepted by A. F. Leach in his first book on English schools; in his last, he emphatically recanted it — but in vain: already it had been absorbed into historical orthodoxy.[1] The idol of Cardinal Gasquet crumbled beneath the scientific punctures of Dr. Coulton — too late, for the good Abbé Constant had already innocently carried a few germinative relics abroad. And how

[1] The article, by J. S. Phillimore, 'The Arrest of Humanism in England', was published in the *Dublin Review* 1913. Chambers seized upon it (*Sir Thomas More*, p. 379) as 'a vital essay, to which every student of More is under a heavy debt'. It was exposed by Professor Douglas Bush in his article 'Tudor Humanism and Henry VIII' (*University of Toronto Quarterly* 1938). Nevertheless, it was revived and made a central argument in Mr. A. C. Southern's *Elizabethan Recusant Prose* (London 1949).

they have germinated! This, with its sister-doctrine that Protestantism is the ideology of capitalism, has proved grist to other than Roman mills. The Marxists have ground tediously away on it; Anglo-Catholics have surreptitiously gleaned up a few morsels; and many a sentimental Fabian history still owes its spurious cottage flavour to the residue.

In fact this false doctrine is not new: it is as old as the time itself, and it was partly to refute it that Fuller compiled his careful lists of public benefactors. In fact, in England as in Roman Catholic countries, the Elizabethan Age was a great age, not only of private wealth, but of private charity. Even the most unscrupulous politicians, even the most rapacious courtiers, paid that tribute to society. Unlike the nineteenth-century millionaires, who regarded their wealth by itself as sufficient proof of their virtue, they felt the need to excuse their sudden fortunes. So there arose colleges, grammar-schools, hospitals, almshouses, to apologise for aristocratic opulence; and the fashion thus set at court was followed competitively in the City and the country, by Lord Mayors and bishops, merchants and gentry. Especially the bishops deserve remembrance, those hard-working, harassed Protestant bishops whom Papists and Puseyites have so long conspired to dishonour. In spite of their families, their compliances, their alleged meanness, all founded something for society: Archbishop Parker a grammar-school at Rochdale, Archbishop Grindal a grammar-school at St. Bees, Archbishop Whitgift a hospital and free school at Croydon, Archbishop Sandys a grammar-school at Hawkshead, Archbishop Hutton a grammar-school in Lancashire, Bishop Pilkington a grammar-school at Rivington — which of their loudly puffed Laudian successors did as much as this? High churchmen have never forgiven Archbishop Abbott for his puritan views, or for keeping Laud so long out of Lambeth: let them look, in Guildford, at his noble hospital, 'the apogee of the architecture of charity,' and then search their own record for a parallel. Well might a contemporary observe that 'hardly any age in former times may compare with this of ours (since this Church was happily purged from Popery) for public expressions of charity'.

Of course this was a provocative statement, and the Belloc of those times, the Jesuit Edward Knott, could hardly let it pass.

Hospitals indeed? he would not even allow them to be named: they were 'a few mean nurseries of idle beggars and debauched people'. This was the phrase which, casually read, outraged that good, worthy, moderate man, Dr. Fuller. Though he would never be able himself to found a hospital, he protested, at least he would commemorate those whose foundations had been thus ignorantly slighted. So, while he travelled round England as a chaplain in the royalist army, he kept his eye specially open for 'benefactors of the public', and, to refute this 'Romish Goliath' who had defied 'our English Israel', deliberately distinguished those — the greater number — who had flourished since the Reformation. On other topics prudence might stay his pen — for 'when men's memories arise it is time for history to go to bed' — but on this he was not afraid to risk a contemporary comment: he would rescue from oblivion not only dead but living founders — Lady Anne Clifford who, during the Civil War, that 'earthquake of ancient hospitals', had founded 'a beautiful hospital, stately built and richly endowed' at Appleby; and Sir Thomas Adams, draper, one of the twelve Lord Mayors who, in 150 years, had come out of Shropshire, founder of a free school in his native town of Wem, who still 'liveth in due honour and esteem, and I hope will live to see many years, seeing there is no better *collyrium* or eye-salve to quicken and continue one's sight, than in his lifetime to behold a building erected for the public profit'.

The refutation is indeed complete: it is surprising that Fr. Knott's sneer was ever thought worth reviving, or cooking up into a social theory; but since it has been so revived, and since Fuller's *Worthies* have now been reprinted (while we still hopefully await Professor Jordan's *History of English Charity*) it may well serve us as a convenient reminder that the Jacobethan age, so far from being an age of selfish individualism and spoliation, was the great age of collectivism, of social construction, of educational and charitable endowment. Of no age are the worthies still so vivid to us. In hundreds of parish churches we still see their marble or alabaster effigies, recumbent or praying, under great canopies, with their quarterings, their pedigrees and their children complacently grouped around them. Enraged High Church incumbents may protest at the sacrilege — as indeed did the good Bishop Hall at the time, who did 'not hold God's house a meet repository for the dead bodies of the greatest saints'; virtuous precisians may protest at hush-money paid to society — as indeed did Dr. Donne when he warned his rich city congregation against seeking to bribe God with a hospital or a fellowship or a pious legacy; but at least, from whatever motive, they all, lawyer or merchant, peer or gentleman, Anglican or Puritan, founded something for that society of which none ever forgot his membership. As for the source of their income, what has that to do with the question? As Fuller himself once wrote, 'should a secret scrutiny be made how all founders of monasteries came by their wealth,' who would escape scatheless? Men get how they can; it is in their spending that they illustrate their philosophy.[1]

[1] The seventeenth century controversy about Protestantism and charity was begun by the Jesuit Edward Knott alias Matthew Wilson in his *Charity Mistaken* . . . 1630. He was answered by the Anglican Christopher Potter, *Want of Charity Justly Charged* . . . 1633, and himself returned to the fray with *Mercy and Truth or Charity Maintained by Catholics*, 1634. Fuller first took up this challenge in his *Church History*, 1655 (ed. J. S. Brewer, 1868, v. 429), and returned to it in his posthumous *Worthies*.

CHAPTER XX

JAMES I AND HIS BISHOPS

The Bishops of any generation, being, as it were, the general staff of the established Church, reflect the nature of the government under which they serve. They reflect it by their own general character: by what they have in common, as a group. Take the Elizabethan bishops, for instance. We all know their character. It is described, vividly as usual, by Mr. A. L. Rowse: 'when one looks at their portraits, high-shouldered with their furred tippets, their puffy, lined faces with their atrabilious, constipated expressions, always grave, often sour, one cannot find them congenial'.[1] The Elizabethan bishops, as a class, were earnest, Protestant-minded, worried men, burdened with duties, uncertain of their position in a society which was both revolutionary and conservative, and labouring under a double disapproval: of the Queen, who disliked their wives, and of the Puritans, who disliked their doctrines. It is difficult not to find them dull, but it is difficult not to sympathise with them. They were unable to preserve the wealth of their sees, for which they have long and unfairly been blamed by high-churchmen; but they defended, almost alone, a vital position in the Church; and when they died they founded, by their wills, grammar-schools and almshouses and charities of every kind which ought to preserve of them a more fragrant memory.

Also we all know the Caroline bishops, the Laudians — at least in the idealised form which their order has acquired from the character and aims of Archbishop Laud and the catastrophe which overtook them all. Severe high-churchmen, rigid disciplinarians, 'arminian' — that is, in some respects, liberal — in doctrine, constant assertors of those two very different policies which, in the reign of Charles I, were accidentally united: clericalism and the royal supremacy. When we look a little below the surface, we find that this general picture needs

[1] A. L. Rowse, *The England of Elizabeth* (1950), p. 415.

serious modification in detail. The bishops could not live up to this severe standard. Nevertheless, so complete was the domination of Archbishop Laud in those years, so well understood was the attitude of the court under a prim, fastidious, clerically-minded monarch, that the ideal remained clear and constant, and the bishops can be judged by the amount of service (or lip-service) that they paid to it. It gives them still their 'character'.

But what of the Jacobean bishops? They are not often considered as a class. Nevertheless, I think it is worth considering them, because the reign of James I was, I believe, of enormous importance in English social and institutional history. It was then that the structure of society was so weakened that Puritanism became the powerful political doctrine of the Opposition, and the belated attempt of Strafford and Laud to reanimate the old structure so disastrously foundered. Moreover, this weakening of the structure was largely the fault of the Crown; and since the Crown appointed the Bishops, the Jacobean bishops both reflect this weakening in themselves and created for their successors the problem which ruined them. It was partly the fault of the Jacobean bishops that the question of episcopacy was so prominent, indeed fundamental, in the struggle between Crown and Parliament.

Perhaps I should amplify this point a little. Some historians suppose that the crisis of the seventeenth century was caused entirely by social and economic changes which no political action could have corrected. According to this view, the Stuart Kings are comparatively guiltless — or at least, James I, who sagaciously drifted along with the inevitable tide, is more guiltless than Charles I, who foolishly resisted it. Now I cannot quite accept this view. It seems to me that the political problem which faced the Stuarts was not at all insoluble: it was probably easier than that which had faced Elizabeth. James I inherited institutions which he could have applied to the solution of that problem. But he did not apply them: he allowed them to decompose; and when Charles I sought to revive them and apply them again, he found that they were either fatally rusted or had been converted to other uses. These institutions were both lay and clerical. They included both the Privy Council in the State and, in the Church, the Bench of Bishops.

For James I, it should be remembered, was a foreigner when he came to England. He was quite unfamiliar with English institutions. Now England, in the sixteenth century, like other European countries, had developed a new form of government: centralised, institutionalised, 'bureaucratic'. That is what 'the new monarchies' meant in practice. But Scotland, from which he came, was one of the few countries where no such change had occurred. There was no 'new monarchy' in Scotland. In Scotland the art of kingship did not mean the art of governing the country through bureaucratic institutions: it meant the art of personal survival: of not being imprisoned, blackmailed, defeated, deposed or murdered (as had happened to most of the Stuart sovereigns) by overmighty subjects. Consequently when James I inherited the English throne, he had no personal experience of the English system of government or of anything like it. His boasted omniscience in the art of government was a positive disadvantage: although in fact he only understood the art of survival, he satisfied himself that he had nothing left to learn.

The political consequences of this fact were, as it seems to me, enormous. Queen Elizabeth, like all her family, had been an excellent judge of men, and she had made the Tudor bureaucracy work by choosing the right men for the jobs and keeping them there. But James I saw in this strange new bureaucracy a means not of government but merely of patronage. He did not choose men for his jobs but bestowed jobs on his men. The whole apparatus of Tudor government became, in his reign, a system of outdoor relief for the courtiers of an ever more extravagant, ever more expensive court. This important fact did not reveal itself at first, for at the beginning of his reign James was dependent on the great Elizabethan officials whom he had inherited and indeed to whom he owed his succession — in particular, on Sir Robert Cecil in the state and Richard Bancroft in the Church. But in 1610 Cecil lost effective power with the King in consequence of his project (which the King rejected) to sell out the feudal dues, and in the same year Archbishop Bancroft died. Thirty years later the disastrous nature of both these events was recognised. Clarendon then singled out the enforcement of the feudal dues as the prime social cause of the

Great Rebellion, and referred back sadly to 'the never enough to be lamented death of Dr. Bancroft'.

Thus in 1610 the real 'Jacobean era' can be said to have begun. As it began late, so it ended late: it was protracted beyond the King's death in 1625, like twilight after sunset, by the survival of his favourite the Duke of Buckingham. It was not till the assassination of the Duke of Buckingham in 1628, followed as it was by the dispersal of Parliament and the new course of 'Thorough', that it can be said to have ended. It is therefore with this period, from 1610 to 1628, that I shall be dealing in this essay.

The new personal policy of this era can be seen at once, in both Church and State. Let us consider the State first. In 1612, when Cecil died, a number of great offices became vacant. Perhaps the most important was the Secretaryship, the linchpin of Tudor government. Ever since Thomas Cromwell's tenure of it, the Secretaryship had been held by one of the ablest politicians of the time: Paget, Burghley, Walsingham, Cecil. But after 1612 this tradition was broken. James I had talent to choose from, but he did not choose it. 'The King in this distraction', wrote a contemporary, 'makes no haste to nominate any, but says he is prettily skilled in the craft himself and till he be thoroughly weary will execute it in person.'[1] Of course he was soon thoroughly weary; but he never returned to the Tudor system. The Stuart secretaries, unlike their Tudor predecessors, were lightweights, barely known to history.

Another great office vacated by the death of Robert Cecil was the Mastership of the Court of Wards. This was an office of the greatest social importance, offering great opportunities and requiring great discretion: the royal revenue and the loyalty of the nobility and gentry alike depended on it. Founded by Thomas Cromwell, it too had always been held by great officers of State: William Paulet, Marquis of Winchester, Lord Burghley, Robert Cecil; but on Cecil's death the Tudor tradition was broken here too. 'For the mastership of the Wards', we are then told by a gossip-writer, 'the King saith he hath groped after one in the dark and will make trial if a meaner man cannot perform

[1] *The Letters of John Chamberlain.* Edited by N. E. McClure (Philadelphia 1939), I, 355.

it as well as a great; and yet he means not to trust him too far, but will make him provisional. . . .' After two such 'meaner men', the same observer wrote, 'if the two late Lord Treasurers could look out of their graves and see these successors in that place, I think they would be out of countenance with themselves and say to the world *quantum mutatus*!'[1]

In everything it was the same. King James regarded positions in Church and State not as offices of trust but as sinecures to be bestowed or perquisites to be sold to the highest bidder. The bureaucracy became a vast system, or market, of patronage; the court became separate from the country; and responsible men, being disgusted, turned to parliamentary opposition in the State and Puritanism in the Church. This patronage, moreover, was not operated by the King himself: it was operated in his name by royal favourites. The private empires which gave such importance to James I's favourites were empires of patronage: the Scottish Earls of Dunbar and Somerset, the English Howards and the Duke of Buckingham were the rulers of gigantic systems of jobbery — sale of offices, sale of benefices, sale of titles; and in this vortex of patronage the real purpose of government was often quite forgotten. Such a system was of course very convenient to those fortunate enough to profit by it. The endless incense-laden clouds of flattery which were offered up to the King and to Buckingham by successful or aspiring courtiers are evidence of that. Well might the most famous and fashionable of his preachers, at the King's funeral, single out, as the principal cause of courtly lamentation, the final atrophy of that once liberal hand, 'that hand that had signed to one of you a patent for title, to another for pension, to another for pardon, to another for dispensation. . . . It was not so hard a hand when we touched it last, nor so cold a hand when we kissed it last. That hand which was wont to wipe all tears from our eyes, doth now but press and squeeze us as so many sponges filled one with one, another with another cause of tears'.[2] 'So many sponges'— the metaphor is peculiarly apt. The court of James I was a court of sponges. There were lay sponges and clerical sponges, and his death did indeed create a great weeping in the sponge-

[1] *Ibid.*, I, 354, 392.
[2] Donne, *Fifty Sermons* (1649), no. XXXIII,

bed. But outside those limits the cry was very different. The cry of growing puritanism was the cry of Jugurtha at republican Rome: Woe to the state where everything is for sale!

Turning from the State to the Church we find exactly the same situation. Archbishop Bancroft was one of the greatest of ecclesiastical administrators, and the work which he carried out in his brief reign at Lambeth has justly been described as 'the reconstruction of the English Church'. He reformed abuses, recovered Church property, restored Church discipline, and published the canons by which the Church of England is still ruled. During Bancroft's lifetime, James I seemed to agree with his policy: at least he agreed with his dictum 'No Bishop, No King'. But when Bancroft died, what did the King do to ensure the continuity of that policy? The answer is instructive. To him the Archbishopric of Canterbury was just another perquisite happily at his disposal, and who should have it but George Abbott, the bereaved chaplain of his late Scottish favourite, the Earl of Dunbar? So Abbott was given the post and told to 'carry his house nobly', i.e. to live splendidly, as befitted a courtier of that opulent, extravagant court. The fact that Abbott's elevation meant a complete reversal of Bancroft's work does not seem to have troubled King James: it was no doubt more important to him that the new archbishop shared his own passion for hunting.

It troubled Bancroft's disciples profoundly. For twenty-two years Abbott reigned at Lambeth and all the devoted work of their master was allowed to slide into ruin. It was not merely that Abbott was somewhat Calvinist in his theology. That was true enough; but so also had Whitgift and many other Elizabethan bishops been, who however had been efficient governors of the Church. The fatal fact was that he was simply indifferent, negligent, secular. In English history he is known for two things only: for keeping Laud out of office for so long, and for his famous hunting accident. This happened in 1621 when the Archbishop, aiming at a stag in Lord Zouche's park at Bramshill, accidentally killed a keeper. It was an accident, of course. The King quickly absolved him: 'an angel', he said, 'might have miscarried in that sort.' But it was not only Puritans who doubted whether angels did or bishops should go hunting and who were shocked to observe that, once pardoned by the King, the Archbishop snapped his fingers at ecclesiastical objections, and showed 'no feeling of so great and heavy a misfortune to fall upon a man of his rank and profession in such a manner'. One other fact about Archbishop Abbott's reign should perhaps be noted. A skilful courtier, he realised that the best way in which the Archbishop of Canterbury could keep in with the Head of the Church was by inserting a personable young man into the royal bedchamber; and it was he who thus introduced George Villiers into that important apartment. His letter of practical advice to his young *protégé* is a model of its type. The rival faction of the Howards of course struck back in kind. They found another young Adonis, washed his face every morning with posset-curds, and thrust him under the King's eye. But the Archbishop was the abler tactician: his candidate romped home, and within ten years George Villiers, Duke of Buckingham, was disposing of every bishopric in England.

'Indifferent, negligent, secular. . . .' This, it must be admitted, could be said of almost all James I's bishops. Take another, the most prominent after Abbott himself: John Williams, bishop of Lincoln. Williams was a political careerist who chose, or rather deviated into, a clerical career merely by accident. A supple Welshman, he observed with a sagacious weather-eye the changing climate at court, and in 1620 he decided finally to invest in the favour of Buckingham. The position is stated with engaging frankness by Williams's chaplain and biographer. 'The King', says Dr. Hacket, 'was the fountain of honour indeed, but there was one pre-eminent pipe through which all graces flowing from him were derived'; and so Williams, in another metaphor, decided that though he had already 'crept far, as I may say, for ground ivy, he must clasp on this tree or none to trail and climb'.[1] Within a year, thanks to Buckingham's support, he had climbed into the deanery of Westminster, the bishopric of Lincoln, and — in secular politics — the Keepership of the Great Seal in succession to Francis Bacon. A few months after netting these great offices, he was writing to Buckingham soliciting the Bishopric of London; and then, when the ink of this letter was scarcely dry, learning of Archbishop

[1] J. Hacket, *Scrinia Reserata* (1693), I, 39–40.

Abbott's hunting accident, he was following it up with another, suggesting that 'a man of blood' could hardly continue as Archbishop of Canterbury and reminding his patron that 'His Majesty hath promised me, upon my relinquishing the Great Seal, or before, one of the best places in this Church'.

Williams did not become Archbishop of Canterbury. Like most of these worldly Jacobean bishops he went, in the reign of Charles I, into eclipse. Deprived of political office, forced to retire to his bishopric, he there conducted a long aristocratic resistance-movement against the new policy of Archbishop Laud; and though defeated, emerged again on Laud's fall to become Archbishop of York. Then, when the whole episcopal order foundered in revolution, he retired to his native Wales, took to the profession of arms, and organised the defence of North Wales for the reception of an army of Irish Catholics. For Williams, patron of puritans and papists as opportunity required, had no real interest in religious positions. His attitude towards the functions of a bishop is illustrated by his suggestion to King James that he provide for his infant grandchildren by making them Bishops of Durham and Winchester. Deputies, he said, could always be found to do the work 'for a laudable allowance', while 'the fruits' sustained the royal infants in the style appropriate to their rank. Altogether Williams (says a modern Welsh historian) would have been more at home 'in a full-bottomed wig among the latitudinarian bishops of the next century than he was among the theological heats of his own'.[1]

Indeed, the more one looks at the Jacobean bishops, the more one is reminded of the Whig bishops of the eighteenth century. And rightly; for their social basis was fundamentally similar. In both cases the royal patronage in the Church was regarded as a mere extension of its secular patronage, and bishops and deans were simply courtiers in clerical clothes. Sometimes they did not bother much about the clerical clothes. Williams, for instance, was painted in cloak and ruff and broad-brimmed hat, like his friend Francis Bacon. Sometimes they were not even in orders. Adam Newton, for instance, Prince Henry's tutor and treasurer, who built the beautiful Charlton Hall in Kent, though never a clergyman, was rewarded with the deanery of Durham; and

[1] A. H. Dodd, *Studies in Stuart Wales* (Cardiff 1952), 98.

after fifteen years as dean, sold the benefice, as if it had been a lay office, in order to buy a baronetcy. Nor did aspirants to clerical office feel that it was necessary to have spiritual qualifications: their begging letters are as shameless as those of any layman begging a sinecure or a pension. They have expensive wives, numerous children, are in debt . . . these are the reasons they advance for preferment in the Church. 'I hear the Bishop of Worcester is very sick,' the Rev. Richard Montagu wrote; 'if my Lord of St. David's might succeed, and I him, I should be half-delivered.' 'My Lord,' the Bishop of Llandaff wrote to Buckingham, 'I am grown an old man, and am like old household-stuff, apt to be broke upon often removing. I desire it therefore but once for all, be it Ely or Bath and Wells, and I will spend the remainder of my days' — not, be it noticed, in performing his episcopal duties, but 'in writing an history of your good deeds to me and others, wherein I may vindicate you from the obloquy of this present wicked age.' In distributing bishoprics, Buckingham was of course no more concerned with their religion than the bishops themselves. His favoured clerical clients did not belong to any doctrinal party. They included such incompatible figures as Laud and Williams, Godfrey Goodman, who was thought to be a secret papist, and the Puritan John Preston, 'the greatest pulpit-monger in England' whom Buckingham at one time nominated as Lord Keeper, and who even proposed the abolition of deans and chapters as 'fat, lazy and unprofitable drones'. To Buckingham, as to the bishops, clerical promotion was not a matter of doctrine but — like lay offices and titles of nobility—very often merely of cash: it was bought and sold.

But let us not be too hard on these Jacobean bishops. If they were really lay courtiers holding clerical sinecures, it is perhaps fairest to judge them without reference to their religion. They were not, as the Elizabethan bishops were, and as bishops perhaps ought always to be, a class apart from the lay governors: no one could describe them as 'puffy', 'atrabilious', 'constipated', 'sour'; they were, like the eighteenth-century bishops, a representative section of the governing class — higher civil servants whose duties sat lightly upon them, worldly, literate clubmen, dabblers in fashionable intrigue, diners-out in fashionable society. Some of them were perhaps too worldly. Bishop Williams, for instance, was generally distrusted as too sharp by half in matters of intrigue; and Bishop Mountain was obviously a *bon-vivant* and a wit, but little else. Milton cited him as the type of the 'swan-eating and Canary-sucking prelate'; and he won promotion to the archbishopric of York by a happy *bon mot.* Consulted by the King as to the most suitable candidate for that post, he had listened for a time in patience while other names were canvassed, but then, unable to contain himself longer, had exclaimed, 'Sir, if you had faith even as a grain of mustard-seed, you would say unto this Mountain, Go and be removed into that See!' But, in general, seen as professional intellectuals and entertainers, as fashionable broadcasters and television performers subsidised by the court, the Jacobean bishops do not make too bad a showing; and this, perhaps, is the rôle in which we should envisage them.

Bishop Williams, for instance, was a great patron. At his parsonage house at Walgrave, where he 'lived like a magnifico', and at his episcopal palace at Buckden — that beautiful red-brick fifteenth-century palace which he rebuilt and enlarged, adding galleries and bowers and raised walks and planting exquisite gardens — he entertained lavishly. 'Nobles and gentry with their retinues called in at that palace in their passage, and found a sumptuous table and a cellar free, if not' (admits his admiring chaplain) 'too open.' They also found the sons of great noblemen serving as pages in an 'academy of good manners', and scholars and poets living there in an academy of learning. The poet William Alabaster was one of them; others included the two most highly reputed English scholars of the day, John Selden and Patrick Young, and the three foreign scholars who had the greatest influence on English educational ideas and inspired the founding of the Royal Society: the Scot John Dury, the German Pole Samuel Hartlib, and the Czech Comenius.[1] In the evenings at Buckden there were musical performances in which the Bishop himself took part: for, being a Welshman, he was fond of singing and had a fine voice. There were also comedies,

[1] For Williams' patronage of Hartlib, Dury and Comenius, see R. F. Young, *Comenius in England* (1932), pp. 25–51; G. H. Turnbull, *Hartlib, Dury and Comenius* (1947); Miss R. H. Syfret, 'The Origins of the Royal Society' in *Notes and Records of the Royal Society*, vol. 5, no. 2.

acted in the great hall by the Bishop's household: profane comedies like the *Midsummer Night's Dream* which, to the scandal of the Puritans, was acted on a Sunday after the Bishop had despatched an ordination. Even in his political eclipse, 'the Bishop of Lincoln', Charles I was told, 'lived in as much pomp and plenty as any cardinal in Rome for diet, music and attendance'.

Other bishops similarly had non-theological intellectual interests. Bishop Thornborough of Worcester, for instance, was an enthusiastic propagandist of Anglo-Scottish union and an enthusiastic amateur mineralogist. He published works on both these subjects and was an active participant in the coal-industry;[1] but his pen did not deviate into religion until his eightieth year. Bishop Goodman of Gloucester was a philosopher of some importance: his controversy with George Hakewill on 'the Decay of Nature' touched one of the central philosophical problems of his century;[2] and his posthumously published book on the Court of King James I is a work of great value to historians, unrivalled in the modernity of its outlook. Because of his religious views, Goodman has had a bad press from high and low churchmen alike; but intellectually he was probably the profoundest of his contemporary bishops.

And then there were the poets. Joseph Hall, Bishop of Exeter, was not, strictly speaking, a Jacobean bishop, for he was advanced to the bishopric of Exeter in the twilight period after James's death, in the last years of the rule of Buckingham; but he was patronised by James I and certainly owed his elevation to Jacobean, not Laudian, influences. Hall's early satires — he claimed to be the 'first English satirist' — were consigned to the bonfire for their 'licentiousness' by the stricter Anglican hierarchy in the reign of Queen Elizabeth and were afterwards castigated, for their style, in the reign of King Charles, by the Puritan Milton. To-day, Hall is chiefly remembered because of his famous defence of limited episcopacy, and the controversy with Milton in which it involved him; but this was a sudden venture of his old age: in his middle years, in the Jacobean days,

[1] See J. U. Nef, *History of the British Coal Industry* (1932), I, 247; II, 213–19, for his patent for refining coal and his projects for regulation of the coal-trade. He later moved on to gold and wrote a book *Λιθοθεωρικός* on the transmutation of metals.

[2] See Victor Harris, *All Coherence Gone* (Chicago 1949).

it was as a poet, an aphorist and a satirist that he was best known. He was 'the English Seneca'; and it was as such, no doubt, that he had received his promotion.

The greatest of all the Jacobean clerical poets was never a bishop: but as a benefice, the Deanery of St. Paul's was hardly less valued than a bishopric; and the career of John Donne perfectly illustrates the attitude of King James to the Church. For Donne had no clerical vocation; he had been brought up as a Roman Catholic; his early poems were far from religious; and his ambitions were entirely secular. Unfortunately, although he succeeded in attracting the royal notice, King James, who saw in him the talents of a fashionable preacher, absolutely insisted that he go into the Church: Mr. Donne, he said, should receive church preferment or none at all. For years Donne held out. He clutched at a patron — Robert Carr, Earl of Somerset — and angled desperately for a diplomatic post. It was only when all his attempts had been rebuffed and his patron disgraced that Donne finally surrendered and took holy orders. Thereupon the stopper was removed from the royal bounty, and Donne's wonderful talents, as a poet, as an orator, as an actor, found a new expression in that fashionable extension of the theatre then in its golden age: the Jacobean pulpit. The career of another distinguished poet was very similar. Throughout the reign of King James, George Herbert sought to realise his talents in diplomacy and at court; it was only on the death of the King that he gave up hope and found that he had another vocation after all.

Another important deanery was the deanery of Windsor. James I's bestowal of this distinguished benefice provided one of the many scandals, or comedies, of his reign. In 1618 he presented it to a suitably learned and literary Italian who had not only written a treatise on optics but had also deserved notice by his spectacular conversion from Popery. This was Marcantonio de Dominis, formerly Archbishop of Spalato. De Dominis had had a violent tiff with Pope Paul V, apparently over money-matters (a subject on which he was always sensitive), and had ended by repudiating his allegiance, publishing ferocious tracts against the Popish Babylon, and bargaining his way to England, where he had a great reception. Unfortunately, after four years as Dean of Windsor, Master of the Savoy and Rector (by his own presentation) of West Ilsley, he found the English climate disagreeable, and observing that the new Pope was an old friend and kinsman of his, he scraped up the profits of his English visit (which were considerable) and bargained his way back to Rome. His hopes, however, were soon dashed. In spite of his bargains and his palinodes (for once safely across the Channel he had published an eloquent tract against the abuses of Anglicanism), he soon found that the Pope could double-cross as well as he. He died in the prison of the Inquisition, which had to be content with burning his dead body and his anti-Roman books. In spite of this last honour, the Church of England does not count him among its martyrs.

Donne, the great convert-dean, was a genius apart: we cannot take him as typical of the higher Jacobean clergy — although we can take James I's attitude towards him as typical of royal policy in church-preferment. Another and far smaller poet who sought to profit by the same policy was Richard Corbett, a *bon vivant* friend of Ben Jonson, who, being conveniently placed in Christ Church, Oxford, pressed himself, by means of flattering verses and convivial habits, upon the notice of aristocratic patrons. In 1620, thanks to that universal patron, the Duke of Buckingham, he became Dean of Christ Church; and in 1628, thanks to the same patron, Bishop of Oxford. As dean and bishop he continued both his convivialities and his poems; and indeed, it must be admitted, he had little other claim to distinction. Nothing that he wrote, in prose or verse, betrayed the slightest interest in religion; even his sermon before King James at Woodstock was only famous because it proved such a fiasco. It was as the poet of his patron and of the taphouse, as 'an high wit and most excellent poet', that his contemporaries knew and admired him. When Corbett was followed by John Donne into a deanery, it was remarked 'that if Ben Jonson might be made Dean of Westminster' — an appointment which the writer perhaps did not think improbable — 'that place, Paul's and Christ Church should be furnished with three very pleasant poetical deans'; and when he died, as Bishop of Norwich, he was lamented as 'the best poet of all the bishops of England'. No doubt he was. Some of his poems have indeed great charm and felicity, and one of them, 'Farewell Rewards and Fairies', is famous; but unlike Donne, Corbett never wrote any 'Divine Poems'. When he wrote about religion it was generally to poke fun at 'the Distracted Puritan' and his brethren, at their foibles and phobias, their consciences and their politics, their hatred of maypoles and stained-glass windows, their fear of Damnation and the Pope, and the Cambridge seminary, 'the pure house of Emmanuel', where they were bred. To Bishop Corbett, Puritanism was a great joke.

Alas, Puritanism was not a joke. It had its excesses, of course; but fundamentally it was the religious and secular outlook of serious-minded men who believed that men had 'a calling from God' and must 'discharge their trust'. It was not only a 'left-wing' movement: there was a Puritanism of the 'right' also, a Puritanism of Archbishop Laud as well as of Oliver Cromwell. As the reign of James I drifted on, and the great racket of the Duke of Buckingham's private empire became ever more scandalous, men found themselves protesting more and more indignantly against the frivolity, the irresponsibility, the extravagance of that gay, heedless court where offices had become sinecures and government had been forgotten. Statesmen demanded that the old Tudor bureaucracy, which had been rotted with patronage, should be cleaned and repaired: there should be working privy councillors, working bishops; such were the views of Strafford and Laud. Radicals demanded that the same bureaucracy, since it had become rotten, should be destroyed: there should be no privy councillors, no bishops — or at least different privy councillors, different bishops; such were the views of Pym and Cromwell. Both parties were serious. Though their political aims differed, they had much in common: much more than they thought. Between them they were to put an end to the Jacobean era, which they both detested with a real, serious, moral detestation.

It was the Puritanism of the right which struck first, and it was one of the Jacobean bishops who led the attack; but it was not one of the bishops whom James I himself had willingly advanced. The King saw well enough that William Laud was very different from those genial, pleasure-loving wits and scholars, boon-companions and hunting-men whom he liked to admit to the fat slumbers of what a contemporary critic called his

'Church dormant'. Laud was too serious, too religious, too dynamic: in short, a trouble-maker; and therefore the King had kept him down, in an Oxford college. But Laud was determined to rise, and he knew the way to rise in that court where, as Bacon wrote, all rising was by a winding stair. Attaching himself to patron after patron, he gradually found his way into the good graces of that universal provider, the Duke of Buckingham, and clung to him with unremitting tenacity, fighting against his fellow-clients (and in particular Williams) with neurotic jealousy. His very dreams were of Williams and Buckingham. 'To-night', he recorded in his diary, 'I dreamed that the D. of B. came into bed with me and was very gracious to me.' Then there was the satisfactory entry: 'The Marquis of Buckingham was pleased to enter upon a near respect to me; the particulars are not for paper.' From then on, as Clarendon wrote, 'he prospered at the rate of his own wishes'; and when his patron was murdered, he emerged into the open as Bishop of London, leader of a party already entrenched in power, determined to resume the work of Cecil in the state, of Bancroft in the Church: the work which, for eighteen years, had been so disastrously suspended.

For the Jacobean bishops that was the end. They were sent packing from court to their dioceses, told to govern their flocks, to husband their estates, to remember their 'trusts'. If they were remiss (as they often were) in these novel duties, they found themselves spied and sneaked upon by Laudian agents. The mineralogical Bishop Thornborough found his inadequacies reported by a succession of Laudian deans; the English Seneca in Exeter found men 'set over me for my espials: my ways were curiously observed and scanned'. Abbott was by-passed at Lambeth; Williams exiled to Buckden; Corbett at Norwich, having now no patron, gave up poetry and contented himself with drinking-bouts in the palace cellar; Goodman, who had so acutely analysed the court of King James, had no opportunity, in the depths of Gloucestershire, to continue his studies into the court of King Charles. And as each old bishop died, his place was taken by a new 'Laudian' bishop, of a very different kind: a Piers, a Wren, a Montague, vigorous administrators of their sees, tenacious stewards of their property, firm asserters of their rights, formidable harriers of Dissent: men with little time or inclination for poetry or satire, court-history, *conversazioni* or the philosopher's stone.

It was no good, or perhaps it was too late. The Laudian attempt to restore a working bureaucracy in the Church and State failed, and the Puritans of the Left, the residuary legatees of the indignation against the Jacobean court, moved to the attack, with their more radical programme. In the Great Rebellion, the agents and the instruments of Tudor government were destroyed. But although it was the Caroline Privy Council and the Laudian bishops who actually crumbled under that attack, it is worth remembering that it was the Jacobean council and the Jacobean bishops who, by their irresponsibility, had first invited it. The moral indignation of Puritanism had not been aroused by the chaste, severe court of Charles I, nor by the disinterested energy of Laud: indeed, when the Puritans were in power, their reign was in many ways similar to the rule of 'Thorough'. The men who gathered in Parliament in 1640, determined to do away with a whole system, were already by that time elderly men who had conserved their indignation since their last assembly in 1629: indignation which the active policy of 'Thorough' had merely held at bay for eleven years, but which had originally been mobilised against the indolent, inactive rule of James I and Buckingham. It is customary to blame the Laudian bishops for the overthrow of episcopacy in England. They have their share of responsibility. But a large share is also due to their predecessors who had so undermined the system that it called for such rigid, desperate defenders: to those worldly, courtly, talented, place-hunting *dilettanti*, the ornamental betrayers of the Church, the Bishops of King James.

CHAPTER XXI

THE JEWISH DISPERSION

Anti-Semitism is as old as the Semites. From Pharaoh to Hitler tyrants have oppressed or expelled that indigestible people; neither Antiochus nor Caligula nor the Inquisitors of Spain could convert them; and even their own God, who had so arbitrarily chosen them, found them (since he had made them in his own image) stiff-necked and unmanageable. No people in the world has had so long and so consistent a history of nonconformity as the Jews, whose first record in mythology is an expulsion from Paradise and whose last record in history has always been an expulsion from somewhere else.[1] In the eleventh century the German crusaders, finding the Turks too distant, turned to slaughter the Jews at home; in the twelfth the Moslem fanatics rose up to expel them, the Almohads from Spain, the Shi'ites from Arabia; in the thirteenth they were sent packing from England; in the fourteenth, the Franciscans in Italy, the Dominicans in Spain incited the mobs against them; in the fifteenth they were driven out of the Peninsula; in the sixteenth the Dominicans roused Germany also against them; in the seventeenth they were massacred in Poland and banished from Vienna; in the eighteenth the edict of expulsion hovered over them in Prague; and if, in the nineteenth, through the Napoleonic whirlwind, they were at last emancipated, how brief that emancipation has been! Experience soon proved the philosophers wrong. Legal emancipation did not make the Jews as other men: they remained indigestible still; and in the twentieth-century whirlwind the rulers of Europe, weary of the attempt to tolerate, have returned to the time-honoured course of oppression.

What is the effect, upon a people's history, of such continual exile and repeated persecution? First, a heightened consciousness, a closer discipline, and, through fear of trespass, a timor-

[1] *Letters from Jews throughout the Ages*. Edited by Franz Kobler (London 1952).

ous, illiberal Church. In the Middle Ages Jewry, like Christendom, was an international organisation, and from the safety of the rich and tolerant Moslem lands its Popes, its *Geonim*, sent out their oracular answers to rabbis vigilantly preserving faith and morals in the precarious ghettos of Europe. Sometimes, in those easier lands, liberalism might prevail. It was in Cairo, the Athens of the Islamic world, that Moses Maimonides, the most famous of all his tribe, the new Aristotelian Moses who 'drew his people out of the waters of error' to the truths of Greek philosophy, compiled his great work, *The Guide of the Perplexed*. But Maimonides, comfortably established as court-physician to the enlightened Sultan Saladin, could afford to be liberal; for the faithful in bigoted Europe it was different. Just as, in the Christian world, the liberalism of Renaissance bishops would founder on the bigotry of proletarian friars, so the rationalism of Maimonides and his disciples was broken by the frightened obscurantism of the European ghetto. 'O lord and master to whom there has been no equal since the days of the Judges, since Jerubbaal and Bedan,' so an alarmist rabbi of Montpellier, a century after Maimonides, addressed a pillar of his church in Barcelona, 'how canst thou look on when the sanctuary is being consumed by rotten books? Gird thy sword around thy loins, lift thy stick and strike at their heads!', and the rabbi of Barcelona, agreeing that his people had become 'infatuated with alien sciences, Sidonian and Moabitish, and pay homage to Greek books', duly and solemnly banned to the young the dangerous study of science and philosophy. It is the voice of the Inquisitor, the monk, the Spanish *cristiano viejo*, raised in protest against the Erasmian enlightenment. And it was raised successfully. Two centuries later, apart from a brief flicker in Italy, the humanism of the European Renaissance scarcely touched the Jews of Europe in their timorous seclusion — for 'why', asked a Polish Jew in the seventeenth century, 'should we nibble at the bones of later authors when we can feast on the meat upon the golden table of the Talmud. . . .?' Their greatest thinker before the Emancipation, Spinoza, was an excommunicate: among his numerous learned correspondents the piety of philosophers has not discovered a single Jew.

Secondly, in the artificially narrowed field to which they were confined, oppression generated a heightened industry, which sometimes made the Jews essential to the governing classes of foreign lands. Joseph, as Pharaoh's factor, managed for him the economy of Egypt; Nehemiah was a favoured courtier of Artaxerxes; and how often, in later centuries, have these examples been followed, at Moslem and Christian courts alike. 'Our King', wrote the great Jewish minister Hasdai ibn Shaprut from the Moorish court of Córdoba, 'has collected very large treasures of silver, gold and precious things such as no king before. His yearly revenue is 100,000 gold pieces, mostly derived from merchants who come hither from various countries and islands; and all their trading is placed under my control.' In medieval England the Jews, hated by the populace, were 'the King's Jews'; and what magnificence did the King of Castile's Jews both earn and exhibit in fifteenth-century Spain! And when they were expelled, behold! still keeping to their national mysteries of commerce and finance, medicine and diplomacy, customs-farming and army-contracting they became the Sultan of Turkey's Jews, organising the resources of a new empire. Even when kings turned against them, noblemen often continued to protect such useful subjects. Just as the Spanish Moriscos, also an indigestible minority, had often been protected against the hatred of the people and their tribunes, the friars, by the nobles of Aragon who profited by their unnatural industry, so, for the same reason, the Jews often found similar patrons. German dukes and bishops protected them from the German crusaders; Protestant grandees in Germany, England and Sweden became known, in the seventeenth century, as philosemites; and in the eighteenth Bohemian noblemen, officials and corporations protested to Maria Theresa that to expel the Jews would be to strike at public and private revenues.

The Empress yielded; hers was an aristocratic society; but except in such happy societies noble patronage alone is a slender support; and when Popes and Kings allied themselves with the blind prejudices of the Church and the mob, such patronage availed the Jews no more than the Moriscos of Spain or the Huguenots of France. Whither then were the persecuted remnant to turn for relief? Whither indeed but to that stock refuge of the oppressed: mysticism, the Messiah, the Millennium. As the defeated humanists of Spain sank into private ecstasies, as the *marabout* on his African dunghill promises a *Mahdi* to the dejected beduin, as the Anabaptists of the seventeenth century manipulated their Scriptural logarithms to hasten the Apocalypse, so also the Jews of the Dispersion deviated into mystical heresies, counted the days to the Millennium, or discovered the Messiah. He appeared to the persecuted Jews of the Yemen in the twelfth century; a Portuguese Jew announced him in Italy in the sixteenth century; and in the middle of the seventeenth, in those propitious days when the English millennarians had already pin-pointed the Second Coming and Manasseh ben Israel was reviving the hopes of his people, there arose in Turkey the most spectacular of all such Messiahs, Sabbataï Zevi of Izmir.

What lunacy overcame the whole Jewish world in the days of Sabbataï's antics! A Polish prostitute, having boasted her reservation for the Messiah, was fetched unseen from Leghorn to be his bride; a high-powered secretariat proclaimed his mission throughout Europe and the East; and prosperous jewellers and grain merchants in Hamburg and Amsterdam giddily declared that Sabbataï Zevi would 'take the royal crown from the Sultan's head and place it on his own'. 'Like a Canaanitish slave', they repeated, 'shall the King of the Turks walk behind him, for to Sabbataï is the power and the glory.' Even the tolerant Sultan found this rather too much. Summoned to the Palace at Constantinople, and offered the choice between Islam and the bowstring, the new Messiah and his wife promptly and prudently chose to survive, and sinking, under the new names of Mehemet Effendi and Fatima Radini, into Moslem obscurity, left their embarrassed disciples to explain away, as best they could, their prophetic miscalculations.

Such was one emotional response to the hostility of the world; but was there no other — nothing more positive than the timorous cohesion and exaggerated industry of tender minorities, nothing more practical than millennarian enthusiasm? There was. Always in the back of the Jewish mind lurked the hope of a new independent state on earth, a new Temple, a new terrestrial Zion. In the tenth century Hasdai ibn Shaprut heard in Córdoba of the Caucasian kingdom of the Khazars, those Tartar converts to Judaism whose reputed survival, in 1942, set to Himmler's extermination-squads in Russia a nice problem of racial casuistry. Delighted, Hasdai saw therein an answer to the ancient taunt that the Jews alone had no kingdom on earth. 'Blessed be the Lord of Israel,' he wrote (if, indeed, his letter is genuine[1]) 'who has not left us without a kinsman as defender nor suffered the tribes of Israel to be without an independent kingdom'; and he asked the King of the Khazars, 'whether there is among you any computation concerning our final redemption'. Centuries later the harassed Jews of Europe listened to tales that the lost ten tribes had been identified in Tartary or America, and when they found in Turkey their great haven from the oppressions of Europe, it was in that hospitable land of freedom and plenty that they saw a new hope of a new Jewish state. 'O Israel, wherefore sleepest thou?' one of the earliest Jewish immigrants to Turkey wrote back to his compatriots in Germany; 'arise, and leave that accursed land for ever!' Within a century the Sultan's great Jewish financier, Joseph Nasi, Duke of Naxos, was planning a Jewish kingdom, under his sceptre, in Cyprus; and his successor, Don Alvaro Mendez, Turkish Duke of Mytilene, was working to found a Jewish state of Tiberias. Thus, after roving over Asia and America, the eyes of exiled Jewry came to rest, at last, on an area from which Christendom had been expelled: its original home.

At the time, such ambitions came to nothing. In the seventeenth century, that century of recession and retreat from the adventures of its predecessor, the Jews were content more modestly to reconstruct their shattered communities; stage by stage they crept back, and again became factors to the rulers of England, Austria, Germany — even (concealed as 'Portuguese') of Spain. Then came the great experiment of Emancipation. But to-day, now that emancipation seems to have failed and Europe reverted to its older practice, while another three centuries have passed without either a Messiah or a Millennium, it is once again to the East, to the relics of the hospitable Turkish Empire, that the Jews have turned, to realise at last the third of their romantic dreams: the terrestrial Zion.

[1] The authenticity of Hasdai ibn Shaprut's correspondence with the King of the Khazars has been disputed; but D. N. Dunlop, in his *History of the Jewish Khazars* (Princeton 1954), concludes that Hasdai's letter is most probably genuine.

CHAPTER XXII

THE SEPHARDIM IN ENGLAND

Three great movements set out, in its golden age, from the Iberian Peninsula. First there were the conquerors, Portuguese and Spanish, who gathered up in turn archipelagos and continents in East and West; then, in their wake, were the missionaries, Dominicans and Jesuits, both Spanish orders, whose sudden empires were scarcely less surprising. Both these were aggressive, radical, crusading movements. The third was not. Timid, unobtrusive, conservative, its history was nevertheless extraordinary: the dispersal of the Peninsular Jews, the Sephardim.

Nowhere had the medieval Jews so prospered as in Spain. There, outside Galicia and Catalonia, all commerce seemed to have gravitated into their hands; they were the intermediaries between Moslem and Christian rulers; physicians, *litterati*, diplomatists, financiers, they formed almost the official class: chancellors and treasurers, sometimes even (if converted) archbishops and Inquisitors of Castilian kings. To Erasmus the whole Peninsula seemed to have become a Jewish colony. Then, in the sixteenth century, all was changed. Already in 1492 professing Jews had been expelled from Spain, and in 1496 from Portugal. The Christian converts — the Marranos — remained, but not for long. With the Inquisition behind, and greater opportunities before, they drifted away. Though many Marranos stayed — and indeed in the next century became once again an economic *élite* in the Peninsula — the most active had gone, to be replaced, for a century, by the Genoese. Most of them went at once to the rudimentary empire of Turkey, crying for their expertise to feed and provision its armies and finance its government. There they settled, in Salonika and Cairo, Aleppo and Alexandria and Istanbul, Smyrna and the Ægean islands, universal providers in the East; thence they emerged as diplomatic envoys of the Sultans of Turkey and Morocco; there the most spectacular of them, Joseph Nasi, Duke of Naxos, became the financier and adviser of the Sultan Selim. Others gathered in old Venice and new Leghorn, the twin mercantile capitals of the Mediterranean; or moved westward to the Canary Islands and Brazil and the Caribbean, to prosper there under more tolerant Spanish and Portuguese governors; and, in the next century, to those new portents of the North, London, Hamburg, and, in particular, Amsterdam.

For a century, with interruptions, there had been Sephardim in England when the law courts, as a by-product of Oliver Cromwell's war with Spain, implicitly repealed the ban of Edward I and a group of rich Jewish merchants suddenly revealed itself in London: Antonio Carvajal, the contractor from the Canary Island who had supplied the Parliamentary armies with corn; Simon de Caceres, a migrant from Amsterdam, who, having interests in Jamaica and Chile, proposed to Cromwell the conquest of both countries; David Dormido, also from Amsterdam, eager to recover his lost interests in Brazil. Within a year these men had a synagogue in Creechurch Lane. Astutely they survived the Restoration. One of them, Augustin Coronel Chacon, proposed to Charles II the Portuguese marriage and (after baptism) was knighted as a reward; others, Alvaro da Costa and the brothers da Silva, handled the bride's huge dowry; and, in Fernando Mendes, Charles II, like Queen Elizabeth before him, had for his court-physician a Portuguese Jew. Protected by the new court the Sephardim flourished. They organised themselves into a community, self-taxed, self-governed, self-disciplined. In 1662 an astonished English visitor was introduced into their synagogue. It was, he declared, 'a strange and barbarous show'; nevertheless, when he thought of

> the Wonders which God wrought for their fathers in Egypt, and who heard the Voice of God speak to them out of the midst of the fire on Sinai . . . I was strangely, uncouthly, unaccustomedly moved and deeply affected; tears stood in my eyes the while, to see those banished Sons of Israel standing in their ancient garb, veiled, but in a strange land, solemnly and carefully looking East toward their own country.

And he noted that whenever the rabbi mentioned the rival tribes of ancient Syria, Edomites or Philistines or such, those rich London goldsmiths, hatted and veiled and glittering with jewels ('for they are the richest jewellers of any') stamped their feet with such tribal passion 'that all the Synagogue sounded'.

Patronised in turn by Cromwell, by the Stuarts, by William III — in whose wake a new colony came over from Amsterdam — the English Sephardim seemed set to prosper; but in fact, in spite of a few great fortunes and famous names, their progress was slow. City rivalry and native prejudice reduced the effect of royal need and court favour, and the growing power of Parliament and City was reflected in the decline of these new 'King's Jews'. The first professing Jew to become a freeman of the City was Samuel da Veiga in 1663; but he had few successors, and after 1738 there was no Jewish freeman for nearly a century. Alvaro da Costa owned land in England under Charles II, but eighty years later Samson Gideon, whose loans had saved Hanoverian rule during the '45, secured a private Act of Parliament before daring to imitate him. The first knighted Jew was Sir Solomon de Medina in the reign of William III; but even Samson Gideon could not aspire to imitate him (though he obtained a baronetcy for his son, a schoolboy at Eton, prudently baptised for that purpose). Not till Sir Moses Montefiore, in the reign of Queen Victoria, was another practising Jew knighted in England, although the Emperor of Austria had given baronies and marquisates to his Sephardi financiers. In 1753, when the Whig government, partly out of gratitude to Samson Gideon, sought to permit the naturalisation of foreign Jews, public pressure forced it to retreat. Jews could not receive commissions in the British forces till 1829 nor sit in Parliament till 1858. It was the first appearance, not the later progress, of the English Sephardim that was spectacular.

Hence throughout their history, so long as they formed an independent community, the English Sephardim retained a conservative character. Excluded from commercial privilege, they concentrated on special trades. Their West Indian and Oriental connexions led them to specialise in sugar and silk; many were jewellers or bullion and bill-brokers — like the Mocatta dynasty, brokers to the Bank of England from its foundation; most of all they were army-contractors. Antonio Carvajal had supplied the army of Oliver Cromwell; William III in Ireland relied on the Amsterdam firm of Machado and Pereira who had already provisioned the Spanish and Dutch armies; Sir Solomon de Medina supplied Marlborough's armies in Flanders and Joseph Cortissos those of Lord Galway in Spain; and Abraham Prado sustained the British armies in the Seven Years' War. Neither in England nor in Holland did the Sephardim contribute significantly to general trade; they were specialists within it, sometimes parasitic upon it: an oligarchy of plutocrats, separated by race and religion from the world in which, by casual favour, they precariously contrived to prosper.

Hence, too, they were a timid conservative oligarchy. Numerically weak, dependent upon favour, above all they feared the disruption of their small society, the withdrawal of their privileges, the invasion of an always hostile world. Extreme conservatism was the philosophy of their ruling Elders, a rigid formalism of doctrine, an absolute fear of adventure. Lest they should be compromised by their members, the Elders exercised over them an intolerable censorship (even a Portuguese dictionary, or an English translation of their liturgy was suppressed); they clung with the conservatism of despair, until the nineteenth century, to an obsolete constitution and the forgotten Portuguese language; they sought to prevent the foundation of new synagogues; they resisted even the movement for Jewish Emancipation; and above all, while they sought by absurd sanctions to prohibit secessions from their faith, they absolutely forbade, under heavy penalties, any attempt to convert others to it. Was not this, they incorrectly repeated, the condition of their privileges? In effect no proselyte was admitted to the Sephardi community till 1877. By that time the community, though it remains a congregation, was, as a historical phenomenon, extinct.

In the seventeenth century the Sephardim had been the aristocrats of the Diaspora; by the nineteenth they were its reactionaries. Their best spirits — David Ricardo, Isaac Disraeli — influenced by English liberalism, had seceded; and their numbers were already swamped by a new immigration, the Ashkenazim, followers of another rite, Jews of Central Europe, claiming to inherit their usages not from the Babylonian Captivity but from the returning followers of Ezra and Nehemiah.

One by one the Sephardi communities were engulfed, or dwindled into obstinate minorities. Perhaps it is a mistake to idealise them. Perhaps they were never aristocrats, merely timorous stockbroking freemasons, tenacious only of economic advantages and meaningless rites. Certainly — though their great age was the age of Newton and Locke — the Sephardim contributed nothing to it comparable with the work of those German Jews who have replaced them — Marx, Freud, Einstein, revealers of new worlds (and new abysses) in human thought. Their greatest figure, their only international genius in that, their golden age, was Spinoza; and him they excommunicated. In the following centuries the sect may have produced many parochial worthies, but it has never contained a great man.

Nevertheless, even in their decline, the English Sephardim remain a colourful minority, retaining their native iridescence even in their last fantastic mutation. For in three centuries their nature as well as their circumstances gradually changed. The first Sephardim, whether they came direct from Lisbon or indirectly from Amsterdam, had been predominantly Portuguese, who had fled to the prosperous North, as they had also fled to prosperous Italy and the colonial Levant, from the declining economy of the Peninsula. By the eighteenth century the opportunities of the Mediterranean were also contracting and on London, as the capital of world commerce, there now converged fugitive Sephardim from mouldering Venice, declining Leghorn, the decaying Ottoman Empire. Peninsular names — Henriques, Andrade, da Costa, Pereira — gave way to Italian — Soncino, D'Israeli, Piperno, Montefiore — and Levantine — Aloof, Abecasis, Bensusan and to the proletarian stream that flowed through the new British port of Gibraltar, birthplace of the most suddenly famous of all British Sephardim, Don Pacifico. So the great figure among the nineteenth-century English Sephardim is no longer a Carvajal or a Samson Gideon (*alias* Abudiente) but that splendid figure, the millionaire Messiah Sir Moses Montefiore from Leghorn; and when Montefiore died, after celebrating, in his private synagogue at Ramsgate, his hundredth birthday, a new portent was already rising among the English Sephardim: the Bombay family of Sassoon.

CHAPTER XXIII

THE JEWS AND MODERN CAPITALISM

An interesting study could be made of the fertilising effect of error in the intellectual world. What a revolution has been caused in historical studies by the enormous errors of those misguided but prolific Germans, Karl Marx, Max Weber, Werner Sombart! The importance of these men is that they obliged scholars to ask new questions: the fact that their own answers were erroneous is a secondary matter. Immediate falsities were soon exposed; ultimately a whole new science was born and more scrupulous thinkers gave exacter answers. Indirectly the new science and the exacter answers owe their existence to the first challenge.

The errors of Werner Sombart were certainly heroic. Himself an economist, not a historian, erudite indeed but careless of evidence, he was suddenly inspired by Max Weber's thesis about the relation of the Protestant ethic to capitalism to offer an alternative answer. Why, in the sixteenth century, had the centre of economic power shifted from Southern to Northern Europe, from the Mediterranean to Antwerp, London, and Amsterdam? The discovery of America and the East Indies is no answer — is Hamburg really nearer to the Far East than Venice? Some other explanation is required. Weber had supplied one ideological explanation: Protestantism had created the capitalism of the North. In search of another, Sombart hovered briefly over a desperately insufficient understanding of history, and then, seeing it, or thinking he saw it, pounced. In 1492 the Jews had been expelled from Spain, in 1495 from Portugal, and later from some Italian cities. Whither had they gone? Some few had gone to Northern Europe. What need of further argument? The thesis is stated: 'modern capitalism is nothing more nor less than an expression of the Jewish spirit'; it only needs to be illustrated. Sombart's book *The Jews and Modern Capitalism*, which appeared in Leipzig in 1911, is the illustration of it, rich, suggestive, intellectually irresponsible, and in its political consequences ultimately disastrous. Himself a Gentile, an admirer of the Jews, he became involuntarily a Founding Father of anti-Semitism.

To maintain his thesis Sombart made a number of suppositions. First, he supposed that the Jewish religion was inherently capitalist (all the 'capitalist' elements which Weber had detected in Puritanism were conveniently found by Sombart to have been borrowed from Judaism). Then he assumed that all medieval commerce in Europe had been in the hands of the Mediterranean Jews. Then he supposed that the economic expansion of Northern Europe followed the sudden arrival of these exiled Mediterranean Jews. Finally, to round off his thesis, he supposed that all the greatest financiers and merchants of these new economic centres were really Jewish. Unfortunately all these suppositions are totally and demonstrably wrong.

Sombart's definition of Judaism as an essentially 'capitalist' religion is as clearly erroneous as Weber's similar definition of Calvinism. Religions in fact have no essential or immutable character: they respond to social circumstances and are subject — although of course the faces of the dogmatists are saved — to radical change. Calvinism may at one time have served the capitalist bourgeoisie of Antwerp; but in the end it proved most appropriate to the backward crofters and fishermen of Scotland and Zeeland. The economic doctrines of Christianity were developed in a period of natural economy, in the Dark Ages; but they were soon adjusted to the needs of a fiscal empire, a commercial society. Similarly Judaism, first formulated among primitive pastoral tribes in landlocked hills, was only afterwards adapted to the cosmopolitan commercial life of a scattered people. This dependent aspect of religion was totally overlooked by Sombart as by Weber: consequently both were obliged to select their evidence. They selected such evidence as seemed to support their theories: they could easily have selected such as would ruin them.

Sombart's evidence that medieval European commerce was controlled by the Jews is just as selective, and the conclusion deduced therefrom consequently just as wrong. 'Already in the Middle Ages', he writes, 'we find that everywhere taxes, saltmines and royal domains were farmed out to the Jews.' To whom did the French and English kings farm out their taxes, their mines, their domains? To the Florentine bankers, the Franzesi, the Scali, the Frescobaldi. To whom did the Pope of Rome farm out his taxes, his alum-mines, his domains? To a succession of great Florentine houses culminating in the Medici, and then to the Fugger of Augsburg. The same can be said of every European prince who needed the help of international finance. In Italy, the centre of medieval capitalism, the Jews played no part at all, and it was Italians, not Jews, who developed capitalism in the rest of medieval Europe. Sombart's ignorance of medieval Italian capitalism is extraordinary. Faced with the inescapable figures of the great Genoese financiers of the sixteenth century, he simply refuses to believe in them. To suppose that members of the old Genoese aristocracy, Grimaldi and Spinola, really indulged in profitable trade is, he declares, self-evidently absurd: clearly it must have been immigrant Spanish Jews who, in the sixteenth century, 'brought new blood into the decrepit economic body of Genoa'. The fact that the Genoese aristocracy, the Grimaldi and Spinola themselves, so far from being a decrepit caste, had been a mercantile oligarchy, governing a great trading empire for continuous centuries, is simply ignored. Indeed, for his medieval assumptions, Sombart consistently ignores not only Italy but all Europe outside Spain and Portugal. There, for special reasons, the Iberian Jews had largely controlled the trade of the Peninsula; but the Iberian Peninsula neither was nor is Europe.

Further, even if capitalism was developed in those Northern cities which received some (and only some) of the exiled Peninsular Jews, did this development in fact follow their arrival? When were the Jews first allowed to resettle in England? Timidly and tentatively they were readmitted by Cromwell in 1655, but it was still many years before they could trade freely or exercise financial power; and the City of London had been a great money market long before Cromwell. As for the specific instances advanced by Sombart, they are totally false. He states that the English Long Parliament was financed by Jews and that it was the Spanish Jew Carvajal who supplied the English Republic with funds. The financial methods of the Long Parliament and of Cromwell are well known: they were excise, land tax, capital sales, and loans from privileged companies and a few great financiers, all known and all English: there is no evidence that Carvajal (an army contractor and luxury merchant) ever lent them a penny. The same can be shown of Antwerp and Amsterdam, the basis of whose prosperity long preceded the arrival of the exiled Jews. In fact it is clear that the Jewish *émigrés* resorted to the Northern capitals not to create prosperity but to participate in it. They did indeed specialise and become rich in certain trades — in bullion, jewellery, luxuries, and army contracts — but even here their greatest contribution was not to the already developed economy of Northern Europe, in which they merely found themselves private corners: it was in the backward Turkish Empire, whither — ignored by Sombart — the majority of them had gone.

Finally, Sombart's use of evidence to prove that every great financier, every great financial discovery, was really Jewish is utterly irresponsible. Essential to his thesis is the Jewish character of the Dutch East India Company. To prove this desperate assumption would seem impossible — but not to Sombart: a glance at the portraits of the early governors is enough to convince him of their Jewish birth. And then there is the great Dutch imperialist, the founder of the company's empire in the East, Jan Pieterszoon Coen. Surely his real name was Cohen, and he a Jew — just as the real name of John Law, the Scottish founder of French banking, was presumably (as surmised by an anti-Semitic writer in the days of the Dreyfus case) Levi? And then there is Columbus — has not he also been claimed as a Jew? Indeed, since his expeditions were financed, in part, by confiscated Jewish goods, the discovery of America was really a Jewish achievement, and 'Columbus and the rest were but managing-directors for Israel'. One might as well say that Nazism was a Jewish movement since it too was financed, in part, from confiscated Jewish property.

What need of further words? Sombart's thesis, as a thesis, is rubbish, and even the incidental truth which it may sometimes contain becomes, by his authority, suspect until tested at the source. Nevertheless, in a preposterous way, the book is a classic, for Sombart stated a problem which others have answered less wildly than he, and are answering still. His claims may be absurd, but at least we cannot deny the economic importance of the Jews — whether of the aristocratic Sephardim, the exiled Peninsular Jews, on whom Sombart based his theory, or of the far different German Jews by whose later activities he so indiscriminately illustrated it; and if we now give less lurid illustrations, less naïve explanations of that fact — explanations drawn not from belief but from environment, from that self-conscious independence of surrounding society which the Jews have shared with other economically successful groups: Syrians in Rome, Armenians in Persia, Parsees in India, Moriscos in Spain, Huguenots in England, Quakers in England and America — at least we owe to Sombart part of the occasion for such an answer; and this, I have suggested, is the function of a classic.

Unfortunately Sombart achieved something else also. When Weber and he advanced their theories, each thought he was claiming a triumph for his chosen class. Was not capitalism itself a triumph, the basis of wealth and liberty and culture? Weber offered to the Protestants, Sombart to the Jews, the splendid boast of its paternity. Alas, our generation has reversed the formula. Capitalism which is indeed the basis of our civilisation, has been identified by resentful ideologues with its incidental abuses and the very word has become almost an insult. Who now wishes to be the father of that child? Instead of gratefully adopting the claim which Weber too generously offered them, Protestants now indignantly deny the charge and impute it, as incorrectly, to the protesting Jesuits. But these are the disputations of schoolmen: in the real world no one has suffered more cruelly from an intended compliment than those whom Sombart thought that he was honouring: the Jews. The clients of Weber have merely been denounced as capitalists and plutocrats; those of Sombart have been massacred.

CHAPTER XXIV

RUBENS IN POLITICS

To-day, in our economically-minded age, secret, unprofessional diplomats tend to be business-men. In the theologically-minded past they were priests. In one age of history they were artists. In the early seventeenth century we often come across painter-diplomats — a Balthasar Gerbier or an Endymion Porter — flitting across frontiers on secret missions. And towering above them all there is always that prince of painters, Peter Paul Rubens, whose tomb in Antwerp commemorates him less as an artist, 'the Apelles of our age', than as the ambassador who made peace, in 1630, between his friends and patrons, the art-loving Kings of England and Spain.

Nor were Charles I and Philip IV the only royal æsthetes in that art-loving age. In Paris the Queen-Mother, Marie des Médicis, intrigued against Richelieu in the auction-rooms as well as in the palace, and Cardinal Mazarin, dying, would sigh not for the past sins of his soul but for the future loss of his picture-gallery. In Munich the Elector Maximilian built up a famous collection of Dürers. In Prague reigned his great rival, the most magnificent and eccentric of collectors, the Emperor Rudolf II. And in the far North there was that fabulous bluestocking, Queen Christina of Sweden, whose armies would soon bring home to Stockholm the rifled treasures of both Munich and Prague.

How furiously these monarchs contended against each other in their cultivated zeal! How lamentably they sacrificed their political duties to their collectors' mania! How scandalously they cannibalised the galleries of their unfortunate brethren! Was the Duke of Buckingham being impeached for his political incompetence? Never mind, wrote Rubens, for 'all the machinations of his enemies have never struck so near his heart as to divert his taste for pictures and *objets d'art*'. Next year the Duke's expedition to the Isle of Rhé foundered dismally, and the clamour against him rose yet higher. Why had he failed? Because, protested the royal banker, the King had suddenly required him to divert all funds to a greater objective: the Duke of Mantua's famous picture-gallery, whose sale (to replenish the ducal circus of Polish and Hungarian dwarfs) sent a thrill of horror through Europe. The citizens of Mantua cried out in protest. Rubens, who had once served in Mantua, exclaimed that the Duke should have died first. But it was no good. Secretly outbidding both the Queen-Mother and the Cardinal of France, Charles I swiped the prize. It was, he thought, his greatest triumph. Twenty years later his rivals had their revenge, in that tragic sale when Cardinal Mazarin, the King of Spain and the Governor of the Netherlands sent their agents to Whitehall 'to get shares in the spoils of a murdered monarch'.

In their love of art the Princes of the Church were not behind the Princes of the World. Defying the iconoclasm of the Reformers, the Catholic Church had resolved that art must be a new weapon of orthodoxy, and as it reimposed its rule over lapsed provinces it demanded for altar and palace new pictures to symbolise its dogmas, its victories and its power. The Jesuits and their great doctor Baronius supplied the subjects; the Inquisition jealously controlled the details; and the faithful, now restored to obedience and *taillables à merci*, paid the price. Buoyant, confident, dynamic, the Church called for an art that would reflect its mood. Nowhere was this more obvious than in the reconquered Southern Netherlands to which Rubens returned from Mantua in 1609. In that year a twelve-year period of peace began in which Church and State could repair the ravages of war. The New Order must advertise. Recovered by Spain, the Southern Netherlands not only enjoyed (for a brief time) the patronage of a resident archducal court: they were also the advance-guard and the shop-window of Catholicism in the infidel North.

Such were the opportunities of Rubens's career. How splendidly he responded to them! 'Each according to his gifts,' he once wrote; 'my talent is such that no undertaking, however vast or various, has ever surpassed my courage.' And so he filled the new or rebuilt churches of Flanders with the triumphs of the Cross, the heroism of the saints, the mysteries of the Faith; at the same time he was court-painter to the King of Spain and the Princes of his far-flung *clientèle* — the Queen-Mother of France, the King of England, 'the Archdukes' in Brussels, the Dukes of Mantua and Neuburg, the Republic of Genoa; and finally, since it was an age in which art and politics could not be separated, he found himself the political agent of that system of states which then seemed so firm but which the genius of Richelieu was soon to shake.

This intermixture of art and politics is admirably illustrated by Rubens's correspondence, now collected, translated and excellently edited by Dr. Magurn.[1] Did Rubens the diplomat go to Madrid to report and be instructed? Then we find him incidentally painting an equestrian portrait of the King and making friends with Velasquez. Did Rubens the painter go to Holland to meet another painter sent by Charles I and the Duke of Buckingham to consult him on art-purchases? Then we find them discussing the possibility of a peace treaty. And when Rubens the ambassador arrives in London, what do we find? His time is spent visiting and marvelling at the unexpected culture of that Northern court, 'so remote from Italian elegance'. King Charles descends upon him, eager to know and honour 'a person of such merit', and in the intervals of negotiations he dashes off a couple of masterpieces and prepares to decorate Inigo Jones's Banqueting House at Whitehall. As for Marie des Médicis, if he supported her politics, how could he do less for so magnificent a patron? She had commissioned for her new Luxembourg Palace a great cycle of his works, while her hated enemy Richelieu had sought to transfer the commission to a politically sounder artist. Connoisseur though he was, the Cardinal was no more able than his contemporaries to sever art from politics.

Was Rubens then simply the propagandist of Spain and the Counter-Reformation? Certainly not. His letters reveal too keen a political intelligence for that. Devout though he was, he could write with real hatred of the Jesuits, 'who breathe out their venomous contagion against all those whose virtues they envy'. Loyal though he was to the court of Spain, he was too much of a

[1] *The Letters of Peter Paul Rubens*. Edited by Ruth Saunders Magurn (Harvard 1955).

cosmopolitan, too much of a Fleming, to agree with it in all things. He distrusted its wooden severity, its lethargy and, above all, its refusal to leave the Netherlands in peace. Why could not the King of Spain abandon his impossible Northern ambitions, so ruinous to loyal Flanders? Why could he not treat with the Dutch 'simply as allies of the King of England, without mention of liberty or any other title odious to His Majesty'? The Archdukes, his patrons, understood the needs of the country they governed. So did Ambrogio Spinola, Marqués de los Balbases, the great Genoese general who fought — and financed — the Spaniards' battles there. It was Spinola and the Archdukes who, in 1609, had obliged Spain to make peace in the Netherlands and had thus opened the golden age of reconstruction for Flanders. It was Spinola and the surviving 'Archduke', the Infanta Isabel, who, after the return of war in 1621, found themselves once again the leaders of the peace party. To Rubens Spinola was 'one of my greatest friends and patrons in the world', second only to the Infanta in his devotion — what a pity he had such poor taste in art, understanding 'no more about it than a street-porter'! Such was the peace-party of which Rubens was a member. It was a cosmopolitan party: the Infanta was a Spaniard; Spinola was an Italian; Rubens a Fleming. They sought peace alike in the interest of Spain, Flanders and Europe.

Unfortunately, the Court of Spain thought otherwise. Olivares and his friends had more glorious ambitions. So had the Court of Rome. They thought of reconquests and crusades: the reconquest of the Northern Netherlands, a crusade against the heretics of both Holland and England. Such schemes filled both Rubens and his patrons with hatred and contempt. Why could not 'these young men who govern the world to-day live in friendship with each other instead of throwing all Christendom into confusion by their whims'? As for the ideologues who preached the crusade against Protestantism, 'they are the scourges of God who carry out his work by such means'. In 1627, when the crusaders got their way, Rubens did not despair. He wrote direct to the enemy, to his former patron, the Duke of Buckingham. The policy of peace, he said, was not merely his own private venture: it was the considered policy of the Infanta and Spinola who, 'notwithstanding the completely adverse results, still persevere in their opinion and do not change their minds at the caprice of fortune'. All depended on them. If only they could prevail against 'the King of Spain and his ministers, who appear to have sunk into a profound lethargy' — 'if only Her Highness, with the help of the Marquis, could govern in her own way, everything would turn out very happily, and we would soon see the greatest changes, not only among us, but everywhere. For to-day the interests of the entire world are closely linked together. Unfortunately countries are governed by men without experience and incapable of following good advice from others'.

Rubens's great opportunity came in 1628 when the Court of Spain agreed at least to make peace with England and he himself was sent as ambassador to London. He hoped that this was the beginning of a general peace; but in fact it soon became clear that Olivares only wished to free himself from one enemy in order to strike harder at the other. Spinola went to Madrid to urge peace in the King's Council; but he urged in vain. Rubens, in London, tried once again to make policy on his own. He paid a secret, unauthorised visit to the Dutch ambassador, Albert Joachimi, and suggested a private peace between their two countries, to 'bring quiet and rest after long war to all the seventeen provinces'. But it was no good. There was but one way to bring peace to the Netherlands, Joachimi answered him, and that was 'by chasing the Spaniards from thence'. It was only when all such plans had failed — when Spinola had died, defeated, in Italy, and Richelieu had raised up a coalition against Spain and driven Marie des Médicis as a refugee to Brussels — that the disillusioned apostle of peace would underwrite the policy of Olivares and urge him, as the chosen instrument of Heaven, to establish the Pax Hispanica by force against the infamous Cardinal 'who, in truth, has always devoted all his industry and power to undermine, insult and abase the monarchy of Spain'.

Thus, if Rubens succeeded as a diplomatist, he failed as a politician. But ultimately he was neither diplomatist nor politician. He was an artist: the greatest, boldest, most variously gifted genius of the late Renaissance. Like Erasmus, like Voltaire, he became the friend and counsellor of kings, but was never corrupted by royal patronage. And so, when he had achieved his London Treaty, he resolved to escape from that 'labyrinth' of diplomacy. The King of Spain, pleased with his success, would have made him a regular ambassador. But the professionals distrusted him as one who 'practised an art and lived by the product of his work', and the Flemish nobility hated him as a mushroom of the court: 'all I have to say', the Duke of Aerschot wrote to him, 'is that I should be glad that in future you should learn how persons in your position should write to those of my rank.' So, as Rubens wrote,

> I decided to force myself to cut this golden knot of ambition in order to recover my liberty. . . . I threw myself at Her Highness' feet and begged, as the sole reward for so many efforts, exemption from further duties. . . . This favour I obtained, with more difficulty than any other she ever granted me. . . . Now for three years, by divine grace, I have found peace of mind, having renounced every sort of employment except my beloved profession.

Thus released, Rubens married again. Pressed to make a court marriage, he refused. He had had enough, he said, of aristocratic insolence, 'and so I chose one who would not blush to see me take my brushes in hand'. His last ten years were filled with prodigious artistic activity. He painted his new wife; he painted his castle of Steen and the Flemish landscape around it. If he thought of the great world in which he had once moved, it was always to remember, in the worst years of the Thirty Years' War, his vainly pursued ideal, the ideal of peace 'not only in Flanders, but also in Germany and throughout Christendom'. At the height of his public career he had painted for Charles I the apotheosis of his father, *Rex Pacificus*. In his years of retirement he painted for the neutral Duke of Tuscany his great canvas *The Horrors of War*.

CHAPTER XXV

GUSTAVUS ADOLPHUS AND THE SWEDISH EMPIRE

In the 1620's Protestant Europe awaited its deliverer. For sixty years Rome and its Habsburg champions had been pressing their counter-attack: revolt had been frustrated in Austria and Bavaria; France, after forty years of civil war, was once again a Catholic monarchy; Poland and the Rhineland and Bohemia had been reconquered; Flanders had submitted again, and finally, to its old masters; and now the imperial armies stood even on the shores of the Baltic. Where was a champion to be found? Queen Elizabeth — at best a reluctant crusader — was dead and her successor had renounced the heroic part of her inheritance; the German princes were weak and cautious, dismayed by the frolics and failure of the 'Winter King'; the King of Denmark, that outrageous royal æsthete Christian IV, was of dubious fidelity to the cause, and when appetite rather than faith had led him into the war, it had led him only to disaster. Desperately, in that messianic age, men sought guidance from the Kabbala and the Apocalypse, from astrologers and witches; and finding, among the portentous lunacies of Paracelsus, a prophecy concerning 'the Lion of the North' who would conquer the Eagle and institute, in time for Christ's Second Coming, a golden era, they turned their gaze upon Sweden. In 1629 Gustavus Adolphus, King of Sweden, made peace in Poland and marched into Germany. In a trice the balance of power was convulsed: from Brandenburg to Alsace, from Mecklenburg to Munich, his seven mercenary armies terrorised Germany; excited Protestants everywhere hailed him as the Messiah; and in Vienna the imperial eagle indeed trembled in its nest. The Lion of the North, the Protestant deliverer had come.

And what was the end of it? Twenty years later, when the long war was at last over, the ideological mirage had evaporated: the ghoulish nightmares of Popish and Protestant blocs seemed in retrospect absurd hallucinations; but the Swedish empire was a reality. On the loot of Germany, on the tribute of the Baltic ports, Queen Christina, the daughter of the Protestant Hero, sustained — until her unfortunate conversion to Popery — her extravagant court, her exciting intellectual patronage, her princely art-collection. For fifty years Sweden was a great, and often a terrible, power. Such was the most obvious consequence of the glorious Protestant crusade.

It was indeed a triumph of war and diplomacy. For the brief Swedish empire, like the larger Spanish and Turkish empires, had little economic power of its own. Armaments were its only industry: it depended on foreign tribute, foreign capitalists, foreign servants. How then did it happen? What native power supported and supplied the genius (or madness) and energy of those incalculable, domineering, unscrupulous, inspired Vasa Kings? How did a power which in 1560 was the Cinderella of the Baltic become, within a century, its undoubted mistress? And why, within another half-century, did that empire so totally collapse? These are questions which Mr. Roberts, in an excellent new work of scholarship, enables us to answer.[1]

Without good administration, declared St. Augustine in his magisterial way, what are empires but great robberies? And they grow, he added, through fear of diminution. The Swedish empire nicely illustrates his apophthegm. In 1560 the collapse of the Teutonic Orders and the decline of the German cities had created, in the Baltic, a vacuum of power and trade tempting to some, dangerous to others of the riverain states. If Russia, suddenly installed in the great market of Novgorod, or Poland, now dominating the rich cornlands of Lithuania, or Denmark, already controlling the entrance and the sea routes of the Baltic, were to gather up that inheritance, what would be the prospect for Sweden, a new power bottled impotently up in a blind alley of that inland sea? To prevent his neighbours from cornering the Muscovy trade, the King of Sweden had therefore pounced upon the free city of Reval. But Reval, to be safe, needed Narva, and Narva Estonia, and Estonia Livonia; and if the Muscovy trade were to avoid Swedish control by leaking out through

[1] Michael Roberts, *Gustavus Adolphus*, vol. I, 1611–1626 (London 1953).

Pernau and Riga, then Pernau and Riga must — in self-defence of course — be occupied too. And soon there would be the threat from the King of Poland, a Catholic Vasa expelled from the Swedish throne and now meditating revenge. To prevent a Danish stranglehold on Baltic trade, or a Polish invasion of Sweden, or Russian support to Poland — was not this a purely defensive policy, even if it entailed a series of aggressive wars against all three powers?

In 1621, Gustavus Adolphus had captured Riga and diverted the tolls of the river Dvina into his absorbent treasury. His neighbours trembled: was he not now seeking for himself *dominium maris Baltici*? Nonsense, retorted the injured innocent: 'if I draw a bucket of water from the Baltic, must I be accused of thirsting after the whole sea?' Eight years later, to defend his Livonian gains, he had acquired the Prussian tolls also, thus increasing his whole revenue of state by 50 per cent, and the modest aphorism about the bucket of water was happily forgotten: 'all the harbours of the Baltic,' wrote his triumphant chancellor, 'from Kalmar to Danzig, throughout Livonia and Prussia, are in His Majesty's hand!' Thereupon the defensive war was carried farther into Germany; and twenty years later, when peace had returned, the same chancellor could be even more triumphant: Sweden could now exploit, he cried, 'all the rivers of the Baltic — the Neva and the Narva, the Dvina and the Oder, the Elbe and the Weser, besides many incomparable fair and rich harbours in the Baltic, the North Sea and the Kattegat'. The looted libraries of Riga and Braunsberg, Würzburg and Mainz, the looted picture-galleries and imperial treasures of Prague might illustrate Swedish victories — they had been looted from Papists; it was the tolls of the Baltic, wrested often from Protestant powers, which financed them.

Conquest may find its motives in fear, its resources in victory; but it also needs the intoxication of a doctrine. Protestantism might serve well enough against a Popish enemy, but what when the victims were themselves Protestant? A robber-state requires a more exclusive ideology, a claim of absolute racial superiority which will justify any aggression. To the subjects of Gustavus Adolphus such a doctrine was fortunately to hand. Incidentally they were indeed Protestants, but fundamentally, they now remembered, they were Goths, authentic scions of those ancient Goths who, descended through Magog from Noah, had once colonised and civilised all Europe; whose hundred kings had all been exactly chronicled by Johannes Magnus; and whose heroic poets could be proved by their works (if these had not unfortunately perished) to have been greater than Homer. To Gustavus, as to Hitler, the conquest of Europe was never aggression; it was the restitution of that cultural hegemony to which the Swedes were, by their history, entitled; and to avoid any misunderstanding on that point he created the post of Antiquary-Royal and instructed his professor of poetry to declaim, among other topics, 'upon the deeds of the old Gothic men'.

And who were the new Gothic men who now, under him, profitably resumed this ancient mission? It must be admitted that their Gothic character was not very obvious. They were aristocrats, often foreign in origin, Italian by education, and Swedish only by accident or adoption. For it was the age of aristocracy, and in Sweden, as in England and Spain, the nobility were challenging once again the strong monarchy which had recently cowed them. The first Vasas, ruling their primitive state through bailiffs and secretaries, had based themselves on peasant support and distrusted and ignored their rural nobility; the usurper Karl, Gustavus's father, finding that they had acquired 'constitutional' views, had oppressed and murdered them; but in the weakness of Gustavus's early years they had returned to power, and had returned the more surely because, in the meantime, they had trained themselves carefully for it. They had educated themselves. They might pay lip-service to runes and rubbish, but they studied seriously abroad, read Machiavelli, wrote to each other in Italian, sought passionately after learning, and competed to serve, and by service to control, the state. Gustavus, the conciliator of the classes, who was also the educator of Sweden, the founder of the *gymnasia*, the refounder of Uppsala University, welcomed such service and paid for it — since their leader was his chancellor and constant adviser — handsomely. So, through grants and privileges and offices and exemptions casually given and systematically taken, the profits of conquest enriched and strengthened not the Gothic King but a cosmopolitan aristocracy, and the new Swedish court-nobility — that is, the French de la Gardies, the Estonian Wrangels, the German Königsmarcks, the Scottish Hamiltons and the Liégeois de Geers — quietly broke the royal monopoly of power and patronage, art and architecture. In that dismal land they built for themselves Mediterranean palaces and pleasure-gardens, Medicean galleries and Burgundian *Wunderkammern*, and they listened, in their cold northern churches, to dull Lutheran sermons inappropriately preached from gilded baroque pulpits, among effigies and crucifixes and the apparatus of idolatry. To the ambassador of the Puritan Republic of England this also was a surprising end to the Protestant crusade: 'None could see a difference', he declared, 'betwixt this and the Papists' churches'.

Thus behind the conquest of empire lay, as always, a social transformation: behind the strange, quixotic, Cromwellian genius of Gustavus the patient administrative industry of his aristocratic chancellor, Axel Oxenstjerna; and when the King had perished on the field of Lützen, and his halo had evaporated, the triumph of his chancellor showed clearly through its dissolving wisps. Sweden had changed its character. While Queen Christina, with princely hand, dissipated the Crown revenues, the Crown lands and ultimately the Crown itself, the government of the country was in other hands. It had become an oligarchy: an oligarchy of great, foreign, pensionary peers.

Unfortunately, in history, one social transformation is seldom enough. An oligarchy made the Roman Empire, but a further revolution was necessary to govern it — to give it that 'good administration' without which it would have remained merely 'a great robbery'. This second revolution the Swedish Empire never fully underwent: whatever its social form at home, abroad it remained a robber-empire, financing itself not by native industry but by tolls and spoil. 'It must make no difference', Gustavus once wrote, 'that the Livonian peasantry complain, for we are less concerned with the welfare of the country than with the provision of our soldiers who by faithful service have helped to conquer it.' The later Vasa despots might recover power from the oligarchy; they might resume Crown lands, recover (with arrears) Crown revenues, reimpose the rule of the Crown; but they could not forget their policy of conquest. And what when conquest failed to sustain itself? Like later Germanic conquerors they were to find that even a combination of an armament industry, an ideology and a formidable army is not quite enough. It once pleased Oxenstjerna to say that it takes very little wisdom to rule the world. His successors were to learn that it takes just a little more than they thought.

CHAPTER XXVI

A CASE OF CO-EXISTENCE: CHRISTENDOM AND THE TURKS

To us the great fact of the fifteenth and sixteenth centuries is the expansion of Europe by the spectacular discovery of new continents; to contemporaries it was its diminution by the spectacular advance of the Turkish Empire. In France, between 1480 and 1609, twice as many books were published upon the Turks as upon America, and the greatest of the observers of Turkey, the Belgian Busbecq, complained that the nations of Christendom were gathering worthless empires at the end of the world while losing the heart of Europe. Throughout the sixteenth century Europeans were alternately fascinated and terrified by the Turks; by their silent, invincible, victorious armies, by their mixture of cruelty and toleration, their system of political slavery and their private moral virtues. Alternately the rulers of Europe preached crusades and practised appeasement of this terrible enemy, whom only his eastern enemies, first Tamerlane, then the Sophy of Persia, seemed to restrain from swallowing up their whole continent: 'When the Turks have settled with Persia', wrote Busbecq,

> they will fly at our throats, supported by the might of the whole East; how unprepared we are, I dare not say . . . Constantinople, once the rival of Rome, is now laid low in wretched slavery. Who can look on without pity, without reflecting on the mutability of human things? Besides who knows whether the same fate may not now be threatening our own land?

For already, when he wrote, the bastions of Eastern Europe had crumbled: Belgrade had fallen by land and Rhodes by sea; the Turkish armies had conquered the plains of Hungary and their fleets dominated the Western Mediterranean from Algiers.

The Europeans had reason to be fascinated by the Turks, for these new conquerors were unlike any others they had known. They were not a nation: they were a host of peoples, an imperial family, and a system. The Sultan's subjects were of diverse conquered races, his invincible Janissaries had all been born Christians, his terrible sea-captains were almost invariably renegades, his technicians, his financiers, his merchants were Christians or Jews. What power had made these men desert their natural traditions and uphold a slave-empire so utterly at variance with European society? For European society was an aristocratic and landed society, a society of hierarchy, heredity and privilege: the Ottoman Empire knew no aristocracy, no class loyalties, no hereditary privilege outside the Sultan's own family, whose privilege was limited to the alternative of the throne or the bowstring. Wherever the Turks imposed direct rule, the old aristocracies were liquidated and a new social system was implanted on their ruin. In Budapest Busbecq saw the splendid palaces of the Hungarian nobles, recently so powerful, all in ruins; in Bulgaria he found descendants of the royal house married to ploughmen and shepherds; in Constantinople he saw members of the imperial families of Palæologus and Cantacuzene reduced to menial trades. These were the few who had survived the general massacres of the nobility, and Busbecq was one of the few who could see them: for in general the Turks, having conquered a country and imposed their social system, protected it by an iron curtain from profane eyes. Were it not for the all-penetrating power of money, he remarked, 'their country would be as inaccessible to foreigners as those lands which are said to be uninhabitable through heat or cold'. On crossing the frontier from Vienna to Budapest he felt as if he was entering another world, so different was it from the old Europe of which so lately it had been a part.

A hideous system, Europeans thought; and yet, since it had been accepted willingly by so many of their former subjects, they were obliged to concede its merits, or their defects. Why, they asked, had it so triumphed? The answer stared them in the face. Europe, in the days of Turkish conquest, had not only been politically divided: it had been full of social unrest. The aristocratic system in Eastern Europe had become intolerable. Landlordism on the continent, colonialism and *monoculture* in the islands, had everywhere bred a mutinous native peasantry ready to welcome the Turk as a deliverer from social bondage. The fifteenth century was an age of peasant revolts, and the feudal oppressions of the Hungarian and Frankish nobles, the Byzantine and Italian 'despots', were no more hateful to their subjects than the mercantile rule of the Venetian aristocracy in Salonika, Eubœa and Cyprus, or of those private capitalist companies — the *Maona* and the Bank of San Giorgio — to which Genoa had surrendered or sold its colonies in Chios, Corsica and the Crimea. The Hungarian chivalry which went down fighting in the valley of the Danube, the Venetian galleys which watched the loss of Greece and its islands, were the forces of an alien oligarchy whose subjects preferred — or thought they preferred — the Turks. Constantinople itself — a medieval Shanghai controlled by Venetian and Genoese concessionaires — hardly resisted its change of masters. Three years after its fall, a German popular play, the *Türkenspiel*, represented the Sultan coming to Nuremberg as the Messiah of the poor peasants. Eighty-five years later Luther, whose great hymn *Ein feste Burg* may well have been written to inspire an imperial crusade against the Turks, nevertheless declared that the German peasantry, crushed by noble landlords, might well prefer Turkish rule to that of such Christian lords.

Thus, for some two centuries, from the disastrous crusade of Nicopolis in 1396 to the peace of 1606, the aristocratic society of Western Europe, like the liberal society of Western Europe to-day, looked with apprehension on the portentous new power in the East: a power of huge military strength which, exploiting every social discontent, had advanced into the heart of Europe, imposed a new social system, and protected it behind an iron curtain: a power, moreover, which, by its very success, fascinated many of those who sought to resist it. Half the contemporary books on Turkey are inspired by admiration as well as by fear and hatred. Even the imperial ambassador could not withhold his respect from the civic virtue, the charitableness, the frugality, the public works and the *carrière ouverte aux talents* which he found in the Ottoman Empire, and grudgingly admitted that slavery, after all, has its social utility. From overpopulated Southern Europe there was a constant stream of emigration to those hospitable lands of opportunity where, it was noted, there were no beggars; and persecuted intellectuals

— Jews of Spain and Germany, Protestants of Italy — fled, or dreamed of fleeing, to that tolerant Empire where religion at least was free. To the rulers of Western Europe all this was an added source of alarm. What were they to do? The answer was given by their traditional oracle, the Pope of Rome: Christians unite! Prepare for a crusade against the ideological enemy, the conquering tyrant!

And what did they do in fact? Alas, as Miss Vaughan's learned and closely packed diplomatic narrative shows,[1] they did no such thing. They quarrelled among themselves, split Christendom in two, mopped up empires overseas, and while all vying with each other in denouncing the infamous Turk, each secretly made, or sought to make, alliances with him against the others. The King of France, by his alliance, obtained profitable concessions for his subjects and, in return, welcomed a Turkish army in France: 'Christian captives were openly sold in Toulon market-place, and while French Protestants were undergoing savage persecution, Turks on French soil turned unmolested to Mecca to pray'. The King of Spain taxed his subjects regularly for the crusade and as regularly pocketed the proceeds. Venice for the sake of old markets, England for new, managed and supplied the infidel. Lutheran Germany, suspicious of all papal crusades, insisted that

> to reform our ways and works
> is the best defence against the Turks.

The Jesuits, having once got a footing in Constantinople for the purpose of missionary work, quickly changed their tune and concentrated on the more congenial task of denouncing Protestant and Greek Christians to the common enemy. As for the Pope himself, when it came to the point he always found himself too poor for any action — perhaps even (like Alexander VI) he was in receipt of a Turkish pension. . . . It was all very unedifying and ought, of course, as Busbecq foresaw, to have led to a Turkish conquest of Europe. In fact it did not. Whereas a crusade might have proved as disastrous as the crusade of Nicopolis, this refusal of a crusade led to a long practical co-existence, until suddenly, in the seventeenth century, it became clear that

[1] Dorothy Vaughan, *Europe and the Turk* (Liverpool 1954).

the danger was past. Europe, in full internecine vigour, then observed the decay of the Turkish empire, and having failed to unite against the tyrant in his prime, soon had to unite to prop him up when he had become 'the sick man of Europe'.

How had it happened? The rise and fall of nations remains a historical mystery which cannot be solved in a paragraph. We know very little of Turkish history, and what we know is almost entirely drawn from the imperfect observation of foreigners: for the Turks themselves have, until recently, been incurious in such matters. As Busbecq wrote, 'they have no idea of chronology and dates and make a wonderful mixture and confusion of all the epochs of history'. Probably the breakdown was institutional: the collapse of that system of privileged slavery which, under able Sultans, had given a formidable but temporary cohesion to an otherwise ramshackle empire. Perhaps it was also economic: the Turkish, like the Roman and the Spanish empires, created no new wealth: it lived parasitically on foreign wealth and faltered when that supply ran out. Possibly a complex 'liberal' society has, after all, greater staying power, because greater resilience, than a 'classless' tyranny. We cannot say. But even so, even if we must leave this deep question open, at least there is one negative conclusion that we can draw from this historical precedent. The theory that the world cannot live 'half slave and half free', that a frontal struggle between opposing systems is sooner or later inevitable and might as well be hastened by an ideological crusade, is simply not true. Europe and the Turk, with their opposing ideologies and opposing social systems, faced each other for centuries. There were diplomatic relations and local struggles, as between Christian powers, but there was no crusade, and when the system which had once seemed so formidable began to disintegrate, it was through inner weakness.

To-day these facts are worth remembering. Our Marxist historians like to compare the opposition between Bolshevism and the West with the struggle between barbarian Christianity and the decadent pagan empire of Rome. They do so because they know that the barbarians prevailed. Professor Toynbee likes to remember the time when Rome and Carthage faced each other in uncompromising frontal struggle

in dubioque fuere utrorum ad regna cadendum
omnibus humanis esset terraque marique

and his disciple, James Burnham, deduces therefrom the necessity of a preventive crusade.[1] This also was Hitler's view, but it did not prove correct. Thus the doctrinaires seek out the parallel that best suits their doctrine. All historical parallels are imperfect and therefore dangerous; but those who use them would do well to remember one which, being inconvenient, they too often forget: the parallel of co-existence, of Europe and the Turk.

[1] Mr. Burnham's Toynbeean premises are set out in his book *The Struggle for the World* (1947), his crusading conclusions in *The Coming Defeat of Communism* (1950).

CHAPTER XXVII

THE COUNTRY-HOUSE RADICALS 1590–1660

For centuries the country houses of England have been regarded as centres of conservatism. By their solidity, their comfort, their former traditions, their present uninhabitability, they remind us regularly of the past, and the past in England has, on the whole, been, or seemed, a good past, at least for those who built such houses, lived in them, and, in every generation until this, signalised their prosperity by improving and enlarging them. It is therefore difficult to envisage a period in which this apparently comfortable and conservative class of Englishmen was in fact, as a class, politically and socially radical. Nevertheless, in English history, the period between 1590 and 1640 was, in my opinion, such a period. It was a period first of gentry mutterings, then of gentry conspiracies — the plot of the Earl of Essex in 1601, the Bye Plot and the Main Plot in 1603, the Gunpowder Plot of 1605 — and finally of gentry revolution — the Puritan 'Great Rebellion' which was launched by the Long Parliament in 1640 and brought first a gentry republic, then a gentry dictatorship: the rule of Oliver Cromwell.

This is not the conventional interpretation of the period. The most advanced historians interpret it differently. But in my opinion they have failed to see the underlying unity because they have over-emphasised superficial distinctions. Particularly they have over-emphasised the religious distinction between Puritanism and Popery. The little rebellions were popish rebellions, the Great Rebellion was a Puritan rebellion. Further, there is a fashionable (but in my view quite erroneous) theory that these religious differences corresponded with differences of social status and philosophy, so that the popish rebellions are assumed to be different in origin and character from the Puritan rebellion. Finally, because of the loudly denounced practice of enclosure, the landed gentry of this period are widely supposed to have been 'rising' at the expense of their peasantry, so that a crisis of their class seems by definition absurd. In fact, of course, enclosure (since it required no capital outlay) can be the resort of the desperate as well as the investment of the prosperous, and this theory of the rise of the gentry class is, in my opinion, an illusion. In my opinion the gentry — using the word in its exact sense, of non-noble landlords living mainly on agricultural rents — were often in economic difficulties; and compared with this uniting factor the divisions between the popish and the Puritan gentry are unimportant.

The difficulties of the provincial gentry are obvious from the large contemporary literature of complaint; nor is the reason far to seek. First, since 1540 the value of money had rapidly declined while customary rents had only slowly risen; secondly, fashions of ever-increasing extravagance were being set by a favoured minority within the class: a minority who had learnt to profit, not to suffer, by the changes of the time, and upon whose example the popular illusion of a general 'rise of the gentry' has been based. And who were these fortunate few? They can be summarised in two words: the Court and the City. Under the Tudors both the Court of Westminster and the City of London had immensely grown — indeed 'Tudor despotism' had been defined as the domination of London over the provinces — and the laments of the provinces, of 'mere country gentry' who resented the invidious ostentation of those old or new neighbours enriched by official fortunes, and of borough merchants from 'decaying' towns like Norwich or Beverley who resented the monopolisation of foreign trade by the City of London, were both loud and long. To see the phenomenon at a glance one only has to look at the great new houses, or the splendid new tombs, which were everywhere being built in this period. They were not being built — as in the eighteenth century — by 'mere' country gentry, rising effortlessly upwards on the rents of improved land. In almost every case in which we can discover the economic basis of such extravagance, it is found to be Court or City money. Take a relatively remote county like Yorkshire. Nostell Priory was built by an official — a President of the Council of the North; Temple Newsam by a City financier; East Riddlesden by a cloth-merchant dependent on the City market. . . . It is the same story everywhere. Among all the great houses of this period I can only think of one — Althorp — which seems to have been built primarily upon the profits of land. In general it was officials and London merchants who were the 'rising' gentry: the 'mere' gentry — i.e. the gentry who relied upon rents alone, or primarily upon rents — were in decline. It was not that they were poor (that is to introduce an anachronistic term): it was that they could not maintain the 'port' to which they felt committed and consequently, in that ostentatious and competitive age, felt unbearably humiliated and eclipsed. 'It is impossible', declared one of them, 'for a mere country gentleman ever to grow rich or raise his house. He must have some other vocation with his inheritance, as to be a courtier, lawyer, merchant or some other vocation. If he hath no other vocation, let him get a ship and judiciously manage her, or buy some auditor's place, or be vice-admiral in his county. By only following the plough he may keep his word and be upright, but will never increase his fortune. Sir John Oglander wrote this with his own blood, June the 25th, 1632.' 'With what comfort can I live', asked another, 'with seven or eight servants in that place and condition where for many years I have spent three or four hundred pounds yearly and maintained a greater charge?'

What was such a 'mere country gentleman' to do? First and most obviously, he would do his best to obtain an office. But offices were few and claimants many, and there were always bound to be a host of disappointed suitors, especially when (as happened throughout Europe in that century) competition drove up the purchase-price of offices and the fortunate possessors sought, and often contrived, to make them hereditary in their families. Failing an office, the 'mere country gentleman' had to resort to some other expedient. He might 'get a ship and judiciously manage her' — i.e. become a privateer; consequently, as this depended on a state of war, the 'mere' gentry featured throughout this period as the party favouring war with Spain. 'Are we poor? Spain is rich; there lie our Indies!' was their cry. Or, if he stayed at home on his estate, the 'mere gentleman' might try desperately to stave off insolvency by raising his rents and enclosing his lands, regardless of those clamours from his tenants which a more comfortable landlord would have heeded. Finally, he might emphatically reject the society into which he could not obtain admittance and, making a virtue of necessity, signalise his rejection by repudiating its religion. Anglicanism, in the reign of Elizabeth, was a new religion: its roots seemed shallow; it had not yet acquired that *mystique* which must be drawn from the catacombs in the days of persecution; and to many of her subjects it seemed merely a state-religion, the religion of the Court. Thus those who repudiated the Court could repudiate its religion as readily as those who were admitted to the Court would assume its religion, and, repudiating it, they looked for a 'purer' faith appropriate to those who had not the wish, or the means, to compete in that fashionable, expensive, superficial world. Some turned to Romanism, revived since 1580 by the Jesuit missionaries: it was in the country houses of the provincial gentry or the unfashionable, uncourtly, impecunious peers that the priest-holes were to be found. Others turned to Puritanism, which was by no means a commercial religion as has so often been stated (although the City of London made an opportunist alliance with it for a brief time) but the religion, in England as in Holland, of the backward impoverished gentry, who despised, partly because they could not afford, the expensive frivolities of the Renaissance court from which they were excluded. Socially, I believe that Romanism and Puritanism were not opposite but to a large extent rival ideologies, appealing to different members of the same class, the declining gentry. The chief difference was that whereas an anti-court family, if it chose Romanism (as was more natural under the Protestant Queen Elizabeth), thereby deprived itself of political opportunities and was reduced to despair and conspiracy, a similar family, if it chose Puritanism (as was natural under the 'romanising' Stuarts), still had access, through Parliament, to political influence and could therefore sustain hope and plan more prudently for change. Thus the period of Romanist Opposition, from 1569 to 1605, is a period of desperate conspiracy while the period of Puritan Opposition, from 1605 to 1640, is a period of skilful political manœuvre. But the social basis of opposition in both periods was the same: the crisis of the gentry.

Such, then, was the social background: how did it reveal itself in political action? At first the political skill of Queen Elizabeth and her ministers controlled the situation. The backward North indeed, for which Tudor centralisation meant an invasion of 'carpet-baggers' from the South, rebelled under Roman Catholic leaders in 1569; but that rebellion — a rebellion against the monopolisation of patronage by the Cecil and Dudley families and their numerous clients — was crushed, and after its suppression the colonisation of the North continued a an increased pace. Then, about 1590, a second outbreak threatened. Not only was the plight of the gentry now worsened by war-taxation and economic slump, but death was beginning to make gaps in the government — the Dudleys were dead, Walsingham was dead, Lord Burghley was verging to the grave, and the Queen herself was old — and rival and younger politicians were ready to speculate upon impending change. This was the situation which the Earl of Essex sought to exploit when he challenged Robert Cecil for Lord Burghley's inheritance and raised against him what one historian has called a 'revolt of the squires'. But Essex was not a sufficient politician to contend with Robert Cecil, and his squires were, in general, too provincial to compose a solid or organised party. They came, once again, from the backward areas, from the North, still mutinous against the 'Cecilian' carpet-baggers, and from Wales, where Essex's own power lay. It was not in these remote areas that effective gentry opposition could be organised — and indeed, after these failures, the gentry of the North and West, who were mainly recusant, became quietist and were largely royalist in the Civil War. With the defeat of Essex and the peaceful accession of James I the centre of gentry radicalism changed; from now on it was not the North or the West, but that other area of chronic social pressure: the Midlands.

Since the middle of the sixteenth century at least, the Midland counties, dependent almost entirely upon agriculture, had been a centre of unrest. There the declining gentry, less qualified than their more maritime brethren to 'get a ship and judiciously manage her', had sought to raise their rents and enclose commons, and had thereby, in that area of conservative open-field farming, provoked peasant discontent; and on the other hand, since the Midlands were near enough to London, there the great *nouveaux riches* of Court and City had regularly established themselves at the expense of the resident gentry. Contemporaries continually referred to this fact. In Northamptonshire, the Dukeries of the Jacobean era, 'most of the ancient gentlemen's houses', wrote Sir Edward Montagu of Boughton, 'are either divided, diminished or decayed. . . . There hath been within these three or four years many good lordships sold within the county, and not a gentleman of the county hath bought any, but strangers, and they no inhabitants'. In Nottinghamshire, too, 'foreigners' — London aldermen and Court grandees — were said to have squeezed out the resident gentry; in Worcestershire there were said to remain 'few gentlemen of antiquity'. Such was the state of the Midland counties when King James I, by increasing yet further the burdens upon the already groaning gentry of England, gave a new stimulus to the organisation of radical conspiracies in both the papist and the Puritan country houses.

For the organisation already existed. The gentry of the Midland counties were politically more alert than the gentry of the North and West, and if we study either the Recusant Underground or the Puritan Underground in the days of Elizabeth, we soon see how closely both were organised around a nexus of Midland country houses. From Warwick Castle and Kenilworth the two Dudley brothers maintained aristocratic control over their Puritan party, whose secret printing-press issued the Marprelate tracts from Fawsley in Northamptonshire, the country house of the Knightley family, themselves for the next sixty years patrons of Puritan gentry-opposition. On the other hand, the Jesuit John Gerard travelling in the same country also 'had so many friends on my route, and so close to one other, that I hardly ever had to put up at a tavern in a journey of 150 miles', and near Henley the Stonors of Stonor Park harboured the only secret papist press outside London. Thus both parties among the radical gentry had already shown themselves capable of organisation when the failure of Essex and the accession of King James, pledged now not to break but to continue the 'Cecilian' monopoly, drove them both alike into action.

How did King James exasperate the English gentry? Almost everything he did was an offence to them. His extravagance necessitated heavier taxes upon them, especially the 'feudal' tax of wardship which was conveniently outside Parliamentary control; his swollen court was maintained by 'purveyance' — that abuse which even under the frugal Queen Elizabeth had only been contained by the skill of the even more frugal Lord Burghley; in his confidence that no bishop meant no king, James I also reversed the policy of his predecessor and defended the property of the Anglican Church against gentry encroachments; and finally, he made peace with Spain and thus ended the opportunities of privateering which for twenty years had provided so useful an outlet for gentry discontent. The early years of King James were the heyday of the Court of Westminster, that vast, extravagant, costly Court to which he welcomed back the peers whom Elizabeth had alienated and invited the Scots peers whom Elizabeth had never known; and they were the heyday of the City of London, thriving as never before in the great boom-time of the Spanish peace; but they were lean days for the 'mere gentry' of England, whom King James never wooed or sought to woo or even bothered to notice, and who paid the cost of Court and City alike and resented alike the immunity of the Anglican Church and the immunity of the Spanish treasure-fleets now sailing safely home.

What were the radical gentry to do? The Puritan gentry, who had Parliament as their engine, could afford to act cautiously. Through Parliament they organised opposition and clamoured for relief: absolute relief through the abolition of the non-parliamentary taxes which they could not control — wardships and purveyance — and relative relief through the shifting of their burdens on to other shoulders. In particular, they sought to transfer the burden to the unrepresented members of their own class, the recusants. In other words, they demanded the enforcement of the recusancy fines; and the recusants, being unrepresented, and therefore unable to resist by constitutional means, panicked and resorted to conspiracy.

Thus began the series of Catholic plots which disturbed the first years of the seventeenth century. In Sherwood Forest in 1603, throughout the Midlands in 1605, the recusant gentry rose hopelessly against the government. Kirby Bellers in Leicestershire, Rushton in Northamptonshire, Hinlip in Worcestershire, Coughton in Warwickshire, Chastleton in Oxfordshire, Gayhurst in Buckinghamshire, Stoke Dry in Rutland — these were the country houses in which the plans first of the Bye Plot, then of the Gunpowder Plot, were laid — for though Guy Fawkes and a few others came from the North, survivors of Essex's party there, the majority of the conspirators came from the Midlands, which were the scene of their intended triumph and actual ruin. And when the conspirators themselves were ruined, what then? The families they had intended but failed to rescue from decay irresistibly declined; some of them sought to stay the process by yet harsher exploitation of their peasantry, and thereby provoked the Midland Peasant Rising of 1607; in the end they surrendered and a new generation of courtiers and citizens moved into their deserted manor-houses: Erasmus de la Fountaine, merchant of London, replaced the Markhams at Kirby Bellers; Brian Ianson, citizen and draper of London, replaced the Catesbies at Ashby St. Ledgers; Walter Jones, clothier of Worcester, replaced the Catesbies at Chastleton; Sir William Cokayne, alderman of London, replaced the Treshams at Rushton. The popish gentry of the Midlands had failed and failed finally; it was left to the Puritan gentry of the Midlands to try again.

They tried, and, unlike the recusants, they succeeded. Unlike the unrepresented papists, the Puritan gentry, whose background and grievances were so similar but whose means and language were so different, could afford to wait. They had Parliament as their instrument, and they waited till, by skilful exploitation of government mistakes, they had found supporters both in Court and City, to weaken the government and finance themselves. They struck, not blindly and desperately like their rivals, but cautiously, constitutionally, politically. When the first blows failed, others were planned; and with the attack on Ship-Money — devised at Fawsley in Northamptonshire, first aimed at Broughton Castle in Oxfordshire, and finally delivered at Great Hampden in Buckinghamshire — they turned the tide in their favour. Ultimately it flowed too fast for their courtly allies, their City financiers; but the exasperated gentry of England would not be halted by Court and City, who were in truth their real enemies. In the end they destroyed both, and set up in England, on their ruins, that brief, disastrous experiment: the republic of the gentry.

A brief, disastrous experiment? Some historians would reject this description. Was not the Puritan Republic a stage in the progress of liberty and democracy, in the emancipation of the *bourgeoisie*, in the development of Parliament, in the adoption of religious toleration? In my opinion it was no such thing. Beginning, so long as it was under the control of dissident but enlightened members of the Court and the City, as a progressive movement, it quickly became, once it had triumphed over its own leaders, a meaningless *jacquerie* of unconstructive radical gentry, who knew well enough what they hated, what they wanted to destroy, but knew no more. Their slogans on the way to power, their fumbling actions while in power, all made that clear. Away with the Court, they cried, with its officials, its lawyers, its pensioners, its privileged monopolists! Away with the peers — they hoped they would 'live to see never a nobleman in England'. Away with the City, the merchants who penetrated to their counties and drove them from their estates: 'this nation', they complained, 'was falling into the rickets, the head bigger than the body'. Away with feudal taxes, wardships and purveyance! Away with the Anglican Church, the Court Church, that sought to recover from them those lands and tithes with which they had refreshed themselves since the Dissolution of the Monasteries. Away with the Spanish Peace, King James's Peace, which had put an end to the glorious days of privateering, the days of 'Queen Elizabeth of glorious memory', when a country-gentleman, in default of office, could 'get a ship and judiciously manage her. . . .' All these things, in their radical mood, they attacked and destroyed. They abolished the Monarchy and the House of Lords, purged the City, sold up the Church, and broke the peace with Spain; but when it came to construction, what did they do, where did they aim? Their own leader, Oliver Cromwell, himself a declining gentleman, adequately expressed their philosophy when he answered that question with the enigmatic but in his own case true words, 'None climbs so high as he who knows not whither he is going.'

So the experiment failed. All that the radical gentry of England gained by their revolution was, in the end, another court

— the court of Cromwell, that fastuous expensive court which made even the court of King James seem cheap and cheeseparing — with its inevitable complement of other office-holders, other great financiers, heavier taxes. In 1660 an exhausted country welcomed back the old royal line. Just as the radical popish gentry, after their vain risings in 1603–5, had relapsed into popish quietism and become the most devoted royalists, so many of the radical Puritan gentry, after their failure to establish a republican government, relapsed into Protestant quietism. They became the royalist Anglican 'young squires' of the Convention and Cavalier Parliaments, the squires of the October Club, the high-flying non-resisting Tories. It is from then, and then only, that the country houses of England have been, as they have seldom ceased to be, conservative.

CHAPTER XXVIII

THE OUTBREAK OF THE GREAT REBELLION

Every great revolution has both its profound social content and its immediate political cause. Some revolutions lack the former, but these are not great revolutions: they are palace revolutions, which may nevertheless, like the Glorious Revolution of 1688, be surgical and salutary. Sometimes the latter element is lacking: then we have a 'revolutionary situation' but not revolution, as in England in the 1840's; for in the unbroken political crust the smouldering subterranean embers find no vent. But in 1640 both elements were present in fatal combination and then England experienced its only great revolution: those twenty years of war and anarchy which Clarendon happily named the Great Rebellion.

How did it break out? Miss Wedgwood, narrating the events with faultless scholarship and graceful style,[1] does not admit any profound problem. 'I have not attempted', she says,

> to examine underlying causes, but rather to give full importance to the admitted motives and the illusions of the men of the seventeenth century . . . the behaviour of men as individuals is more interesting to me than their behaviour as groups or classes.

But is it true that the men of the seventeenth century declined to admit underlying causes? And was the revolution made only by those public men whose behaviour as individuals can be studied? I think not. The controversy about its profound causes is as old as the Revolution itself. James Harrington, long before Professor Tawney, sought its origin in the days of the Tudors, and his contemporary Clarendon, by implication, answered him, declaring that 'I am not so sharp-sighted as those who have discovered this rebellion contriving from, if not before, the death

[1] C. V. Wedgwood, *The King's Peace*, 1637–41 (London 1954).

of Queen Elizabeth'. And between the great theorist and the great statesman, thousands of lesser men, whose participation in the struggle made it revolutionary, admitted their motives. It was not because they disapproved of 'unconstitutional' taxes or the imposition of the Prayer Book in Scotland that men who were neither taxpayers nor Scots first protested, then rebelled, against both government and society. They had — and avowed — other, social reasons for their discontent.

To isolate particular social causes is always speculative, but in the Great Rebellion one grievance soon became pre-eminent: the state of the law. To the ruling classes the Common Law, the guarantee of property, was as respectable as the Bank to-day: it was, said its greatest and most prosperous exponent, Sir Edward Coke, 'divinely cast into the hearts of men and built upon the irremovable rock of reason'. But when the thin crust of the ruling class was broken and other voices were heard — the voices of poor gentry, of younger brothers, of peasants and artisans, 'the people of England' who bore and resented the burden of that top-heavy courtly society — what an outcry arose against 'the corruption and deficiency of the laws of England' and those 'insatiable cannibals' the common lawyers! 'Reformation of law and clergy' was the slogan which united all the Independents, radical and conservative alike; after the Battle of Dunbar, Colonel Pride hoped to hang up the lawyers' red gowns with the captured Scots colours as spoils of war in Westminster Hall; and to reform 'wicked and abominable laws' was one of Cromwell's most constant ambitions, for 'the law, as it is now constituted', he said, 'serves only to maintain the lawyers, and encourage the rich to oppress the poor'. Such was the real feeling of hitherto inarticulate classes about the laws of England, whose voice, however, and whose 'admitted motives', Miss Wedgwood does not hear — or how could she assure us that the law in England was regarded with 'affection' and say that 'there is little evidence at this epoch in England of any real fear of the law . . . the law remained popular and serviceable in spite of all'?

Such social grievances made up the tinder of rebellion, and rebellion itself sometimes made them more inflammable; but mere tinder, however combustible, cannot cause a conflagration and in other countries similar matter lay often, and long, unlit. The economic depression was a European phenomenon. Fiscality, sale of offices, and the straits of the gentry exercised Cardinal Richelieu in France. The expensive racket of the Court, the growth of entails, the plight of younger brothers, were deplored as vocally in Spain as in England. And yet in France and Spain there was no such revolution because the tinder there lacked the essential spark. In England there was a spark: the spark created by the violent political friction between the two parties into which, in the 1630's, the ruling class found itself split.

This political cause of the Rebellion is Miss Wedgwood's real subject. In this she is on the side of Clarendon as against Harrington. And yet whereas even Clarendon, if he would not look back as far as Queen Elizabeth, at least went back to the 1620's to explain the Rebellion, Miss Wedgwood begins her narrative in 1637, when the parties were already organised for action and their deeper motives buried in the past. This, I think is unfortunate. For in 1637 'the grand contrivers' of the rebellion, as Clarendon called them, were already elder statesmen, and if we are to do justice to their motives and understand the intensity of their feelings, we must know the circumstances and experiences which had formed and still fed them. And in fact the more we study them, the more we are led back, with Clarendon, to the 1620's, to the reign of the Duke of Buckingham. It was then that the extravagant rackets of the Court had most affronted the country, then that so many of the outrages afterwards listed in the Grand Remonstrance had been perpetrated, then that parliamentary privileges had been most forcibly asserted and most violently broken and members of Parliament illegally imprisoned, even to death. The elaborate precautions and sometimes sharp practices of Pym and his allies in 1640–2 are not fully intelligible unless we remember the fear behind them: a fear neither hypothetical nor unreasonable, for it was based on a bitter recollection of past treatment. The parliamentary leaders of 1640 had been the parliamentary martyrs of 1629: most of them had suffered then in one way or other. For eleven years thereafter they had organised themselves for revenge — in country houses, in Puritan societies, in trading companies, in legal actions; and now, having learnt by experience the character of their enemies and recovered the initiative against them, they were determined, this time, not to fail.

And who were their enemies under the Crown? First there was Archbishop Laud, 'that little active wheel that set all the rest on motion', 'the centre from whence our miseries do flow'. But Laud was now an old and broken man, a bureaucrat without a party, deserted by all the sorry creatures he had vainly raised up. Once in prison he was no danger and could be ignored. Far different was Strafford, 'Black Tom Tyrant', whom the Opposition hated the more as an ally who had deserted them. Strafford is still Miss Wedgwood's hero; and, indeed, the tragedy of his power, his mission and his betrayal must always give him something of heroic stature. Moreover, unlike Laud, he has a romantic appeal: commanding, fearless, and with the gift of style. The doctrines of absolutism acquired, in his mouth, a warmth and majesty which Laud, the 'little meddling hocus-pocus', could never give them. 'The authority of a King', he once wrote, 'is the keystone which closeth up the arch of order and government, which, once shaken, all the frame falls together in a confused heap of foundation and battlement'; that authority, he thought, the Puritans 'would have circumscribed and brought under the government of their narrow and shrivelled-up hearts'; and when he set out, in the crisis of his own and his master's fortune, 'with more danger beset, I believe, than ever man went out of Yorkshire, yet', he wrote, 'my heart is good and I find nothing cold within me'.

Nevertheless it is, I believe, a mistake to idealise this romantic but primitive figure. With his rough methods, his contempt for legitimate interests, and that unscrupulousness which idealists so easily excuse in themselves, Strafford was a disaster in the mature politics of England. He offered to conquer Scotland with an army of Irish barbarians and to impose upon it an English governor; to cow the City of London by hanging a few aldermen; and to subject England with the help of Spanish money — for with 'the debts of the Crown taken off', he once told Charles I, 'you may govern as you please'. No wonder he was universally distrusted by those who wished to defend English institutions against an erratic and arbitrary authority.

No wonder, in 1641, they felt safe only through his death. They knew their King too well. They knew he would play for time and then, by hook or crook, at a favourable moment, dissolve the Parliament and bring Strafford, if he were alive, back to power; and then Pym, Hampden and the rest, like Eliot in 1629, would be sent to the Tower to die. The execution of Strafford was judicial murder, but what of the death of Eliot? Pym and his friends, whose political life went back to the outset of the reign, remembered Eliot; Miss Wedgwood, going back only to 1637, does not.

This shortness of memory, and this idealisation of Strafford, seem to me to harm Miss Wedgwood's history. They take the genuine passion out of it. Eager to do justice to all, to put the best construction on their acts, she fails to recreate the long tension, the accumulated history of personal oppressions, suspicions and betrayals, the inveterate determination of those now experienced men to bring their frivolous and shifty King, at whatever cost and by whatever methods, back again into the ancient ways. Instead of this, Miss Wedgwood sometimes seems to describe only unfortunate mutual misunderstandings in the polite society which Sir Antony Van Dyck painted and Sir John Suckling sang, with an undertone of less dignified clerical bickering below the shapely Jacobean salt-cellar. This seems to me to do justice to the honesty of men's intentions, but perhaps not to the seriousness of their problem.

For the political problem which faced the Puritans in 1640 was indeed serious, and they faced it seriously. Indeed, they nearly solved it. Had the Earl of Bedford's settlement, in 1641, been acceptable, England would perhaps have escaped those twenty years of 'blood and confusion'. Unfortunately, as it turned out, 1641 was already too late. After sixteen years in the wilderness the 'grand contrivers' were at last in power, and then, before they could complete their work, Death took them, one by one. In that very year the greatest of them, Pym's patron and master, the Earl of Bedford, died. Two years later Pym and Hampden followed him. Meanwhile, the irresponsible King lived on. With those deaths, and that continued life, the problem darkened, the solution receded. Bloody and untidy in its course, futile and desperate in its aims, the Great Rebellion drifted on, and Strafford was proved right in his formula: the crumbling royal authority did indeed bring down with it 'a confused heap of foundation and battlement', and the high-piled social tinder was set alight. But in the application of his formula Strafford was wrong. It was not the 'narrow and shrivelled-up' Puritan limitation of that authority but the irresponsible royal exercise of it which caused the convulsion. In this respect at least the accidents of personal history were more important than either social tinder or political spark.

CHAPTER XXIX

THE SOCIAL CAUSES OF THE GREAT REBELLION

The social interpretation of the Great Rebellion, or Puritan Revolution of 1640–60, is one of the most controversial subjects among English historians to-day. Not only conflicting, but entirely opposite and incompatible, views are held about it. But before considering these views, let me remind readers briefly of the course of events to which they apply.

The Great Rebellion began in 1640 with the summoning of the Long Parliament which, having forced Charles I to end his period of 'personal rule', and having removed the ministers who had governed in his name, enacted a series of constitutional reforms. Unfortunately, the Parliament had just grounds for distrusting the King's good faith, and this distrust, combined with certain political accidents, led, in 1642, to Civil War. In order to win this war the Parliament was obliged, in 1645, to create a new army, and this new army soon became the instrument of a new party in the country. This new party, the party of the Independents, soon showed itself as a revolutionary party which made all previous politics obsolete: it overpowered the Parliament, executed the King, destroyed the monarchy, and set up, under Oliver Cromwell, a military régime which did not founder until after his death.

Now in the social interpretation of these events the crucial question is, who were these Independents? What social forces did they represent? What did they seek to do? What did they succeed in doing? And this is the question which has elicited the most various answers.

The classic answer, which has been underwritten by some of the most distinguished historians and promptly accepted as the orthodoxy of the Schools, is that of the doyen of English social and economic history, Professor R. H. Tawney. This view rests on three major premises. First, Tawney accepts, at least in some sense, the view of Max Weber that Puritanism was the ideology of capitalism, that 'capitalism was the social counterpart of Calvinist theology'. Secondly, he supposes that the period from 1540–1640 was a period, in England, of continuous economic advance by the 'capitalist' and Puritan classes, who, with increasing prosperity, became increasingly resentful of the paternal restrictions imposed by the state. Thirdly, he supposes that the gentry was a force on the side of capitalism. The gentry, he argues, by introducing capitalist principles of land-management, became a rural branch of the bourgeoisie, a continuously 'rising' class, unlike the aristocracy, who, being committed to obsolete methods, were rapidly declining into debt and ruin. On the basis of these premises, Tawney interprets the Great Rebellion as the last, violent episode of the victory of the prosperous, self-confident, impatient bourgeoisie over the old order, impoverished, anachronistic, but tenacious. According to this view, the crown and the aristocracy were a debtor class, the merchants and gentry a creditor class; and the Great Rebellion was a kind of forcible foreclosure of impatient *nouveau-riche* creditors on evasive aristocratic debtors: 'It was discovered, not for the last time, that as a method of foreclosure war was cheaper than litigation'.[1]

Now this view, which of course I have greatly (but, I think, not unfairly) simplified, has recommended itself to a very wide range of historians. Roman Catholics, seeing Protestantism equated with capitalism by scholars, and capitalism turned into a word of abuse by socialists, have been quick to seize their advantage and declare that the Protestant Reformation in England is thus proved to have been 'a rebellion of the rich against the poor', leading to all the ills that modern socialists complain of. Marxist historians, declaring summarily that the equation of Puritanism with capitalism is one of 'the irresistible conclusions of modern research', announce that the Puritan Revolution was the crucial victory in the world struggle of capitalism to

[1] Professor Tawney's views are given most clearly in his essays on 'Harrington's Interpretation of His Age' (British Academy Lecture 1941) and 'The Rise of the Gentry' (*Economic History Review*, 1941). His 'The Rise of the Gentry, a Postscript' (*Economic History Review*, 1954) does not seem to me to meet my objections to this thesis, or even to recognise their nature.

burst its 'feudal' bonds: it was 'the decisive shift' from a generally feudal to a predominantly capitalist society. . . . Had the English revolution failed, as so many other revolutions in the seventeenth century failed, it is entirely possible that economic development might have been long retarded. As it was (they say) 'the Revolution triumphed, with portentous results': the Puritan onslaught broke down the resistance of feudalism and by its success secured the victory of capitalism in the world. The army of Cromwell provided the shock-troops of the bourgeoisie.[1]

Now my interpretation is very different from this view of the Tawney school. It could hardly fail to be, because I disagree fundamentally with all three of its major premises. First, I do not think that there is any exclusive connection between Puritanism and Capitalism: I find that the English Puritans included strong anti-capitalist forces, and that orthodox Calvinism, so far from being the ideology of the merchant classes in the seventeenth century, prevailed largely — in Protestant countries — among backwoods squires, as in Scotland and Gelderland. Secondly, whatever may be said of the period before 1590, I do not think that the years 1590–1640 were a period of growing general prosperity in Europe, or even in England (though certain special trades, centred in London, brought prosperity to certain great London merchants and, of course, government financiers). Thirdly, I do not think that the gentry were 'rising' in that period: on the contrary, I find evidence of general decline among those whose income came solely or largely from land. In fact, I do not think that 'capitalism' played any great part in the Revolution: the City of London was royalist and had to be drastically purged four times in order to keep it in line with the rebels, and the parliamentary boroughs, whose support to the opposition has been claimed as evidence of mercantile feeling, did not represent merchant feeling at all: they were 'rotten boroughs' controlled by great magnates whose opposition was far from mercantile in character.

[1] See, particularly, Christopher Hill, *The English Revolution* 1640 (1940, reprinted 1949); E. Hobsbawm, 'The Crisis of the 17th Century' in *Past and Present*, Nos. 5 and 6 (May and Nov., 1954). The phrase about the 'irresistible conclusions of modern research' is from Christopher Hill, 'Society and Andrew Marvell', in *The Modern Quarterly*, No. 4 (1946).

Finally, I do not believe that the Revolution 'triumphed with portentous results'. I believe that it failed.

I shall not use space here in destructive argument. In this essay I propose to consider the social nature of the revolution by asking two questions of fact: first, what was the economic position of the gentry, who, since they dominated both Parliament and local government, were the essential social class in any parliamentary and national movement? and, secondly, what were the most insistent claims of the 'Independents' who provided the revolutionary force in this movement? Fortunately, in the increasing quantity of local and family history, in the parliamentary records and vast pamphlet literature of the period, we have abundant evidence on which to attempt an answer to this question.

First, what was the economic state of the gentry? In my opinion, Tawney has misrepresented this problem by selecting, as instances of a general economic 'rise of the gentry', only those families whose fortunes, in fact, can be shown to have come not from land but from office. Office-holders naturally owned land; but land was not the source of their wealth: it was not even necessarily an economic investment: it was a social asset — it may even have been an economic liability. If we wish to learn about the state of the gentry, we must not consider such office-holding gentry but the 'mere gentry', '*les pauvres gentilhommes*', as Cardinal Richelieu called them, '*dont le bien ne consiste qu'en fonds de terre*'. If we do this, I think we discover overwhelming evidence that such men, in England as in France, were in economic difficulty.

Wherever we look, it is the same. In North Wales, the gentry were all declaring themselves ruined. In Staffordshire, between 1600 and 1660, half the land was said to have been sold. It was out of the estates of decayed northern gentry that the Countess of Shrewsbury and Lord William Howard endowed the noble houses that they founded, and in 1614, when the first Earl of Cork wanted to establish his family in his home county, he was told that he could please himself 'for half of Herefordshire is for sale'. In the same year, 'most of the ancientest gentlemen's houses' in Northamptonshire were declared 'either divided, diminished or decayed'. In the last few years, many good manors had been sold, but 'not a gentleman of the county hath bought any, but strangers and they no inhabitants'. In Nottinghamshire, in 1625, the sheriff reported that the resident gentry had been much diminished, bought out by strangers. The lands in Berkshire were likened to skittish horses which often threw their owners. Modern scholars have shown that the gentry of Devonshire were almost universally in debt in the 1630's, that those of Lincolnshire were almost all declining, and that, in Bedfordshire, Buckinghamshire and Northamptonshire, one family in three among them, between 1600 and 1640, was selling its land. Clearly the decline was not merely local: it was general, throughout England.[1]

And who were the 'strangers' who are named as thus buying up the decaying gentry? The Earl of Cork, the Countess of Shrewsbury, her son the Earl of Devonshire, Lord William Howard — officers and grandees of the court; Alderman Soame, Alderman Craven, Alderman Cokayne, Sir Thomas Middleton, Sir Arthur Ingram, Sir Baptist Hicks — great merchants and government financiers from the City of London. It is an oligarchy of metropolitan plutocrats, aldermen of London and courtiers of Whitehall, who are sucking the life out of the 'mere gentry' and 'decayed boroughs' of the provinces. For it is because boroughs are economically 'decayed' that they become politically 'rotten', and sell their independence to aristocratic patrons. Thriving towns, like Newcastle-upon-Tyne, linked to London by the coal trade, or Bristol, the port of Western trade, continue to elect their own representatives.[2]

What were the gentry to do in such circumstances? In Spain, the impoverished *hidalgo* had a solution: *iglesia o casa real o mar*, office in Church or Court, or the sea. The English gentleman thought in the same terms. 'It is impossible', wrote one of them, 'for a mere country gentleman ever to grow rich or raise his house. He must have some other vocation with his inheritance,

[1] See A. H. Dodd, *Studies in Stuart Wales* (Cardiff 1952); Erdeswicke, *Survey of Staffordshire*, 1717, supplement; Chatsworth MSS., Boyle Papers (kindly communicated by Mr. T. O. Ranger); T. Hallinan, 'The Changing Composition of Landownership in Bucks., Beds. and Northants, 1540–1640' (MS. D.Phil. Thesis, Oxon, 1955); and sources quoted in my 'The Elizabethan Aristocracy' (*Economic History Review*, 1951), pp. 294–5, and 'The Gentry, 1540–1640' (1953), pp. 40–1.

[2] On this, see J. E. Neale, *The Elizabethan House of Commons* (1949), p. 163.

as to be a courtier, lawyer, merchant or some other vocation. If he hath no other vocation, let him get a ship and judiciously manage her, or buy some auditor's place, or be vice-admiral in his county. By only following the plough he may keep his word and be upright, but will never increase his fortune. Sir John Oglander wrote this with his own blood, June the 25th, 1632.'[1] It was no accident that the first thirty years of the seventeenth century saw an unprecedented scramble for office, an unprecedented and rising market in office, a desire to make office hereditary, as in France; and that, in the 1630's, when the more parsimonious government of Charles I cut down the opportunities at court, there was an unprecedented emigration of the gentry to North America. Nor is it an accident that the gentry, who thus embarked on colonial schemes, were Puritans and became the leaders of the Independents. Puritan austerity was often the religion not of rich capitalists, saving to invest, but of poor gentry, saving to make ends meet, and morally disgusted at the ostentation and extravagance of a court from which they were excluded and which flourished at their expense. It was appropriate that the leader of these gentry, when they became revolutionary, should have been Oliver Cromwell — the representative of a former court family, now reduced to their lands and obliged, in his youth, to sell their great house in Huntingdonshire to a new family drawing its income from office and the law.

Thus the Great Rebellion, in my opinion, is not the clear-headed self-assertion of the rising bourgeoisie and gentry, but rather the blind protest of the depressed gentry. In the 1630's, incidental political factors increased this depression, and the radical gentry willingly supported the aristocratic politicians who sought, by parliamentary pressure, to bring the King back into the ancient constitutional ways. Unfortunately, these aristocratic leaders afterwards proved unable to contain their radical followers. Under the pressures of fear and civil war, the aristocratic leadership crumbled; and, in 1645, the Independents stood forth, mobilised, invincible, revolutionary, demanding satisfaction.

[1] *A Royalist's Notebook, The Commonplace Book of Sir John Oglander of Nunwell*, 1622–1652, ed. Francis Bamford (1936), p. 75.

What were the demands of the Independents? Socially they are clear enough. They wanted independence from Court and City, the two swollen products of Tudor centralisation to which the provinces — the 'mere gentry' and the 'decayed boroughs' — had so long been sacrificed. They wanted decentralisation of government — the Cromwellian government would cut down the borough seats in Parliament and treble the county seats; decentralisation of religion — toleration instead of a centralised Anglican or Presbyterian Church; decentralisation of trade — that is to say, the break-up, not the formation of that national market which is essential to capitalism — 'I thought', protested a West Country gentleman, 'that long ere this we should have trade dispersed all the nation over, but this City, it seems, must have all the trade'; decentralisation of law — local county registries, local courts; decentralisation of education — local schools, local universities. It was in the reign of the Independents that universities were projected in Wales and Cornwall, at York and Manchester, and a short-lived university founded in Durham. Socially, the Independent revolt was a revolt of the provinces against a century of Tudor centralisation: against that enslavement of the country by the Court and City to which the depressed gentry ascribed their present plight.

But what of their political claims? When we ask this question we soon find that they were entirely negative. The Independents knew what they hated. They hated the Court, with its office-holders, its lawyers, its pensioners, its monopolists, its archaic taxes; they hated the Lords, those great courtiers — he hoped, Cromwell once said, to live to see never a nobleman in England; they hated the centralised Church, which had tried, under Archbishop Laud, to rob them of their patronage and their tithes. They hated the all-absorbent City — 'this nation', they said, 'was falling into the rickets: the head bigger than the body'. And, in their radical mood, they duly destroyed these things. They executed the King, abolished the House of Lords, sold up the Church, purged the City.

But what were their positive alternatives? They were not republicans, or whigs or mercantilists. A little 'whig' republican group, which did obtain the leadership in Parliament for a time, was soon eliminated. The Independent gentry had no positive theories: one form of government, they said, was as good as another; they would really prefer to be governed than to govern, to be 'tolerated' by a paternal government, under which they could prosper, than to exercise direct power, which they found too difficult. As to the form of that government — if pressed, they thought that 'a government with something monarchical in it' was probably the best thing. On second thoughts, Lords were a good thing too: 'we would keep up nobility'; and so was an established Church — they had never wanted to separate from the Anglican Church but only to live more comfortably in it than Archbishop Laud had allowed. The only thing that was *not* good was government by or for capitalists. Every aspect of Cromwell's rule aroused squeals of despair from the mercantile classes; but when they protested, he told them sharply to keep to their counting-houses. A whig champion of the merchant class really answered the theorists of the capitalist revolution, long before they had spoken, when he entitled his diatribe against the economic policy of the Protectorate 'The World's Mistake in Oliver Cromwell'.[1]

In truth, the Independents did not know what they wanted in politics. As Cromwell himself once said: 'none climbs so high as he who knows not whither he is going'. Or rather, what they wanted was so vaguely envisaged that they could not think of any constitutional formula to achieve it. What they wanted was 'a commonwealth'. The conception of 'the commonwealth', of an organic, almost a collectivist society, had been a commonplace under the Tudors and the great Tudor statesmen, Thomas Cromwell and Lord Burghley, and their social philosophers, 'the Commonwealth men', had sought, however imperfectly, to realise it. But with the coming of the Stuarts, those feckless Scottish kings, this ideal had been rejected by a government of irresponsible courtiers and favourites and had been inherited instead by the Puritan opposition to government: an opposition not only inflamed by gentry grievances but also fired by a just indignation against feeble, bad and irresponsible government, the betrayal by selfish governors of 'the honest part of the

[1] For references see my essay 'The Gentry', pp. 42–4. For Cromwell's utter indifference to mercantile interests in his foreign policy, see Menna Prestwich, 'Diplomacy and Trade in the Protectorate' (*Journal of Modern History*, 1950).

nation'. Hence the cult, by the Puritans, not of new or mercantile or republican ideas, but of a vague, romanticised English monarchy such as they supposed had existed under the last sovereign of the old dynasty, 'Queen Elizabeth of glorious memory'. When the Independent Army reasserted itself and effortlessly drove out of power the little côterie of 'whig' republicans who had usurped authority in its absence, the essential justification for that act was that the republican government thus overthrown was not, as it called itself, a 'commonwealth', but 'an oligarchy, detested by all men that love a commonwealth'. And so Oliver Cromwell and his Independents replaced the policy of *laissez-faire* at home and mercantile aggression abroad against England's trade rivals, the Dutch, by an anachronistic revival of 'Elizabethan' policy: paternal government, enforcement of poor law and tillage laws, leadership of the 'Protestant interest' in Europe, a protectorate over the Netherlands, a piratical war in the West Indies to tap the American treasure of Spain.

The Independent ideal was thus essentially an archaism. Unfortunately, the Independents could think of no institutions in which to crystallise and preserve such an archaism. Their philosopher, James Harrington, the author of *Oceana*, proposed a parliament of gentry holding office by rotation. That would prevent the rise of a privileged bureaucracy. More radical, Thomas Hobbes advocated the preservation of the old Tudor hierarchy and 'degree' — which alone, according to the Tudor philosophers, prevented man's natural wickedness from destroying the commonwealth — by an open resort to naked, unsanctified power. Both Harrington and Hobbes conveniently ignored the existence of mercantile classes. But in fact even these desperate philosophies could not recreate that obsolete ideal. After a series of short-lived constitutional experiments, the Independents threw up the sponge and submitted again to the time-honoured rule of King, Lords, Commons and Established Church. Harrington died and was forgotten. Hobbes survived and was tolerated, in the new age, as a harmless old crank. The whole world of the Independents was rejected and became, in gay Restoration England, something of a joke. It is difficult to describe this as 'success' or 'triumph'. 'Success' by the Independents would have been a kind of decentralised anarchical gentry-republic, a Polish Diet. It is just as well that they failed.

And yet, protest our theorists, whatever the *nature* of the revolution, surely the *result* of it was a capitalist advance? If a new class had not come to political power, may it not nevertheless, behind the appearance of political continuity, have occupied the seats of social power? For, at the Restoration, one great change that had taken place was not reversed: the great transfer of land by enforced private sale. Now of the purchasers of these lands, says the Marxist historian Archangelsky, fifty-one per cent were London merchants; and thus, says another scholar, the Restoration settlement was economically 'a triumph for the "new men" — men who may best be described . . . as business men who had thriven under the Commonwealth'.[1] But alas, even this conclusion cannot now be sustained. Recent research has shown that the 'new men', of whom Marxist historians have made so much, were, to a very large extent, merely agents, buying back their lands for the old families, and that the land settlement of the Restoration passed through a royalist Parliament so easily because, in fact, the net effect of these sales had been insignificant.[2] Socially, as politically, the Revolution had been a failure, and the history of England after 1660 was a continuation of its history before 1640. The Interregnum was merely an untidy interruption. The only permanent changes were a few constitutional changes that could have been, and sometimes had been, achieved by peaceful legislation, and certainly did not require civil war, revolution and military dictatorship.

Thus I conclude that the Great Rebellion was not a 'capitalist' rising, nor did it 'succeed' in any sense, nor in any way directly forward the advance of capitalism in England. It was the blind revolt of the gentry against the Court, of the provinces against the capital: the backwash against a century of administrative and economic centralisation. Since they were animated by passion, not by positive political ideas, and since they soon either lost by death, or overpowered and destroyed their poli-

[1] H. E. Chesney, 'The Transference of Lands in England, 1640–1660' in *Trans. R. Hist. Soc.*, 1933, p, 210.

[2] Joan Thirsk, 'The Sale of Royalist Lands' (*Economic History Review*, 1952); 'The Restoration Land Settlement' (*Journal of Modern History*, 1954).

tical leaders, the radical gentry, when they were in power, found themselves without a policy. Ultimately, after a period of fumbling expedients, they gave up the effort, accepted back the old political system, and sank into political quietism. They might still grumble about Court and City; but, instead of arming themselves with radical ideas, they consoled themselves with conservative ideas: they became high-flying tories, preachers of non-resistance and divine right.

Thus, in my opinion, whatever results followed from the Great Rebellion followed not from its success but from its failure. The rebellion itself was a blind rebellion, which took place because a failure of political ability coincided with a general economic crisis. There were reformers; there were capitalists; there were political thinkers; and, had there been no rebellion of the gentry, these might well have achieved their aims by peaceful progress. But the rebellion of the gentry, a rebellion of mutinous, impoverished, backward-looking provincial squires, gave them no chance — at least until that rebellion had consumed itself and outlasted some of its causes. Perhaps *indirectly* the rebellion may have forwarded the undoubted change of mentality between the early and the late seventeenth century in England: by burning up both itself and its mental fuel, it may have cleared the way for the progress of new and very un-puritan ideas. But, equally, it may have impeded that progress for a generation. We cannot say. What we can say — or, at least, what I am prepared to say — is that it was not, in itself, a successful stage in the rise of the bourgeoisie. As in most revolutions, much of its momentum was self-generated; but in so far as it can be reduced to simple, fundamental terms, it was a protest, by the victims of a temporary general depression, against a privileged bureaucracy, a capitalist City.

CHAPTER XXX

THE MYTH OF CHARLES I: A TERCENTENARY OCCASION

On January 30, 1649, King Charles I was executed, and cries of horror arose from an outraged world. There had been revolutions before, and kings had been murdered, but never with such dreadful formality; nor could it occur to the prosperous Bourbons or the barbarous Romanovs who denounced it that such a deed could be repeated. The murderers were ready to defend themselves. They uttered magniloquent phrases about Divine Providence and the will of the people which doctrinaire republicans of the nineteenth century (when it was quite safe to be republican) were ready to swallow; but they deceived no one at the time. All recognised that the act had been perpetrated by a hated and despotic Army, mindless and afraid, and a small parliamentary rump, its creature.

No judge would sit in the new High Court of Justice. Soldiers dominated its sessions in Westminster Hall, and its President wore a bullet-proof hat throughout the proceedings. When he called upon the King to answer the charge made 'in behalf of the good people of England', Lady Fairfax called from the gallery, 'No, not half of them! It is a lie!' Her words were cut short. 'Down with the whores, shoot them!' ordered the colonel of the guard. When the King demanded to be heard, the rhythmical cry of 'Justice, Justice, Execution, Execution!' drowned his words, as arranged by a Puritan clergyman; and when the death warrant was drawn up, intimidation and forgery were required to complete the list of signatures.

On the day of execution staples were fixed to the platform in Whitehall to tie the King down in case he struggled — an absurd precaution, as anyone should have known who knew him. Soldiers around the scaffold prevented him speaking to the crowd, who expressed their indignation with sullen groans and had to be dispersed by cavalry. Even the Army shrank from the act they carried out; a promise of £100 and promotion could not find a soldier to be executioner, and the common hangman who finally carried out the sentence — a skilled practitioner who had prepared himself in childhood to inherit his father's office by decapitating cats and dogs — died of remorse within a few months. Arbitrary power was not concealed, it was merely consecrated by the solemn barbarities of religion and the blood-curdling texts of a buffoon-preacher.

Martyrologists will no doubt take this occasion to dwell upon the details of martyrdom. Historically it is more interesting to enquire how such a revolutionary situation came about. Charles I's failure was a double failure — a failure of government, which destroyed his personal rule, and a failure of personality which brought him to his death. The first failure was not merely his; it was the failure of a whole system. He had neither devised the system nor carried it out; he had merely approved of it and been carried along by it as a decorative parasite; and since he felt no intimate connection with it, he did not defend it when it wavered, but saw its architects removed to the Tower and the block. It was the system of Thorough, the system of Laud and Strafford, which had collapsed through internal weakness and could never be restored. But Charles I's second failure was purely personal. Irresponsible, unpolitical, convinced, as he said in his last speech, that 'a sovereign and a subject are clean different things', he had persuaded himself that no compact with his subjects could limit his ultimate freedom. Worse still, he took no pains to conceal this view. At any stage in his progressive defeats in politics and war he could have recognised the facts of power and made a practical bargain with serious, practical men who wanted nothing better than 'a good correspondency' with him. But Charles was not a practical man. His tongue could compromise, as a tactical manœuvre, but not his heart, and he showed it. The practical men could find no basis of settlement, or of their own future safety, and if they could not become revolutionary they were thrust aside by others who could. Thus the voice of reason stammered and was drowned by a cry for the death of 'Charles Stuart, that Man of Blood'. It seemed the only way to settle the business.

Thus not only tyranny but weakness brought Charles I, as it

was to bring Louis XVI and Nicholas II, to his pompous death. Nevertheless, his fate in our insular revolution has a dramatic quality which even the greater significance and more universal character of the French and Russian Revolutions cannot give to theirs. It is an artistic difference. While they were dull and ordinary men, Charles I had a touch of quality which they lacked. He was an æsthete. His court was the last Renaissance court in Europe, and himself perhaps the greatest royal patron that art has ever found. Even the fragments and recollection of his great picture-galleries bewilder us. His taste seemed universal; while bidding for old masters he could detect a living genius, and while he commissioned Rubens he could invest in Rembrandt. Neglecting politics, he seized every artistic opportunity. On his romantic visit to Spain he missed the Infanta but secured a set of Titians. When Rubens visited England as an ambassador he was made to decorate the Banqueting Hall of Whitehall.

Through his own ambassadors, through cosmopolitan financiers and travelling virtuosi, Charles continually enriched his collection, and his purse was refreshed by questionable taxation only to be exhausted on works of art. In Rome Bernini carved his head from a triptych by Vandyck: Vandyck who, more than any other, has captured the elegance and refinement of that doomed Cavalier generation. Nor was it only painting that Charles patronised. Inigo Jones was his surveyor of buildings, Henry Lawes his musician; and if the great poets — Milton and Marvell and the metaphysicians — were too serious for his taste, he took care of the lesser, granting them here a benefice or a bishopric, there a pension or a perquisite — Herrick and King, Suckling and Lovelace, and those fashionable academic poets, Strode and Randolph, Cleveland and Cartwright, whose reputation has long evaporated. From the King's court the fashion of culture spread outwards to the lesser courts of the nobility. The Earl of Arundel would return from Vienna with marbles and pictures; the Earl of Pembroke gathered more Vandycks than anyone else in the world; Milton's *Comus* and Lawes's music were played in the Earl of Bridgewater's castle; Palladian houses and Italian gardens enclosed a privileged life which seemed exempt from revolution; and in the romantic Cavalier Montrose that exquisite generation contrived to produce a poet even in Scotland — the last poet ever to arise in that prosaic peninsula.

An æsthete need not be an intellectual. Charles I had perfect taste, but he was not interested in thought, and in literature as in life he sought not meaning but sensuous beauty and theatrical effect. In religion he sought not a rule of conduct but a graceful liturgy. Above all literature he preferred the drama and the masque. Oxford was his spiritual home; at Cambridge they thought too much, but in Oxford Laud had corrected that. Oxford was 'the only city of England that he could say was entirely to his devotion'. Thither he went in his prosperity to see plays and yet more plays, on new stages where the genius of Inigo Jones had contrived mechanical billows and shifting scenes; thither he went in adversity, as to a refuge, to be received 'with that joy and affection as Apollo should be by the Muses'. There he sadly forecast his fate from a prophecy in Virgil and at the news of the poet Cartwright's death, 'it is not to be forgot that His Sacred Majesty dropt a tear'.

To the end he retained his love of masques and pictures, poetry and plays. A prisoner at Hampton Court, he commissioned a portrait from the newly-found Dutch painter Lely; and immured 'in his doleful restraint in Carisbrooke Castle' he consoled himself with Tasso and Ariosto, George Herbert and Edmund Spenser and a book of plays. Driven from comedy to more melancholy thoughts, he turned to religion. In the days of Laud he had been somewhat inattentive, for the archbishop had made Anglicanism, like himself, practical and boring. Even his plays at Oxford had been made tedious by politics and morality. Now, with bishops abolished and church-lands for sale, it was too late to be practical. The busy, complacent, persecuting Church of Laud had gone, and religion had become consolatory and devotional, the gentle ministrations of Juxon and the consecrated phrases of the Book of Prayer. Charles's taste for religion, his taste for drama, and his refusal to compromise all combined at the end. He managed his last act with flawless taste; Inigo Jones could not have designed more perfectly that final *mise-en-scène*.

When mythology is sustained by art, history strives in vain. The regicides, when they cut off King Charles's head, sealed their own historical doom. If the King's faults were personal, his death logically ended them; they could not invalidate the claims of the monarchy. By destroying him the rebels had destroyed his liabilities, which were their own assets and sole justification, and had to fight against the myth which they had enabled him to create. They sought to liquidate the monarchy and the Church. They sold their lands and property, but they could not dispose of their intangible assets. They sold King Charles's pictures, and kings and cardinals and bankers sent their agents to so memorable a sale. They nearly sold all the English cathedrals for scrap. And they protested, ever more shrilly, the virtues of republics, the justice of the deed, and the clarity of their consciences. But it was no good; they convinced no one. 'They were an oligarchy, detested by all men,' was the reply of a real republican. And meanwhile Dr. John Gauden, a prudent clergyman who contrived to write an Anglican best-seller while drawing the salary of a Presbyterian minister, was plying his indefatigable pen. Within a few days of the execution his *Eikon Basiliké, the Pourtraicture of His Sacred Majestie in His Solitudes and Sufferings* appeared as the genuine work of the royal martyr. Conquered and frustrated people hunger for a myth, and provided they have a symbolical figure and a dramatic immolation they are seldom fastidious about the literal truth or authenticity of the gospel. *Eikon Basiliké* supplied the need; it ran through edition after edition. The function of a myth is to compensate for the loss of reality; and when the royal Government and Church returned, shorn of their old powers, and the happy author was blackmailing his way from bishopric to bishopric, doubtless there were many who found in his skilful mythology balm for their final defeat. Perhaps there are still some. If so, they ought to celebrate this tercentenary not for the death of a reality but for the birth of a myth.

CHAPTER XXXI

'EIKON BASILIKÉ': THE PROBLEM OF THE KING'S BOOK

The books written by Kings and Queens of England (or ascribed to them) have been very few. They have also been very controversial. The Tudors, our most literate dynasty, were too prudent to publish. King James I, less prudent in everything, provoked indignation in England by his *True Law of Free Monarchies*, and in Scotland by his *Basilikon Doron*. Queen Victoria's *Leaves from the Highlands* was discontinued as discrediting the monarchy. I doubt if the Duke of Windsor's published Memoirs, *A King's Story*, will prove an exception to the rule. But the most controversial of all such works is the only best-seller among them, the *Eikon Basiliké* of Charles I. For 300 years the true authorship of this famous book has been disputed and the evidence of scholars has been converted into the ammunition of political and religious partisans. Even now (since Whig and Tory are perpetual characters) the smouldering embers sometimes burst into flame. Now, thanks to the existence of a new and scholarly bibliography of the work,[1] we are in a good position to re-examine this famous controversy.

Eikon Basiliké or the Pourtraicture of His Sacred Majesty in His Solitudes and Sufferings was first published a few days after the execution of Charles I. In purpose it was political propaganda: an apologia of the king's policy, a vindication of his religion, in the form of explanations, meditations and prayers apparently composed by him. Furthermore, as propaganda it was highly effective. In 1640 the people of England had clamoured for reform; by 1649 they were overwhelmed by an outrageous military revolution, and King Charles, once their 'tyrant', had become their most exalted fellow-victim, whom, in their tragic

[1] F. F. Madan, *A New Bibliography of the Eikon Basiliké* (Oxford Bibliographical Society, 1950).

mood, they were willing to romanticise as their martyr. *Eikon Basiliké* exploited that mood; and, as long as that mood lasted, it was a best-seller. It ran through 36 editions in its first year; it was published abroad and translated into five languages; and thereafter, in spite of the Republican censorship, four more editions were secretly printed and circulated as part of the King's works. Then, in 1660, the monarchy was restored; the sentimental mood of defeat dissolved in the new climate of victory; and *Eikon Basiliké*, from the Gospel, became the shibboleth of the royalist party. It ceased to be read; but the great controversy about its authorship began.

From the beginning the royal authorship, triumphantly proclaimed by the royalists, had been denied by their adversaries; but these denials had rested entirely on expediency, not on evidence. The Republican authorities, eager to discredit the book, had summoned the printer to Whitehall and urged him, with bribes and threats, to deny that it had been sent to him from the King; but he insisted that it had come in the King's name. John Milton, the poet, had been commissioned to write a counterblast to it, and in *Eikonoklastes*, following an earlier, anonymous pamphleteer, he had ascribed it to a royalist forger; but, as he could not name this forger, his argument fell somewhat flat. Then, at the Restoration, the 'forger' named himself. Promptly, in 1660, John Gauden, the former Presbyterian dean of Bocking in Essex, came forward to claim an Anglican reward.

Gauden first advanced his claims as the author of *Eikon Basiliké* to Charles II and the Duke of York, bringing with him highly-placed witnesses to prove his veracity.[1] From their later statements we know that both the royal brothers admitted his claims, and Gauden was rewarded with a royal chaplaincy and the bishopric of Exeter. But Exeter, he soon discovered, was a dismally impoverished see; and, having once visited it, he immediately began a series of plaintive letters to the Lord Chan-

[1] The interview in which Gauden advanced and established his claim before Charles II and the Duke of York is described independently by Gauden himself, in a letter to Clarendon dated January 21, 1660–1, and by the Duke of York, as quoted by Burnet. Gauden's witnesses at this interview were the Duke of Somerset and the Earl of Southampton, who both admitted that they had acted as intermediaries between Gauden and Charles I and had carried Gauden's *Eikon* to the King at Newport. The Duke of Somerset's part as an intermediary is confirmed by Mrs. Gauden and by Anthony Walker, Gauden's curate at Bocking.

cellor, the Earl of Clarendon, protesting against so poor a reward for such signal, if secret, services. For some time Clarendon took no notice of these repeated hints. Then Gauden became explicit. The *Eikon Basiliké*, he said, was 'wholly and only my invention, making and design, in order to vindicate the King's wisdom, honour and piety'. Had not Bishop Morley, Charles I's chaplain, acquainted Clarendon with the facts, 'for so Dr. Morley told me, at the King's first coming, when he assured me the greatness of that service was such that I might expect any preferment I desired'?

This positive claim, clearly and insistently advanced, was as embarrassing to Clarendon as it has since been to the modern advocates of the royal authorship, who now claim that Gauden was a mere impostor, 'a disreputable prelate' whose claims should be totally disregarded. If this were so, Clarendon would no doubt have disregarded them — for since Charles I's intimate advisers and attendants were still alive, a false claim could easily have been disproved. But Clarendon did not disregard them. Instead he wrote to Gauden, admitting that he had been told the fact and begging him to keep it secret. It had been communicated to him, he said, under oath of secrecy, so that he had not felt at liberty to take notice of it; 'and truly, when it ceases to be secret, I know nobody will be glad of it but Mr. Milton. I have very often wished I had never been trusted with it.' Within a few months Gauden was comforted with a new bishopric. He had wanted Winchester, but in the end Worcester sufficed to keep him quiet. Next year he opportunely died, and the secret remained buried for the time in the private papers of Gauden and Clarendon. Clarendon's own silence is almost heroic. It is an extraordinary fact that his great *History of the Rebellion*, which he left in manuscript, contains absolutely no reference to the famous work which had been so effective in those years as the gospel of his party. There seems only one reasonable interpretation of such silence: that Clarendon disbelieved in the royal authorship but was unwilling, even in a work written for posterity, to divulge the secret which would have pleased no one except the shade of Mr. Milton.

But if Clarendon was thus conscientious, other more highly-placed persons could afford to be less discreet. In 1673 the Duke of York, afterwards James II, surprised his confidant the Rev. Gilbert Burnet by telling him categorically that the *Eikon Basiliké* was not the work of his father. 'Dr. Gauden writ it', he said firmly, and described the interview in which, at the Restoration, Gauden had established his claim. Burnet's account of this conversation, however, was not published until 1723; thus, on this side, too, the secret was kept for another fifty years.

Meanwhile there was another leakage. In 1686 died Arthur Annesley, first Earl of Anglesey, a prominent politician and virtuoso, famous as the first English peer to build up a great private library. On his death his library was sent to an auctioneer, Mr. Millington, to be sold; but when Millington examined Anglesey's copy of *Eikon Basiliké* he found written upon one leaf of it an extraordinary and alarming note. It was an autograph note by Anglesey himself, and it stated that in 1675 both Charles II and the Duke of York had personally assured Anglesey that the *Eikon* was not by their father at all 'but made by Dr. Gauden, Bishop of Exeter'. The auctioneer, fearing to pass on to a casual purchaser so explosive a document, tore that leaf out of the volume and sent it, as a state paper, to Whitehall. There it was casually seen by the Rev. Simon Patrick, a chaplain in waiting, who recorded the fact privately in his diary and afterwards in his autobiography, but himself published nothing. His autobiography was not published till 1839. Once again, it seemed, the secret was preserved.

But not for long. For although the original had thus been suppressed, and was perhaps destroyed, by authority, documents, as Sir Lewis Namier has remarked, have nine lives: for there are always copies. Now it happened that one of those who attended Lord Anglesey's sale was William Ashurst, a well-known London alderman, of strong Whig sympathies; and when Ashurst saw the interesting inscription in the late Earl's copy of *Eikon Basiliké*, his interest was at once aroused. He instantly made a copy; and this copy, in Ashurst's own hand, certified by him as a true copy taken from the original in the Earl's own hand, survived to reveal the facts even after the original had disappeared. For some time Ashurst kept his secret from the public. In the reign of James II it would no doubt have been imprudent to divulge it. But in 1688 the Glorious Revolution sent King James into exile; in 1689 Ashurst (now Sir William) was returned as Whig member of Parliament for London; in 1690 an opportunity occurred for the Whigs to reveal the secret which they had thus secured.

For in 1690 a Whig publisher thought it seasonable to reprint Milton's *Eikonoklastes* — that attack on the Stuart kingship which was incidentally the most famous challenge to the royal authorship of the *Eikon*. It is clear that the publisher — who pretended to be in Amsterdam but in fact was almost certainly in London[1] — did not know about the Anglesey Memorandum: he merely saw, in the Whig triumph, an opportunity of profit or propaganda. But when his book was printed, and some copies of it had already been sold (one of them to Sir William Ashurst), someone suddenly showed him a copy of the memorandum and told him its history.[2] At once the publisher seized his chance. Printing a number of copies of the Memorandum, he pasted them into such copies of *Eikonoklastes* as had not yet been distributed, and thus published, together with Milton's book, the one essential piece of information which Milton himself had lacked — the name of the royalist 'forger': Dr. Gauden.

The Anglesey Memorandum, as I have shown, is not the only evidence of Gauden's authorship; but it was the first evidence to reach the public, and consequently it bore the brunt of controversy. Even now it is sometimes dismissed as a forgery. The only serious evidence for such a verdict is the fact that Anglesey's son, Lord Altham, afterwards declared that his father had never mentioned to him the information which he was supposed to have inscribed in the Memorandum. This, of course, proves nothing — for why should Lord Anglesey have passed on to his son a secret confidentially told to him by the King? And besides, if the Memorandum is a forgery, who forged it, and when? It can only have been forged between the time of Lord Anglesey's death and the time when Sir William Ashurst saw it at the

[1] The edition bore an Amsterdam title page, but such devices were a regular method of evading the English censorship (*Eikonoklastes* being banned in England). In any case, the book was, of course, printed for the London market.

[2] The facts about Ashurst's part in this affair, as shown by his own MS. note in his copy of the 1690 edition of *Eikonoklastes*, are revealed by Mr. Madan in a letter to *The Times Literary Supplement*, August 31, 1956.

sale, or (if we disbelieve him) when Simon Patrick saw it at Whitehall — in other words, on the way to the auctioneer or while it was in his hands. But why should the auctioneer wish to forge a document which he then immediately sought to suppress? Why should anyone seek to forge it in so extraordinary a place and manner, with no reasonable prospect of publicity? And by what curious chance did such a forger so fortunately and exactly anticipate the evidence only afterwards to be revealed by the private papers of Gauden, Clarendon and Burnet? Is it not really more rational to suppose that the document was genuine, and agrees with the other evidence for the simple reason that it is true? The suggestion that it is a forgery is supported by neither evidence nor probability.

Thus, in 1690, the controversy was at last launched and the air was once more darkened with pamphlets animated by Republican or Royalist zeal. Evidence on both sides was furiously sought and triumphantly produced. The Gauden family papers were unearthed and publicly exhibited at the Rummer in Fleet Street in 1692, and part of a valuable account by Mrs. Gauden was published in 1699. Unfortunately the personal witnesses, who might have been cross-examined on the subject, were by this time either dead or doting, and much of the evidence ascribed to them is indirect or indistinct. One fact, however, is clear. In all the evidence elicited by the controversy, though there is much mention of the King's name, and some apparent conflict of evidence, there is nothing to invalidate the evidence of Gauden's authorship which I have given: nothing to explain why Clarendon should have accepted Gauden's claim if it were false, or why Bishop Burnet and Lord Anglesey should have independently ascribed identical observations to Charles II and the Duke of York if those observations had not been made. These facts remain insurmountable obstacles in the way of those who still seek to reject Gauden's authorship. Besides, since then another argument, almost as decisive, has been advanced in favour of Gauden: an argument this time not historical but literary.

After 1660 the *Eikon* had been much discussed but little read. Even Bishop Burnet, who had been 'bred up with a high veneration of this book', seems to have been singularly unfamiliar with its contents. But in 1883, G. E. Doble and in 1907 J. A. Farrer independently drew attention to these contents as evidence of authorship. Analysing the style of *Eikon Basiliké* and of the undisputed works of both Charles I and Gauden, they showed that, whereas between the style of Charles I — a plain but elevated style — and that of the *Eikon* there is no similarity, between that of Gauden and the *Eikon* the similarities are both numerous and remarkable. Both show the same passion for alliteration, the same meretricious verbal tricks and affectations, the same exotic or recondite words and phrases, the same metaphors, the same quotations and interpretations — sometimes curious interpretations — of Scripture and the classics. The cumulative effect of these similarities is overwhelming; even the bigots of neo-Royalism have not sought to deny it, but desperately suppose that Gauden must have had 'the opportunity of tampering with the *Eikon*'. But how Gauden obtained such an opportunity, or could be responsible for the style of a work which they nevertheless ascribe exclusively to the King, these enthusiastic gentlemen prudently do not seek to explain.

For these reasons, then, all serious scholars now regard Gauden's authorship of the *Eikon Basiliké* as certain, and most scholars have been content to leave the matter thus decided. On the other hand there remain serious difficulties of detail. How did Gauden, himself a stranger to the King, nevertheless convince well-informed contemporaries that his book was genuine? If his style is that of an affected literary hack, his ideas undoubtedly seemed the King's ideas: the book has an elevation absent from Gauden's other works. Further, although the evidence of detail was given so late, there is no good reason to disregard it, and this evidence not only suggests a more complex history than could be explained by mere straightforward forgery: it also suggests that the King had a definite though limited part in that history. For it suggests, first, that the King, too, had written something, and secondly, that before Gauden conveyed his text of the *Eikon* to the King's court, something which the King had written had been conveyed to Gauden.

Of the King's literary activity during the Rebellion we have many scraps of evidence. We know (from a pamphlet of 1649) that he had long intended to write a vindication of his politics.

We know that papers written by the King were captured at Naseby and afterwards restored. We know, from three different sources, that the King was engaged in some kind of literary composition at Holmby. We know that 'loose papers' in his hand, left behind at Hampton Court, were ordered by him to be set in order and sent after him. However certain it may be that Gauden was the author of the published *Eikon Basiliké*, clearly we cannot disregard the substantial weight of evidence which suggests that the King, too, was writing something similar, and at the same time.

Further, there is evidence that, at this crucial moment, Gauden himself had access to those papers. The link is the Rev. Edward Simmons, the servant of the King, who had been a clerical neighbour of Gauden in Essex, and who, on his return from exile in the summer of 1647, had joined the King at Hampton Court. We know, from Gauden's own servant, William Allen, that Gauden sat up one whole night, copying a manuscript of the King's which had been brought to him by Simmons. All the evidence shows that Simmons remained an important intermediary in the matter. He was himself a literary champion of Royalism and had published a *Vindication of King Charles*; it was to him that the King, as a reward for this *Vindication*, presented a manuscript of the finished *Eikon*, taking it out, at Newport, from under his 'blue-watchet waistcoat'; and it was he who took the *Eikon* to the printer who, since it was brought by the King's servant, 'never knew but that it was of His Majesty's own penning'.

From this summary of the later evidence it is clear that no exclusive solution is satisfactory. If the Royalist claim that Gauden was a mere impostor is ridiculous, the Whig claim that he skilfully forged the whole text of the *Eikon* is obviously inadequate: for it requires us to reject all the evidence of the King's own writing and of Gauden's copying of the King's manuscript. It is obviously better to reconcile than to reject such evidence; and this is what Mr. Madan, in his new bibliography, has done. With infinite patience and judicial skill — he has himself been a judge and can weigh exactly the value of testimony — Mr. Madan has examined every reference, every deposition, every text, every printer's device which can possibly illustrate the history of the book; he has traced every mention of every relevant manuscript known or said to have been handled by the King or his servants or Gauden; and he has reconstructed therefrom a history which, at last, is both consistent in itself and fits all the known evidence: a history which indeed leaves Gauden the author of the *Eikon* but satisfactorily explains both the origin of his material and the reason for its plausibility.

Briefly, it would appear that the idea and execution of the *Eikon* were, as he claimed, due to Gauden, but that Gauden used as the raw material for that purpose manuscript notes which the King, in the intervals of politics (and especially while confined in Holmby House) had compiled. These notes were undoubtedly seen at Hampton Court by the King's servant Simmons who, as the author of the *Vindication of King Charles*, would appreciate their value; and Simmons showed them to his friend, John Gauden. Thereupon Gauden saw his opportunity. King Charles, in the midst of his adversities, would probably never finish or publish his apologia; but Gauden, a facile literary journalist, could easily polish them up and present them in a form that would be of immense psychological value to the cause to which he had been converted. Borrowing the papers from Simmons, he copied them in a night, and from that copy elaborated the finished literary work which he then sent to the King at Newport with a full explanation of the plan.

Of the King's reception of Gauden's text there we have abundant evidence. Both Gauden and Mrs. Gauden (who, according to Gauden, was privy to the whole affair) afterwards described it in detail; and of the two principal intermediaries, the Marquis of Hertford and Bishop Duppa, the former personally gave evidence which convinced Charles II and the Duke of York in 1660, and the latter was still alive in 1661 when Gauden named him to Clarendon as a witness of his veracity. The manuscript was actually delivered to the King by the Marquis of Hertford. At this time the work was entitled *Suspiria Regalia*, 'The Sighs of a King'. The King had passages of the book read to him by Bishop Duppa and 'did exceedingly approve of them'; but he had to be persuaded that it should be published in his own name. In the end, having 'both corrected and heightened' Gauden's draft, he agreed; the title of the book was changed, perhaps at the suggestion of Jeremy Taylor, to *Eikon Basiliké*; and it was sent to the printer, through the agency of Edward Simmons, as 'the King's Book'.

Such, we can now say, was the history of *Eikon Basiliké* — the real history of its composition, long obscured by the controversy which it aroused. The hero of it, in a sense, is Gauden who for so long has been vilified by both parties. In fact, as he claimed, Gauden was the author of that great literary triumph. He did not forge the King's thoughts: he presented them, and presented them so skilfully that his book, as he claimed, 'was an army, and did vanquish more than the sword did'. In this there is nothing disreputable; and perhaps we may now, if we read his plaintive letters to Clarendon after the Restoration, feel more sympathetic towards him than the rival denouncers of his forgery or his imposture. After all, he was entitled to his reward, and Clarendon, when he at last broke his silence, freely admitted that Gauden was asking no more than he had deserved and had been promised. That service, as Bishop Morley had said, was such that he might have expected any preferment that he desired.

CHAPTER XXXII

THE QUAKERS

Three hundred years ago, in 1652, George Fox, the first Quaker, wandering westwards through the Yorkshire dales, came to Pendle Hill, 'and was moved by the Lord to go up to the top of it'. From that moment a new religion can be dated: for thence, as he afterwards wrote, 'I saw the sea bordering upon Lancashire, and there, on the top, I was moved to sound the day of the Lord, and the Lord let me see in what places he had a great people to be gathered'. This promised land was the remote peninsula of Furness, cut off from England by hills and moors and the treacherous tidal sands of Morecambe Bay. Thither Fox went, walking, as always, in his famous leather breeches, and testifying on the way; there, at Swarthmoor Hall, the home of Judge Fell, he was received and entertained; and there he made the great conquest without which it is impossible to conceive the later history of his movement.

Margaret Fell, the Judge's wife, had had 'a vision of a man in a white hat that should come and confound the priests'. Now she met him. That evening, she afterwards wrote, Fox 'opened us a book that we had never read in, nor indeed had never heard that it was our duty to read in — the Light of Christ in our consciences'. A few days later Fox walked suddenly into the parish church before the sermon and began to speak. 'I stood up in my pew', wrote Margaret Fell, 'and wondered at his doctrine, for I had never heard such before.' From that time Margaret Fell was a Quaker and Swarthmoor Hall was the centre and headquarters, as it is still one of the holy places, of Quakerism. There the early Quakers had their meetings, thence they went out on their astonishing pilgrimages, thither they returned as to a home and a base. It was the cradle, the springboard, the office, the registry, the library of the movement; from it the missionaries, many of them local men, went out to convert Scotland and Ireland, Holland and Germany, Turkey and Egypt, the redskins of America and the subjects of Prester John; and always they were organised by George Fox and corresponded with Margaret Fell, and the correspondence was copied and filed at Swarthmoor Hall. By all contemporary observers Quakerism was regarded as a north-country movement. 'Those that come from the North', declared an indignant south-country member when Parliament was first disconcerted by their antics, 'are the greatest pests of the nation'; and a member for Cumberland admitted, among less accurate statements, that they swarmed particularly in his constituency. 'They meet', he said, 'in multitudes and upon moors, *in terrorem populi.*'

Certainly, these new apostles frightened the conservative classes: were they not radicals, the irrepressible heirs of those Levellers and Anabaptists who had so nearly plunged England into a new revolution? In fact, they were not: but the error was venial. For the Quakers had indeed started as just another of those numerous proletarian sects which, directed by some local prophet, exploiting the principle of toleration, and appealing to the equalitarian principle of the Inner Light, had sought to canalise a private rivulet of radical discontent. As for George Fox, his own record of his early life hardly differs from that of the lunatic Fifth-Monarchy saint, John Rogers. He would walk alone all night, making strange noises, or sit all day in hollow trees. He would call down the wrath of God, for no apparent reason, on the 'bloody city of Lichfield'; like any other radical he would denounce humane learning, tithes and the law; and he would unctuously chronicle (or imagine) the repeated evidence of his own election, the lingering diseases and painful deaths of those who doubted it. No wonder the provincial squires of Cromwell's parliaments failed to distinguish Quakers from other proletarian radicals. In 1656, when Fox's disciple James Naylor had 'run out into imaginations', those champions of religious toleration vied with one another in holy ferocity. Let his tongue be bored, cried a colonel; and his lips slit, added a major-general; let him be whipped, urged an alderman, from Westminster to the Old Exchange. Some would send him to the Scilly Isles, some to the Isle of Dogs. 'We are God's executioners,' declared a retired clergyman, 'and ought to be tender of his honour.' 'I shall speak no more,' said a medical man, 'but let us all stop our ears and stone him.'

And yet, if squires and colonels turned purple at the name of Quakerism, finer spirits, in spite of its extravagancies, were drawn gradually towards it. Irresistibly it spread; it won converts far outside its original social frontiers; and in 1660, when the other sects evaporated overnight, it survived and prospered, a world movement: indeed, the only world movement to have been generated by our provincial Revolution.

What was the cause of this unique success, this spectacular survival? Partly, of course, it was the personality of its founder, that strange, compulsive personality which caused his enemies so often to charge him with witchcraft. Throughout his life it shone through his disorderly expression and made converts even among his enemies, who, though they sometimes thrust him into gaol, beat him unconscious, and threw him over walls, into ponds, and down pits, would sometimes also (as he complacently records) part to make way for him crying, 'Oh he shines, he glisters!' But even more it was his message: the message by which the Inner Light became not, as with the other sectaries, the right to unlimited private interpretation leading to unlimited compliance and special pleading, but the duty of absolute integrity: let your Yea be Yea and your Nay Nay. Never was the need for such integrity more widely felt than in the last days of the Puritan Revolution.

Periods of revolution are sometimes supposed to liberate heroic actions and profound thoughts. The evidence for this supposition is very tenuous. More often they generate political corruption and intellectual dishonesty. Traditional restraints dissolve, new fears and new opportunities are more easily indulged, and high ideals, which sometimes fire a revolution, are easily adjusted in the course of it. This is that *trahison des clercs* which M. Benda supposed a new phenomenon of our century but which in fact is to be found in all unquiet periods. In the Puritan Revolution every victorious group had in turn adjusted its ideals to its interests, and consequently, as each in turn failed in its politics, it found itself without moral virtue upon which to fall back. So, while the leaders made their terms, their followers abandoned them and, accepting the fact of political defeat, looked for consolation to religion. They wanted leaders whose religious integrity was untainted by political compromise, independent of political hopes, unaffected by political defeat: consistent men to whom, even in failure, they could still offer a spiritual allegiance.

They found the Quakers. First the other sectaries, disgusted with the greed and scramble of their old leaders, the 'jangling Baptists', turned in shoals to Quakerism. Others followed. In 1657 John Lilburn, the defeated Leveller leader, deserted by his allies, died a Quaker. In the same year Isaac Pennington, whose father had once, as Lord Mayor, financed the rebellion but was now foundering in bankruptcy, listened to a sermon by Fox and became a Quaker. Sir Henry Vane, the defeated Republican, tired of his crooked career, maintained, during his disgrace at Raby Castle, a household of Quakers. Elizabeth, Princess Palatine, the daughter and granddaughter of Kings, after years of exile, became a Quaker. Elizabeth Claypole, Oliver Cromwell's favourite daughter, in the height of her father's power, became a Quaker. And Cromwell himself, always genuinely tolerant, genuinely searching for religious truth, received Fox at Whitehall, suspended State business while he talked with him, kept him to dinner, and in the end sent him away, with tears in his eyes — those tears which, according to his enemies, he could so skilfully produce — saying, 'come again to my house, for if thou and I were but an hour of the day together, we should be nearer one to another'.

Such was the Quakerism which survived the year of Restoration to enjoy, in a new, more confident climate, a second efflorescence. Nevertheless, the second stage was different from the first. In 1688, the year of aristocratic revolution, George Fox was still alive; so was Margaret Fell who, the Judge being dead, had become his wife; but the leadership was already sliding into other hands, and the second founder of the movement, William Penn, came from a different class. His youth had been spent not in hollow trees in Leicestershire but in the *beau monde* of Paris and the viceregal court of Dublin; and when he went to America, it was not, like Fox, to wander preaching through the perils of the Indian wilderness (perils which lose nothing in the Founder's telling) but as Lord Proprietor of Pennsylvania, to settle a pacifist colony among the equally pacifist Delaware Indians. Even Fox, in his old age, like so many successful founders, began to disclaim his early radicalism and after his death friends took care to expurgate from his writings that evidence of unseemly enthusiasm, social challenge, and questionable egotism which later, more historically-minded Quakers have since, with equal care, restored.[1]

Thus the Quakers too, like those other sects whom they had once absorbed and survived, compromised gradually with that society against which they had once protested. Little by little, as a movement, they ceased to challenge, they preferred to ignore the difficult facts of human organisation. In colonial America, as now in Europe, they blindly advocated the appeasement of threatening tribes; and if their wealth had begun, in the days of George Fox, through their scrupulous observance of that medieval concept, 'the just price', it was continued, by some of them at least, by more usual commercial practices. Consequently they soon lost their original appeal, but by the same compromise they gained once more the world they had renounced. Instead of a spiritual they became an economic *élite*. It had happened before to such movements. As the great Czech historian, Anton Gindely, wrote of his native quietists, the Bohemian Brethren, 'those who, in conformity with Pauline doctrines, favoured celibacy, accepted no office, allowed themselves no luxury, tolerated no wealth, put out no money at interest, and abhorred war — these men produced very wealthy capitalists, very honourable husbands, very decorous burgomasters and jurymen, as well as very able generals and statesmen'. With but a slight change (for the Quakers did not preach celibacy or produce generals), the same might be said of the Quakers.

But in truth we should not be surprised. Humanity can be transcended only in moments, not in continuity, and a great protest is seldom renewed within the same movement which it has first launched. Nevertheless, it is the strength of any great tradition that some men within it can always refresh themselves

[1] For this expurgation see especially *George Fox's Book of Miracles*, ed. Henry J. Cadbury (Cambridge 1948)

by turning again to its original sources. The long political servility of Lutheranism was broken by the protest of Niemöller; the Quaker acceptance of society was challenged again by Elizabeth Fry. But who to-day, among that quiet and prosperous community, is likely to challenge, as boldly and eccentrically as George Fox, our *trahison des clercs*?

CHAPTER XXXIII

HUGUENOTS AND PAPISTS

Minority religions resemble one another. There is a similarity of circumstance and experience which overshadows many differences of content and teaching. Take the French Protestants, the most self-conscious of Protestants; their history is very similar to that of the English Catholics, the most self-conscious of Catholics.

In the sixteenth century the French Huguenots, like the English recusants, seemed the majority of the country. When power in the State was secured by their opponents, both alike dwindled. From the 1680's, with the Revocation of the Edict of Nantes in France and the Glorious Revolution in England, both alike gave up hope of ever controlling the State, and a period of quiet attrition began. Eighteenth-century religion, in the upper classes at least, minimised doctrinal differences and recusant peers in England, Huguenot noblemen in France, found it easy to slide into the communion of the majority. If they persisted in their minority beliefs, it was by tradition rather than conviction. For such a tradition they were no longer persecuted, but they paid a price. Both alike were excluded from the service of the State, from the national education. The recusants sent their sons to Douay and worshipped at the chapels of Catholic Embassies in London; the Huguenots sent their sons to England and Holland and worshipped at the chapels of Protestant Embassies in Paris. The question was, whether the family tradition was worth the price? Some decided that it was not, and relapsed. Others, unwilling to desert their traditions, sought to have the price reduced. They advertised their exemplary behaviour. Gone were the days when Calvinists preached revolutionary republicanism against Catholic Kings and Catholics the papal deposition of Protestant Kings. What Englishmen more loyal even to the Hanoverians than the recusant nobility and gentry and their chaplains? What Frenchmen more loyal even to Louis XIV than the Huguenot noblemen and their pastors? Thus they hoped to earn relief from remaining disabilities. At the close of the century they obtained it. In 1778 the English Parliament passed the first Catholic Relief Act; in 1787 Louis XVI published, for the Huguenots, his Edict of Grace. On the eve of the Revolution religious differences seemed to have died. The 'Cisalpine' English Catholics, like the loyal French Huguenots, seemed almost a department of the Established Church.

And after the Revolution, in the new climate of the nineteenth century? We all know of the Catholic revival in England, how that moribund, residuary, tolerated religion, shifting its basis from the cold-blooded aristocracy to the fanatical Irish peasantry, reasserted itself, gathering recruits, preaching defiance, and causing dismay to the Establishment; and we tend to think that Catholicism, as such, then showed a greater vitality than Protestantism. But when we look at France, what do we find? In 1830, the year after the Catholic Emancipation in England, Louis-Philippe came to the throne and inaugurated a new age of Protestant ascendancy. The Crown Princess was a Protestant; so was the Prime Minister Guizot; so were two other ministers, Gasparin and Pelet de la Lozère. They dominated the government, the markets, the salons. In 1852, the year after the 'Papal Aggression' in England, the *Société de l'Histoire du Protestantisme* was founded, a fertile source of commemoration and propaganda. Then came the Third Republic, bringing even greater triumphs. The Protestant minority provided two Presidents of the Republic. They dominated and reformed the system of Education. They controlled high finance. They made spectacular conversions. And in the 1880's, just as Cardinal Manning in England sought to proclaim a social catholicism, so, in France, the pastor Tommy Fallot founded the movement of social Protestantism which still flourishes under the name of *Christianisme Social*. The freethinker Quinet, the Catholic Renan, declared that only through Protestantism could France be revitalised; and Ernest Renauld, surveying with alarm the ascendancy of Protestants throughout the national life, published his rallying cries, first *le Péril Protestant*, then *la Conquête Protestante*.

It is easy, when one makes such a comparison, to conclude that religions do not in themselves, or at least in their practical expressions, differ very much: that such external facts as establishment, or independence, or persecution are more significant than doctrine or internal discipline. And this indifferency can be fortified if we stop to observe the Christian Churches silently and secretly stealing each other's doctrinal clothes. But before sinking into such a sceptical conclusion, it is as well to test it by looking beyond similarities to differences. Fortunately, in respect of French Protestantism, we are now singularly well equipped to do so. Two new books, different but complementary, provide us with ample evidence and stimulating suggestions. One is by a distinguished French Protestant historian, M. Emile G. Léonard[1]; the other by an American student of politics, a Christian Marxist who has also been influenced by the work of that great French sociologist, himself an Alsatian Protestant, André Siegfried.[2]

For beyond all questions of quantity — the response of parties or Churches to the policy of the State or the movements of the age — there is the question of quality. Quantitatively the English Catholics, now ten per cent of the nation, compare favourably with the French Protestants, now one per cent; and their fluctuations have been similar. But what a difference in quality and achievement! At no time have the English Catholics been an active or progressive element in the nation. They may expand within society, but they do not animate any part of it. On the other hand, the French Protestants have always been an active force. Henri IV, even after his conversion, filled his court with Huguenots. He had a Jesuit confessor, but his ministers, his advisers, his men of affairs were Protestants: 'I trust them more around my person', he said, 'than any of my new religion'. Their names are famous: Sully, Laffemas, Montchréstien, Olivier de Serres. Protestants built the Paris of Henri IV as they afterwards rebuilt the Paris of Napoleon III. Cardinal Richelieu similarly relied on Protestant advisers; so did Mazarin, so did Colbert; and when Louis XIV revoked the Edict of Nantes, what talent the Huguenot *Diaspora* carried over Northern Europe! Is there anything like it among the recusant

[1] E. G. Léonard, *Le Protestant Français* (Paris 1953).
[2] Stuart R. Schram, *Protestantism and Politics in France* (Alençon, 1954).

exiles under our Queen Elizabeth? The question only has to be asked to be dismissed.

When one turns to the nineteenth century it is the same. The Catholic minority in England expanded also in that century; but who were its recruits? They were the casualties of change: intellectuals tired of thinking, aristocrats unable to compete in society, worldlings weary of the world. How well one knows the face of certain converts to Catholicism — that smooth, exhausted look, burnt-out and yet at rest, as of a motorist who, after many mishaps and mounting insurance-premiums, has at last decided to drive himself no more, and having found a chauffeur with excellent references, resigns himself to safer travel in a cushioned back-seat. Very different were the expanding Protestant minority in nineteenth-century France, the creators of the Third Republic, the educators of modern France.

Turning to politics, we find the same difference. French Protestantism has a dynamic which Catholicism has not, or has lost. English Catholics solicit pity for their past 'sufferings'; French Protestants boast that they always hit back. Under Louis XIV two Marshals of France and 25,000 regular soldiers took two years to suppress a few hundred Protestant peasants in the Cevennes. Throughout the eighteenth century, when its social leaders had fled abroad or were conforming, the 'Protestantism of the Desert' refused to yield, and while the men went to the galleys, the women, locked up in the *Tour de Constance* at Aigues-Mortes, carved the slogan '*Résister*' in their prison-stone. In 1870 it was the Protestant ministers who refused capitulation to the Prussian army; and in the last twenty years the pattern has been repeated. While the Roman Church complied with fascism, or only resisted in defence of its own sectarian interests, and while Vichy and the Church propped each other up and sought to undo the great educational work of the Republic, the French Protestants prepared once more to resist. From 1935 French Protestants in the universities organised for the defence of freedom of conscience. In 1940, of the seven members of General de Gaulle's committee for political re-education after victory, five were Protestants.

In France itself, or at least in the *Midi*, the geography of the Resistance coincides remarkably with the geography of Protestantism. And while the French hierarchy complied with Vichy and its masters, the President of the Reformed Church never bowed the knee to Baal. Ordered to broadcast in favour of the German requisition of skilled workers, Pastor Boegner firmly refused. 'I am distressed to observe', the head of the Vichy radio service wrote to him, 'that, although your Catholic colleague has found powerful arguments in the Gospel for rendering to Cæsar that which is Cæsar's and to God that which is God's, I have listened in vain for any sign of such efforts by your pastors'; nor could all the threats of the German authorities persuade Pastor Boegner to imitate the Catholic cardinals and archbishops in denouncing Allied bombardments. The Catholic Church sometimes resisted Fascism; but it waited till it was directly attacked and then it resisted only in defence of the rights of Catholicism. The French Protestants resisted from the start; and they resisted (as Pastor Boegner showed by his famous letter on the persecution of the Jews) in defence of the rights of man.

What is the source of this difference, of this Protestant dynamism which so contrasts with the defensive character of Catholic minorities? Is it essentially a Calvinist force — for the record of Lutheran Germany is very different? But the Lutherans of Alsace have provided French Protestantism with as much of its vigour as the Calvinists of the *Midi*. Is it then the special individualism of the French — for even the Catholics in France have, to their credit, given a good deal of trouble to the Pope? Possibly; but even so, this individualism is undoubtedly made sharper, more positive, more radical by Protestantism. The French Protestant is, above all, an *active* individualist; collectively, his community is not a tribe but an *élite*. In his character and social behaviour he is, as Professor Léonard says, *un noble*. Among the peasants of the *Midi*, as in Ireland, the Protestants are the admitted aristocracy. A modern Swiss writer has noticed it: they are, he writes, '*très conscients d'une supériorité qu'ils ne peuvent attribuer au rang social, ni au salaire, c'est evident, mais à la réligion*'. And in the sixteenth century Agrippa d'Aubigné described the Protestants of the South as '*Princes qui règnent sur eux-mêmes*'. Perhaps all genuine Protestantism has something of this proud self-respect which reaches its grim logical form in Calvin's doctrine of the Elect. Even in England, converts to

Popery are generally regarded as socially *déclassés*. Newman's *Apologia* may excite pity: it cannot command respect. An *élite* never asks for pity: the concept is self-contradictory. Rather it moves to the attack and becomes a party of revolt. Its slogan (when it needs one) will be, Keep Left.

Such observations do not answer so large a question; but perhaps it is something to have posed it. In the past the practical effect of doctrinal difference has often been exaggerated. More recently it has been attenuated. I believe that it has been rightly attenuated. Much that was formerly ascribed to direct teaching can be shown, if we make fair comparisons, to have been caused by external circumstances. Yet the genuine differences remain. Nowhere are they shown more clearly than in these two minorities whose external history has been so similar, the English Catholics and the French Protestants.

CHAPTER XXXIV

THOMAS HOBBES

When Thomas Hobbes, at the age of eighty-four, looked back on his life, he found the key to it in fear. 'Fear and I were born twins,' he wrote; for his birth had been premature, hastened by the panic of the Spanish Armada. Fear characterised his personal life, making him twice a fugitive. Fear is the basis of his political philosophy, as of all dictatorships; the very word tolls like a minute-bell throughout the *Leviathan*. But philosophical systems do not spring from obsessions only. The mind of a revolutionary thinker is rarely simple, And the extraordinary boldness of Hobbes' intellectual method requires some less facile explanation.

Like many great revolutionaries, Hobbes was a convert. His early studies were desultory. In his youth, he loved music, and the lute. At Oxford, he left his books to snare jackdaws. As tutor to the Cavendish family, he hawked and hunted in Derbyshire, and wrote a poem on the wonders of the Peak. His intellectual interests were with the humanists. He jotted notes for Francis Bacon in the stately gardens of Gorhambury. He read Aristotle and translated Thucydides, corresponded with philosophers and conversed at Great Tew. He had already passed his fortieth year, ingenious but infertile, a witty conversationalist and pleasant companion for his aristocratic friends, before he reached that intellectual crisis, which to most men occurs, if at all, at least ten years earlier. Travelling abroad with his patron, he picked up a text of Euclid, and opened it at the forty-seventh proposition. From that moment he was 'in love with geometry'; it was 'the only science that it hath pleased God hitherto to bestow upon mankind'.

Whether his conversion was really as simple as this, we cannot say. Such incidents are usually the culmination of a long and painful process, not a substitute for it. But from that time Hobbes gradually turned his back on his intellectual past, and trod a new path, which he never forsook. Aristotle, he now discovered, was no better than a country bumpkin; nothing could be more absurd than his Metaphysics, nor more repugnant to government than his Politics, nor more ignorant than his Ethics. Henceforth logic was the only intellectual method which he allowed. The baggage of the past — experience, tradition, observation — was jettisoned. He read little. Had he read as much as other men, he said, he would know no more than they. Instead of reading, or observing, he thought, logically. He walked in France with a pen and inkhorn in his stick, and a notebook in his pocket, 'and as soon as a thought darted, he presently entered it into his book, or otherwise he might perhaps have lost it'. Thus the *Leviathan* was written.

The axiom, fear; the method, logic; the conclusion, despotism. Such is the argument of that extraordinary book. Man, says Hobbes, is by nature unpolitical and unoriginal, a mechanical creature moved by strings and springs. This was the view of the Benthamites after him, and it is no accident that it was they who, in the nineteenth century, revived and edited his works. But the 'springs of action' which Hobbes postulated were simpler than those of Jeremy Bentham: they were fear and emotions derived from fear. 'The cause that moveth a man to become subject to another is fear of not otherwise preserving himself.' Man does not move towards positive ends, but away from fear. It is fear that urges him to 'a perpetual and restless desire of power after power, that ceaseth only in death'. Of all the horrors of the state of nature, so grimly catalogued, the worst of all is 'continual fear and danger of violent death'. And if a man turn to philosophical speculation, what comfort has he?

> As Prometheus (which interpreted is, the Prudent Man) was bound to the hill Caucasus, a place of large prospect, where an eagle, feeding on his liver, devoured in the day as much as was repaired in the night; so that man which looks too far before him, in the care of future time, hath his heart all the day long gnawed on by fear of death, poverty, or other calamity, and has no repose, nor pause of his anxiety, but in sleep.

What is the answer to this terrible, this obsessive problem? One answer is given by the Churches, which exploit fear, and particularly 'the fear of darkness and ghosts, which is greater than other fears', building thereupon a pretentious superstructure of myth and mummery only 'to keep in credit the use of exorcism, of crosses, of holy water, and other such inventions of ghostly men'. This answer Hobbes utterly rejects. Religion is not a safeguard against fear, but a parasite on it. Though his prudence made him an Anglican, and his logic an erastian, Hobbes was, in fact (as his enemies maintained), a complete atheist, regarding all religion as a deliberate fraud invented by priests to fool the people. Ill in France, he was pestered by the clergy of three denominations, begging him to die in their communions. 'Let me alone,' he replied, 'or I will detect all your cheats from Aaron to yourselves.' And he attributed 'all the changes of religion in the world to one and the same cause; and that is, unpleasing priests'.

The trenchancy of Hobbes's anti-clericalism, which makes him so readable, suggests that in this, too, he may have been a convert. It is interesting that his contemporaries believed (perhaps on the evidence of his writings) that he was afraid to be alone in the dark; and though his friends denied this, the vividness and frequency of his allusions to supernatural fears suggest that he may not always have been exempt from them. The man who described Brutus, haunted by the ghost of Cæsar —

> For sitting in his tent, pensive and troubled with the horror of his rash act, it was not hard for him, slumbering in the cold, to dream of that which most affrighted him—

and who, in a series of contemptuous paragraphs, likened the whole apparatus of the Roman Church to the imaginary world of spooks and hobgoblins, at least knew some sympathy with the emotions he disclaimed.

Hobbes's answer is therefore a purely secular answer. To escape the consequences of his bestial and timid nature, man must erect a civil authority of terrifying completeness: a state based on naked, and wielding absolute power, with no other function than to wield power; whose effectiveness alone is its legitimacy; whose opinions are truth; whose orders are justice; resistance to which is a logical absurdity. This is 'that great Leviathan, or rather (to speak more reverently) that mortal god, to which we owe, under the immortal God, our peace and defence'.

The *Leviathan* is a fantastic monster, such as is sometimes cast up, with other strange births, in political, as in marine, convulsions. It is an isolated phenomenon in English thought, without ancestry or posterity; crude, academic, and wrong. Its axioms are inadequate, its method inapplicable, its conclusions preposterous. How seldom in history has any reality corresponded with it! Hobbes's whole system was based on huge errors, uncorrected, because untested, by observation. He had learnt nothing of experimental methods from Bacon, nothing of historical understanding from Thucydides. A vivid impression of civil strife is perhaps all he preserved from the profound wisdom of that greatest of historians. To compare him with Machiavelli is absurd; for Machiavelli tests and illustrates every thesis by historical analogy. Hobbes despised the evidence of the past. It was no better, he said, than prophecy; 'both being grounded only on experience'. He cannot even be regarded symptomatically, as a commentary on contemporary events; for his fundamental ideas were developed before civil war had broken out in England or France. He is a typical, academic *Gelehrte*; which is perhaps why his most enthusiastic commentators have all come from Germany.

Why then is he important? First, for his style. Hobbes was no spellbinder. A complete nominalist, he used words as tools, not as charms. He was contemptuous of fine, meaningless phrases. St. Thomas Aquinas had called eternity '*nunc stans*, an ever-abiding Now'; 'which is easy enough to say,' remarked Hobbes drily, 'but though I fain would, yet I never could conceive it; they that can are happier than I'. 'Words', he said elsewhere, 'are wise men's counters, they do but reckon by them; but they are the money of fools.' Nevertheless, though Hobbes could never lose himself in an *O Altitudo*, the stock from which he drew his counters was that wonderful, rich vocabulary of the early seventeenth century, the vocabulary of Milton and Donne and Sir Thomas Browne; and by the boldness with which he used them, by the monolithic temper of his mind, and the formidable logic of his argument, he wrote a book which is as striking in its singleness of purpose, its defiant language, its inspired iconoclasm (and sometimes its dullness), as the poem of Lucretius.

Secondly, he concentrated his doctrines into a single, timely and complete work. Many of those doctrines had already appeared in the works of French lawyers and English pamphleteers, and in Hobbes's other English and Latin works; but in the *Leviathan* they are brought together in a logical system that allows no further development. And this book, by an accident of date, acquired a terrible significance. In 1651 the ingenuous author presented his academic thesis to the exiled Charles II. Two years later, Cromwell seized power in England, and Hobbes's outrageous doctrines suddenly corresponded, or seemed to correspond, with a fearful reality. Already 'the father of atheists', he now appeared as the theorist of the usurper, made yet more dangerous and detestable by the ringing phrases, the exultant nihilism, with which he swept away the tinselled rubbish of traditional thought in order to make room, in the desolate void which he had created, for his grim, impersonal idol. Humane, conventional, practical, religious men — whether Puritan or Anglican — saw what he had done and trembled. No voice was raised in his support. The universal horror which he inspired became yet another argument for conservatism, for a royal restoration.

Nevertheless, his work — at least his work of destruction — could not be undone. The idol might have crumbled, but the great void remained, and pious hands were never again able to reassemble the old intellectual *bric-à-brac* which he had swept away. So, when King and Court returned to authority, the execrated philosopher somehow survived. The royalist clergy might snipe timidly at the old pachyderm as he brushed through their shady preserves; Dr. Beale, in his court sermon, might still dispute the old question, whether angels have beards, and decide learnedly that they have; the theorists of Divine Right might mumble away about Noah and Nimrod; the bishops might 'make a motion to have the good old gentleman burnt for a heretique'; the Presbyterian Baxter might join with high-flying Anglicans against him: but it was all rather ineffective. Besides the old man was so genial, so witty, so entertaining: one could not really dislike him. And he had royal support: Charles II preferred wit to orthodoxy, and protected his former tutor. As for the philosophers, they might keep his unpopular name from their books, but they could not exclude his achievement from their minds. He had cleared political thought of its ancient, biblical cobwebs, and set it firmly on the secular basis of human psychology. That his psychology was inadequate, elementary, and wrong is an irrelevant objection. The function of genius is not to give new answers, but to pose new questions, which time and mediocrity can resolve. This Hobbes had achieved. By one great thunderstorm he had changed the climate of thought; and his achievement is not the thunderstorm, but the change.

After the storm, the old philosopher enjoyed his ease. He was back in Derbyshire, still with the Cavendishes, the friends and patrons of seventy years. Erect and sprightly, his health improving yearly, he still played tennis at seventy-five; after which a servant would rub him down in bed. Then, in the privacy of his chamber, the old bachelor would lift up his voice and sing prick-song, for the health of his lungs. It would prolong his life, he believed. Certainly he went on living. He seemed immortal, like Satan himself; a genial Satan. At eighty, he wrote *Behemoth*, incorrigibly erroneous. At eighty-six, feeling bored (for conversation at Chatsworth was sometimes thin) he dashed off an English translation of the *Iliad* and the *Odyssey*. At ninety, he was still going. His face was rubicund; his bright hazel eye glowed like an ember; and when he took his pipe from his mouth, he delighted all by his brisk and decisive repartees. Only the flies disconcerted him, settling on his bald head. Of the *Leviathan*, that product of his headstrong sixties, he did not speak. There has never been anything to add to its utter finality.

CHAPTER XXXV

THE ANTI-HOBBISTS

In 1651, cruising with majestic indifference through the political Deluge that had submerged their society, bewildered Englishmen suddenly sighted a new and terrifying monster. It was the *Leviathan* of Thomas Hobbes, who himself soon afterwards arrived from France to join his creature. What new cataclysm could this beast portend? Two years later, when Oliver Cromwell set up his military dictatorship, muddle-headed royalists thought that they knew. Of course they were wrong. Hobbes was as hated by the Puritans as by the Royalists, and indeed by everyone else — as soon became clear. For a whole generation every shelf and sandbank in the receding flood contained a fisherman. Most of them were elderly men, in old-fashioned clothes; many of them wore clerical collars; all were equipped with complicated tackle and jars of curious bait. They were engaged in the new national pastime; catching the *Leviathan*.[1]

First on the bank was the squire, Sir Robert Filmer, an angler of established reputation. Aged sixty-three, cœval with Hobbes himself, and a rival expert on sovereignty, he studied the monster with a professional eye. As the oracle of patriarchal rule he approved its absolutist conclusion ('for we do but flatter ourselves if we hope ever to be governed without an arbitrary power'), but he differed on the basis of that power, which ought, of course, to be the patriarchal power of Stuart Kings consecrated by the Anglican Church; and having thus disposed of the *Leviathan*, the squire resigned his stretch of water to another experienced angler, the parson. The parson — the Rev. Alexander Rosse — waded a little deeper, and having carefully set up the vast, ornamental, archaic intellectual fishing-tackle of the Jacobean age, which, in its time, had engaged many a doctrinal herring, returned to the Angler's Arms to boast of

[1] John Bowle, *Hobbes and his Critics* (London 1951).

Leviathan Drawn out with a Hook and demonstrate that the creature (which had got away) had been merely a synthesis of all those polysyllabical heresies which the Church had long ago condemned. Of two other angling parsons, the Rev. William Lucy and his younger colleague the Rev. Seth Ward, little need be said. They did but tickle, with home-made gear, and their efforts (as Aubrey said of Lucy) were 'but weak ones'. However, they did not fish altogether in vain. Though they failed to catch the *Leviathan*, each in the end netted a bishopric.

Who indeed could catch the *Leviathan*? Roused by the challenge, two far greater men now addressed themselves to the task. Both were elderly and conservative, but both were men of the world, statesmen and thinkers of real stature, strenuous before and powerful after the Flood. Furthermore, both knew the monster well and had been present at its birth. In 1658 John Bramhall, Bishop of Derry, arrived confidently at the waterside; he was followed in 1676, at a slower, more dignified pace, by Edward Hyde, Earl of Clarendon. Their style was different. Clarendon, now once more an exile, was a graver man — and indeed there is a tragic dignity in his emphatic rejection, addressed to Charles II, of Hobbes's 'false and evil doctrine' that a banished man owes no allegiance to the sovereign who has banished him. Bramhall, an out-of-doors bishop accustomed to Irish conditions, intended to enjoy the sport. He would adopt, he said, the methods of the Greenland fishermen who, after harpooning the Leviathan and then

> giving him line and space enough to bounce and tumble up and down and tire himself out and try all his arts . . . at last draw this formidable creature to the shore or ship, and slice him in pieces, and boil him in a cauldron, and tun him up in oil.

In the bounce and tumble the *Leviathan* gave the episcopal angler a few sharp knocks, but in the end, as another bishop complacently observed, Bramhall's *Catching of the Leviathan* 'hit him hard . . . the hook is still in his nose. Good judges have thought he hath not licked himself well of those wounds the Bishop of Derry gave him'.

Bramhall and Clarendon both attacked Hobbes from a conservative position. Having themselves loyally followed their own unfortunate sovereigns through defeat and banishment, they saw Hobbes as a mere turncoat who, by recognising only such sovereignty as could effectively protect him, 'doth take his sovereign for better but not for worse'. Had he not himself deserted the helpless Charles II in order to court the odious usurper? But to refute him they did not rely on tradition alone: they attacked the heart of his philosophy. Fundamentally, Hobbes had begun by rejecting the Aristotelian doctrine that man is by nature a social animal. Aristotle, he had declared, was no better in politics than a country bumpkin, and society, far from being natural, was an artificial structure imposed upon men to correct the disastrous consequences of their anti-social nature. Bramhall and Clarendon, as conservatives, returned to the wisdom of the past which Hobbes had so vulgarly spurned. 'Whatever errors may have been brought into the world by Aristotle,' said Clarendon sharply, 'no man ever grew a rebel by reading him.' All other philosophers, said Bramhall more explicitly, 'do derive commonwealth from the sociability of nature which is in mankind — most truly'; but Hobbes

> will have the beginning of all human society from mutual fear. . . . Let him tell me what mutual fear of danger did draw the silly bees into swarms, or the sheep or doves into flocks . . . and I shall conceive it possible that the beginnings of human society might be from fear only.

Further, if the basis of Hobbes's theory was false, so was the method of his conclusion. Hobbes had presumed man to be naturally anti-social but naturally rational, and politics to be a mathematical art, consisting 'of certain rules, as doth arithmetic and geometry, and not, as in tennis-play, in practice only'. Both Bramhall and Clarendon, from their practical experience, contemptuously rejected this view. Men are not rational: 'We have too much cause to believe', said Clarendon, 'that the major part of mankind do not think at all.' As for government by arithmetical formulæ, they laughed aloud at such academic folly. 'I should be glad', wrote Clarendon,

> that Mr. Hobbes might have a place in Parliament, and sit in Council, and be present in courts of Justice and other Tribunals, whereby it is probable he would find that his solitary cogitations, how deep

soever, and his too peremptory adhering to some philosophical notions, and even rules of geometry, has misled him in the investigation of policy. . . .

In truth Hobbes was not the philosopher of the Cromwellian or any other revolution, and the *Leviathan*, that terrifying monster, was in fact only a pedant's Chimæra. It had scattered some older phantoms, but when exposed to the real world had itself in turn dissolved, leaving to later philosophers only a few disconnected intellectual stage-properties. Man is not rational: no system of politics can govern him without some mystique; and experience — which Hobbes despised — has shown that the least mystical, most utilitarian system of government is in fact not despotic but liberal. When the greatest of liberal philosophers picked up from the wrack of the *Leviathan* the concept of the social contract, he did not even think it worth while to mention the rest of the decomposing carcase; indeed, with polite disdain he pretended not to have noticed it; Filmer's *Patriarcha* then seemed a more serious adversary.

And yet, although two elderly conservative statesmen had landed the *Leviathan*, it was perhaps not they who persuaded the younger generation of its weakness. After all, the younger generation did not listen much to Bramhall and Clarendon. Bramhall only survived the Restoration by three years, in 'the declension of his age and health', reminding Jeremy Taylor of 'the broken heaps of Pompey's Theatre, and the crushed Obelisks . . . venerable in their very dust'; and Clarendon outlived him only to taste another exile. If the *Leviathan* was dead by 1680, perhaps he had not died of his wounds in that famous anglers' contest: perhaps he had died a natural death: death by exposure on the bank after the Deluge had subsided.

For after 1660 there was in England a new intellectual climate, in which the whole basis of Hobbes's philosophy seemed out of date. For Hobbes's underlying fear, his belief in the fundamental wickedness of man, was not peculiar to him: it was the commonplace of his generation. The early seventeenth century was an age of intellectual gloom: Roman Catholics lamented 'the last era of a declining and gasping world'; Anglicans like John Donne and Sir Thomas Browne dwelt magniloquently on worms, urns, and the apparatus of mortality; and Puritans rejoiced (if at all) only at the imminence of that Eternal Damnation from which they alone would be exempt. But after 1660, Englishmen were not afraid, they were confident; and perhaps the magisterial reproofs of Bramhall and Clarendon were less effective than the gay dialogues of the Rev. John Eachard, who, in 1673, rendered the dismal philosophy of Hobbes, with its state of nature, 'the war of all against all', not heretical but ridiculous.

Timotheus: Well met, Philautus, how does your best self this morning? What stout and hearty? . . . Shall we take a turn or two in the walks?

Philautus [*Hobbes*]*:* No, I thank you, unless I know your tricks better: You may chance to get behind me and bite me in the legs. . . .

The man who began thus, mocking the portentous philosopher for his chronic fear of being 'affronted, abused, choused, defamed, flung downstairs or tossed in a blanket', knew that his readers were already on his side. In such a climate the *Leviathan* did not need to be hooked and played, bounced and tumbled to an elaborate death: it could not live. Unfortunately for its clerical adversaries, neither could their rival doctrine: Original Sin.

CHAPTER XXXVI

CLARENDON AND THE GREAT REBELLION

Edward Hyde, first earl of Clarendon, was not a great statesman. As a member of the reforming Long Parliament he had handled an important piece of legislation; as minister of Charles I in his adversity and Charles II in his exile he had shown constant dignity in eclipse; aided by events, he had achieved his ultimate masterpiece, a bloodless restoration on the best of possible terms; but as Lord Chancellor of the monarchy thus restored he was a failure and his life ended in a second and more bitter exile. Every incident heightened the tragedy of that second failure: the long-delayed triumph and the sudden 'gust of envy' which reversed it; the ingratitude of his royal master expressed in that brief and heartless phrase, 'Bid the Chancellor begone'; the hustled flight; the seven wandering years in an inhospitable country while his letters begging leave to revisit England remained unacknowledged; and finally the undismayed magnanimity of the old man who, in humiliation and defeat, composed one of the serenest, most majestic narratives that any man has ever written of events which have engulfed him: *the History of the Rebellion.*

Of course, Clarendon's history has its faults. A historian of his own time does not always use the language, or answer the questions, which posterity will require of him: he takes much for granted and assumes, in his readers, an equal familiarity with at least the background of his story. It would be vain to seek in Clarendon anything comparable with Macaulay's famous third chapter. Further, Clarendon's work is often — like the Revolution it describes — formless: for it was not written at one time, or for one purpose, or in one pattern. Begun in the Scilly Islands in 1646 and continued during the next two years in Jersey, its first chapters had carried the story down to 1644 only, and had never been intended for publication. Rather, they were confidential memoranda to instruct future ministers in past errors. Then, for twenty years, this document had been laid aside. The opportunity to instruct the ministers of the Crown was never given to Clarendon, and in exile no minister would have heard him. He was, anyway, separated — finally as it seemed — from his papers and his friends. He therefore decided to begin again and instruct instead his own children. In Montpelier in 1668 he resumed his autobiography — a vast work, whose original manuscript, never yet published in full, still rests in the Bodleian Library. Then, in 1671, when he had carried the story down to the Restoration, his son was at last allowed to visit him, and brought out to him from England the unfinished manuscript of his earlier *History*. Clarendon re-read that half-forgotten work, and, like Swift, was astonished at his own genius. Turning aside, in its turn, from his uncompleted *Life*, he resolved to use it now as a mere quarry from which to resume work upon his long-abandoned *History* — not now as a manual for politicians seeking to cope with old problems, nor as a vindication of the political career of a statesman who would soon be dead, but as the work of an English Thucydides: a monument of history written by one who, from start to finish, had participated in it; who had understood its causes and traced its consequences; who had familiarly known its great actors and great victims; and who, having tasted, in equal measures, the alternating extremes of fortune, had arrived at that magnanimous philosophy which alone can judge the complex revolutions of human politics. Thus, in 1674, when Clarendon died at Rouen, his heirs inherited a finished manuscript. Thirty years later it was published, and the University of Oxford, to which, as Clarendon had written in his moving letter of resignation, no other Chancellor could ever be more affectionate than he, was unexpectedly enriched by the best-seller of a century.

History changes, historians ask new questions and offer, with temporary certainty, new answers. The history of the Great Rebellion in England has been re-interpreted a dozen times since Clarendon. And yet, when these fashions of interpretation have evaporated, how much more modern does he still appear than they! Carlyle's heroic Cromwell 'bathed in the Eternal

Splendours' is as extinct as the great auk; Gardiner, for all his evidential accuracy, can never now persuade us of his constitutional and religious conclusions; and the Marxist doctrine of the seventeenth century class-war is foundering in turn beneath the evidence it has generated. Through the tatters of these dissolving theories the great work of Clarendon still looms in undiminished stature and forces us to ask, what is the quality which gives to this seventeenth-century lawyer and politician a modernity which no later historian of his period has contrived to retain?

Partly it is the very formlessness of his work, which, unconstrained by any rigid doctrine, excluded nothing as irrelevant. Modern historians, devoutly seeking the social and economic causes of great revolutions, find these omitted by their immediate predecessors, who worshipped at other shrines, and are pleased suddenly to discover them, clearly set out, in the vast and comprehensive pantheon of Clarendon. This is not mere accident, of course, for Clarendon, like most of his contemporaries, had a sharp economic sense. He was careful to assess the economic interests of all his characters, including himself: he recognised this as one of the springs of action. Further, as a London company-lawyer, he knew the politics of the City, which later historians have so strangely ignored. He also analysed the social divisions in the country: the political opposition of old and new landlords and the parliamentary sympathies of corporations. The Great Rebellion was formerly regarded primarily as a religious movement, and Sir Charles Firth could complain of 'the fundamental defect' of Clarendon's work, that it is 'a history of a religious revolution in which the religious element is omitted'. Modern social historians will regard such an omission rather as a virtue, a sign that Clarendon was as perspicacious as they.

In fact he was more perspicacious than many of them: for he did not share their greater illusions. Himself a politician, who had often seen a whole train of consequences launched by some chance incident — by 'the never enough lamented death of Dr. Bancroft'; by the 'untoward and in truth unheard of accident' of the non-election of the Speaker; by the inopportune and prejudicial death of the Earl of Bedford — he could never have entertained the academic error of determinism. He understood, as modern doctrinaire historians do not, that economic interests are abstractions which cannot mobilise themselves; that their force depends on personal manœuvres, temporary alliances, procedural devices; that the study of politics is in fact always also the study of politicians. And since he was by choice a student of men, whose whole life illustrates a genius for human understanding, he looked through his political microscope and saw political parties not as solid blocs but as shifting groups only casually held together by perpetual human adjustment. He saw the vast revolution of his time not (like Carlyle) as a cosmic act, nor (like the Victorians) as a struggle for principles, nor (like the Marxists) as a crude class-war, but as the operations of politicians only imperfectly in control of their material. Every character was to him half an agent, half a victim, in the avalanche so imprudently set sliding, and every character therefore required — and received — a just and careful portrait.

What brilliant portraits they are! To those who read history for pleasure, not instruction, Clarendon's work seems often a mere endless tapestry of wonderful portraits in the great age of such portraiture, in an age of humanism, when every educated man polished his personality and sought to shine as a virtuoso. To this passionate interest in character Clarendon owes his splendid magnanimity: it enabled him (since he agreed with Gibbon that history is the record of the crimes and follies of mankind), while visiting the crimes with judicial severity, to shed a humanising light at least upon the follies. Buckingham, to more censorious judges the new Sejanus, the tyrant-favourite, was for him 'of a most flowing courtesy and affability to all men who made any address to him', only reprehensible to the inconsiderate profusion of his benevolence; Archbishop Laud, the 'little meddling hocus-pocus', achieves from him, an adversary, his most sympathetic portrait; even the Earl of Warwick, the grand patron of rebellion, appears in his pages as a genial rogue; even John Hampden, who, 'as was said of Cinna, . . . had a head to contrive, and a tongue to persuade, and a hand to execute any mischief', receives from him an unfeigned appreciation; and as even the funeral panegyric of the murdered king is qualified by the admission that 'his kingly virtues had some mixture and allay that hindered them from shining in full lustre', so even the final sentence on the grand regicide, Oliver Cromwell, is mitigated by a reluctant concession: 'in a word, as he had all the wickedness against which damnation is denounced, and for which hellfire is prepared, so he had some virtues which have caused the memory of some men in all ages to be celebrated; and he will be looked upon by posterity as a brave bad man'.

So, as we follow Clarendon's great history through those long, rich, serpentine, polychromatic sentences which heighten its majestic quality, we see the double character of historian and politician, combined in his greatest virtue: his study of men. Like Boswell, Clarendon 'ever delighted in that intellectual chymistry which can separate good qualities from evil in the same person'; therefore he was at his best, both in politics and in literature, as a conciliator. If any man could have reconciled King and Parliament in the critical years 1640–2 it was Clarendon; when the breach was irreparable his influence declined, but we can trace it still, in his state papers, reconciling, with infinite tact and understanding, mutually suspicious groups of exiles and conspirators. His greatest work in politics — the Restoration Settlement — was again a work of conciliation; and if he was unable through political insufficiency, to consolidate that achievement, the same quality secured for him in literature a more permanent triumph: his *History*, thanks to human understanding and an incomparable style, has reconciled posterity to him as to no other historian of the English Revolution.

CHAPTER XXXVII

MACAULAY AND THE GLORIOUS REVOLUTION

Success was the end of Macaulay's career, confidence the means to it. All his life he knew what he meant to do, and it was not a vulgar ambition. He knew the price, and paid it; knew the rewards, and savoured them. For the long journey to India he chose his books with purpose: 'Richardson, Voltaire's works, Gibbon, Sismondi's *History of the French*, Davila, the *Orlando* in Italian, Don Quixote in Spanish, Homer in Greek, Horace in Latin . . .'; and he read them all. In India he planned his economy: from his salary of £10,000 a year as a member of the Supreme Council he saved, in five years, £30,000 on which to live in comfort while he sat in Parliament and wrote his *History*; and that *History*, the ultimate aim of it all, was the most carefully planned of all. It was to be popular — 'to supersede the last fashionable novel on the tables of young ladies' — but permanent, resting on permanent merits. It was to be perfectly clear — 'how little the all-important art of making meaning pellucid is studied now! Hardly any popular writer except myself thinks of it'; and it was to be as accurate as research and method could make it. Such finality is not cheaply acquired. Infinite pains were devoted to it. Macaulay studied the methods of the great historians critically, revised his views of Tacitus and Thucydides ('the *ne plus ultra* of human art'), and sought the lost secret of narrative style. Methodically he estimated his programme: eighteen months of reading and travel, in Holland, Belgium, Scotland, Ireland, France; the Dutch and French archives to be ransacked; thousands of pamphlets to be read. Then he would start writing, two pages a day (for easy reading means hard writing) for two years. 'Then I reckon a year for polishing, retouching and printing.'

To ensure success he refused cabinet office and gave up political life; and when the book at last appeared his fame was instant and immense. Byron and Scott were eclipsed. 'Is that Mr. Macaulay?' exclaimed two girls at the Zoo. 'Never mind the hippopotamus!' When the third and fourth volumes were published, Longmans sold 26,500 copies in ten weeks and sent the author a cheque for £20,000 in the eleventh; and the author, broken in health but sure of immortality, retired to Kensington, there, with his elegant villa and rolling lawn, his carriage and four men-servants, to impress the pilgrims who came to question, to admire, to be entertained. His entertainments were famous. On Anglicans he would press the Michaelmas goose, on Dissenters the fillet of veal, 'the recognised Sunday dinner in good old Nonconformist families'; to both he would recite such passages from the *Almanach des Gourmands* as that 'after the seventh dozen oysters cease to whet the appetite'. Once he was even visited by a deputation of five Quakers, eager to refute his strictures on William Penn. He recorded the incident with his usual complacency. The Quakers, he said, were routed: 'they had absolutely nothing to say.' As Sir Charles Firth remarked, this is probably because they never had a chance to speak. In fact they were right and Macaulay, on this occasion, demonstrably wrong.

The crown of a man's career is his biography. In this, too, Macaulay was wonderfully successful. Gibbon was his own best biographer; Macaulay's real liberalism, genuine humanity and disinterested love of learning would never have been revealed by his own too brisk and rhetorical pen. By supreme good fortune he found, in his own nephew, his perfect biographer. Sir George Trevelyan's *Life* is one of the great biographies in our language; and having read it we feel, as after reading Gibbon's autobiography, genuinely glad that the subject was so successful.

The world is jealous of confidence and success: it loves to detect the occasional ignorance of the omniscient, the trivial errors of the infallible; and since Whig views of history lost their absolute supremacy, Tories, Marxists and Catholics have presumed a gleeful revenge. 'The Macaulay view of history' has become, in their vocabulary, one of the great exploded myths, as obsolete, they would suggest, as the systems of Ptolemy or Bishop Bossuet. And yet what is this 'Macaulay view of history'?

A little examination shows that wherever else his critics may have found it, it was not in the works of Macaulay. Macaulay certainly made errors, as every historian does — though surprisingly few — and he further erred in assuming, as no historian can, the finality of his conclusions. He made errors of fact, as over Schomberg's funeral and William Penn, and errors of method, condemning Marlborough on evidence which he found to be mere libel when it condemned William III; he exaggerated for effect and by exaggeration sometimes missed the narrow shades of truth; and his treatment of foreign affairs, compared with that of Ranke, is amateur and provincial. But 'the Macaulay view' as supposed by his modern opponents — the view that there was, in the seventeenth century, an accepted constitution which the tyrannical Stuarts broke and the virtuous Whigs defended — he never held, and one only has to read him to know it. Like all great historians he seems, as it were, to have reinsured himself against future changes in historical philosophy, and the blows which doctrinaire adversaries have aimed at him damage not him but his inferior imitators. His own philosophy is much less easy to assail.

In politics Macaulay believed in three things whose value seemed to him self-evident: honesty, reason and sense. Political honesty was partly the contribution of those great nineteenth-century Evangelicals, the Clapham Sect, to which his own family belonged, and Macaulay, though proud of such a tradition, never claimed for it an earlier pedigree. Rational politics — the politics which removed ancient restrictions, liberated mercantile enterprise, and led to that prosperity upon which any liberal culture must rest — he ascribed to the defeat of the Stuart kings. Political sense consisted, to him, in the recognition that the aim of politics is economic prosperity and liberal but effective administration, not artistic achievement, the triumph of doctrine, or the spread of mumping mysticism. On such views the Revolution of 1688 was indeed a Glorious Revolution, however achieved, and it was quite unnecessary to maintain either that it was an exclusively Whig achievement or that its makers were necessarily inspired by abstract virtues. Not constitutional precedent but actual consequence was its justification, and Macaulay, convinced that the consequences were indisputably good, was ready to make any concession of fact that the evidence required: evasion of inconvenient evidence he could afford to leave to his neo-Catholic, neo-Tory rivals, who would need it.

If Macaulay allowed himself a luxury in his writing, it was not distortion or evasion, but emphasis and relish. Hence those famous passages on James II and his supporters, the backwood squires and parsons, the irreducible rump of the *Ancien Régime*, which caused such an outcry in the manor-houses and rectories of Victorian England. The seventeenth-century squire, said Macaulay, was 'a man with the deportment, the vocabulary and the accent of a carter, yet punctilious on matters of genealogy and precedence'; his wife and daughter were 'in taste and acquirements below a housekeeper or a still-room maid of the present day'; and the chaplain in a great house was traditionally 'the resource of the lady's maid whose character had been blown upon, and who was therefore forced to give up hopes of catching the steward'. Was this to be borne? cried the prosperous Tory gentry, the comfortable Tory clergy of 1850. Unfortunately, it has to be. Controversy and research have modified, but not altered Macaulay's generalisation, produced exceptions but not invalidated the rule. His offence, it is clear, was not in reaching wrong conclusions but in so obviously relishing the conclusions that he reached.

For in the end Macaulay is always vindicated by his sense. He understood politics because, like so many of the great Whigs, he had taken part in them. Academic historians have their advantages, but sometimes they can be very silly. Carlyle was fundamentally silly. Macaulay's modern rivals are often silly. Macaulay never was. Essentially a practical politician, he had no use for abstract theories, no sympathy with emotional indulgences, and therefore a restricted understanding of those subtle moods and colours which also illuminate history. Archbishop Laud's careful record of his superstitious dreams filled him with disgust, and he dismissed that protomartyr of Puseyism as 'a ridiculous old driveller', 'a poor creature who never said or wrote anything indicating more than the ordinary capacity of an old woman'. George Fox, the founder of Quakerism, whose compulsive personality shed around him an almost magical illumination, was to Macaulay an indecent exhibitionist, 'too much disordered for liberty and not sufficiently disordered for Bedlam'. Even Harrington, whom modern Fabian historians have built up into the greatest political thinker of his time, he dismissed with contempt; even Locke, the great doctor of the Revolution, he passed over almost in silence. It was not because he disagreed with their views that Macaulay passed over these philosophers — with Locke, after all, he would have agreed. It was because he was fundamentally uninterested in abstract thought. His mind was hard, practical, empirical.

This hard, practical quality was perhaps Macaulay's greatest limitation: it made him an insensitive critic of art, ideas and religion, on which he nevertheless dogmatised. Even as a historian it limited him: he saw prosperity and good government as the culmination of historical development, and condescended (it is his most tiresome habit) towards the less successful past. Gibbon also believed in his own age, in 'the full light and freedom of the eighteenth century', and looked back with complacency on the dark centuries of 'Christianity and barbarism'; but Gibbon at least recognised, in the age of the Antonines, a civilisation as mature as his own, and his philosophic mind, which could regard history as 'the register of the crimes, follies and misfortunes of mankind', was proof against vulgar self-satisfaction. Place Macaulay beside Gibbon and he seems as parochial as Froude beside himself. And yet, since Macaulay was writing not about art, ideas or religion, but about politics, these are but incidental limitations: the boundaries which exclude the beliefs and absurdities of men still preserve the essentials of political history; within them (and they are wide enough) he remains supreme. He chose the most colourful period of English political history and devoted to its understanding and presentation all his incredible resources of industry and memory, sense, experience and narrative skill. Success so bought is well earned and he remains, after a century of indefatigable historiography and philosophical change, uneclipsed. Besides, he could write, and took trouble to learn the art of writing. Which of his modern critics can claim as much?

CHAPTER XXXVIII

THE MARQUIS OF HALIFAX

The age of Louis XIV was the age, in France, of the aristocratic writers, of de Retz and Hamilton, of St. Simon, and La Rochefoucauld; urbane and polished authors, illuminating, by their lucid memoirs and sceptical aphorisms, the politics which they had known and left. England is poorer in this class of writers, and for good reason. The French aristocracy had tasted power, and been defeated; it was in a long and opulent retirement that those brilliant memoirs were written, that Attic style perfected. But while the French nobility was being driven from politics to the *salon*, the English was busy ensuring its long tenure of power; improving estates, pushing commerce, dominating the provinces, packing legislatures, and shuffling kings. As a class, it had no time for the pen. Only its casualties turned to literature: Clarendon, whose great *History* was written in exile; Bolingbroke, whose too bright career fizzled out in long banishment and the *Patriot King*.

To this generalisation there is at least one important exception. George Savile, Marquis of Halifax, was the English La Rochefoucauld. His *Maxims* have the same dry, sceptical flavour, the same deadly penetration:

> Generally speaking, a trowel is a more effectual instrument than a pencil for flattery.
>
> A man had as good go to bed to a Razor, as to be intimate with a foolish friend.
>
> When a Prince trusteth a man with a dangerous secret, he would not be sorry to hear the bell toll for him.
>
> Men who borrow their opinions can never repay their debts.
>
> It is flattering some men to endure them.

But unlike La Rochefoucauld, Halifax was consistently successful in politics. His writings were the fruit, not of failure and disgrace, but of a bold and dangerous political career. In consequence they are few; but they are also untinged by the bitterness of disappointment. If he saw through the vulgar charms of power, it was not with envy, as unattainable, nor with disgust, as sour; it was with the same intellectual judgment of one who has known and valued it at its proper estimation:

The government of the world is a great thing; but it is a very coarse one, too, compared with the fineness of speculative knowledge.

It is this intellectual temper, exercised successfully in an age of unscrupulous politics, that makes the career of Halifax at once so consistent and so distinguished. His contemporaries thought differently. To them he was an enigma. His experience, his politics, his values were different from theirs. By birth a Cavalier (he was the nephew of Strafford), he had been saved by the Civil War from a conventional education. His great house gutted, his family lost or scattered, he had spent his youth wandering abroad, in France and Italy; not a complacent aristocrat on the Grand Tour, nor a penniless *émigré* following an exiled court, but a free observer of international struggles and revolutionary politics. In France he had not only fallen in love with the works of Montaigne; he had seen the real nature of aristocratic faction. And when he returned to England, not (as so many Royalists) to faded splendour and confiscated estates, but to increased opulence and prospects of power, he had already shed many illusions in which older exiles had only been confirmed. From this vantage-point of wealth and experience, he intervened continually in the vertiginous politics of the Restoration. His interventions seemed often random, and his enemies called him a Trimmer. By another bold intervention, he appropriated the term, and in his most famous pamphlet, *The Character of a Trimmer*, he vindicated both his politics and his consistency:

This innocent word *Trimmer* signifieth no more than this, That if Men are together in a Boat, and one part of the Company would weigh it down on one side, another would make it lean as much to the contrary; it happeneth there is a third Opinion of those, who conceive it would do as well, if the Boat went even, without endangering the Passengers. Now 'tis hard to imagine by what Figure in Language, or by what Rule in Sense, this cometh to be a Fault, and it is much more Wonder it should be thought a Heresy.

Halifax's interventions in politics well illustrated his thesis: they were always bold, and generally decisive. His friends thought him imprudent, his enemies irresponsible. He could be unscrupulous. He told Temple that whether the Popish Plot were true or false, it must be handled as true, and threatened that 'unless he would concur in points so necessary to the People's satisfaction, he would brand him everywhere as a papist'. But when the Whigs used the Plot as an excuse to alter the succession, Halifax again intervened, this time on the other side. Alone, or almost alone, he opposed the majority in the House of Lords. Swords were drawn around him, and he was threatened with death; but at the end of the day his oratory had prevailed, and the Whigs, unable to exclude the Heir Apparent, sought vainly to exclude his champion. A few years later, it was again his intervention (this time literary, with his *Letter to a Dissenter*) that was decisive in ruining the plausible schemes of James II. Throughout the complicated history of the Revolution, he acted with the same conspicuous independence, made more hazardous by his incautious wit. When some zealous but unimportant grandees applied for high offices in reward for their services, 'I remember to have read in history', replied the caustic nobleman, 'that Rome was saved by geese; but I do not remember that those geese were made consuls'. Applicants are not deterred from application by such rejoinders: but next time they apply elsewhere.

A few contemporaries, more inquisitive or less sensitive than the rest, risking such shafts, sought to understand that enigmatic personality. They were not very successful. Since he despised rank, why, asked the pertinacious but pedestrian Bishop Burnet, did he accumulate titles? And was he really, as was generally believed, 'a bold and determined atheist'? But Halifax, who 'was never better pleased than when he was turning Bishop Burnet and his politics into ridicule', gave no satisfaction on these important points. He was a Christian in submission, he said; 'he believed as much as he could, and he hoped that God would not lay it to his charge if he could not digest iron, as an ostrich did, nor take into his belief things that must burst him'. Not perhaps a very satisfactory apologia in the eyes of those High-Churchmen whose elastic credulity and obsequious politics he loved to satirise, those 'silken divines who, one would think, do practise to bow at the altar only to learn to make the better legs at court'. His private aphorisms were even less orthodox:

> The people would not believe in God at all, if they were not permitted to believe wrong in Him.
>
> Men must be saved in this world by their lack of faith.

Courageous intervention in times of crisis, independence of party loyalties, a pungent wit — these are excellent qualities, but without an intellectual consistency and a political purpose they cannot be claimed as virtues; and it was precisely Halifax's consistency and serious purpose that his contemporaries were least qualified to understand. While Whig and Tory fought their often irrelevant struggles over often factious issues, Halifax was one of the few Englishmen, indeed Europeans, who from the start had seen and apprehended the growing power and insatiable ambition of Louis XIV. It was once supposed, and is by some still believed, that the seventeenth-century Whigs were the party of liberty and national resistance. It is a vain and desperate supposition. Such liberties as were then attained were the direct achievement of neither Whigs nor Tories, but the consequence of their often deadlocks, their rare agreements. As for national resistance, if the Stuarts were content to be Louis's satellites, the Whigs (even their canonised martyrs) competed to be his pensioners. Imbecility in foreign affairs was no more a monopoly of one party under the Stuarts than under Baldwin and Chamberlain. Then, as later, the real issues were seen, and faced, not by parties, but by individuals: by the Dutch William, by the Austrian Lisola, by the Englishmen Temple and Halifax. 'The greatness of France', protested Halifax, 'has made all old politics useless'; but old politics have a fatal fascination, especially for old politicians.

Two characteristics, both equally rare in his time, determined Halifax in this policy. They are the same characteristics which inspire his writings: a burning patriotism, and an intellectual contempt for mere power. When the Trimmer looked abroad, to Versailles and Marly, he saw only a vain creature 'grazing among his flatterers and receiving their false worship', 'blown up into an ambitious dropsy', 'not only an encumbrance, but a common nuisance to mankind'. 'The King of France', he wrote in 1680, when Louis was at the zenith of his power, 'hath great pleasure to see how all the world trembleth under him, for I suppose it is satisfaction suitable to his heroick mind; but for my own particular, was I in his place, I could find out a hundred things that would please me more than to keep Flanders and Germany from sleeping for fear of him.' And when he looked at England, he found 'a smell in our native earth better than all the perfumes of the East'. The most eloquent, the most anthologised passage in his works describes the Trimmer's idolatry for the earth of England, how 'he would sooner die than see a Spire of English Grass trampled down by a foreign Trespasser'.

Clearly Halifax's patriotism was no abstract emotion. He was a great aristocrat, a great proprietor; and the fragrant land which he would defend against intrusive trespassers was an extension of his own Nottinghamshire estate, of Rufford Abbey, now enlarged and restored. In the dust of London, in the intervals of politics, his mind reverted instinctively to Rufford, to his plantings and prunings, his improvements and conversions. In his letters to his younger brother (a delightful correspondence, the image of a delightful relationship), among the variety of gossip and politics, among the details of those nine per cent annuities in which he so successfully traded (and in which John Churchill so successfully invested), 'poor old Rufford' is the constantly recurring theme. 'If I had my choice free,' he wrote from Windsor, 'I should prefer being there before this place with all its glory.' 'Your retreat to Rufford', echoed Henry Savile, from the court of Louis XIV, 'I do not only approve of, but envy more than all the places and dignities any court upon earth can give.'

But like all who combine a love of the country with intellectual or political interests, Halifax found that one had often to be sacrificed to the other, and it was Rufford that was sacrificed. 'Content to the mind', he once wrote, 'is like moss to a tree: it binds up so as to stop its growth'; and at Rufford he was too contented. Hence those nostalgic phrases, which his brother sometimes returned with mockery: 'when a lover is absent by his own choice, it is a sign of a very moderate passion'; if the monks were to return and reclaim their abbey, it would be no more than a just judgment on its owner, who did not spend eight months of the twelve 'in that Paradise of the whole North (if Paradise can lie northward)'. But in truth there was no pretence in Halifax's love of the country:

Poor old Rufford mourneth that she could not see you. Now she hath her best clothes on, she hath little to brag of, yet she saith her flies are harmless, and the air is clear; and if it were possible for a statesman to love ease and quiet and silence you would rather enjoy them with bilberries than eat melons in the crowd and dust of a wandering court.

So I may at the same time lament for my own sake, and congratulate for yours (he wrote to his son-in-law) that you are returned to your state of happiness, where your birds have no doubt made a new tune to bid you welcome, and your flowers strew you with your perfumes, to cleanse you from any remainder of London air which may yet hang about you.

Il n'y point de déguisement qui puisse longtemps cacher l'amour où il est, ni le feindre où il n'est pas, says Halifax's French counterpart; and this is not the language of affectation. It is precisely because Halifax (unlike La Rochefoucauld) had honest political aims and humane private enthusiasms; because he could write his delightful and sympathetic *Advice to a Daughter*, and his indulgent, though penetrating *Character of Charles II*, that we can freely relish his dry and sceptical *Maxims*. Lacking the bitterness of personal frustration, his writings are always contemporary. His life had not been a failure: he lived to see, if not the victory, at least the solidity of the Grand Alliance, and though his last days were spent in retirement, there was consolation in the parting compliment of William III, that usually ungracious monarch: 'The King said, he was still a Trimmer, and would continue so'.

XXXIX

THE SPANISH ENLIGHTENMENT

Spain is a country of extremes, of desperate opposition, absolute alternatives. Spaniards strain after impossible achievement; or they stagnate in Oriental timelessness. *Todo o nada*, prince or peasant, for them there is nothing between these opposite poles; and every century bears witness to the same uncompromising antithesis. In the sixteenth century, they thought to conquer the world: they lived at a heroic tension and performed unforgettable feats; in the seventeenth they washed their hands of greatness and their country became a byword for helpless apathy. To that sense of grandeur, that confidence that their empire was *la mayor cosa que ha sido después de là creación del mundo*, there succeeded that disdain for life, that disgusted indifference, that *menosprecio de la vida*, which had never been far beneath the solemn, magnificent surface. In the eighteenth century the same opposition was continued. On the one hand the society of Spain remained incredibly stagnant: astonished travellers described a medieval society, two centuries behind the rest of Europe, without industry or honesty, roads or justice. On the other hand, in the same century, there arose in Spain an *élite* of Reformers who sought to create a new country, to bring Spain once more into contact with Europe, to import into it the ideas — political, economic, intellectual — of the European Enlightenment, and thereby to reconquer again for their country the primacy of the past. The activity, the writings, the enthusiasm of these men is still inspiring. It is no less inspiring because they failed. The old Spain swallowed them up, as it has swallowed up all its reformers in turn. The most that they can say of themselves is the epitaph which Don Quixote wrote for himself, *Si no acabó grandes cosas, murió para acometerlas*: if he did not achieve great things, he died in the pursuit of them.

Which are we to admire most, the obstinate conservatism of the people, that complacent, proud, insular, invincible loyalty to ancient habits, which always absorbs those who set out to change it, or the heroism of those who defy its force? Two books have recently been published on eighteenth-century Spain, both excellent works, full of learning and scholarship, and yet very different, even opposite in their motivation. Señor Antonio Domínguez Ortiz[1] is a loyal Spaniard. He is not much interested in ideas. The Reformers make but little appeal to him. In his eyes, they did less than the price-rise of the 1760's for Spanish prosperity. Moreover (since he distrusts foreigners) their foreign inspiration, if it must be admitted, seems to him a reason for suspecting them. As for the Bourbon Kings of Spain, that French dynasty for whom French historians have made such proud claims, if he allows any credit to them it is not because they imported the light of Europe, and particularly of France, into a benighted province, but because they enabled Spain to discard the incubus of a European empire, liberated it from that fatal inheritance, drew it back from those corrupting embraces, and furnished it, in the end, with an army which was capable, in 1808, of fighting back against the jacobinical French invaders. It is native Spanish society, not the cosmopolitan *élite*, which interests him; and of that society he draws a detailed, rich and sympathetic portrait, scholarly, alive and full of interesting suggestions, which clearly marks him out as an important Spanish historian — the first, perhaps, to recapture eighteenth-century Spain from the French historians who have so long and so forcefully occupied it.

Very different is M. Jean Sarrailh, Rector of the University of Paris.[1] To him, as to the Frenchmen of the eighteenth century, Spanish society is interesting only, or mainly, as the unpromising, unyielding material which the great reformers sought to change. He is interested in books, ideas, and the prophets of ideas. To him, as a European, the eighteenth century is the glorious century of the Enlightenment, and his enthusiasm is quickened when he thinks of the great Spaniards who sought to apply the ideas of the Enlightenment at home and thereby to animate the stagnant, primitive society whose character Señor Domínguez so piously traces. Between these two historians,

[1] Antonio Domínguez Ortiz, *La Sociedad Española en el Siglo XVIII* (Madrid 1955.)
[2] Jean Sarrailh, *L'Espagne Eclairée* (Paris 1954).

therefore, there is a fundamental opposition of interest. The one is a French rationalist, the other a Spanish conservative, and both hold their views with a zeal which shines through their cool, scholarly prose. Nevertheless, there is no need to take sides between them. Though they approach it from opposite sides, the problem is the same, and their approaches to it are complementary. Perhaps we see it better when both sides of it are so well illuminated.

Certainly Spanish society in the eighteenth century was stagnant. All the social forces which had given Northern Europe such vitality in the last century were absent, or seemed dead, in Spain. The population had declined; the land was increasingly deserted; the middle class, always weak and small, had no awareness of its identity or mission. Spanish society was a rural society of landlords and peasants, lawyers and priests, usurers and beggars. Its economic life had always been in the hands of foreigners, first Jews, then Genoese; but these immigrants who had been drawn to the wealth of the Empire had moved, or been driven, away from its poverty. In the seventeenth century, as the impoverished Crown sold out its rights and gave up its powers, the nobility and the Church had gained in power and in wealth; but it was not a cultivated nobility or a vigorous Church. A few great magnates, whom court office had carried abroad, might patronise European learning; but these were exceptions. The indolent, indebted rural landlord, the useless, parasitic monk, still reading equally pernicious romances of chivalry or lives of the saints — these were the regular types of Spanish society. Higher education was neglected, learning condemned. Astronomy, geology, biology, anatomy were banned as dangerous subjects in the universities, the teaching of Descartes, Gassendi and Newton condemned as further than Aristotle from revealed truth. In 1705 only four books, and those trivial, were published in the whole of Spain. On the other hand elementary schools pullulated throughout the country, turning out a semi-literate clerical proletariat to lower still further the level of popular education. And this seedy society was still held back from economic progress by ancient taboos. More important even than *hidalguía* was racial purity, *limpieza de sangre*; and a whole series of useful professions were by their nature declared 'indecent'. Clerical or municipal office or membership of a gild was unattainable even to the son of a former actor or innkeeper, butcher or miller. On the other hand no social stigma attached to the honourable profession of begging. It was only the honest apprentice, not the idle beggar, whose activity was regarded as ignoble. No doubt this cult of holy poverty is very praiseworthy in merely rural societies; but, as Bernardo Ward pointed out, it is not the way towards economic growth. The child who sees his mother kiss the hand of a useless begging friar insensibly adopts a religion of idleness, whereas 'in the countries where there are no mendicant orders and no pilgrims, and where poverty is never represented as meritorious, the popular contempt for begging is a powerful force on the side of industry'.

Such was the society which the eighteenth-century reformers set out to reform. They were economic reformers: they sought to increase the trade of the country, build up its industry, release the natural wealth which lay unexploited at hand. 'In Spain', wrote their pioneer Bernardo Ward, 'three things which must support the greatness and wealth of any powerful monarchy lie almost neglected: land, men and money. . . . Ten thousand leagues of excellent land, two or three millions of idle hands, and many millions of pesetas buried in private hoards — is there a richer mine than this in the world?' But how could such a mine be exploited? It required not only a change of economic policy but a change of human character. The ancient character of Spain, its pride, its indolence, its caste-system must be changed before the social consequences of that character could be altered, So the reformers found themselves not only economic but social and educational reformers. They were philosophers; and being philosophers they looked also to the end of their reforms. The economic reforms which were to begin with education and to be carried through by an enlightened, centralising state, inspired by them, were not directed merely to the vulgar accumulation of wealth, but to the physical and moral improvement of man. The essential motive throughout, the simple (but novel) key which would set in motion one beneficent process after another, was human reason. Reason showed the way. Reason solved each problem on the way. Reason would unlock the barren womb of Nature. Reason would enrich the people of Spain. 'Numerous are the streams that lead to social prosperity,' wrote the greatest of all the reformers, Jovellanos, 'but all spring from the same source, and that source is public education.' Reason would ensure the freedom of thought, the freedom of trade; by destroying the false, misguided causes of war, it would lead to peace; and finally it would liberate human nature from the yoke of superstition, from the limitations of ignorance, from the cramp of poverty. 'Is there any sadder spectacle', asked Jovellanos, 'than the sight of man, who was born to be the lord of nature, conquered and enslaved by it?' Such was the philosophy, one may almost say the religion, which inspired the great works of Spain's enlightenment, the reception of new ideas from the liberal North, the attack on the old habits of the Church, the old privileges of the nobility, the old prejudices of society.

Of course the old order resisted: that was to be expected. The Inquisition, that great instrument of xenophobia, that armed defender of obscurantism, scholasticism and *limpieza de sangre*, though it had become cautious, was still strong; the Jesuits, by concentrating on courtly manners and literary grace, were the worst, because the most insidious, enemies of the education they professed to serve. But it would be wrong to suppose that the Church, as such, was opposed to reform — or at least to the kind of reform which was advocated by the Spaniards of the Enlightenment. The truly Spanish clergy — the home-bred monks and the Inquisition — might resist all improvement, but the more cosmopolitan clergy, now as in the past, had accepted more liberal ideas. It is well to remember that the acknowledged Father of the Spanish Enlightenment, Feijóo, was a Benedictine monk; that the most influential educational reformer, El Barbadiño, was a Portuguese priest; and that if the great triumph of the Reformers was the expulsion of their enemies, the Jesuits, they found allies in the Augustinians and the Dominicans. If they earned clerical distrust, they were not attacked, even by the clergy, as 'atheists': they were attacked as 'Jansenists' — or royalists.

For the great, the essential ally (or instrument) of the Reformers was always the Crown. It was by means of an enlightened ruler that the Reformers of the eighteenth, as of the sixteenth century sought to realise their programme; and when they found him, in Charles III, they were no less excessive in their adulation of his virtues than their predecessors had been in praise of many an equally undeserving, but fortunately docile, prince. Charles III looks down upon us from the portraits of Goya like a Spanish George III: bucolic, kindly, stupid, with his dog and his gun. But to the Reformers he was the demiurge sent from Heaven and no praise was too high for him. 'It was reserved for Charles III', wrote Jovellanos, 'to make good use of the light which the economists had revealed in their books. To him were reserved the happiness of diffusing that light throughout his kingdom and the glory of converting his whole people to the study of economy. . . . The sanctuary of Science is open to a little group of citizens only; it is they who dedicate themselves to the silent study of Nature and her mysteries, to reveal them to the nation. It is you, great King, who have the mission to receive their oracles, to spread the light which they have kindled, and to use it for the good of your subjects. The Science of Economics belongs exclusively to you: to you and to the ministers of your authority.' The Reformers were liberal men. They denounced the slave-trade and the oppression of the American Indians; they protested against the harsh persecution of the gypsies; they opposed the social inequalities of their times, the privileges of nobility, the subjection of women, the iniquity of the law. But against one privileged authority no voice of protest was raised in Spain. The despotism of the Crown was not challenged. Spain had always been known as a country of infinite loyalty. 'The loyalty of Spaniards', says Señor Domínguez, 'was an ocean which neither incompetence nor severity could drain.' Now this vulgar loyalty of the people was not diminished but swollen by the tributary streams of eloquent adulation which the highly educated Reformers poured into it. It was through an enlightened, dynamic, authoritarian state, and through that alone, they thought, that the obscurantist, stagnant, obedient society of Spain could be regalvanised. In the end, on the eve, as it must have seemed, of success, the machine broke in their hands: but it only broke when an overmighty minister, having usurped the authority, could incur, as a scapegoat, the penalties which none would think of exacting from the Crown.

Such was the Spanish Enlightenment, that movement which makes the eighteenth century, like the sixteenth century, one of the great centuries of Spanish history. Whence did it come? The French historians, strong in possession of the field, are seldom in doubt about the answer. Was not the whole European Enlightenment a French movement, inconceivable except in connexion with the names of Voltaire, Diderot, the Encyclopædists? Was not the new dynasty which enabled it to reach Spain, which favoured its leaders and was in turn extolled by them, the Bourbon dynasty which reached its culminating point in the reign of Charles III, itself a French dynasty? From the very beginning, Frenchmen and courtiers of the Bourbons have harped upon this string, ascribing to the house of Austria the decline of Spain and its revival to the house of Bourbon. François de Cabarrús, himself a French immigrant and a courtier of Charles III who was to become the founder of the Bank of Spain, could find no good to say of any of the Habsburg kings: to him the greatest and most splendid were no less disastrous to their country than the latest and least fortunate, weak bigots sunk in trivial pleasures and lethargic prayer. How different from the enlightened Bourbons, the reanimators of the Peninsula! Even M. Sarrailh, in his admiration for the Reformers, quotes without qualification, and therefore seems to share, their royalist enthusiasm. It is left to Señor Domínguez to redress the balance by pointing out that the loudly praised Bourbon kings of the eighteenth century were really no better than the unfairly denigrated Habsburg kings of the seventeenth century: that Philip V oscillated between imbecility and madness, spent whole days in bed, and refused, for months on end, to change his malodorous clothes; that Ferdinand VI similarly passed from lethargy to lunacy; that Charles III, the hero of the Reformers, was vain, feeble and reactionary, in love only with the idea, or illusion, of his own power, and Charles IV semi-imbecile; and that whoever brought the Enlightenment into Spain, it was not the new French dynasty which had preceded it by sixty years. 'Many of the current opinions on the eighteenth century in Spain', he says summarily, 'are based on the events of the reign of Charles III, arbitrarily extended over the whole century.'

In fact Señor Domínguez is surely right to reject these French claims. The Spanish Enlightenment was not exclusively French in origin. It is easy to be blinded by the greatness of the Encyclopædists, and that philosophic influence which, radiating from Paris, dazzled the petty courts of Germany; but it is well to remember that France was not the only source, nor French courts the only channel, of that transmission. The economic liberalism and the scientific methods of the eighteenth century were derived mainly from England and Holland: the French physiocrats had, by comparison, a very limited influence. The political concept of enlightened despotism was Italian or German, not French: France is one of the few European states in the eighteenth century which never knew an enlightened despot. Among the seventeenth century kindlers of the eighteenth-century Enlightenment, Hobbes and Locke, Petty and Newton, are as important as Descartes and Mersenne. Voltaire himself drew much of his inspiration from England. Berkeley and Gibbon, Hume and Adam Smith were formed in a native, not a French school. And there was an Italian Enlightenment, too: the Italians of the Renaissance had their disciples in the eighteenth century in the Naples of Giannone, Filangieri and Vico — that brilliant intellectual Naples whose character Benedetto Croce, with exquisite patriotic malice, has contrasted with the obscurantist court of Piedmont, its later master. If Spain, in the eighteenth century, rose again after its decline, may it not have owed such foreign influences as it received as much to England, to which it was bound by seaborne trade, and to Naples, to which it was bound by history and dynasty, as to France?

It may indeed. If the influence of Colbert, Buffon and the French physiocrats can be traced in the Spanish reformers, English and Italian influences are just as clear. If Cabarrús was a Frenchman, Bernardo Ward, the adviser of Ferdinand VI and Charles III, whose *Proyecto Económico* remained the bible of the economic reformers, was an Irishman who looked to English examples. So was his successor Guillermo Bowles. In their emphasis, above all, on science, empiricism, and the 'useful' arts, the Spanish reformers showed a natural preference for English models. Jovellanos himself was an admirer of Gibbon, an enthusiast for Adam Smith. As for politics, there Italy was the master-nation. Charles III had himself been King of Naples before he succeeded to the throne of Spain, and even after moving to Madrid he continued to use Neapolitan ministers. The Neapolitan Squilace followed him to Spain to become his minister of finance; the Neapolitan Tanucci remained, at a distance, his political confidant and adviser. Another Italian, the Genoese Grimaldi, succeeded as foreign minister to the Irishman Wall. The court of Charles III, like the intellectual life of his country, was not French but European: it took its politics from Italy, its economics from England.

But if it was cosmopolitan it was also Spanish: indeed, even in this it was Spanish, for what court had been more cosmopolitan than the Burgundian and Italian courts of Charles V and Philip II? The historians who conveniently break up Spanish history into centuries — the *Siglo de Oro*, the century of Habsburg decline, the century of Bourbon revival — do violence to its continuity and often ascribe a spurious novelty to ideas or experiments which are really old. If we forget the artificial distinction between Habsburg and Bourbon Spain, we find that many of the 'new', 'French' ideas of the eighteenth century are in fact a continuation of seventeenth-century projects. Did the Bourbon ministers suppress internal tolls, did they seek to attract foreigners and to build up the fishing industry as the nursery of sea-power? All these policies had been urged by the statesmen and economists of the early seventeenth century: Gondomar, Navarrete, Saavedra Fajardo. Did the eighteenth-century Reformers urge the reduction of monasteries, the abolition of superfluous schools, the lifting of taboos against trade? Philip IV, that much-maligned ruler, had done all these things. Did the Bourbons, at last — perhaps fatally — centralise the government of Spain? What else had been the policy — perhaps the error — of that much-maligned minister, the Count-Duke of Olivares? Did the new men of the Enlightenment turn with enthusiasm to rediscover their own country, surveying and recording its flora and fauna, its minerals, its agriculture, its customs, its history? They were but resuming the interrupted work of Philip II, of whose great geographical, historical and statistical survey of Spain the fifteen folios lie still unpublished in the Spanish archives. In these and a dozen other ways we find, if we look, that the 'innovations' of Bourbon Spain really represent a resumption of Habsburg policy, Habsburg ideas. The new spirit of the late eighteenth century is the old spirit of the early seventeenth century, revived after an intermission of a hundred years.

This native character of the Spanish Enlightenment is perhaps best seen in the matter of Church reform. What particularly characterised the French Enlightenment, separating it sharply from other national manifestations of the same spirit, was its uncompromising freedom of religious thought, its clear, logical 'infidelity'. But in Spain this element was almost entirely lacking. If the Spanish reformers attacked monasticism, it was indolent, useless or evil-living monks, not their religion, that they condemned. 'We do not suppose', says M. Sarrailh, 'that in Spain in the second half of the eighteenth century there was anyone who would seriously have denied the existence of God in the manner of d'Holbach, Diderot or La Mettrie.' 'The slightest acquaintance with the ideas of Campomanes, Roda, Floridablanca and Jovellanos is enough', says Señor Domínguez, 'to show how little these men were attracted by the frivolity, the voltairian satire, the impudent atheism of Helvetius and d'Holbach.' Even the most outspoken advocates of Reason against the Church in Spain — Aranda, Olavide, Azara — never went so far as the French philosophers with whom they corresponded and whom they professed to admire. Aranda, whom Morel-Fatio described as 'an infidel, perhaps the only real infidel among them all', died in the bosom of the Church. Olavide, who refused to allow monasteries in his model villages in the Sierra Morena and was denounced to the Inquisition for eating meat on Friday, collecting nudes and corresponding with Voltaire, soon recanted and published his contrite work *The Gospel Triumphant or the Converted Philosopher*. Azara, who wrote from Rome his excoriating attacks on that sink of corruption, was described as 'profoundly religious, and therefore profoundly shocked to see at such close quarters the vices of that

Roman clergy which should be the first to preserve the purity and humility of the Church'. In fact, if we analyse the religious views of the Spanish reformers we find, once again, that they have a good Spanish and a good European, rather than a French pedigree. They attack the wealth and ostentation of the Church, the overgrown numbers of the clergy, images, processions, pilgrimages; and they extol lay piety, 'interior religion', Biblicism: in short that 'Erasmianism', that *Philosophia Christi* which, in the sixteenth century, had also flourished, thanks to European contact, on Spanish soil. It is surely no accident that the heroes of the Spanish reformers — even of priests like Fray Isla and el Barbadiño — included the hated heretic Erasmus and his great Spanish disciple, Luis de León.

One reason why the Spanish reformers were less 'infidel' than the French was perhaps that the Spanish Church gave them less cause. The monastic orders might be sunk in sloth and bigotry, but the bishops and parish clergy — all observers agreed — if unenlightened in their views, were at least creditable in their lives. 'The courtly, frivolous, extravagant prelates, such as flourished in France', says Señor Domínguez, 'were hardly to be found in Spain. Even those who owed their benefices to favour led exemplary lives.' A French traveller said of them, 'they seldom go out of their palaces and never seek out women. Their great revenues are not consumed at table, to which they invite only their vicars-general and occasional priests. Episcopal wealth is known only by continuous alms-giving. Were it not for the honourable signs of their rank, bishops could hardly be distinguished from the rest of the clergy'; and he added that bishoprics were not, as in France, monopolised by the nobility. When the French Encyclopædists dwelt complacently on the 'obscurantism' of Spain, Antonio Cavanilles could justly retort that there were some useful lessons which 'enlightened', 'philosophical' France could still learn from retrograde Spain. For instance, that benefices in the Spanish Church were not sold, that humble birth there was no obstacle to a career, and that Spain did not know that 'proud barrier between the higher and the lower clergy' which, a few years later, was to prove, in France, one of the causes of the great revolution: a revolution which was indeed carried to Spain, but which Spain, in many ways, did not need. The social basis for such a revolution was absent — except in the minds of the Encyclopædists, whose superficial propaganda led Napoleon, that 'former jacobin, indoctrinated with all the old anti-Spanish truisms', to undertake what he supposed would be 'the easy conquest of a country brutalised by the rule of priests'.

Of course Spain was backward; but it may be argued that it is not backward countries which need revolutions. Being backward, Spain had not yet developed those internal strains which made France, with all its enlightenment, a social volcano. Consequently, whereas in France a few reformers, scratching the surface of society, liberated a dreadful explosion from beneath, in Spain a dedicated band of Reformers, working desperately to modernise society from above, in the end achieved very little. Like the Spanish Erasmists before them, they were a great generation, an influence in their day, a memory afterwards; but like the Erasmists they were defeated. M. Sarrailh commemorates their teaching, but Señor Domínguez pronounces their epitaph. In spite of all the reforming zeal of the reign of Charles III, 'barely one of its great problems was decisively solved. Neither the seignorial system, nor the *Mesta*, nor the gilds were abolished. . . . Torture was not formally abolished, though in practice it gradually died out. There was no important change in the condition of *limpieza* and nobility. . . .' Instead of the radical improvement of which they dreamed, the Reformers only paved the way for 'the palace despotism' of Godoy and, indirectly, for the blood and confusion of the French invasion.

Why did they fail? Even before these political misfortunes overtook Spain, they were defeated by the sullen resistance of society, the absence of any well-defined middle class to support them, the obstinate conservatism of the rural classes, the natural strength of the old institutions, and, above all, that profound characteristic of the Spanish people: its hatred of change, of *novedad*, its refusal to think in what Europeans consider a 'rational' way, its unwillingness or incapacity to organise, to realise, to bring to completion the ideas which it may entertain. How many excellent projects, in Spain, dissolve uncompleted into dusty nothing! How many ideas, once adopted, degenerate into mere moods, emotions, sensations! How many parties, or institutions, formed for action, are atomised into individuals before the work has begun! If Spain has contributed little to science, that, says a modern Spanish writer on the subject, is not for lack of scientific ideas, but through refusal to pursue, realise, institutionalise those ideas. Even in religion, says Señor Américo Castro, Spanish Catholicism is what is *felt* by Spaniards, not what is *understood* by Rome: the only Spanish contribution to popular religion is the passive quietism of Molinos. And in Spanish politics there are no parties, only 'movements' and individuals: even on the extreme Left, elsewhere so disciplined, there are not communists but anarchists. Against such difficulties the boldest reformers may well fail. The great eighteenth-century reformers, who sought to change a stagnant society by developing a dynamic state, found that in the end the machinery crumbled in their hands. Nor, for that matter, did the revolutionary invaders achieve more durable success. Whenever the 'modern', 'rational', 'European' forms of society are set up in Spain, they tend to tumble down again. As soon as the tension is relieved, the pattern dissolves, and we are back where we were, swallowed up once again in that ancient, unthinking conservatism which still dominates, even to-day, that Oriental society.

XL

THE FAUSTIAN HISTORIAN: JACOB BURCKHARDT

How much European heresy owes to Switzerland, the refuge from orthodoxy throughout the centuries! The European reformers of the sixteenth century, the defeated republicans of seventeenth-century England and of nineteenth-century France all fled thither; Erasmus, Calvin, Rousseau, Gibbon, all challenged there the orthodoxy of their times; Voltaire, for his greater safety, encamped upon its frontier; and Mussolini, Nietzsche and Lenin all hatched there the violent doctrines which have since proved so terrible. These men have shaken the world. It was in Switzerland also that the shaking of it was foreseen most clearly. It was foreseen from two rooms above a baker's shop in Basel, by Nietzsche's university colleague Jacob Burckhardt, once regarded only as a historian of art, now recognised, thanks to his posthumously published lecture-notes and correspondence,[1] as one of the profoundest of historians.

Unlike most of the great thinkers who have written in Switzerland, Burckhardt was himself Swiss, and he drew from Switzerland part of his character. For Switzerland is not only a miniature cosmopolis, it is, more particularly, the meeting place of German and Italian culture. Through its passes German armies have passed constantly into Italy, Italian baroque art and ideas have penetrated into Austria and Bavaria. As a Swiss, Burckhardt was captivated alike by German and Italian culture. 'It seemed to me at times', he wrote of a visit to Florence when he was twenty, 'as if I were Faust, full to overflowing with yearning. . . . Before me lay the riches of nature and art, as though the Godhead had passed through the land like a sower, *Und alle Näh und alle Ferne befriedigt nicht die tiefbewegte Brust*'; and when

[1] *The Letters of Jacob Burckhardt*, translated and edited by Alexander Dru (London 1955).

he went to Germany to study under Ranke and Droysen, to that brilliant, intellectually re-awakened Germany of the 1840's which we are now so tempted to forget, he could pour out his enthusiasm like an authentic German nationalist. 'What can I tell you about Germany?' he wrote to his sister.

> I am like Saul the son of Kish, who went out to look for lost asses and found a King's crown. I often want to kneel down before the sacred soil of Germany and thank God that my mother-tongue is German. I have Germany to thank for *everything*! . . . What a people! What a wonderful youth! What a land — a paradise.

'Now', he wrote to a German friend, 'I recognise the embrace of our common great Fatherland which I, like most of my fellow Swiss, used to mock and repel. . . . I will make it my life's purpose to show the Swiss that they are Germans.'

But Burckhardt did not in fact become a German nationalist. Closer study soon cured his enthusiasm. It is a great mistake, he afterwards wrote, to idealise the Emperor Frederick II, *Stupor Mundi*, who so dazzled the nationalists; and as for Wagner and his ideals, they seemed to him 'utterly loathsome'. Burckhardt saw through much of German erudition and remained a Swiss, and therefore a cosmopolitan. His great works, *The Age of Constantine* and *The Civilisation of the Renaissance*,—the terminal fragments of a vast design — were about Italy and the Mediterranean, not the Barbarian North. Moreover, he was more than a Swiss: he was a Burckhardt: that is to say, an aristocrat in the oligarchical city of Basel where he had been born, to which he returned as a professor and in which he stayed, resisting even the call to succeed Ranke in Berlin. In the past, for over a century and a half, one of the two burgomasters of Basel had always been a Burckhardt; but his own lifetime saw the change. In 1833 the aristocracy preserved their rule in the city only by surrendering their authority over the surrounding country. In 1847 democracy triumphed in Basel, and with it a new Switzerland, the old patricians were submerged and Basel, the city of Erasmus and his printers, became the great, rich, materialist, industrial railway-junction which it has remained. It is tempting to ascribe to this social change another and fundamental element in Burckhardt's philosophy: his deep prophetic pessimism, his profound distrust of the masses. Like his great contemporary, Alexis de Tocqueville, he saw more clearly the price of democracy by being himself, in his family tradition and intellectual outlook, one of its victims: an aristocrat.

For if one looks for the heart of Burckhardt's philosophy, it always comes back to this: civilisation is a delicate and precarious thing which only an educated and perhaps unscrupulously self-preserving hierarchy can protect against the numerical revolt of the masses with their materialism, their indifference to liberty, their ready surrender to demagogic power; and the crises of civilisation consist in precisely that revolt of the masses which, however, can never prevail against the strength of conservative institutions unless it is aided from within by moral and intellectual decay. His 'liberal' contemporaries welcomed the revolution: Burckhardt despised the easy, idiotic optimism with which they danced giddily on to the bandwagon heading for destruction. 'We may all perish,' he wrote as the portents accumulated before 1848, 'but at least I want to discover the interest for which I am to perish, namely the old culture of Europe.' After 1848, he felt, the triumph of materialism and the masses was assured; the educated classes had fooled themselves and betrayed their old ideals; numbers would now prevail; and the history of Europe was heading for 'a fundamental change'. One of those 'general crises' had come in which, as in the last days of Rome 'things can only be changed by ascetics, men who are independent of the enormously expensive life of the great cities. . . .' The sick civilisation of Europe could perhaps only be saved by a new generation of anchorites.

For the rest of his life, while lecturing on art and history in Basel, Burckhardt himself became something of an intellectual anchorite. From his 'Archimedean point outside events' he studied the crisis of his time in its historical context. How few such crises there had been in the past! Throughout Antiquity there was no such 'general crisis', no such 'historical transition through the despotism of the masses' until the collapse of the Roman Empire: only then had the ruling classes lost control. At the Reformation a crisis could have been avoided — as it was by Henry VIII and the Counter-Reformation Princes who never admitted the masses to the mysteries of state. But now the crucial step had been taken and Burckhardt could only see, in the future, either 'complete democracy' or 'absolute lawless despotism'. Possibly the architects of the new age would be great men: for single men had sometimes personified in themselves historical change; and he pointed to Genghiz Khan, who had converted a nomadic horde into an empire, and to Frederick the Great, whose iron will, in the years 1759–63, had 'determined the course of all subsequent European history'. More probably Europe would see bogus messiahs like Napoleon III and Boulanger, whom he so despised, or, far more dreadful, *Gewaltmenschen*, 'the *terribles simplificateurs* who are going to descend upon poor old Europe' and to create, out of the blind assent of the masses, a hideous ideological tyranny. One thing was certain: they would not be the old legitimate dynasties 'who are too soft-hearted'.

> People do not like to imagine a world whose rulers ignore law, prosperity, enriching work, industry, credit, etc., and who rule with utter brutality. But these are the people into whose hands the world is being driven by the competition among all parties for the participation of the masses on any and every question.

Nor had Burckhardt any doubts in which country this portent would most formidably appear. It was in Germany, that once liberal Germany whose very soil he had worshipped as holy ground. 'I have a presentiment that may now seem completely mad but yet will not leave me', he wrote to a German official: 'the military state must become a large-scale industrialist . . . the development of a crafty and enduring tyranny is still in its infancy: it is in Germany that it will probably first grow to maturity.'

Of course I have selected only one strand from the rich historical understanding which Burckhardt so casually entrusted to his lectures and his occasional correspondence. But it is pertinent to ask by what technique of historical study he was thus able to prophesy, as no other of his contemporaries, what then seemed 'completely mad' but has since become so terribly true. The answer, I think, is twofold. First, he rejected the cramping systems which have imprisoned other 'universal historians'. Secondly, unlike them, he was a humanist.

For who are the other 'universal historians' who have sought to compare civilisation with civilisation and prophesy the future by analogy with the past? From Hegel to Toynbee we see the monstrous series, crushed beneath their useless armour of abstractions, like ancient cataphracts. For all his brilliant intuition, Marx, by his impersonal economic laws, never deduced the rise or even the possibility of Fascism; and what he did prophesy shows no sign of coming to pass. As a historian he is dead as mutton, or at least as dead as Orosius, Baronius and Bossuet. But Burckhardt, because he was a humanist, because he saw human behaviour not merely as a blind response to vast impersonal systems but as evidence of itself, of the variable causes and matter of history, was proof against such prodigious errors. 'History', he once wrote, 'is the most unscientific of all the sciences'; and he did not seek to make it scientific. 'My poor head', he wrote to Nietzsche, 'has never been capable of reflecting, even at a distance, as you are able to do, upon final causes, the aims and the desirability of history.' Nor was he, like so many systematic theorists, secretly bewitched by mere power. All power, he believed, priestly or lay, was evil, and as for Nietzsche's supermen, he saw them as *flagella Dei*, scourges of God, 'whose precise psychological construction I willingly leave to others, for it is a point on which one can be most astonishingly mistaken'. Indeed one can.

Where then is the real evidence of human history to be found? Burckhardt answered that if man is the agent, not the mere dead matter of history, then his historical character must be revealed in his work, not in the neuter systems of which he is said to be the victim. In other words, human art, being the lasting expression of man's ideas at any time, is more valuable to the historian than abstract philosophical theories. I agree. What a flood of light can be shed on human motives, on the changing patterns of human thought in different ages, by art-history: by those wonderful volumes, for instance, of the late Emile Mâle! Marx assumed that men's motives were always the same; Toynbee assumes that they play no part in history which is a superhuman mechanical process. Burckhardt saw man as an artist, constantly varying the interrelation of his interests. He asked the same great questions as the other philosophers of history; but remembering that man was the measure of all things, he answered them differently. He did not write ten volumes on historical process: he wrote a great work on *The Civilisation of the Renaissance* and, in his lecture-notes and these letters, a few general observations on human history whose profundity has been emphasised, not diminished, by time.

XLI

LYTTON STRACHEY AS HISTORIAN

About 1918 Lytton Strachey, then 38 years old, turned from the study of literature to the study of history. He had made an important discovery. He had discovered that the Victorian Age was not dull, not conventional, not stuffy: it was baroque, bizarre, even funny. It was useless to announce such a paradox suddenly in Bloomsbury. The dullness and conventionality of the Victorian Age was an accepted orthodoxy of the time, admitted with that absolute finality with which one age customarily judges its immediate predecessor. What was the evidence, they would have asked, for so preposterous a heresy? And if he had pointed to that seemingly infinite series of ponderous, official, commendatory, many-volumed collections of lives and letters which weighed like multiple tombstones upon the grave of every politician or bishop or headmaster, they would have derided such a view; for who could persevere, in the reign of George V, through those notoriously tedious works of hagiography, as remote and unreadable as the Benedictine folios, or the Lives of the Saints?

Lytton Strachey did not waste time in giving such advice; he followed it. A fine scholar, an exquisite stylist, a disciple of the Age of Reason but a lover of the Baroque, he turned from the studies in which his mind had been trained and seasoned and diving to the bottom of that deep and apparently dull sea, the nineteenth century, he emerged with small bucketfuls of strange polyps and fantastic sponges, as samples of its astonishing submerged variety. In so doing he became, from an essayist and a student of literature, an historian; and the success of his two immediate works, *Eminent Victorians* in 1918 and *Queen Victoria* in 1921, made him, in the public mind, and in spite of his disclaimers, an historian of the Victorian Age. It is as an historian, at least in part, that he must be considered, and his reputation judged.

He would not himself refuse such a condition. He not only

wrote history, he wrote on historiography; he extracted its principles, defined its methods, and awarded their place to his predecessors, Gibbon and Hume, Macaulay and Carlyle, Froude and Creighton. The rules of historiography, he declared, with the firm finality of the expert, are few and obvious: 'a capacity for absorbing facts, a capacity for stating them, and a point of view'. The criterion seems to me dubious: a capacity to interpret facts seems at least as important as a point of view which may precede the facts and may be desperately erroneous. Sir Charles Firth, I believe, was in all respects a greater historian than Mr. Hilaire Belloc, and Mr. W. H. Chamberlin's history of the Russian Revolution is more luminous than that of Trotzky. Still, such was Strachey's conclusion, and it was one by which he would willingly be judged: for he would certainly emerge successful.

Strachey certainly had a capacity for absorbing facts. Those great commemorative volumes, unread and unreadable by his contemporaries, he eagerly devoured, and anyone who attempts to read them after him must be astonished at the unremitting sensitivity of that vast appetite. Course after course of heavy and sometimes windy fare is swallowed, and yet nothing relevant is missed, every trace of flavour, however slight or subtle, is instantly appreciated and accurately distinguished. In all his writings, Strachey once told a friend, there was only one occasion when he had consciously yielded to the temptation of supposing a fact for which he lacked evidence or authority. That supposition was the shortness of Dr. Arnold's legs: for that detail he had no evidence, only a conviction that, on the general grounds of a rational universe, it must have been so. Apart from that one deviation Strachey felt that his reputation for scholarship and accuracy was above reproach.

He also had a capacity for stating facts. Seldom has a writer been more compelling in his presentation, and even if all his facts had been as speculative as the shortness of Dr. Arnold's legs, we should still read him, not for information but for pleasure, as we read Herodotus and parts of the Bible, and other works of mythology. Strachey was a brilliant narrator, a brilliant portrayer of character. He shows it not only in his central figures — in his wonderful portraits of Lord Melbourne or

Mr. Gladstone; there is not a character in his works, however secondary or peripheral, who does not assume an individual reality and complexity. And all those characters and their interrelations are drawn together in perfect prose, a prose that is coloured and yet clear, subtle and yet firm, sparkling and only occasionally vulgar.

But what of Strachey's point of view? He had a point of view of course: it was his point of view that informed his style and made it so irresistibly readable. It is also his point of view which ultimately disqualifies him as an historian.

Lytton Strachey was a humanist: he was interested in human motives and human eccentricities, awake to every instance of human absurdity or inconsistency. Like some skilful Jesuit confessor of the Baroque Age, he could explore, with seemingly infallible technique, every quaint recess and dark corner of the labyrinthine human mind. But this interest, this technique, so useful for the exposure of human behaviour, did not extend to the analysis of impersonal or social facts, which also are the material of history. To Strachey historical problems were always, and only, problems of individual behaviour and individual eccentricity. He read big biographies and wrote little biographies: Boswell was the model for his reading, Aubrey for for his writing; but historical problems, the problems of politics and society, he never sought to answer, or even to ask. He read the five volumes of Sir Theodore Martin's *Life of the Prince Consort*, and distilled from it every drop of essence that could possibly heighten the flavour of his own work, but he skated timidly past the political significance of that patient, central, administrative career — its effect on the power of the Crown. He read the six volumes of Monypenny and Buckle's *Life of Disraeli* and contented himself with an incredibly superficial verdict. Because of a few personal eccentricities, Disraeli is dismissed as a mere egoist, a vain, trivial figure of 'rococo futilities', an 'absurd Jew-boy' visible under all his trappings to the very end. Disraeli's political achievement — a social and political revolution silently achieved, by brilliant tactics, under the forms of immutable conservatism — is never noticed: it is on a senile passion for Lady Bradford that the statesman's whole career must finally be judged.

Further, even within his own limits Strachey shows certain fatal defects. The worldly Jesuit confessor, so confident in his skill, sometimes made shocking errors. It is the danger of any apparently infallible technique. History — even personal history — is often dull. Strachey could not bear to be dull; and therefore he strained unreasonably to be funny, to sustain a drama of conflicting personalities and grotesque incidents even beyond the capacity of his material. Having made the important discovery that the Victorians were not dull and conventional but strange and complex creatures, he could not resist the temptation to make them, by judicious interpretation of motives and skilful manipulation of doubt, just a little stranger, just a little more complex. Hence those brilliant portraits, those wicked contrasts, those touches of exquisite extravagance and occasional cheapness which seem for a moment to invalidate even the best of his works. The effect is unfortunate, for in fact Strachey is much more reliable than he seems. Mr. F. A. Simpson has shown that in one instance, in his life of Cardinal Manning, Strachey has succeeded in creating a false impression where he could not have ventured to state the equivalent fact. Many readers might deduce from this that his whole portrait of Manning is invalid. The reader of Strachey's principal source, Purcell's *Life of Cardinal Manning*, knows that this is untrue. Purcell's devastating book is, in form, the antithesis of Strachey's essay. It is very long, and it never offers an opinion. And yet this apparent panegyric, this officially commissioned biography of the cardinal, is packed with secret dynamite, whose detonation, in 1896, had shattered the unnaturally smooth front of Popery in England. Against the documentary revelations of Purcell the defenders of Manning were helpless, and it is instructive to look back at their agonised and desperate writhings. Strachey, by his excessive zeal in converting unassailable facts into questionable judgments, supplied an unexpected defence. Manning's supporters could thenceforth discreetly forget the name of Purcell and complacently dismiss his revelations as being 'only Lytton Strachey'.

A more significant instance of Strachey's excess is provided by his treatment of General Gordon. His account of Gordon in the Sudan, retiring into his tent 'for days at a time' for secret communion with the Bible and the bottle is the richest flourish in his brilliant picture of that strange, unpredictable, complicated character. It so pleased Strachey that he repeated it in his essay on the Memoirs of Li-Hung-Chang: Gordon there reappears as 'the half-inspired, half-crazy Englishman, with his romance and his fatalism, his brandy-bottle and his Bible'. In fact, as Mr. Bernard Allen has pointed out, this picture is a total fiction. Strachey had seized eagerly on a passage in Chaillé-Long's memoirs, twisted a passage from an article by Burton to match it, and the Bible and the brandy-bottle were the result. In fact the brandy-bottle, the ultimate crown of the whole literary structure, never existed. Long had invented it, in his spiteful seventies, when, filled with hatred of Gordon, he was improving his own already published and anyway unreliable memoirs. The real object had been not a brandy-bottle but a prayer-book. Unfortunately, 'brandy-bottle' is funnier than 'prayer-book'; Strachey could not resist that final touch of absurdity; and his brilliant portrait of a crackpot crusader is, by that one dangerous detail, overdone.

This reduction of all history to personal history, this desperate straining after effect, accounts also for Strachey's occasional vulgarity — his reduction of serious problems to merely personal terms and the bathos with which his essays almost invariably end. These qualities appear most forcibly in his third historical work, *Elizabeth and Essex*. The Victorian Age, if it was remote in one sense, was near in another. It was near in time: Strachey had grown up in it; and it was near in place: it might have evaporated in Bloomsbury but it could still be recaptured in less quickly-changing parts of the metropolis. Such nearness is a useful corrective for a historian. But the Elizabethan Age was in every sense remote, and Strachey, who was never able to breathe a foreign climate, created, in seeking to recapture it, not history but an historical novel, almost as distant from reality as *The Black Arrow* or *Ivanhoe*. The success of such a romance was instant. In America it sold by the hundred thousand. It was both the crown and humiliation of his career. It has brilliant portraits — the portrait of Bacon, like a swaying cobra, holding his breath 'in the midst of some great sentence, some high intellectual confection . . . in a rich beatitude, fascinated by the deliciousness of sheer style'; the portrait of the aged Burghley seeking vainly 'with trembling arguments and venerable aphorisms' to appease the outraged Queen; there are ingenious caricatures, as of Philip II and Antonio Perez, luminous phrases and dreadful vulgarities, and a total strangeness from the subject. The age of Elizabeth was an age which Strachey, isolated in his twentieth century Enlightenment, simply could not understand.

To have written a best-seller (it is said) is a chastening experience, and after *Elizabeth and Essex* Strachey (I am told) suffered from humiliation and remorse. What he might afterwards have done we cannot say, for he died four years later, having only written essays in the interim. But it is probable that his best work was still to come. He had ventured into a foreign climate: the experience had been exhilarating, even intoxicating; but on retrospection his antics had seemed to him somewhat absurd and possibly indecent. After such an adventure it would have been natural to return home. Strachey's home was not the Elizabethan Age; it was not even the Victorian Age in which he had been an inquisitive and somewhat mischievous observer from across the frontier. It was the Eighteenth Century. There he was in harmony with his contemporaries; there he had no occasion to postulate absurd motives or mock incomprehensible emotions; and across the rearward frontier of that age he could still observe, with sharp sceptical eyes, yet another more truly Baroque era to engage his wit and fascinate his mind. It is a pity Strachey did not take back his perfected style to the eighteenth century — or rather to that elongated century, the Age of Reason, which extends from the rise of Louis XIV to the fall of Metternich. There he had achieved some of his best, least popular work, in *Landmarks in French Literature* and *Books and Characters* — early works which by their sympathy seem more mature than his later, more famous studies. Unfortunately he died early, leaving imperfect work in an experimental and perhaps mistaken field. His imitators observed his apparent success but not his real failure. Not having written best-sellers they were unchastened by humility; and they sought to continue his adventures into history. Fortunately, they are now all quite dead. They lacked what will preserve even his errors: style.

XLII

KARL MARX AND THE STUDY OF HISTORY

History, it seems, is the modern Queen of Sciences. From the humble position to which Dr. Johnson relegated it as the mere industrious collection and arrangement of facts it has come, in this century, to be the most controversial, the most combustible of studies. Every political party, every ideological movement has its historical theory. There is orthodoxy, there are heresies. The greatest orthodoxy (in the eyes of believers), the greatest heresy (in the eyes of unbelievers) is the Marxist theory of history which now dominates historical thinking in communist Europe and Asia and has many powerful advocates even in the unconverted West.

What is this Marxist theory of history? Why is it now so powerful? I think it is easiest to take the second of these two questions first. For it is partly because there is a general demand for 'philosophies of history' that the particular kind of historical philosophy called Marxism has achieved such success. Its own merits may enable it to compete with similar but rival philosophies, but the public taste for such philosophies naturally precedes these particular and competing attempts to gratify it.

One obvious reason for this change of taste in historical matters is what may be called the drying-up of the classical stream of historiography. With the vast increase in the mere bulk of historical evidence caused by the opening of archives in the last century, a kind of hopelessness has overcome many conventional historians. For how, they ask, can one ever compete with the enormous weight of this ever-lengthening, ever-deepening past? Their answer has been to draw in their horns. Always seeking finality, fearful of giving any answer which some new document will reverse, and only too conscious that such new documents are continually being unearthed by their colleagues, they have become narrow specialists, knowing more and more about less and less, and saying less and less about it. And this timidity of the specialist in turn intimidates the layman. For when the experts are unable to master even such minute periods of history, how can the layman, who lacks their training, hope to understand any historical problem? Besides, the answers of the expert seem to the layman not only uncertain, but trivial. For if history is to interest the layman at all, it must be because it has some general significance. The professional historians, disputing about a cabinet crisis in a petty European court in the eighteenth century or the style of knitting in a medieval nunnery, answer no general question. Therefore laymen turn away from them and look for someone who will rise above this detail, range more easily over the ever-extending centuries, and find, in this bewildering mass of matter, with which they do not wish to encumber their minds, some general significance.

This process has been happening for some time, but it has been greatly accelerated in our own days by a new fact which has caused us to revise much of our attitude towards history. I refer to the general crisis which — at least since 1945 — we all feel in the West. In the nineteenth century there were historical prophets who rejected the comfortable optimism of their contemporaries and foresaw alternatives to endless progress; but they went unheeded. Carlyle, whose terrible legacy we have seen in German Nazism, seemed to the Victorians, in their safe world of expanding liberalism, merely an eloquent crank. Lord Acton, whom in retrospect we see as one of the great historical thinkers of his time, felt himself isolated, 'absolutely alone', among his contemporaries. Jacob Burckhardt, the great Swiss historian, uttered his profound reflexions unregarded in a provincial university. But now the complacency of the nineteenth century is irretrievably lost. We no longer feel that history is the history of progress, or that our civilisation is unique. We do not even feel that it is superior to other civilisations which have perished, or exempt from their laws of mortality. And so we are now more ready to listen to prophets of woe or at least prophets of change. Faced with the crisis of civilisation we look to history not for detail or for diversion but for serious lessons: lessons which must be drawn not from mere superficial incidents but from the deep roots of history, and from its whole range. We do not look in vain. Standing before us, larger than life, no longer, like their predecessors, neglected by their contemporaries, we see the modern prophets of History: Spengler, Toynbee, Marx.

Moreover, among these three (though all of them are, in my opinion, demonstrably wrong in their reasoning), it must be admitted that Marx is now by far the most effective. Spengler and Toynbee are even, in one sense, his auxiliaries. For all three maintain that the West is irremediably, by historical laws, in decline; but whereas Spengler and Toynbee say so in tones of gloom only mitigated by occasional sighing after a Messiah, Marx says so in tones of confidence. Like the early Christians in the days of the pagan Roman Empire, the Marxists prophesy the collapse of contemporary 'civilisation' not in a defeatist but in an exultant spirit, as men who have a positive alternative to offer. All confidence is catching, and consequently many 'Western' intellectuals whose will to survive is sapped by the vaticinations of a Toynbee find themselves converted to the more positive doctrines of Marx. In less intellectual language, they leap on to the bandwagon. And what a bandwagon it is! Hitler, who in some ways was the disciple of Spengler, maintained that remorseless human will-power — if only it was applied in time — could arrest the otherwise inevitable triumph of Russia.[1] The failure of his huge, feverish effort seemed to prove that in fact nothing could arrest it. Toynbee, who had begun by thinking that Western Christendom might yet survive by returning to its original inspiration and plunging back into medieval Catholicism, now, since 1945, has despaired of even that desperate remedy and preaches a non-European messianism.[2] Only Marxism moves confidently on. The physical conquest of new empires in Europe and Asia seems to the layman, who (like God) is secretly on the side of the big battalions, proof that Marxist history may well be right. Has not the Marxist interpretation of the past been proved scientifically correct by the most exacting

[1] I have sought to show Hitler's systematic philosophy of history, which is consistent with that of Spengler and Toynbee, in my essay 'The Mind of Adolf Hitler', printed in *Hitler's Table Talk* (London 1953).

[2] This radical difference is discernible between the six volumes of Toynbee's *Study of History*, published in 1934–9 and the last four, published in 1954.

of all tests? Applied to the future has it not proved an accurate prophecy of the way we must go, the way we have in fact already half-gone?

Such are some of the reasons which, as it seems to me, make Marxist history acceptable to-day. Though humanly understandable, I do not think that they are intellectually good reasons. I do not believe that truth is necessarily on the side of the big battalions. If it were, Mohammedanism was true in the Dark Ages, Christianity in the sixteenth century. Nor do I think that a mood of defeatism in the West, if there is such a mood, is evidence that Western civilisation is on its way out. There was a similar mood of defeatism in the early seventeenth century, when men also lamented the old age of the world and looked either for the Last Trump or a new Messiah. ''Tis too late to be ambitious,' sighed Sir Thomas Browne; 'the great mutations of the world are acted, or time may be too short for our designs.' The world, philosophers agreed, was then running down, Nature was in decay, and Jew and Gentile alike calculated the imminent year of Armageddon. But in fact this defeatism of seventeenth-century Europe was but a passing crisis of conscience, as ours also may be. I do not think we should judge the truth of theories either by the physical force of those who advance them or by the mood in which they are received. We should judge them by their inherent logic and their empirical validity when tested against the facts. In considering Marxist history I therefore propose to come down to earth and apply to it these simple tests. It claims to be scientific: let it be tested scientifically.

First of all, what *is* the Marxist philosophy of history? Its basic assumption is that human history is conditioned not by ideas or institutions or man-made laws but by the economic organisation of society, which in turn is based on the mechanism of production and exchange of goods. Laws, ideas, institutions may preserve and protect society, but they do not create it: what creates it is the complex system of economy of which contemporaries, who take it for granted, are often unaware, but which historians can discover even if, in doing so, they often oversimplify it. Moreover, this economy which is at the basis of history is not static: it is dynamic; and the motive power which animates it is the class structure and, more particularly, the struggles between the classes which, in any society, are divided from each other by their different relationship to the means of production. History, in fact, if we are to understand and use it, is not the history of courts and cabinets and armies; it is not even, as Gibbon called it, the register of the crimes, follies and misfortunes of mankind. It is the history of the class struggle of which all other developments commonly described as history are but the highly coloured epiphenomena, outward symptoms not inner causes, as the flush is of the fever. For this reason the layman who seeks the 'meaning' of history and seeks to learn a lesson from it may neglect much of the tedious detail in which the 'professional historians' so narrowly specialise. Under Marxist guidance, he can go straight to the 'relevant' part of history: the economic system and the social structure. Such is the first premiss of Marxist history.

But, it will be objected, in what sense is this 'Marxist'? In what sense indeed? It is my first objection against Marxist historians that they falsely claim a monopoly over a historical approach which is in fact quite independent of both Marx and Marxism, which preceded Marx in time and whose modern exponents owe little, perhaps even nothing, to the ferocious systematisation which Marx sought, a century ago, to impose upon it. The theory that political power is simply the reflexion of economic power was advanced in the seventeenth century by the English theorist James Harrington whose axiom 'that empire follows the balance of property' was declared at the time to be 'a noble discovery, whereof the honour belongs solely to him, as much as those of the circulation of the blood, of printing, or of optic glasses to their several authors'. The relationship between economic and political systems was explored by the great Scottish thinkers of the eighteenth century — in particular David Hume and Adam Smith. If the best modern historians are more interested in problems of comparative history, of economic change and growth, of social structure and social adjustment than in 'straight' political history, that is by no means necessarily because they have been influenced by Marx.

It is probable that they would still be pursuing these interests even if Marx had never lived. Their masters may have been, and more probably are, other thinkers — Tocqueville, Fustel de Coulanges, Burckhardt, Pirenne, Dopsch, Hamilton, Keynes, Marc Bloch and many others who have contributed far more than Marx to the study of history as a science (though not, of course, as a dogma), but whom the Marxists now seek, as it seems, to drive out of memory except in so far as they can be turned into precursors or satellites of their master. The result is that much of the credit for the modern interest in social and economic history is arbitrarily claimed for Marx, as if it derived from no one else, and the work of far more important historical thinkers is noticed only as their 'contribution to Marxist sociology', as if it contributed to nothing else.[1]

By any ordinary standards this is a strange perversion of intellectual history, but perhaps it should not surprise us too much. After all, it is very similar to the action of Lenin in political matters. For in politics, too, the men of the nineteenth century discovered new ideas, new approaches. Out of the crisis of their time they evolved socialism, communism, populism and numerous variations of the collectivist idea of society. Some of these variations have had a fertile later history, as European Social Democracy and the collectivist State of Israel still prove. But Lenin, the leader of a particular sect in this movement, violently seized control of it, and by his success as a revolutionary politician in Russia, drove all heretics into subordination or the wilderness; after which he was able to claim for himself and his disciples the sole right to represent that much wider movement which had in fact existed before him as it did beside him and does after him. It seems to me that what Lenin and his followers have done to the course of socialist politics is very similar to what Marx and his followers have done to the course of historical studies.

Thus the first and most necessary step in considering Marxist

[1] This point is clearly shown in the controversy 'Marx as Historian' which took place in the correspondence columns of the *New Statesman and Nation* (London), August 20, 1955 to October 29, 1955. In this controversy, which was provoked by my essay on Jacob Burckhardt (reprinted in this volume, pp. 273–8 above), every Marxist writer argued that Marx was in some way the sole inspirer of the modern interest in social and economic history.

historiography is to drive its exponents back within their proper limits and prevent them from usurping the credit of schools of thought which are in fact quite independent of it. But what are their proper limits? What are the characteristics which give the Marxist historical method its real originality and distinguish it from those other schools of history and sociology of which its disciples now wrongly claim to be the only begetters? The answer to this question was given by Marx himself, and it is worth while to recall his words in case I should seem to have improperly reduced his claims. 'As to myself', Marx wrote to Joseph Weydemeyer on March 5, 1852,[1] 'no credit is due to me for discovering the existence of classes in modern society, nor yet the struggle between them. Long before me bourgeois historians had described the historical development of this class-struggle and bourgeois economists the economic anatomy of the classes. What I did was to prove: (1) that the *existence of classes* is only bound up with *particular, historic phases in the development of production*; (2) that the class struggle necessarily leads to the *dictatorship of the proletariat*; (3) that this dictatorship itself only constitutes the transition to the *abolition of all classes* and to a *classless society*.' This careful isolation of Marxism from those 'bourgeois' social studies which are now so unscrupulously claimed as an inseparable part of the Marxist inheritance was again emphasised by Lenin when attacking 'the miserable philistines and petty bourgeois democrats' like Kautzky who are now claimed as Marxist thinkers. 'The theory of the class struggle', Lenin protested, 'was *not* created by Marx, but by the bourgeoisie before Marx and, generally speaking, it is acceptable to the bourgeoisie. . . . A Marxist is one who *extends* the acceptance of the class struggle to the acceptance of the *dictatorship of the proletariat*. This is where the profound difference lies between a Marxist and an ordinary petty (and even big) bourgeois. This is the touchstone on which the *real* understanding and acceptance of Marxism should be tested.'[2]

These statements could hardly be clearer, and it is most important that they should be remembered, especially by those woolly-minded students who think that one can only study

[1] Marx, *Selected Works* (English translation, London 1942), I. 377.
[2] Lenin, *The State and Revolution*, Chapter 2, quoted in Marx, *Selected Works*, l.c.

social history under Marxist guidance, and that the best modern historians are what they are thanks to the influence of Marx. In fact, as these words of Marx and Lenin show, all that Marx did or claimed to have done was to sweep up the ideas already advanced by other thinkers and annex them to a crude philosophical dogma. It is a strange irony that his followers should now claim for themselves, as the authentic property of their party, the general social ideas which Marx borrowed from his contemporaries, and for which he explicitly rejected any responsibility, and should soft-pedal the philosophical dogma which was his only original contribution and which, according to Lenin, was 'the touchstone on which the real understanding and acceptance of Marxism should be accepted'. However the reason for this *volte-face* is clear enough. The social analysis which Marx merely borrowed and perverted remains, in its unperverted use, a valuable historical instrument; the theory which he invented, and by which he perverted that social analysis, has been disproved by every test to which it can be subjected.

For let us look for a moment at this theory. According to Marx, human history falls into historic phases which are distinguished by different forms of social organisation and which replace each other by a dialectical process: a process which modern Marxists admit to be 'the very backbone of Marxism'.[1] The weakness of this theory, as a general theory, is (as M. Julien Benda once dryly observed[2]) that Marx only gives one instance of its ever having happened. This instance is, of course, the replacement of 'feudalism' by 'capitalism'. But on the strength of that one instance, to which I shall return, he does not hesitate to prophesy as a necessary next stage in the same process, the replacement of 'capitalism' by a new social form, *viz.* the classless society which will be achieved through the dictatorship of the proletariat. Thus the Marxist general theory of history can be said to rest on two mutually corroborative instances, one in the past and one in the future. The accuracy (so far) of Marxist prophecies about the future is said to prove the validity of the

[1] Giuliano Procacci, 'Dal Feudalismo al Capitalismo' in *Società*, Turin 1955, vol. XI, pp. 123 foll.

[2] Julien Benda, *La Trahison des Clercs* (Paris 1927), p. 257

Marxist historical analysis of the past, which might otherwise seem rather abstract, and the profundity of this historical analysis is said to guarantee, in turn, the accuracy of the prophecy about the future, which might otherwise seem rather speculative. This interdependence is interesting; but I think that perhaps it is better not to accept it, but to test the two instances separately. I believe that in both cases we shall find the theory being constantly — and necessarily — readjusted to fit the facts which it is said to govern.

First let us take the past. The crucial period, according to Marxist theory, is of course the period during which the one alleged instance took place, i.e. the period in which capitalism replaced feudalism. But when was this period? It is easy to say (one does not need to be a Marxist to say) that in the sixteenth century European society was still primarily agrarian and aristocratic society which can be loosely described as 'feudal'. It is easy to say that in the nineteenth century it was 'capitalist'. But when and how did the decisive struggle come — if, indeed, there ever was such a struggle? English (and other) Marxists have decided that it came in the English revolution of 1640–60, and I shall therefore look briefly at their treatment of this, to them, crucial subject.

The ablest Marxist historian who has sought thus to interpret the Puritan Revolution is the Englishman Mr. Christopher Hill. In his book *The English Revolution*,[1] which has been several times reprinted since its first publication in 1940, Mr. Hill, borrowing the doctrines of the anti-Marxist Max Weber and the Fabian R. H. Tawney (whom he condescendingly describes as 'not Marxist but very aware of the economic factor' — as if it were unusual for any but a Marxist to think in economic terms), seeks to demonstrate that the English Puritan Revolution was the effective show-down between the buoyant 'capitalist' classes, represented by Oliver Cromwell, and the 'decaying' relics of 'feudalism' represented by Charles I. This view seems to me demonstrably wrong,[2] but I am not here concerned to contest it: here I wish only to show the Marxist method. For

[1] Christopher Hill, *The English Revolution* (London, Lawrence & Wishart, 1940).

[2] I have given my own interpretation in my article 'The Social Origins of the Great Rebellion', reprinted above, pp. 195–205.

Mr. Hill presents his conclusion, that the Revolution was the triumph of capitalism over feudalism, as arising logically and necessarily from the evidence, and this evidence includes the assumptions that the early seventeenth century was a period of economic advance for the 'capitalist' bourgeoisie and gentry and that Puritanism was in some respects a 'capitalist' ideology. Now the interesting point is that both these assumptions have been strongly challenged of late. Recent research has convinced many historians that the early seventeenth century, at any rate after 1620, was a period of economic decline for the bourgeoisie, and that the equation of Puritanism with capitalism simply will not do. It would therefore seem that, if these assumptions are rejected, the Marxist version of the Revolution must also be rejected, as resting on false premisses. But behold, a miracle! In 1954 another English Marxist, Mr. E. J. Hobsbawm, wrote a long article on 'The General Crisis of the European Economy in the Seventeenth Century',[1] in which he accepted the change of premisses and agreed with the arguments of modern French economic historians that production and commerce were in general decline in the early seventeenth century. The seventeenth century, Mr. Hobsbawm argued, was a period of general economic decline in Europe, and 'even in countries which did not decline, there were secular business difficulties'. Indeed, Hobsbawm goes so far as to associate even the messianic movement of the European Jews in the middle of the century with the decline of prices.

It would seem that such a complete reversal of Mr. Hill's premisses would logically entail at least some adjustment of his conclusions. The English Revolution can hardly be painted as a victory for rising capitalism if capitalism is everywhere in decline. But not at all. Mr. Hobsbawm dogmatically tacks the old conclusion on to the new premisses:

> the economic history of the modern world from the middle of the seventeenth century hinges on that of England . . . the English Revolution, with all its far-reaching results is *therefore* (my italics) in a real sense the most decisive product of the sevententh-century crisis.

Thus, using completely different evidence, Mr. Hobsbawm still

[1] In *Past and Present*, Nos. 5–6, 1954.

finds a 'logical' path to the same general 'conclusion': in spite of the reversal of its basis, the English Revolution signified the triumph of the capitalist bourgeoisie. One is forced to assume that the 'conclusion' was not really derived from the evidence at all, but preceded it.

Indeed, the more one looks at the technical method of Marxist historians, the more one is driven to the conclusion that the evidence is simply selected to buttress up immutable and unsubstantiated dogma in this way. The one conclusion that is always kept inviolate, however the evidence may change, is that there was a decisive struggle between 'feudalism' and 'capitalism'. But what precisely are 'feudalism' and 'capitalism'? According to Mr. Hill, the Dutch, in their revolt against Spain, gave the great example of a 'bourgeois revolution'. The Calvinist Dutch therefore represent the 'Puritan capitalist' spirit. But according to Mr. Hobsbawm the Dutch economy was not capitalist but 'feudal'. Similarly, Marxists have not yet been able to decide whether the economy of the medieval Italian cities was 'capitalist' or 'feudal', and it has now become a major industry among Marxists to discuss the real meaning of the terms they have invented.[1] It is a little difficult to see how one can really prove even the existence of a historic struggle between capitalism and feudalism when one has not yet decided what the words mean.

And here I cannot help observing how sterile Marxist historiography must now seem to anyone who is aware of the great advances being made by those non-Marxist sociologists upon whose work it has become so largely parasitic. To turn from the work of (say) the disciples of Marc Bloch in France, or of the followers of Eli F. Heckscher in Sweden or of Earl J. Hamilton in America, and to see the Marxists subordinating all this work and these opportunities to barren arguments about the meaning of the fancy words they have themselves chosen to use (as if words like 'feudalism' or 'capitalism' had any real meaning other than what they are conventionally agreed to mean) is to turn from life to pedantry. The Marxist historians, when they write as Marxists, are now like Byzantine theologians disputing

[1] For this discussion see *The Transition from Feudalism to Capitalism*, a Marxist symposium published by Science and Society, New York 1954. To judge from an article by V. M. Lavrovsky in the Russian periodical *Voprosy Istorii*, No. 8, 1956, this discussion has laid down the new Marxist orthodoxy in these matters.

the cause of *homoousia* or *homoiousia*, or the inhabitants of Lilliput fighting as to which end of a boiled egg should be broken. This is not to deny that there are Marxists who have made contributions to history, but it is never *as* Marxists that they have done so. If they have done so, it is because, although Marxists, they have detached themselves from the distinctive Marxist rules of thinking and written what Marx and Lenin would have called 'bourgeois' social history.

Turning from history to prophecy, we find the same extraordinary indifference to the connexion between evidence and conclusion. Marxists regularly state that thanks to their intellectual system they have correctly predicted the events of this century. It is therefore of some interest to look more closely and see exactly what they have prophesied. In fact we find that in at least four major respects Marx's predictions were so grotesquely inaccurate that they must be regarded as totally invalidating any intellectual system which is credited with 'proving' them.

First, Marx declared that within the capitalist system capitalists would become fewer and fewer and richer and richer while the proletariat became larger and poorer. He thus envisaged a large, growing, undifferentiated proletariat faced by a small, dwindling group of owner-plutocrats whom ultimately it would easily overthrow. In fact, the history of the last century has shown that the proletariat is not undifferentiated — the workers of the world, so far from uniting, are determined to establish and preserve 'differentials' between themselves — and that capitalism, so far from being confined to a diminishing number of plutocrats, has spread downwards, through the medium of industrial corporations, until it has thoroughly penetrated the workers.

Secondly, consistently with this theory, Marx assumed that communism would be established first, and could only be established, in fully industrialised countries. In fact, for the reasons which I have just given, it is precisely the most fully industrialised countries — America and Western Europe — which have been most immune from communism, while it is agrarian countries of Eastern Europe and Asia in which communism has been most successful. The industrialisation of Russia did not precede the communist revolution but followed it.

Thirdly, Marx totally failed to predict the phenomenon of Fascism as an alternative development to communism. In this he showed far less insight than Burckhardt who already, in the 1870's, foresaw the rise of the 'terrible simplifiers' of our day. When Fascism appeared, the Marxists quickly brought their prophecies up to date and explained that this was merely the last convulsion of capitalism and therefore so insignificant a detail that Marx had not thought it necessary to mention it. This seems to me no better than Professor Toynbee's device of dismissing the World War of 1939–45, for which he had not budgeted when he began his study of History, as a mere 'secondary war'. And anyway, it seems to me outrageous to dismiss Fascism, which has dominated a whole generation and nearly conquered the world, as an unimportant detail. It seems to me that a systematic theory of history which has to be so radically adjusted to fit inconvenient facts is simply not worth its keep.

Finally, Marx insisted, as an essential part of his theory, that the dictatorship of the proletariat was simply a temporary phase leading to a classless society. No comment is needed on this 'prophecy'.

In face of these facts we may well ask, how is it possible for Marxists to maintain that their system illuminates either the past or the future? The answer seems to me to be, by pure effrontery. Just as the Russian Bolsheviks shamelessly re-write the history of the Party to eliminate inconvenient episodes or personalities, so the Marxist historians incessantly re-write the history of the past and the future, changing the evidence in accordance with the fashion, or the unescapable facts, of the moment, but always maintaining that the new evidence still leads to the old conclusions. To perform this sleight-of-hand they need to confuse their readers. Hence the oracular ambiguity of much Marxist writing, thanks to which the Marxist oracle, like the priestess of Delphi, can generally be found, in retrospect, to have prophesied whatever has in fact occurred, and the device (which Marxists share with the old Jesuit writers) of writing so much that each of them, whatever he says, can always appeal to a vast army of obscure but deferentially paraded corroborators. Hence also the complete absence of any great Marxist historians. For it is an extraordinary fact that in spite of a century of Marxism, and a vast output of Marxist historical writing, including dozens of regular periodicals supported by endowed institutions, there is, in the field of social history which they claim to have inspired, no Marxist historian whose name can rank with the admitted masters of the subject. All they have produced is an army of obscure scholiasts busily commenting on each other's *scholia* and loudly claiming to have inspired the work of other historians who have long ago left them behind in their barren, circuitous, resonant cave of Adullam. In the dim past of the nineteenth century, when the Marxist dogma was new and untested, it may have inspired some historical research, as new ideas often do, even if they are in fact erroneous. For historical knowledge, like other knowledge, is advanced by theory and only disciplined by facts. But now we are in the mid-twentieth century. Russian communism is indeed a formidable world power. But it is not the Marxist dialectic that has brought it to that height. The relationship is the other way round. Disproved by all intellectual tests, it is Russian power alone which now sustains and irrationally seems to justify the Marxist interpretation of history.

CHAPTER XLIII

ARNOLD TOYNBEE'S MILLENNIUM

Arnold Toynbee's Bible—for so one can reasonably describe his ten-volume *Study of History*—has not been well received by the professional historians. I agree with them in regarding it as untrue, illogical and dogmatic. But in this essay I do not intend to argue its historical truth or falsehood, its logical coherence or incoherence, its empirical validity or invalidity. I intend to consider its significance as a document of our time. For true or false, logical or illogical, empirical or abstract, this book has excited a great deal of attention. Although every chapter of it has been shot to pieces by the experts, and although it is written in a style compared with which that of Hitler or Rosenberg is of Gibbonian lucidity, it has been hailed by the unprofessional public, at least in America, as 'an immortal masterpiece', 'the greatest work of our time', 'probably the greatest historical work ever written'. As a dollar-earner, we are told, it ranks second only to whisky. Its success has carried its already much-travelled author round and round the globe, lecturing, flower-crowned, from China to Peru. Surely this phenomenon requires some explanation. It is not enough to say that the work is intellectually erroneous. We must ask why such error has such a vogue. What is the meaning of Toynbee's message in the context of our time? To answer this question we must look at Toynbee's message in a different spirit from that in which most of his critics have regarded it. They were primarily concerned with its truth. They tested the validity of his arguments. I am now concerned with his meaning. What kind of a future does Toynbee (rightly or wrongly) envisage? What part, in the unfolding of history, does he invite us to play?

To understand Toynbee's message, it is important to remember the stages in which it was delivered and the events which were happening in the world at that time. For Toynbee's Bible was not delivered to the world all at once. It consists of two Testaments, separated from each other by some fifteen years — fifteen years which included the war of 1939–45. The Old Testament, which comprises volumes 1–6, appeared between 1932 and 1939. The New Testament, which comprises volumes 7–10, was published in 1954. Moreover, the New Testament ends with a remarkable volume, which sheds a great deal of light on the purpose and character of the whole work, volume 10 or the Book of Revelation. If we are to understand the message of Toynbee fully, we must examine his Bible in the order in which it was written, beginning with Genesis and ending with Revelation.

Now Toynbee's general message, the message of his Old Testament, is simple and reasonably clear. His Book of Genesis is the story of the Fall of Civilisations. All civilisations, according to Toynbee, are comparable; all pass through similar stages; all flourish and decay according to the same general laws, the same general time-scale of growth and change; all ultimately die. There may be different forms of death. Some civilisations die sudden, violent deaths without living out their time; others may seem to linger on, but in reality they are dead, mere fossils of themselves. For there is no exemption from the law of mortality. Always there is an end, and our own Western Civilisation, which we once thought unique and immortal, is in fact no different from the others. It too must die. As a matter of fact, it must die very soon. Has it not already shown all the signs of senility, as diagnosed by the scientific doctor of civilisations? Did it not reach its peak four hundred years ago? Are not four hundred years the time invariably allotted, by the mystical mathematics of History, to the 'Time of Troubles' which precedes the death of a civilisation? Is not our civilisation already visibly in dissolution? Surely its end is near.

Such is Toynbee's general message. It is a determinist message. But it has another characteristic too. It is also a fundamentally obscurantist message. For although Toynbee, in analysing civilisations, claims to be dispassionate and scientific, in fact his whole analysis is governed by strong emotional prejudice. In spite of its Hellenic training, his mind is fundamentally anti-rational and illiberal. Everything which suggests the freedom of the human reason, the human spirit, is to him odious. This illiberalism again and again distorts his own logic. Terms which, for his 'scientific' purpose, should be neutral, like 'decline' or 'decay', are by him given a moral significance and arbitrarily equated with the processes which he happens to dislike — i.e. the growth of liberalism or rationalism. So, in his Book of Genesis, the Fall of our Civilisation is dated from the time when our ancestors ate the fruit of the Tree of Knowledge and sought to be like gods, knowing good and evil — the time of the Renaissance. To Toynbee the Renaissance was the beginning of the irreversible decline of the West, and every further manifestation of human reason is to him yet another milestone on the road to ruin. Europe's greatest centuries, the centuries of the Reformation, the New Philosophy of the seventeenth century, the Enlightenment, the gradual conquest of disease and famine, are to him its darkest ages. The European Enlightenment of the eighteenth century, that incomparable period of human emancipation, the age of Bach and Mozart, Gibbon and Voltaire, is to him merely 'a spell of low ideological temperature', a weary lull in the otherwise fatal course of Europe's disintegration and decay, a brief respite between 'a first and a second paroxysm of its deadly seizure'. The seizure, we may note in passing, was already deadly even before the lull. Europe's death was already decreed, not when industrialism or communism or the hydrogen bomb arose to threaten it, but when the Renaissance, that great spiritual disaster, descended like a fatal curse upon us. It was then that disintegration set in, then that that sentence of death was passed which is now, after the preordained term of four hundred years, about to be executed upon us.

Is there then no hope? Can nothing stay our doom? No, says Toynbee, nothing. The best we can do is to find our way back into that Paradise of medieval innocence from which, by our fatal presumption, we have been expelled. Since it was the Renaissance and the Reformation which, by opening the eyes and the mind of man, set us on the four-hundred-year slope leading to destruction, let us now seek to go back behind those fatal episodes, deny them and their consequences, pretend that they have never been. Let us confess that, for the last four centuries, we have all been miserable sinners. We have broken the holy eggshell of Catholic unity in which we had been happily and innocently enclosed, insulted the primitive taboos which before had kept us there, and crept out into the fresh, clear light of day. But now, thanks to the inspired 'science' of the Prophet Toynbee, we have discovered that the daylight is misleading, the open air cold. Let us then, with devout hands, piece together the festering relics of that cosy shell and creep back again into its warm darkness. Who knows but that holy old hen, Mother Rome, though understandably somewhat stand-offish after such long insubordination, may consent to sit again upon her naughty but now penitent brood? We shall not reverse the iron laws of History, but perhaps we shall mitigate our doom. By sin came death. We cannot now escape the decree of death; but at least let us repent of our sin.

Such, in general, was the message of Toynbee's Old Testament. It is worth while to consider briefly its pedigree and its application to current affairs. For there is nothing very original about it, except the monstrous systemisation to which everything is subjected. The 'decline of the West' is, relatively at least, an obvious fact — though with certain limitations to which Toynbee pays little attention. That is to say, the technical conquest and organisation of great land-masses by railways, motor power, and air transport has deprived the small maritime powers of Europe of one of their advantages and has mobilised instead the naturally far greater resources of huge, but previously unorganised, countries like America and Russia. But this shift in the balance of power has, of course, nothing whatever to do with the mere flow of time, the 'ageing' of cultures, or the corroding effects of the Renaissance. It was remarked by geographers like Sir Halford Mackinder before Toynbee seized upon the same fact and, separating it from its real causes, ascribed it instead to the cosmic processes which he assumed. These cosmic processes have in turn another pedigree.

It is a German pedigree. The theory that all history is predetermined and that the stages between one predetermined phase and another are marked by catastrophic convulsions seems to be a peculiar product of the German mind. It was advanced by Hegel, by Marx, by Nietzsche; and in the twentieth century, when great catastrophes seemed to be descending with particular force on Germany, it became, in varying ways, the orthodoxy of various German schools. For after the defeat of the First World War, in the aftermath of that exhausting struggle, surrounded by the debris of ancient empires, and faced with terrible social problems, it was easy and even natural for Germans to draw on these native ideas and imagine a universal catastrophe. So the Marxists, hating the 'capitalist' West, announced with glee that a whole age was over. The West, with its culture, was finished, and must be transformed by conquest: conquest which must come from the new, non-Western power that had accepted the German doctrine of Marxism, Soviet Russia. Theirs was a confident message, because they hoped to be the heirs of the West, the beneficiaries and rulers of the new age. On the other hand conservative German intellectuals, drawing on the same tradition, accepted the same conclusions with much less glee. It was with wailing and gnashing of teeth that Oswald Spengler declared that the turn of the West had come: that 'civilisations' were comparable and all mortal; and that the hour of dissolution for our civilisation was at hand.

It was at this point that Toynbee came in. An English amateur, tagging somewhat incongruously along behind these German professionals, he repeated Spengler's general theory. He was also a conservative, and as a classical scholar he loved the past: it was therefore with some sorrow that he envisaged the crumbling of an ancient order. On the other hand, as an obscurantist, moved by a detestation of human reason and its works, he clearly enjoyed a certain Germanic *Schadenfreude* in equating the decline of the West with the rise of rationality. This equation, one may add, was not new: it was a favourite equation of the obscurantist school of writers — Belloc, Chesterton, T. E. Hulme. Incidentally it is also inconsistent with Toynbee's general theory. For since Toynbee ascribes an equal time-span to all civilisations, regardless of their relative rationality, it is clear that decay, to him, is a function of age, not of reason. Still, it pleased Toynbee to make this equation: it enabled him to wring his hands with more prophetic gusto if he could say to a dying civilisation not only, 'You are old, you have one foot in the grave, you shall surely die,' but also, 'You have sinned, your sins have found you out, you deserve to die! I told you so! Repent.'

Thus Toynbee's Old Testament, like the ponderous vaticinations of Spengler, can be seen as the obverse of Germanic radicalism, as the despairing wail of conservative defeatism. 'The old order is perishing,' cried the radicals, 'it is doomed to perish. Let us give it one more knock, and it will be finished. Then the reign of the new ruling class will begin.' Such has been the cry of radical revolutionaries at all times. It was the cry of the Anabaptists of Münster in the sixteenth century, of the English Saints in the seventeenth century. However, society is a good deal tougher than radicals suppose, as the Anabaptists and the Saints quickly found. When radicals scream that victory is indubitably theirs, sensible conservatives knock them on the nose. It is only very feeble conservatives who take such words as true and run round crying for the last sacraments.

For these reasons Toynbee's Old Testament was not taken very seriously in England. It was still only in Germany that such catastrophic views enjoyed any currency. And indeed in Germany they soon achieved a new lease of life. For although the Marxists proved unable to realise their dream of conquering Germany, another anti-Western radical party, which had stolen the Marxist thunder, was soon able to exploit the theory of 'the Decline of the West'. Adolf Hitler, like Spengler and Toynbee, was a student of history. Like them he ranged over the centuries and crammed such facts as he found it convenient to select into a monstrous system. The true facts of geography joined the rubbish of the philosophers in his head, and he saw himself as the Phœnix of centuries, the Messiah who would roll up one age of history and open out a new. The West, he said, was finished; but Germany was not, or at least need not be — if only it would repudiate the West. He would revive Germany by detaching it from the embraces of a dying civilisation. He would breathe into it a primitive, barbarian, irrational spirit. He would wrest from Marxist Russia the leadership of the new, non-Western, non-capitalist, non-rational age and establish a new empire over the ruins of the West. To demoralise his intended victims he assured them that the iron laws of 'historical necessity' were on his side; and having demoralised as many as were frightened by such words, he gathered up his forces and, in 1939, he struck.

When the German legions marched over Europe, trampling on its liberties, it must have seemed to many that Toynbee's dismal prophecies were coming true. Surely this was the end of the West. Was it not written in the Holy Writ? Then if defeat was certain, was it not most sensible to accept it in its least painful form, by prompt surrender? So everywhere in Europe a class of men appeared who were not Nazis, or pro-Nazis, who did not relish the prospect before them, who were in fact conservatives, but who accepted as inevitable 'the New Order' that was threatened from Berlin. The West, they said, was finished: why should it not surrender in the hope of saving at least those elements of Western Civilisation which were worth preserving? Freedom of all kinds could be sacrificed, provided the essentials of civilisation — the social hierarchy and the Church — were saved. We have sinned, such men cried, we have eaten the forbidden fruit; let us repent and retire out of history, leaving the future to the Nazi Millennium. In future let us be good and let who will be clever; we shall not try to think, but only to pray. The patron saint of such men throughout Europe was Marshal Pétain. He was the patron of all those whose will had been sapped by the messianic claims of Hitler and the dismal certitudes of Toynbee. For Toynbee, in so far as he had any influence, was the unconscious intellectual ally of Hitler in the non-Nazi world, the true prophet of European Pétainism.

I say 'unconscious' because in fairness to Toynbee we must admit that he has no particular preference for a German conquest of Europe. He seems not to care who destroys the West, so long as the West is destroyed and thus vindicates his theory. Nor has he ever prophesied who will be its destroyer. Certainly he never foresaw that it might be Hitler. In 1936, after a long interview with Hitler, Toynbee declared himself 'convinced of his sincerity in desiring peace in Europe'.[1] Even in 1939 he was blind, or indifferent, to the particular threat of Nazi Germany. For civilisations, he maintains, always succumb to internal age,

[1] See the interesting account of Toynbee's conversation after this interview given by Dr. Thomas Jones, *A Diary with Letters 1931–1950* (Oxford 1954), pp. 179–181.

not external blows; or at least external blows are only the occasion, not the cause of their dissolution. Even the Incas were not really destroyed by the Spaniards but because their civilisation had reached its logical term when the Spaniards arrived. The apparent destroyer is in fact not a destroyer but merely a demonstrator of internal rottenness. Still, by 1940, Hitler had proved himself a demonstrator of some capacity. If the West was really so rotten that it was about to crumble through natural decay, it was reasonable to expect that the first external knock would complete the process. This is what the Pétainists believed. It was naturally mortifying to them when, in spite of all the blows which it received, in spite of historical necessity, and in spite of the combined eloquence of Hitler and themselves, the West did not merely not crumble: it resisted; it was victorious; it survives.

What was Toynbee to do when faced with this unexpected survival of the civilisation whose doom he had so confidently pronounced? Change his views? That is too much to expect of any prophet. A slight reinterpretation is the most we can reasonably require. And sure enough, this is what we get. In 1954, after fifteen years of silence, Toynbee published his New Testament, and, in publishing it, admitted not indeed error — he has never admitted to any error — but a certain development in his views. In the past fifteen years, he writes, 'my inner world had been undergoing changes which, on the miniature scale of an individual life, were for me of proportionate magnitude' to the vast changes which the great war of 1939–45 had caused in the world without.

What were these inner changes? Something of them had already been revealed, obliquely, in a public discussion which Toynbee had held in 1948 with the most formidable of his critics, the distinguished Dutch historian Professor Geyl. In this discussion Geyl had described Toynbee, on the basis of his Old Testament, as a determinist. To his surprise, he found that Toynbee now indignantly repudiated the charge. 'With the awful warning of Spengler's dogmatic determinism before my eyes,' Toynbee declared, 'I always have been and shall be mighty careful, for my part, to treat the future of our civilisation as an open question.' It was in vain that Geyl protested that this suspension of judgment simply does not exist in Toynbee's book: indeed 'as regards the future, in one place in your book you are very near to drawing, as you put it, "the horoscope of our civilisation" from the fate of other civilisations, and you suggest repeatedly that we have got into the disintegration stage which you picture to us so elaborately in your book as leading inevitably to catastrophe.' Toynbee simply refused to admit this conclusion. All his arguments might lead thither, but now, suddenly, he refused to pronounce the final doom. He did not give any reason for this refusal to accept the only conclusion to which all his 'laws' seem infallibly to lead. All he would say was that although he had established the laws under which all other civilisations have perished, and although he had shown that our civilisation too is subject to those laws and has now reached the stage at which death can hardly be postponed, nevertheless — who knows? Something may yet turn up. What? we ask. But we receive no answer. All we are told is that Toynbee is not a determinist. And he adds ('somewhat testily' we are told), 'I suppose I must be the last judge of what my own beliefs are.' To which one can only answer, 'No doubt: but not of the rationality or consistency of those beliefs.'

What was the escape-clause which Toynbee, by 1948, had discovered in his own determinist system? For answer, we look to his New Testament, which he was meditating at that time in the light of those profound inner changes caused by the war, and which, six years later, was to be published to the world as volumes 7–10 of his *Study of History*. These volumes do indeed add a very significant message to the message of the Old Testament: a message not this time of despair but of hope — of a kind.

It is not that Toynbee sees any prospect of the survival of Western Civilisation as we understand it. On that point his message is unchanged. Not even the events of 1939–45 can change his eagerness to see 'the West' destroyed, and indeed he seems at times positively impatient with those events for their obstinate non-conformity with his theory. Why, he seems to overhear us asking, did the West not crumble finally before the might of Hitler? Poof! he answers. Hitler was no threat at all — how could he have been if even the rotten West did not crumble at his touch? Hitler's armies were phantom armies only: it was only the decadent pacifism of Europe which made him appear formidable. He had not made Germany a military power, he had merely 'coaxed, duped, and flogged' it 'into being one degree less unwarlike than its neighbours.' 'In the realm of the blind the one-eyed man is king.' Nor does Toynbee allow the war of 1939–45 to be a real war — had he not already committed himself to the assertion that the war of 1914–18 was the last major war of which enfeebled Europe, according to the Toynbeean Tables, was capable? So Hitler's war is dismissed as a mere 'supplementary war', beneath the notice of the historical scientist, and therefore unable to disturb the perfect symmetry of those Tables. And finally, if the feeble Hitler let the Professor down by failing to establish universal domination over the ruins of Europe, let us not suppose that that was due to any resistance by the still feebler Europe. No. That was due to 'a chapter of lucky accidents' such as no historian could or indeed should be expected to prophesy, and such — Toynbee adds with relish — as cannot conceivably occur again. Thus Hitler's war, which Toynbee had not predicted in 1939, was written off, after it was over, as an irrelevant 'secondary war', a mere airshot which does not in the least invalidate the general theory that the West is ripe for conquest. It is inconceivable, we are assured, that our next assailant will repeat the 'accidental combination of incidental errors' which led to Hitler's failure. Therefore let us not lose faith — faith in the gospel of our own inevitable defeat.

Where then, we may ask, is the novelty of Toynbee's New Testament? Where is that escape-clause at which he had hinted in his discussion, in 1948, with Professor Geyl? The answer is that the glad tidings of great joy which Toynbee now offers is not that Western civilisation as we know it can be saved. It is that something far more important than our rotten civilisation can be born out of its ruin. In the 1930's Toynbee had lamented the impending death of our civilisation because then, along with much that was rational and therefore bad, the good, irrational elements must also perish. He had therefore hoped against hope that by some modification, some deliberate weakening of the rational and strengthening of the irrational elements, the structure might be preserved. But now Toynbee has admitted the fragility, the logical weakness of any such hope. He has yielded at last to the pressure of his own determinist system. But he has been able to do so without reluctance because he has discovered a new, a very important and — to him — a consoling truth.

The truth which dawned on Toynbee in the years of Hitler's war, the years between the Old Testament and the New, is basically very simple. It is that human civilisations are not, after all, organic wholes. Their elements are detachable and can survive, as vital and vivifying parts, in other civilisations, in the 'universal states' which shall succeed them. Why then, he asks, should we not separate the essential from the inessential elements, the good from the bad, and, having done that,

> *let determin'd things to Destiny*
> *Hold unbewail'd their way?*

Why should not our Western Civilisation go to its doom, the sooner the better, carrying with it the rubbish with which human reason has by now fatally deformed it, provided that the valuable parts of it, its primitive pre-Reformation faith, can be preserved as one of the vitalising ingredients of the new 'universal state'? Surely this is a more logical, more positive, and (to some) more cheering conclusion than that desperate, defeatist proposal so feebly tacked on to Toynbee's Old Testament. Now there is no question of mere reaction. Now salvation will come not by forlorn retreat into the shrivelled womb of Mother Church, but by moving onwards on our predetermined path, which proves not to be so fatal after all. Our civilisation shall indeed perish; but what, after all, is civilisation? 'Civilisations,' we are now told, 'have forfeited their historical significance except in so far as they minister to the progress of religion.' Therefore, what does it matter how soon or by whom Western humanity is decimated, Western justice mocked, Western art and letters snuffed out, Western freedom abolished? Our religion — or rather, one strand of it: for Toynbee still seems to reject Protestantism — shall survive, not indeed alone or exclusive, but as part of a higher religion, the religion of a universal state.

Such is Toynbee's new Dispensation. It is, of course, not entirely new; for Toynbee's whole system is by definition repetitive. Therefore this new Dispensation too has a historical precedent. The precedent is taken, as always, from Græco-Roman civilisation. For although Toynbee claims to base his system on a number of past civilisations, in fact, as the critics have often pointed out, it is based on Græco-Roman civilisation only — the only civilisation which Toynbee has really studied and to whose pattern, as he interprets it, all other civilisations are now arbitrarily told to conform. So now the decline of the West must be made to resemble the decline of Greece and Rome, and the new universal Church, of which Toynbee is the prophet, must resemble the old Christian Church, in the days when it was new. The wheel of history has once again come full circle. The future is once again made clear by the past.

For did not the ancient pagan civilisation of the Hellenic world, obedient to the Toynbeean Laws, duly decompose? Were not its political forms — the independent Greek cities, the Hellenistic monarchies, the Roman republic itself — utterly extinguished? Did not the memory of its poets and philosophers happily fade away, burnt out of human recollection by the purifying fires of clerical bigotry, until the rot of the Renaissance allowed them to return? But did not the more essential parts of that civilisation, its mysteries and mummeries, its sacraments and sacrifices, Isis and Adonis and Mithras, happily survive, gathered up and preserved in that new syncretist religion, 'that quaint Alexandrian *tutti-frutti*', as Norman Douglas once described it, Christianity? Even so, Toynbee tells us, our Western civilisation is now fast decomposing. We shall be conquered, destroyed, absorbed. Our political forms, our liberties, our culture shall be crushed out. But what of that? For our religious beliefs, which alone matter, will be preserved, pickled as one of the ingredients of a new syncretist religion, a new tutti-frutti, 'a mish-mash', as one commentator has described it, 'of the Virgin Mary and Mother Isis, of St. Michael and Mithras, of St. Peter and Muhammad, of St. Augustine and Jalal-ad-Din Mawlana'. Such, we are now assured, is to be the new 'universal religion' which will render political conquest a positive boon and will replace for all mankind the use of human reason and the remembrance of its great landmarks, the Renaissance, the Reformation, the New Philosophy, the Enlightenment.

But how is this new Dispensation to come in? Will our conquerors themselves bring it in? Certainly not. The Roman Emperors did not invent Christianity, they merely created a political system within which it was able to spread. The beginning of the new religion was quite separate. At a certain point in time during the decomposition of Hellenic society there arose a Messiah. The Messiah preached a Word, a Message, which altered the immutable sentence of the Book of Genesis and gave to mankind, predetermined to physical death, a new hope of spiritual life. Around this Message the disciples of the Messiah afterwards assembled and crystallised the miscellaneous mythology of other religions. Even so today the necessity of a new religion requires the appearance of a new Messiah: a new Messiah who, incidentally, has certain advantages over the old. For the old Messiah acted naïvely: he uttered his message, and his disciples slowly did the rest of the work, so that the new religion grew up, as it seemed, spontaneously, over centuries, obedient to impersonal laws. But the new Messiah can do better than that. Knowing the laws, he can himself operate them, or at least further their operation, much more expeditiously. He knows in advance what the final form of the new religion must be. He can foreshorten the centuries of change and preach the new religion, the new tutti-frutti, 'the mish-mash of the Virgin Mary and Mother Isis' all at once.

And who is to be this new Messiah? It surprises me that among so many commentators on Toynbee's work, none (so far as I know) has publicly posed or answered this question. And yet the answer seems to emerge clearly—only too clearly—from the text. It is true the Messiah is never explicitly named; even on this point the Prophet does not deviate into clarity; but discreetly and repeatedly, as the great work nears its end, he is identified until finally there can be no mistake. In the tenth volume of his work, the last book of his Bible, his Book of Revelation, the secret is laid bare: the Messiah steps forth: he is Toynbee himself.

I know that this statement will seem outrageous to some. It will be said that Toynbee is personally a modest and humble man and that this is to ascribe to him *hybris* and blasphemy. I do not wish to ascribe anything to him which does not seem to me to emerge inescapably from his published work. I shall therefore try to document the conclusion I have expressed.

First of all I should say that I am not impressed by Toynbee's alleged 'humility'. It is perfectly true that he himself often praises this virtue. 'Spiritual humility', he says, is one of the distinctive signs of the great historian, and he congratulates himself on being free from that 'blight of egocentricity' which has prevented other historians from seeing as far as he has done. This 'contrite humility, the first of Christian virtues', has, he says, fortified him throughout his superhuman task, and it has also guided his hand in everything he has written; for 'in the writing of a book, as in every other human endeavour, the worst of all vices is the *hybris* that is the nemesis of self-conceit. An author is convicting himself of being past praying for if ever he allows the Old Adam in him to close his mind to a suggestion for some modification of his first draft by answering, What I have written I have written.'

Now this is all very well, but when we look further into Toynbee's work we find it very difficult to discover this 'humility' of which he so regularly boasts. For instance, when has Toynbee ever modified his text in answer to criticism? Some very formidable criticisms were made of some of the arguments used in his early volumes. Has Toynbee ever paid the slightest attention to them or made the slightest modification of those arguments or their conclusions? His only reply has been to include, in his later volumes, a chapter of abuse against those purblind modern historians who, enslaved by a barren devotion to the minutiæ of their technique, have had the '*hybris*', the 'sin', not to admit the validity of his historical laws. As for his claim to be free from 'the blight of egocentricity', it is instructive to look at his last volume of all. There, in the index, it will be found that whereas the entry 'History', which is, after all, the subject of the whole work, occupies only five column-inches, the entry 'Toynbee, Arnold Joseph' occupies twelve column-inches, and there are separate entries for twelve other members of the Toynbee family who owe this distinction entirely to their relationship with the Professor. The 'Acknowledgments and Thanks', too, which cover thirty pages, are awarded not only to the usual suppliers of information, correctors of proofs, and benevolent publishers, but to all who, since the beginning of History, have deserved immortality by contributing, each according to his capacity, to that ultimate creation of the ages, the mind of Toynbee. Æschylus, Pindar, Aristotle are there; the Bible, St. Augustine, Fra Angelico have done their bit; thanks are conveyed to 'the glory of God' and, on either side of it, to the also beneficent city of York and Uncle William Toynbee. Plato is thanked for teaching the Professor 'when, in a mental voyage, I found myself at the upper limit of the atmosphere accessible to Reason, not to hesitate to let my imagination carry me up into the stratosphere on the wings of a myth.' William of Wykeham is thanked for having founded Winchester College and having thoughtfully 'made this provision for me 507 years before I was elected a scholar of his college.' It is clear, from such evidence, that Toynbee regards himself as a portent no less significant than his work. All creation has been groaning and travailing to produce him; Winchester College has at last, in him, achieved its purpose; the ultimate bounds of human reason have at last, by him, been pierced.

All this being so, I do not think we are obliged to ascribe to Toynbee that almost unnatural humility which he so often goes out of his way to claim. Or, at least, his humility must be relative: his own greatness must seem to him so clearly superhuman that it shows remarkable condescension in him to claim, in public, no more than unique mortal genius. As for the humility which he preaches as a necessary virtue of the historian, we are forced to conclude that he is not really thinking of himself at all: he is thinking of his critics. If only *they* were more humble, how much better it would be! Then they would not presume to criticise one who had so splendidly outsoared the shadow of their night.

Thus I do not consider it *a priori* inconceivable that Toynbee should regard himself as the Messiah. And in fact, if we examine the autobiographical part of his work in a little more detail, we can hardly help observing the repeated evidence that this is how he does regard himself. In fact we shall discover that Toynbee, unlike previous Messiahs who were lamentably careless in this respect, has made scrupulous provision for his future devotees. Having himself (since History — as he has shown — repeats itself) tasted almost all the experiences of his prototype, he has contrived so to record these experiences, their dates and places, that there will be no danger of heresy or error in such important matters. Tucked away in the corners of his New Testament, we can find the authentic record of everything that matters in his Life: the minor prophets who dimly heralded his coming; the Holy Family; the precocious Infancy; the youthful Temptations; the missionary Journeys; the Miracles; the Revelations; the Agony. Moreover, looking forward as well as back, he has, by considerately recording the places he has visited and the objects he has touched, made provision for a constant traffic in those pilgrimages and relics upon which the religion of the Mish-Mash, like all true religion, must depend.

Am I serious? Alas, I am. Toynbee's truly monstrous self-adulation, combined with his fundamental obscurantism, does indeed emotionally repel me. But let us not give out all the heat we may feel. Perhaps the subject is best treated with detachment, even if it requires an artificial detachment. So let us interpose the cooling concept of an imaginary century. Let us transport ourselves, in imagination, a century or so onward in time, so that we can look back calmly upon the phenomenon before us. Let us suppose that all has worked according to plan. The Time of Troubles is over. Western Civilisation, long declining, has now at last (thank God) foundered, and all that is good in it, and in other civilisations, has been preserved and pickled in the universal world-state with its universal world-religion of Mish-Mash. From this vantage post I invite my readers to look coolly back at the figure of Toynbee as it will then emerge from his own New Testament and from the glosses with which his disciples, in the course of a century, will naturally have enriched it.

It is noon. The drowsy doggerel of the Founder's Litany 'Mother Mary, Mother Isis, Mother Cybele, Mother Ishtar, Mother Kwanyin, have compassion on us . . .' is rhythmically sounding in all the Churches of Mish-Mash. We know the history of this Litany of course: how the Disciples asked the Master to teach them to pray, and how in 'London, at 6.25 p. m. on 15th June 1951, after looking once more, this afternoon, at Fra Angelico's picture of the Beatific Vision,' the Master obliged by uttering this formula (Vol. X, p. 143). As the unintelligible sounds issue mechanically from his lips, the worshipper will, of course, allow his eyes to stray. Perhaps they will light on a stained-glass window, illuminated from without by the rational daylight. What will it represent? That, of course, will vary with the locality. At Abersoch, in Wales, for instance, a richly painted window will naturally illustrate the great local miracle of the Epiphany: how the Founder, at the age of two, already driven forward by intellectual curiosity and a philosophy of action, 'took and carried out a decision to run into the sea in order to find out what would happen,' and was haled back by an anxious nurse who, though she sprained her ankle in the act, has since been amply compensated by her official beatification. The church at Abersoch is now rich, thanks to the resort of pilgrims eager to baptise their children in those now curative sea-waves, so the window is a fine one, and the artist has not failed to point the moral of the incident. How could he, when the Master has himself so clearly emphasised it: 'There was no benevolently officious nurse to pull him back from the intellectual plunge that he made, six years later, into the Ocean of History' (X. 19).

'Six years later,' the inattentive worshipper may well muse, 'that means that our Founder took his first decisive intellectual plunge at the age of eight. When? Where? In what parish church or rural shrine is this great event worthily commemorated?' On this point, unfortunately, the Scriptures are ambiguous. For the Founder himself tells us (X. 218) that he was only seven when he read, in the Book of Genesis, about Noah's three sons and thence precociously took note of 'the differentiation of the Human Race into divers groups and sub-groups and the historical problems raised by the question how these groups are related to one another'; and again (X. 235) that he was not yet eight when he read *Paradise Lost* in three days and imbibed from it 'the idea of a theodicy'; and it was at the age of seven, too, he tell us, that he received from his mother the inscribed copy of her *True Stories from Scottish History* 'which stands behind his shoulder in his study at No. 45 Pembroke Square, London', and which he has 'just now' taken down (X. 18). . . .

How thoughtful, incidentally, of the Founder always to identify the placing of his books! These helpful details have made it possible to reconstitute his study exactly as he kept it, even down to that translation by Gilbert Murray which he took out of the row on May 11th, 1951 (X. 217); and Aunt Gertrude Toynbee's copy of Mommsen which he received from her in September 1906, which he read in the summer of 'A.D. 1907' (now A.T. 18) and which was 'here on my desk in May 1951' (X. 229); and the four volumes of *The Story of the Nations*, with the bookplate of Grandmother (now the Blessed) Harriet Toynbee in them, which were 'all four of them on my table on this 21st day of February 1951' (X. 219); and the map of Greece which he used on April 26th, 1912, and is still 'lying at his elbow at this moment' on September 23rd, 1952; and the forty-two sheets of an early MS. by himself which, 'as he wrote these words, he took out of a drawer in a bookcase given him by his mother in his study at 45 Pembroke Square, Kensington, London' (X. 22). The study, of course, is now no longer in Pembroke Square. Like the Virgin's House at Bethlehem, which miraculously migrated to Loreto in Italy, it has now been removed intact to the great Toynbeeum in California, and a mere replica has replaced it in Kensington.[1] But London is not entirely without original relics. The three volumes of Grote's work on Plato, for instance, which the Founder 'took down from the shelf in the Athenæum Club' are now preserved in the club in a jewelled reliquary and exposed for the worship of members on the anniversary of the day, April 23rd, 1951 (formerly St. George's Day), on which the Founder records that he touched them (X. 20).

Meanwhile, in other churches throughout the world, similar thoughts must be occurring to other worshippers. At Dunwich, Suffolk, a statue of Mother and Child naturally commemorates the Founder's Mother giving him, when he was five years old, that sagacious tip ('the Wisdom of Dunwich') which enabled him, five years later, to write a better essay than the other boys in his school (X. 41). At the school itself, Wootton Court near Canterbury (now a training college for the Mish-Mash clergy),

[1] Since this essay was first published, a correspondent informs me that in this detail fantasy is behind the facts, since 'a few years ago part of the study at No. 45 Pembroke Square was in fact translated by air to America for a televised theophany.' Given the pace of modern life, I cannot exclude the possibility that some other of these prophecies may already have been fulfilled.

a splendid church is of course dedicated to the Confounding of the Elders in the matter of the Parthian Cataphracts (X. 224). Further afield, in Osaka, Japan, a rich temple marks the spot where the Founder, in November 1929, was inspired by a puppet-show to entertain profound thoughts about determinism and free-will (X. 231). In Greece, in the wild country between Káto Vezáni and Yythion, a rural shrine marks the spot where, on April 26th, 1912, the Founder drank dysentery from an infected stream and thus escaped the dangers of military service. (The lucky stream now cures the disease it then inflicted.) At 12 Westbourne Terrace, London, a fine wall-painting depicts the Founder there listening to his great-uncle Captain (now St.) Henry Toynbee discoursing on the rig of sailing ships (X. 213); and at Arezzo the old daubs by Piero della Francesca have been painted over with more truly devotional frescos representing the Founder fruitfully questioning the rector of the church on 'the affinities of certain forms of headgear' (X. 239). The spot where the Founder swam the Euphrates (IX. 38) is of course a great place of pilgrimage, pickpockets, and baksheesh. In Yorkshire, the less ambitious tourist will find, on Slingsby Moor, the barrow where the Messiah was able to catch 'still unspent reverberations of waves of psychic events' since unrecorded time; and, at Ampleforth Abbey, a noble altar-piece commemorating the Founder's famous Dream in 'A.D. 1936' (A.T. 47) of clinging to the Crucifix: the premonition of his later Passion (IX. 634).

Of these lesser shrines there is no end. For the Founder not only excelled St. Paul and St. Francis Xavier in his travels, he was also considerate enough to supply the faithful with a very detailed record of them. The mere list of places visited by him fills, in his index, three and a half column-inches. But some reference must be made to the seven great centres of the new religion, the Seven Stations as they are now called, where the Founder had his seven direct historical revelations — such an improvement on 'the sole flash of inspiration with which Gibbon was ever visited' (X. 103) — when he was 'rapt into a momentary communion' with incidents in the distant past. The first Station was at Oxford (now Arnoldopolis) in 'A.D. 1911' (A.T. 22). Others were on a peak of Pharsalus on January 10th, 1912 (conducted tours on the anniversary); at Monemvasia on April 23rd, 1912, where 'the quietly browsing goats' (X. 136) are now stylised figures in local art, like the ox and the ass of Bethlehem in Italian painting; and on a peninsula in the Gulf of Chihli on November 24th, 1929, where, in spite of this important event, the ungrateful natives are unhappily not yet settled in the new faith. But the great revelation is the seventh, which took place near Victoria (now 'the Seventh') Station in London. On that occasion the Master 'found himself in communion not just with this or that episode in History, but with all that had been, and was, and was to come. In that instant he was directly aware of the passage of History gently flowing through him in a mighty current and of his own life welling like a wave in the flow of this vast tide' (X. 139). How unfortunate that the Founder 'failed to record the exact date' of this experience. In the absence of evidence the Church has had to name a conventional date for its annual commemoration: the Day of Toynbee's Transfiguration is now kept on December 25th (formerly Christmas).

Of course the Founder's life was not without its frustrations. In his early days there was the Temptation in Buckinghamshire when the Devil, in the form of Uncle Paget Toynbee ('*vivebat* A.D. 1855–1932' — for the Founder always gives these useful biographical data about the Holy Family) and Aunt Helen Toynbee ('*née* Helen Wrigley, of Bury, Lancs.'), sought to divert him at age of seventeen into 'a wrong intellectual turning'. 'Your Uncle Nellie and I', said this plausible old uncle, 'have come to the conclusion that you have been dispersing your interests too widely, and our advice to you is to make your choice of some single subject and to concentrate hereafter on that.' Fortunately the young Messiah had an 'instantaneous conviction that this advice was bad'. He put Satan firmly behind him, and continued to pursue the superficial omniscience which he afterwards so triumphantly attained. Then there was the sad case of the Betrayal, when the Master was 'wholesomely shocked' by the defection of his supposed disciple G. L. Iscariot Cheesman. Cheesman, we are told, so far yielded to 'the dismal orthodox cult of specialisation' that he insisted on learning thoroughly the subject which he was employed to teach. Fortunately the Master survived all these dangers, and now his 'narrow escape from intellectual perdition' (X. 35) is the theme of many a vivid fresco (and many a dull sermon) in the new age. During the years of his mission he was of course past the danger of temptation, although he was never free from carping critics whom, by one of his happy historical parallels, he would designate as 'Scribes and Pharisees'. This, however, was to be expected. Even in his schooldays he had premonitions of his future Agony, 'though I had not yet tasted the cup for myself' (X. 235); nor had he yet — as he was afterwards, like St. Francis of Assisi, to do — received 'Christ's stigmata' (IX. 644).

However, all that is now over. The words, the very names of the critics are now extinct, except in so far as the Master has deigned to take note of them. . . . And here, no doubt, our worshipper's mind will again digress to commend the providence of the Founder who salvaged so much of past literature (in so far as he approved of it) from the wholesome conflagration of the pre-Mish-Mash culture. Readers of Toynbee today sometimes object to his numerous and (to a superficial view) irrelevant quotations from ancient and modern literature. And why, they ask, all these careful references: may one not remark that human projects sometimes 'gang agley' without appending a footnote reference to 'Burns, Robert: To a Mouse, stanza 7'? May not one use the phrase 'eyes that see not' without giving chapter and verse for the nine passages of the (Christian) Bible in which it occurs? A moment's thought should silence these impertinent questioners. Do they not realise that the Master is not writing for us but for our descendants in the Half-Baked Millennium of which he is the Prophet? By then all previous 'pagan' literature will of course have been destroyed, so that only those passages which are, as it were, pickled in the new Bible can participate in its immortality; just as fragments of Hebrew secular literature survive embalmed in the Christian Scriptures. Naturally such detached gobbets from the lost literature of the past will need an explanatory apparatus which to us, who still know the originals, may well seem otiose. Instead of cavilling at the overcrowded pages, we should express our gratitude to Toynbee for allowing so much of pre-Toynbeean literature to enter, in these stormy times, into the Noah's Ark of his Holy Writ.

I have said enough. The temptation of fantasy is irresistible when dealing with this huge, presumptuous, and utterly humourless work, and perhaps I have gone a little further than the orthodox Toynbeean priesthood may go. But the quotations I have given are really enough to prove my point. Has any other writer, however apocalyptic his message, taken such pains to acquaint the public with the trivial details of his own life, the successive signs of his Election, or to represent himself personally as the culminating end-product of one civilisation, the herald, law-giver, and prophet of another? Has any other Christian scholar thus applied to himself the successive incidents of the Christian myth? If the conclusions were stated without the evidence, they would be rejected as incredible. Such egotism leaves the claim of Mohammed, to be the unique prophet of God, nowhere. But then Mohammed, as Toynbee says, was 'a conspicuously unsuccessful prophet'. He only spread his message from China to Nigeria, from Indonesia to Spain. Toynbee, it is clear, is the Messiah of a much wider world.

But let us forget these details. It is not the content of Toynbee's work that interests me. To me it is a matter of indifference whether he read some unimportant book in the library of the Athenæum Club or in No. 45 Pembroke Square, in the summer of 1907 or in September 1952. I am interested in the character, not the content of his work; and I am interested in it because, fundamentally, I find it not merely erroneous — that is not a matter for emotion — but hateful. For Toynbee does not only utter false arguments and dogmatic statements, calling them 'scientific' and 'empirical'; he does not only preach a gospel of deliberate obscurantism; he seems to undermine our will, welcome our defeat, gloat over the extinction of our civilisation, not because he supports the form of civilisation which threatens us, but because he is animated by what we can only call a masochistic desire to be conquered. If Hitler and Stalin rejoiced in the prospect of destroying the West, theirs at least was a crude, intelligible rejoicing. They smacked their lips because they looked for plunder. Toynbee has no such clear interest in supporting a conqueror. He hungers spiritually not for this or that conquest, but for our defeat.

Defeat by whom? Toynbee does not care. To him it does not matter whether it is Hitler's New Order or World Communism which provides the irrelevant secular structure for the religion of Mish-Mash. And so there have been various claimants. For instance, in 1947–51, the American ex-Marxist James Burnham, having swallowed Toynbee's Old Testament whole, declared that 'Western civilisation has reached the stage in its development that calls for the creation of its Universal Empire' and urged the American government to seize its chance by rising and destroying the Russian government, 'if necessary by total war'. This ambition was not very different from that of Hitler. Indeed, if we look closer at Mr. Burnham's policy, we find that it is very like that of Hitler: for he declared that the value of European allies was to be measured not by their attachment to any liberal values, but solely by their hatred of communism. Consequently he rejected all other national leaders except General Franco, General Chiang Kai-shek, General de Gaulle, and the Pope. If this is the measure of virtue, it seems a pity that Hitler had not been left in peace. He was, after all, incontestably anti-communist; and he might have been necessary to reinforce Mr. Burnham's seedy army of crusaders. As it is, it seems unlikely that these three generals and the Pope would make much of a showing against the Red Army, and therefore it is a Russian conquest of Europe that Toynbee must envisage. He envisages it without apparent dismay. The essential thing to him is that a world empire should be established. The secular details are irrelevant. Christianity needed the secular framework of the Roman Empire: what did it matter whether the emperor was Augustus or Nero, Elagabalus or Diocletian? Perhaps in the end, after three centuries, there will even be a Constantine.

Thus Toynbee is still the philosophic ally of any conqueror who will destroy the West. And this, I think, is the explanation of a paradox which certain critics have noted in his work. For although Toynbee always presents himself as a 'gentle' figure, a 'pilgrim' humbly seeking universal understanding, in fact his history is primarily concerned with dynasties and conquests. He is uninterested in the arts and sciences, in trade and industry, in administration and finance. His mind prefers to dwell among the horrors of war, the march of armies, the seizure of empires, the founding of tyrant houses. 'Such preoccupation with violence', says one critic, 'might seem puzzling in so pronounced a pacifist and humanitarian if Freud had not taught us the meaning of ambivalence.' In fact, I fear, the explanation is simple. Like many intellectuals, Toynbee seems fascinated by brute power and longs to surrender to it. And since he identifies himself with the History of the world which he has felt 'gently flowing through him like a mighty current', he wants the whole world to surrender to it too.

Such, I believe, is Toynbee's philosophy. It is a doctrine of messianic defeatism. Toynbee detests Western civilisation because it is basically liberal and rational. Detesting it, he wishes to see it destroyed, and he does not care who destroys it. On its ruins he envisages a new society, or rather, the religion only of a new society. The new society itself, as far as he is concerned, can be the nightmare society of 1984, provided that the religion is the religion of Mish-Mash, of which he is the prophet and Messiah. And this he calls a great hope for the West! Is it any wonder that the greatest of his critics has called it 'a blasphemy against the West'?

For in fact there is no reason to fold our hands and resign ourselves to the inevitable death of Western civilisation. There is, of course, a relative decline in the power of Western Europe: a decline due to the technical achievements of Western Europe in mobilising the resources of the much greater areas which now overshadow it. It is not now conceivable that Western Europe — that is, Britain, France, the Low Countries, and Italy — should dominate the world to the extent that they have done in the past. But who regards 'domination' as an essential mark of civilisation? And anyway this real decline is relative not absolute: it is quite improper to ascribe a 'disease' to a man who, while as healthy as ever, has been outgrown by a giant. Moreover, if we compare Western Europe today with Western Europe in the 1930's, we find that in some respects it is positively healthier today. In the 1930's Germany and Italy were lost to the West. Today all Italy and half Germany are firmly recovered. In the

1930's the social situation throughout Western Europe was rendered precarious by 'the contradictions of capitalism' which both Hitler and Stalin sought to exploit. Today those contradictions have been so largely resolved that no Western country seriously fears revolution. Indeed, the boot is on the other leg. It is in the communist countries of Eastern Europe that the contradictions of communism are now threatening revolution, and the intellectuals of Poland, Hungary, and Russia itself look to Western 'social capitalism' as the answer. In such circumstances to talk of the West as if it were not merely reduced in relative power but a diseased civilisation is not only incorrect: it is absurd.

Those who look to history for lessons should look to both sides of it. They will then find that the West has 'declined' before now. For instance, in the early sixteenth century, Christendom saw itself reduced to frontiers almost as narrow as any it had known since the fall of the Western Roman Empire. The once Christian cities of Asia and North Africa had long been lost; now the Turks had advanced into the heart of Europe. The long-Christian islands of the Mediterranean, the Christian cities of Belgrade and Budapest were all lost. When, men asked, would the remorseless conquest be stayed? Europe only survived, they said, thanks to the Sophy of Persia, who distracted the Turks in Asia. And then, on top of these disasters, came the great schism of the Protestant Reformation. What wonder that the Toynbee of those days, Pope Clement VII, believed that the Last Days predetermined in the Apocalypse were about to come and, in this mood, commissioned Michael Angelo to paint, on the wall of the Sistine Chapel, the Last Judgment? And yet, looking back, it is not this aspect of the sixteenth century which seems to us significant. The sixteenth century, to us, is the beginning of the greatness of the West. Even to Toynbee, who regards the greatness of the West as its decay, the sixteenth century is the beginning, not the end, of the process.

A similar point could be made about the early seventeenth century. Then, too, certain sad spirits supposed that the world was coming to an end. Nature, they said, was in decay, and while enthusiasts looked eagerly for the Millennium, defeatist spirits, repeating, like Sir Thomas Browne, that ' 'tis too late to be ambitious, the great mutations of the world are over', resigned themselves to the impending doom. And yet this was the age of Bacon and Descartes, the beginning of those scientific discoveries which have enriched and alleviated the life of man!

Therefore, let us hear no more of the Decline of the West. Speaking absolutely, not relatively, the phrase has no meaning. The Toynbeean tables are about as relevant to modern historical knowledge as the chronology of Archbishop Ussher. And as for the Messiah and the Millennium, if we think of them at all, let it be only as a bogey. If the politics of 1984 and the religion of the Mish-Mash are all that our new prophet can offer us as the reward of acquiescence in the 'inevitable' ruin which he 'scientifically' predicts, that at least should spur us to throw this Jonah overboard and resist. After all, as some sage philosopher once observed, the irresistible is very often merely that which has not been resisted.

Selected titles: revised June, 1966

harper torchbooks

HUMANITIES AND SOCIAL SCIENCES

American Studies: General

CARL N. DEGLER, Ed.: Pivotal Interpretations of American History TB/1240, TB/1241

A. S. EISENSTADT, Ed.: The Craft of American History Vol. I TB/1255; Vol. II TB/1256

MARCUS LEE HANSEN: The Atlantic Migration: 1607-1860. *Edited by Arthur M. Schlesinger. Introduction by Oscar Handlin* TB/1052

JOHN HIGHAM, Ed.: The Reconstruction of American History △ TB/1068

JOHN F. KENNEDY: A Nation of Immigrants △ TB/1118

ARNOLD ROSE: The Negro in America TB/3048

American Studies: Colonial

BERNARD BAILYN, Ed.: The Apologia of Robert Keayne: *Self-Portrait of a Puritan Merchant* TB/1201

LAWRENCE HENRY GIPSON: The Coming of the Revolution: 1763-1775. † *Illus.* TB/3007

PERRY MILLER & T. H. JOHNSON, Eds.: The Puritans: *A Sourcebook* Vol. I TB/1093; Vol. II TB/1094

EDMUND S. MORGAN, Ed.: The Diary of Michael Wigglesworth, 1653-1657 TB/1228

EDMUND S. MORGAN: The Puritan Family TB/1227

RICHARD B. MORRIS: Government and Labor in Early America TB/1244

WALLACE NOTESTEIN: The English People on the Eve of Colonization: 1603-1630. † *Illus.* TB/3006

American Studies: From the Revolution to 1860

JOHN R. ALDEN: The American Revolution: 1775-1783. † *Illus.* TB/3011

RAY A. BILLINGTON: The Far Western Frontier: 1830-1860. † *Illus.* TB/3012

GEORGE DANGERFIELD: The Awakening of American Nationalism: 1815-1828. † *Illus.* TB/3061

JOHN C. MILLER: Alexander Hamilton and the Growth of the New Nation TB/3057

RICHARD B. MORRIS, Ed.: The Era of the American Revolution TB/1180

A. F. TYLER: Freedom's Ferment TB/1074

American Studies: Since the Civil War

MAX BELOFF, Ed.: The Debate on the American Revolution, 1761-1783: *A Sourcebook* △ TB/1225

EDMUND BURKE: On the American Revolution. † *Edited by Elliot Robert Barkan* TB/3068

WHITNEY R. CROSS: The Burned-Over District: *The Social and Intellectual History of Enthusiastic Religion in Western New York, 1800-1850* TB/1242

W. A. DUNNING: Reconstruction, Political and Economic: 1865-1877 TB/1073

FRANCIS GRIERSON: The Valley of Shadows TB/1246

SIDNEY HOOK: Reason, Social Myths, and Democracy TB/1237

WILLIAM E. LEUCHTENBURG: Franklin D. Roosevelt and the New Deal: 1932-1940. † *Illus.* TB/3025

ARTHUR S. LINK: Woodrow Wilson and the Progressive Era: 1910-1917. † *Illus.* TB/3023

JAMES MADISON: The Forging of American Federalism. *Edited by Saul K. Padover* TB/1226

ROBERT GREEN MC CLOSKEY: American Conservatism in the Age of Enterprise: 1865-1910 TB/1137

ARTHUR MANN: Yankee Reformers in the Urban Age TB/1247

GEORGE E. MOWRY: The Era of Theodore Roosevelt and the Birth of Modern America: 1900-1912. † TB/3022

R. B. NYE: Midwestern Progressive Politics TB/1202

FRANCIS S. PHILBRICK: The Rise of the West, 1754-1830. † *Illus.* TB/3067

JACOB RIIS: The Making of an American ‡ TB/3070

PHILIP SELZNICK: TVA and the Grass Roots: A Study in the Sociology of Formal Organization TB/1230

TIMOTHY L. SMITH: Revivalism and Social Reform: American Protestantism on the Eve of the Civil War TB/1229

IDA M. TARBELL: The History of the Standard Oil Company. *Briefer Version.* ‡ *Edited by David M. Chalmers* TB/3071

GEORGE B. TINDALL, Ed.: A Populist Reader ‡ TB/3069

VERNON LANE WHARTON: The Negro in Mississippi: 1865-1890 TB/1178

Anthropology

JACQUES BARZUN: Race: *A Study in Superstition. Revised Edition* TB/1172

JOSEPH B. CASAGRANDE, Ed.: In the Company of Man: *Portraits of Anthropological Informants.* TB/3047

DAVID LANDY: Tropical Childhood: *Cultural Transmission and Learning in a Puerto Rican Village* ¶ TB/1235

EDWARD BURNETT TYLOR: The Origins of Culture. *Part I of "Primitive Culture."* § *Intro. by Paul Radin* TB/33

EDWARD BURNETT TYLOR: Religion in Primitive Culture. *Part II of "Primitive Culture"* § TB/34

W. LLOYD WARNER: A Black Civilization: *A Study of an Australian Tribe.* ¶ *Illus.* TB/3056

Art and Art History

EMILE MÂLE: The Gothic Image: *Religious Art in France of the Thirteenth Century.* § △ *190 illus.* TB/44

ERICH NEUMANN: The Archetypal World of Henry Moore. △ *107 illus.* TB/2020

DORA & ERWIN PANOFSKY: Pandora's Box: *The Changing Aspects of a Mythical Symbol* TB/2021

† The New American Nation Series, edited by Henry Steele Commager and Richard B. Morris.
‡ American Perspectives series, edited by Bernard Wishy and William E. Leuchtenburg.
* The Rise of Modern Europe series, edited by William L. Langer.
¶ Researches in the Social, Cultural, and Behavioral Sciences, edited by Benjamin Nelson.
§ The Library of Religion and Culture, edited by Benjamin Nelson.
Σ Harper Modern Science Series, edited by James R. Newman.
° Not for sale in Canada.
△ Not for sale in the U. K.

Business, Economics & Economic History

GILBERT BURCK & EDITORS OF FORTUNE: The Computer Age: *And Its Potential for Management* TB/1179
THOMAS C. COCHRAN: The American Business System: *A Historical Perspective, 1900-1955* TB/1080
FRANK H. KNIGHT: The Economic Organization TB/1214
FRANK H. KNIGHT: Risk, Uncertainty and Profit TB/1215
ABBA P. LERNER: Everybody's Business TB/3051
HERBERT SIMON: The Shape of Automation: *For Men and Management* TB/1245
PIERRE URI: Partnership for Progress: *A Program for Transatlantic Action* TB/3036

Historiography & Philosophy of History

JACOB BURCKHARDT: On History and Historians. △ *Intro. by H. R. Trevor-Roper* TB/1216
H. STUART HUGHES: History as Art and as Science: *Twin Vistas on the Past* TB/1207
GEORGE H. NADEL, Ed.: Studies in the Philosophy of History: *Essays from* History and Theory TB/1208
KARL R. POPPER: The Open Society and Its Enemies △
Vol. I: The Spell of Plato TB/1101
Vol. II: The High Tide of Prophecy: Hegel, Marx and the Aftermath TB/1102
KARL R. POPPER: The Poverty of Historicism ° △ TB/1126
G. J. RENIER: History: Its Purpose and Method △ TB/1209
W. H. WALSH: Philosophy of History △ TB/1020

History: General

L. CARRINGTON GOODRICH: A Short History of the Chinese People. △ *Illus.* TB/3015
DAN N. JACOBS & HANS H. BAERWALD: Chinese Communism: *Selected Documents* TB/3031
BERNARD LEWIS: The Arabs in History △ TB/1029

History: Ancient and Medieval

HELEN CAM: England before Elizabeth △ TB/1026
NORMAN COHN: The Pursuit of the Millennium △ TB/1037
CHRISTOPHER DAWSON, Ed.: Mission to Asia △ TB/315
ADOLF ERMAN, Ed.: The Ancient Egyptians TB/1233
F. L. GANSHOF: Feudalism △ TB/1058
DENO GEANAKOPLOS: Byzantine East and Latin West △ TB/1265
DENYS HAY: The Medieval Centuries ° △ TB/1192
SAMUEL NOAH KRAMER: Sumerian Mythology TB/1055
NAPHTALI LEWIS & MEYER REINHOLD, Eds.: Roman Civilization Vol. I TB/1231; Vol. II TB/1232
CHARLES PETIT-DUTAILLIS: The Feudal Monarchy in France and England ° △ TB/1165
HENRI PIRENNE: Early Democracies in the Low Countries TB/1110
STEVEN RUNCIMAN: A History of the Crusades. △
Volume I: *The First Crusade and the Foundation of the Kingdom of Jerusalem. Illus.* TB/1143
Volume II: *The Kingdom of Jerusalem and the Frankish East, 1100-1187. Illus.* TB/1243

History: Renaissance & Reformation

JACOB BURCKHARDT: The Civilization of the Renaissance in Italy △ Vol. I TB/40; Vol. II TB/41
JOHN CALVIN & JACOPO SADOLETO: A Reformation Debate. *Edited by John C. Olin* TB/1239
G. CONSTANT: The Reformation in England △ TB/314
FRANCESCO GUICCIARDINI: Maxims and Reflections of a Renaissance Statesman *(Ricordi)* TB/1160
J. H. HEXTER: More's Utopia: *The Biography of an Idea. New Epilogue by the Author* TB/1195
HAJO HOLBORN: Ulrich von Hutten and the German Reformation TB/1238
JOEL HURSTFIELD, Ed.: The Reformation Crisis △ TB/1267
ULRICH VON HUTTEN et al.: On the Eve of the Reformation. *"Letters of Obscure Men." Introduction by Hajo Holborn* TB/1124
PAUL O. KRISTELLER: Renaissance Thought: *The Classic, Scholastic, and Humanist Strains* TB/1048
GARRETT MATTINGLY et al.: Renaissance Profiles. △ *Edited by J. H. Plumb* TB/1162
J. E. NEALE: The Age of Catherine de Medici ° △ TB/1085
ERWIN PANOFSKY: Studies in Iconology △ TB/1077
J. H. PLUMB: The Italian Renaissance △ TB/1161
A. F. POLLARD: Henry VIII ° △ TB/1249
A. F. POLLARD: Wolsey ° △ TB/1248
A. L. ROWSE: The Expansion of Elizabethan England. ° △ *Illus.* TB/1220
G. M. TREVELYAN: England in the Age of Wycliffe, 1368-1520 ° △ TB/1112
VESPASIANO: Renaissance Princes, Popes, and Prelates: *The Vespasiano Memoirs* TB/1111

History: Modern European

MAX BELOFF: The Age of Absolutism, 1660-1815 △ TB/1062
ASA BRIGGS: The Making of Modern England, 1784-1867: *The Age of Improvement* ° △ TB/1203
CRANE BRINTON: A Decade of Revolution, 1789-1799. * *Illus.* TB/3018
D. W. BROGAN: The Development of Modern France. ° △ Vol. I TB/1184; Vol. II TB/1185
J. BRONOWSKI & BRUCE MAZLISH: The Western Intellectual Tradition: *From Leonardo to Hegel* △ TB/3001
ALAN BULLOCK: Hitler, A Study in Tyranny ° △ TB/1123
E. H. CARR: The Twenty Years' Crisis, 1919-1939 ° △ TB/1122
GORDON A. CRAIG: Bismarck to Adenauer TB/1171
FRANKLIN L. FORD: Robe and Sword: *The Regrouping of the French Aristocracy after Louis XIV* TB/1217
RENÉ FUELOEP-MILLER: The Mind and Face of Bolshevism TB/1188
ALBERT GUÉRARD: France in the Classical Age △ TB/1183
DAN N. JACOBS, Ed.: The New Communist Manifesto *& Related Documents. Third edition, Revised* TB/1078
HANS KOHN: The Mind of Germany △ TB/1204
HANS KOHN, Ed.: The Mind of Modern Russia TB/1065
FRANK E. MANUEL: The Prophets of Paris: *Turgot, Condorcet, Saint-Simon, Fourier, and Comte* TB/1218
KINGSLEY MARTIN: French Liberal Thought in the Eighteenth Century TB/1114
L. B. NAMIER: Personalities and Powers △ TB/1186
L. B. NAMIER: Vanished Supremacies ° △ TB/1088
JOHN U. NEF: Western Civilization Since the Renaissance: *Peace, War, Industry, and the Arts* TB/1113
JOHN PLAMENATZ: German Marxism and Russian Communism. ° △ *New Preface by the Author* TB/1189
PENFIELD ROBERTS: The Quest for Security, 1715-1740. * *Illus.* TB/3016
LOUIS, DUC DE SAINT-SIMON: Versailles, The Court, and Louis XIV △ TB/1250
A. J. P. TAYLOR: From Napoleon to Lenin: *Historical Essays* ° △ TB/1268
A. J. P. TAYLOR: The Habsburg Monarchy, 1809-1918 ° △ TB/1187
G. M. TREVELYAN: British History in the Nineteenth Century and After: 1782-1919 △ TB/1251
H. R. TREVOR-ROPER: Historical Essays ° △ TB/1269
JOHN B. WOLF: The Emergence of the Great Powers, 1685-1715. * *Illus.* TB/3010

Intellectual History & History of Ideas

ERNST CASSIRER: The Individual and the Cosmos in Renaissance Philosophy. △ *Translated with an Introduction by Mario Domandi* TB/1097
ARTHUR O. LOVEJOY: The Great Chain of Being: *A Study of the History of an Idea* TB/1009
FRANK E. MANUEL: The Prophets of Paris: *Turgot, Condorcet, Saint-Simon, Fourier, and Comte* TB/1218
PHILIP P. WIENER: Evolution and the Founders of Pragmatism. △ *Foreword by John Dewey* TB/1212

Literature, Poetry, The Novel & Criticism

JAMES BOSWELL: The Life of Dr. Johnson & The Journal of a Tour to the Hebrides with Samuel Johnson LL.D.: *Selections* ° △ TB/1254

RICHMOND LATTIMORE: The Poetry of Greek Tragedy △ TB/1257

J. B. LEISHMAN: The Monarch of Wit: *An Analytical and Comparative Study of the Poetry of John Donne* ° △ TB/1258

J. B. LEISHMAN: Themes and Variations in Shakespeare's Sonnets ° △ TB/1259

V. DE S. PINTO: Crisis in English Poetry, 1880-1940 ° △ TB/1260

C. K. STEAD: The New Poetic: *Yeats to Eliot* ° △ TB/1263

BASIL WILLEY: Nineteenth Century Studies: *Coleridge to Matthew Arnold* ° △ TB/1261

BASIL WILLEY: More Nineteenth Century Studies: *A Group of Honest Doubters* ° △ TB/1262

RAYMOND WILLIAMS: Culture and Society, 1780-1950 △ TB/1252

RAYMOND WILLIAMS: The Long Revolution △ TB/1253

Philosophy

G. E. M. ANSCOMBE: An Introduction to Wittgenstein's Tractatus. ° △ *Second edition, Revised* TB/1210

HENRI BERGSON: Time and Free Will ° △ TB/1021

FREDERICK COPLESTON: Medieval Philosophy ° △ TB/376

F. M. CORNFORD: Principium Sapientiae TB/1213

F. M. CORNFORD: From Religion to Philosophy § TB/20

WILFRID DESAN: The Tragic Finale: *An Essay on the Philosophy of Jean-Paul Sartre* TB/1030

A. P. D'ENTRÈVES: Natural Law △ TB/1223

PAUL FRIEDLÄNDER: Plato: *An Introduction* △ TB/2017

W. K. C. GUTHRIE: The Greek Philosophers ° △ TB/1008

F. H. HEINEMANN: Existentialism and the Modern Predicament △ TB/28

EDMUND HUSSERL: Phenomenology and the Crisis of Philosophy TB/1170

IMMANUEL KANT: The Doctrine of Virtue TB/110

IMMANUEL KANT: Lectures on Ethics § △ TB/105

IMMANUEL KANT: Religion Within the Limits of Reason Alone. § *Intro. by T. M. Greene & J. Silber* TB/67

QUENTIN LAUER: Phenomenology TB/1169

GABRIEL MARCEL: Being and Having △ TB/310

GEORGE A. MORGAN: What Nietzsche Means TB/1198

MICHAEL POLANYI: Personal Knowledge △ TB/1158

WILLARD VAN ORMAN QUINE: Elementary Logic. *Revised Edition* TB/577

WILLARD VAN ORMAN QUINE: From a Logical Point of View: *Logico-Philosophical Essays* TB/566

BERTRAND RUSSELL et al.: The Philosophy of Bertrand Russell Vol. I TB/1095; Vol. II TB/1096

L. S. STEBBING: A Modern Introduction to Logic △ TB/538

ALFRED NORTH WHITEHEAD: Process and Reality: *An Essay in Cosmology* △ TB/1033

WILHELM WINDELBAND: A History of Philosophy Vol. I TB/38; Vol. II TB/39

LUDWIG WITTGENSTEIN: Blue and Brown Books ° TB/1211

Political Science & Government

KENNETH E. BOULDING: Conflict and Defense TB/3024

CRANE BRINTON: English Political Thought in the Nineteenth Century TB/1071

F. L. GANSHOF: Feudalism △ TB/1058

SIDNEY HOOK: Reason, Social Myths and Democracy △ TB/1237

DAN N. JACOBS, Ed.: The New Communist Manifesto & *Related Documents. Third edition, Revised* TB/1078

DAN N. JACOBS & HANS BAERWALD, Eds.: Chinese Communism: *Selected Documents* TB/3031

KINGSLEY MARTIN: French Liberal Thought in the Eighteenth Century △ TB/1114

ROBERTO MICHELS: First Lectures in Political Sociology. *Edited by Alfred de Grazia* ¶ ° △ TB/1224

BARRINGTON MOORE, JR.: Political Power and Social Theory: *Seven Studies* ¶ TB/1221

BARRINGTON MOORE, JR.: Soviet Politics—The Dilemma of Power ¶ TB/1222

BARRINGTON MOORE, JR.: Terror and Progress—USSR ¶ TB/1266

KARL R. POPPER: The Open Society and Its Enemies △ Vol. I TB/1101; Vol. II TB/1102

Psychology

ALFRED ADLER: The Individual Psychology of Alfred Adler △ TB/1154

HERBERT FINGARETTE: The Self in Transformation ¶ TB/1177

SIGMUND FREUD: On Creativity and the Unconscious § △ TB/45

C. G. JUNG: Symbols of Transformation △ Vol. I: TB/2009; Vol. II TB/2010

JOHN T. MC NEILL: A History of the Cure of Souls TB/126

KARL MENNINGER: Theory of Psychoanalytic Technique TB/1144

JOHN H. SCHAAR: Escape from Authority TB/1155

Sociology

JACQUES BARZUN: Race: *A Study in Superstition* TB/1172

BERNARD BERELSON, Ed.: The Behavioral Sciences Today TB/1127

ALVIN W. GOULDNER: Wildcat Strike ¶ TB/1176

CLARK KERR: The Uses of the University TB/1264

R. M. MAC IVER: Social Causation TB/1153

ROBERT K. MERTON, LEONARD BROOM, LEONARD S. COTTRELL, JR., Editors: Sociology Today: *Problems and Prospects* ¶ Vol. I TB/1173; Vol. II TB/1174

ARNOLD ROSE: The Negro in America TB/3048

PHILIP SELZNICK: TVA and the Grass Roots TB/1230

GEORG SIMMEL et al.: Essays on Sociology, Philosophy, and Aesthetics. ¶ *Edited by Kurt H. Wolff* TB/1234

HERBERT SIMON: The Shape of Automation △ TB/1245

RELIGION

Ancient & Classical

J. H. BREASTED: Development of Religion and Thought in Ancient Egypt TB/57

HENRI FRANKFORT: Ancient Egyptian Religion TB/77

G. RACHEL LEVY: Religious Conceptions of the Stone Age *and their Influence upon European Thought* △ TB/106

MARTIN P. NILSSON: Greek Folk Religion TB/78

H. J. ROSE: Religion in Greece and Rome △ TB/55

Biblical Thought & Literature

W. F. ALBRIGHT: The Biblical Period from Abraham to Ezra TB/102

C. K. BARRETT, Ed.: The New Testament Background: *Selected Documents* △ TB/86

C. H. DODD: The Authority of the Bible △ TB/43

M. S. ENSLIN: Christian Beginnings △ TB/5

JOHN GRAY: Archaeology and the Old Testament World. △ *Illus.* TB/127

The Judaic Tradition

MARTIN BUBER: Eclipse of God △ TB/12

MARTIN BUBER: Moses △ TB/27

MARTIN BUBER: The Origin and Meaning of Hasidism △ TB/835

MARTIN BUBER: Pointing the Way △ TB/103

MARTIN BUBER: The Prophetic Faith TB/73

MARTIN BUBER: Two Types of Faith ° △ TB/75

SOLOMON GRAYZEL: A History of the Contemporary Jews TB/816

JOSHUA TRACHTENBERG: The Devil and the Jews: *The Medieval Conception of the Jew and its Relation to Modern Anti-Semitism* JP/22

Christianity: Origins & Early Development

AUGUSTINE: An Augustine Synthesis △ TB/335

ADOLF DEISSMANN: Paul TB/15

EDWARD GIBBON: The Triumph of Christendom in the Roman Empire § △ *Illus.* TB/46

MAURICE GOGUEL: Jesus and the Origins of Christianity. ° △ Vol. I: TB/65; Vol. II: TB/66

EDGAR J. GOODSPEED: A Life of Jesus TB/1

ROBERT M. GRANT: Gnosticism and Early Christianity △ TB/136
ORIGEN: On First Principles △ TB/310
SULPICIUS SEVERUS et al.: The Western Fathers △ TB/309

Christianity: The Middle Ages and The Reformation

JOHN CALVIN & JACOPO SADOLETO: A Reformation Debate. *Edited by John C. Olin* TB/1239
G. CONSTANT: The Reformation in England △ TB/314

Christianity: The Protestant Tradition

KARL BARTH: Dogmatics in Outline △ TB/56
RUDOLF BULTMANN et al.: Translating Theology into the Modern Age TB/252
SOREN KIERKEGAARD: The Journals ° △ TB/52
SOREN KIERKEGAARD: The Present Age § △ TB/94
SOREN KIERKEGAARD: Purity of Heart △ TB/4
SOREN KIERKEGAARD: Repetition △ TB/117
SOREN KIERKEGAARD: Works of Love △ TB/122
JOHN MACQUARRIE: The Scope of Demythologizing: *Bultmann and his Critics* △ TB/134
JAMES M. ROBINSON et al.: The Bultmann School of Biblical Interpretation: New Directions? TB/251
F. SCHLEIERMACHER: The Christian Faith △ Vol. I TB/108; Vol. II TB/109
PAUL TILLICH: Dynamics of Faith △ TB/42

Christianity: The Roman and Eastern Traditions

DOM CUTHBERT BUTLER: Western Mysticism § ° △ TB/312
A. ROBERT CAPONIGRI, Ed.: Modern Catholic Thinkers I: *God and Man* △ TB/306
A. ROBERT CAPONIGRI, Ed.: Modern Catholic Thinkers II: *The Church and the Political Order* △ TB/307
G. P. FEDOTOV: The Russian Religious Mind: *Kievan Christianity, the 10th to the 13th Centuries* TB/70
G. P. FEDOTOV, Ed.: A Treasury of Russian Spirituality TB/303
ÉTIENNE GILSON: The Spirit of Thomism TB/313
DAVID KNOWLES: The English Mystical Tradition TB/302
GABRIEL MARCEL: Being and Having TB/310
GABRIEL MARCEL: Homo Viator TB/397
GUSTAVE WEIGEL, S. J.: Catholic Theology in Dialogue TB/301

Oriental Religions: Far Eastern, Near Eastern

TOR ANDRAE: Mohammed § △ TB/62
EDWARD CONZE: Buddhism ° △ TB/58
ANANDA COOMARASWAMY: Buddha and the Gospel of Buddhism. △ *Illus.* TB/119
H. G. CREEL: Confucius and the Chinese Way TB/63
FRANKLIN EDGERTON, Trans. & Ed.: The Bhagavad Gita TB/115
SWAMI NIKHILANANDA, Trans. & Ed.: The Upanishads: *A One-Volume Abridgment* △ TB/114

Philosophy of Religion

NICOLAS BERDYAEV: The Beginning and the End § △ TB/14
NICOLAS BERDYAEV: Christian Existentialism △ TB/130
RUDOLF BULTMANN: History and Eschatology ° TB/91
RUDOLF BULTMANN & 5 CRITICS: Kerygma and Myth △ TB/80
RUDOLF BULTMANN and KARL KUNDSIN: Form Criticism: *Two Essays on New Testament Research* △ TB/96
MIRCEA ELIADE: The Sacred and the Profane TB/81
LUDWIG FEUERBACH: The Essence of Christianity § TB/11
IMMANUEL KANT: Religion Within the Limits of Reason Alone. § *Intro. by T. M. Greene & J. Silber* TB/67
K. E. KIRK: The Vision of God § △ TB/137
JOHN MACQUARRIE: An Existentialist Theology: *A Comparison of Heidegger and Bultmann* ° △ TB/125
PIERRE TEILHARD DE CHARDIN: Divine Milieu ° △ TB/384
PIERRE TEILHARD DE CHARDIN: Phenomenon of Man ° △ TB/383

NATURAL SCIENCES AND MATHEMATICS

Biological Sciences

CHARLOTTE AUERBACH: Science of Genetics Σ △ TB/568
LUDWIG VON BERTALANFFY: Modern Theories of Development: *An Introduction to Theoretical Biology* TB/554
LUDWIG VON BERTALANFFY: Problems of Life △ TB/521
HAROLD F. BLUM: Time's Arrow and Evolution TB/555
JOHN TYLER BONNER: The Ideas of Biology Σ △ TB/570
R. W. GERARD: Unresting Cells. *Illus.* TB/541
ADOLF PORTMANN: Animals as Social Beings ° △ TB/572
O. W. RICHARDS: The Social Insects. △ *Illus.* TB/542
P. M. SHEPPARD: Natural Selection and Heredity △ TB/528
EDMUND W. SINNOTT: Cell and Psyche TB/546
C. H. WADDINGTON: How Animals Develop. △ *Illus.* TB/553
C. H. WADDINGTON: The Nature of Life △ TB/580

Geography

R. E. COKER: The Great and Wide Sea: *An Introduction to Oceanography and Marine Biology. Illus.* TB/551
F. K. HARE: The Restless Atmosphere △ TB/560

History of Science

MARIE BOAS: The Scientific Renaissance, 1450-1630 △ TB/583
W. DAMPIER, Ed.: Readings in the Literature of Science. *Illus.* TB/512
A. HUNTER DUPREE: Science in the Federal Government: *A History of Policies and Activities to 1940* △ TB/573
ALEXANDRE KOYRÉ: From the Closed World to the Infinite Universe △ TB/31
O. NEUGEBAUER: The Exact Sciences in Antiquity TB/552
LANCELOT LAW WHYTE: Essay on Atomism △ TB/565

Mathematics

E. W. BETH: The Foundations of Mathematics △ TB/581
H. DAVENPORT: The Higher Arithmetic △ TB/526
H. G. FORDER: Geometry: *An Introduction* △ TB/548
D. E. LITTLEWOOD: Skeleton Key of Mathematics: *A Simple Account of Complex Algebraic Problems* △ TB/525
GEORGE E. OWEN: Fundamentals of Scientific Mathematics TB/569
WILLARD VAN ORMAN QUINE: Mathematical Logic TB/558
FREDERICK WAISMANN: Introduction to Mathematical Thinking. *Foreword by Karl Menger* TB/511

Philosophy of Science

R. B. BRAITHWAITE: Scientific Explanation TB/515
J. BRONOWSKI: Science and Human Values △ TB/505
ALBERT EINSTEIN et al.: Albert Einstein: Philosopher-Scientist Vol. I TB/502; Vol. II TB/503
WERNER HEISENBERG: Physics and Philosophy △ TB/549
JOHN MAYNARD KEYNES: A Treatise on Probability. ° △ *Introduction by N. R. Hanson* TB/557
KARL R. POPPER: Logic of Scientific Discovery △ TB/576
STEPHEN TOULMIN: Foresight and Understanding △ TB/564
G. J. WHITROW: Natural Philosophy of Time ° △ TB/563

Physics and Cosmology

JOHN E. ALLEN: Aerodynamics △ TB/582
STEPHEN TOULMIN & JUNE GOODFIELD: The Fabric of the Heavens: *The Development of Astronomy and Dynamics.* △ *Illus.* TB/579
DAVID BOHM: Causality and Chance in Modern Physics. △ *Foreword by Louis de Broglie* TB/536
P. W. BRIDGMAN: Nature of Thermodynamics TB/537
C. V. DURELL: Readable Relativity △ TB/530
ARTHUR EDDINGTON: Space, Time and Gravitation TB/510
GEORGE GAMOW: Biography of Physics Σ △ TB/567
MAX JAMMER: Concepts of Force TB/550
MAX JAMMER: Concepts of Mass TB/571
MAX JAMMER: Concepts of Space TB/533
G. J. WHITROW: The Structure and Evolution of the Universe: *An Introduction to Cosmology* △ *Illus.* TB/504